Identities and Place

Identities and Place

Changing Labels and Intersectional Communities of LGBTQ and Two-Spirit People in the United States

Katherine Crawford-Lackey and Megan E. Springate

berghahn
NEW YORK · OXFORD
www.berghahnbooks.com

First published in 2020 by

Berghahn Books

www.berghahnbooks.com

Library of Congress Cataloging-in-Publication Data

A C.I.P. cataloging record is available from the Library of Congress
Library of Congress Cataloging in Publication Control Number:
2019037413

British Library Cataloguing in Publication Data

A catalogue record for this book is available from the British Library

ISBN 978-1-78920-479-7 hardback
ISBN 978-1-80539-154-8 paperback
ISBN 978-1-80539-567-6 epub
ISBN 978-1-78920-480-3 web pdf

https://doi.org/10.3167/9781789204797

Contents

Illustrations

Cover Image. The San Francisco Women's Building is a landmark internationally recognized for its mural, *MaestraPeace*, which honors women's contributions around the world. Mural painted in 1994 by Juana Alicia, Miranda Bergman, Edythe Boone, Susan Kelk Cervantes, Meera Desai, Yvonne Littleton, and Irene Perez, and others. Photo courtesy of the Jon B. Lovelace Collection of California Photographs in Carol M. Highsmith's America Project, Library of Congress, Prints, and Photographs Division.

Preface

Katherine Crawford-Lackey

Identities and Place: Changing Labels and Intersectional Communities of LGBTQ and Two-Spirit People in the United States focuses on the recent history of nonheteronormative Americans from the early twentieth century onward and the places associated with these communities. This book and the other volumes in this series are part of a previous publication, *LGBTQ America: A Theme Study of Lesbian, Gay, Bisexual, Transgender, and Queer History*, edited by Megan E. Springate for the National Park Foundation and the National Park Service (2016). *Identities and Place* contains several revised and updated chapters from the theme study, as well as prompts for interactive projects related to the topic material. The chapters for this volume were chosen for their intersectional approach to queer history, demonstrating how such studies contribute to a multifaceted narrative of American history.

Unique to this volume (and the series as a whole) is the focus on historic sites. Authors explore how queer identities are connected with specific places: places where people gather, socialize, protest, mourn, and celebrate. A study of the private residences, social gathering spaces, and sites of protest affiliated with lesbian, gay, bisexual, transgender, and queer (LGBTQ) Americans provides a deeper look at how sexually variant and gender nonconforming Americans constructed identity, created communities, and fought to have their rights recognized by the government. In the 1980s, urban historian Dolores Hayden attempted to commemorate the public spaces associated with women and ethnic minorities by working with local communities in the Los Angeles area. Studying what she referred to as the "politics of place construction," Hayden sought to disrupt the myth that only white heterosexual males had a presence in public spaces.[1] Her work is relevant to this series as it challenges historians to consider how the control of public and private space was (and continues to be) used to reinforce hierarchies of power. The reclamation of meaningful spaces, by extension, is a radical act that can empower marginalized communities.

Queer spaces in both rural and urban America are vital pieces of evidence in documenting and interpreting LGBTQ history. While scholars of queer history rely on historical and archaeological records to study the past, more consideration should be given to the built environment as it reveals how people moved through and interacted with the world.[2] Decades of urban development and renewal have caused a loss in historic structures, particularly those of nonheteronormative Americans with multiple marginalized identities. A lack of knowledge about what constitutes queer spaces causes many urban and rural structures associated with these communities to remain undocumented. There is a need to identify and preserve nonheteronormative spaces to prevent the erasure of queer stories and to identify those not yet told.

Assessing the places associated with LGBTQ individuals and communities requires knowledge of American queer history and culture. Scholarship in this field is relatively new, with early publications dating to the 1980s and 1990s. Research by historians such as John D'Emilio, Estelle Freedman, and George Chauncey laid a foundation for examining how gay Americans first formed communities, created distinct cultures, and established outlets for collective queer thought in the nineteenth and twentieth centuries.[3] Acknowledging and including people whose lives were less fully documented in traditional historical sources, especially women, transgender individuals, and people of color, has been an ongoing challenge for historians. In recent decades, scholarship on lesbian, gay, bisexual, transgender, and queer history has developed to more fully underscore the complexity of identity politics in shaping the lives of those who identified as part of these communities. Foregrounding this diversity of identities has highlighted questions about how queer cultures differed based on regional location, ethnicity, gender identities, and sexual orientation.[4] *Identities and Place* adds to existing literature by exploring how different identities navigated a predominately heterosexual society before and after the emergence of the modern LGBTQ civil rights movement in the late 1960s and early 1970s. By challenging the perception of a monolithic LGBTQ community, the contributing authors reveal how different facets of identity intersect and influence lived experiences. This volume provides an overview of how individuals and communities defined and refined identity over time, and it examines how the process of identity-making is rooted in the physical geography of both urban and rural America.

This volume provides a broad study of different queer identities in order to give a more comprehensive look at different aspects of the queer experience to convey the centrality of all LGBTQ identities in telling a broader narrative of struggle, resistance, and triumph. The authors achieve this by exploring the interdependence of categories of difference, revealing that identity is contingent upon time and place. Their contributions in this volume emphasize the importance of acknowledging the diversity of individuals within the LGBTQ label and how the inclusion (or exclusion) of certain identities changes as social norms and political policies fluctuate.[5] Aspects of identity such as gender and sexual orientation inform our social interactions as well as our ability to partake in society—both professionally and personally. Recognizing that gender and sexuality are socially constructed is an essential foundation when exploring queer identity and history.[6] As demonstrated by the authors in this volume, characteristics of an individual's identity cannot be examined independently; instead, these social categories are contingent upon each other, informing an individual's interactions with society and vice versa. Those with multiple minority identities are more likely to experience prejudice and discrimination in contrast to those with fewer minority identities.[7] It is also important to note that while this book speaks to various queer identities, it does not encapsulate them all.

This inclusive approach to the study of LGBTQ history requires an understanding of the language used when referring to queer individuals and communities. Today, sexually nonconforming and gender variant people are often labeled as belonging to LGBTQ communities. While people who identify as lesbian, gay, bisexual, transgender, or queer are often referred to as a collective, lived experiences are inherently different depending on categories of difference (such as race, class, gender, sexual orientation, ability, and religion). Knowing who identifies as part of these communities is necessary when studying the construction of queer identity. Lesbian and gay Americans are defined by an attraction to the same gender. While "lesbian" refers to women, the term "gay" often refers to men, but can be used when speaking of multiple genders. As author Loraine Hutchins notes, American society has a tendency to categorize people in binary terms (as either heterosexual or homosexual), yet bisexuals have "the capacity to be attracted to and love more than one gender."[8] Her chapter, "Making Bisexuals Visible," reinserts bisexual identities back into the historical narrative and examines how people attracted to multiple genders navigate heterosexual and homosexual society. Susan Stryker defines transgender as "the ways people can live lives that depart from the conventional patterns according to which all bodies are assigned a sex at birth (male or female) and enrolled in a social gender (girl or boy)."[9] Tracing gender nonconforming behavior in America to the pre-revolutionary era, Stryker's chapter, "Transgender History in the United States and the Places That Matter," reveals that gender variant individuals have an integral place in the history of America.

Scholars have debated the use of the term "queer" when referring to nonheteronormative people and behavior. Originally used as a derogatory term beginning in the late nineteenth century, the word queer has recently been reclaimed by a younger generation of Americans. This term is now used to refer to those of us who do not identify as lesbian, gay, bisexual, or transgender but who are also not exclusively heterosexual. The use of the term today recognizes that there are many identities within lesbian, gay, bisexual, and transgender communities. In the spirit of inclusivity, this book series uses the term when referring broadly to nonheteronormative Americans in the past and present.[10]

While the volumes in this series largely focus on the modern history of queer communities, sexually variant and gender-nonconforming behavior was present in North America well before the founding of the United States. However, it was not until the late nineteenth and early twentieth centuries that a collective gay consciousness emerged. Historian John D'Emilio wrote about the formation of gay communities and argued that the "process of urbanization and industrialization created a social context in which an autonomous personal life could develop," allowing gay men and women to meet, socialize, and explore their sexuality.[11] D'Emilio suggested that the rise of capitalism and the free-labor system created opportunities for autonomy and freedom that facilitated the emergence of gay and lesbian culture in the second half of the twentieth century. Urban life introduced men and women to new opportunities for socialization as well as sexual experimentation, and as a result, the meaning of sex changed.

Other scholars, such as Judith Jack Halberstam and E. Patrick Johnson, have challenged the assertion that LGBTQ life is synonymous with the urban cities of the east and west coasts. Halberstam's *In a Queer Time and Place: Transgender Bodies, Subcultural Lives* looks at the queer "way of life" where sexually variant and gender-nonconforming Americans live in a queer "temporality," creating distinct cultures and spaces outside of heterosexual society. The places of LGBTQ individuals and communities are not inherently urban; Halberstam uses the life and tragic death of Brandon Teena, a white transgender teen from rural Nebraska who was raped and murdered, as a way to delve into the construction of queer countercultures in rural settings.[12] While Halberstam focuses on a white transgender teen from rural America to contrast rural and urban queer communities, Johnson notes that there is a dearth of scholarship on the Black queer experience (rural and urban), particularly that of transgender African Americans. Johnson's introduction to *No Tea, No Shade: New Writings in Black Queer Studies* reminds scholars that while more case studies on queer life are necessary, they must also be inclusive of people of color.[13]

Gay communities forming in the late nineteenth and early twentieth centuries also understood their identities differently than queer individuals today. Before the twentieth century, sexuality was not considered an inherent part of one's identity. Instead, it was a behavior. Sexuality, as understood by American society, was fluid. Before the creation of a binary system of categorizing sexuality as either heterosexual or homosexual, engaging in same-sex intimacy did not necessarily make one homosexual, as George Chauncey documented in his study of early-twentieth-century New York City.[14] Instead, sexual acts were evaluated based on the gendered roles individuals adopted during sex.[15] This mentality changed in the mid-twentieth century as homosexual men began to identify themselves as gay on the basis of "sexual object choice rather than gender status."[16] As a result, queer communities changed how they defined themselves.[17]

World War II served as a catalyst for expressing same-sex love and desire and created what John D'Emilio called a "nationwide coming out experience."[18] As homosexuality became more visible during and after the war, gay men and women faced discrimination in both their personal and professional lives. Activists such as Frank Kameny and Henry "Harry" Hay challenged this prejudice and created outlets for queer consciousness, such as the Mattachine Society, Daughters of Bilitis, and ONE, Inc. These early homophile organizations allowed for public expression of gay identity and created the foundation for the later, more radical, activism of the 1970s, including the uprising at Stonewall Inn in Greenwich Village in 1969.[19] That summer, a group of gay, bisexual, and transgender patrons fought back against police brutality, sparking the modern movement for LGBTQ civil rights and paving the way for future acts of civil disobedience. While half a century has passed since the civil unrest at Stonewall, more attention and consideration should be given to queer history and the spaces associated with these communities.

The process of identifying and preserving queer spaces requires the efforts of both amateurs and professionals alike. While those with training in the fields of history, historic preservation, public history, archaeology, and related disciplines have an advantage in accessing tools of documentation and preservation, all citizens have the power to help identify potential sites affiliated with queer history and to pursue various forms of preservation through federal and local designation, adaptive reuse, and more. Participating in the historical process in this way is a powerful act, and as Haitian anthropologist Michel-Rolph Trouillot noted, documenting and preserving history is one way to identify untold stories from the past. His book *Silencing the Past: Power and the Production of History* examines the process of recreating the past (through research and scholarship) and identifies why only a few select narratives are chosen for retelling over others. Many stories have been lost and omitted over time, leaving us with a limited glimpse of the past. As a result, Trouillot cautioned that "the production of historical narratives involves the uneven contribution of competing groups and individuals who have unequal access to the means of such production." The ability to record and interpret the past is an act that is derived from being in a position of power and authority.[20]

To avoid this imbalance of power when talking about the past, citizens today can participate in the process of preservation to make sure the voices of marginalized communities are heard and remembered. To ensure that queer spaces (and by extension queer stories) are not erased, grassroots preservation efforts are needed to preserve the tangible places that speak to the existence and history of LGBTQ people. This book series is intended to empower aspiring professionals, current practitioners, and members of the public to take an active role in learning about and preserving the queer stories of yesterday and today.

One of the challenges in recognizing queer spaces is determining how to document and preserve these places in a way that warrants their survival for the next generation. There are many avenues for recognizing and preserving historic places—some more accessible than others. One way is to nominate a property to the National Register of Historic Places or to designate it as a National Historic Landmark. While the programs are similar, National Register listings encompass locally and regionally significant properties, while National Historic Landmarks are properties deemed significant on a national level. The authors of this book series frequently refer to queer places listed on the National Register and emphasize the need to have LGBTQ historic sites federally designated as National Historic Landmarks. Both programs are managed by the National Park Service (NPS), and as this book series originally began as an online publication for the NPS, there is a notable emphasis on using the National Register and National Historic Landmark programs to recognize and preserve queer spaces.

While there are many historically significant places not listed on the National Register, this program provides certain benefits for property owners. In addition to tax benefits, property owners can also apply for select grants.[21] The National Park Service also uses the history of these places in its official interpretation, which brings greater public awareness about the importance of the properties. The National Register guidelines, however, can be limiting and exclusionary and have in the past favored the histories of white, heterosexual men of privilege.[22]

Despite this volume's emphasis on National Register listings and National Historic Landmarks, there are many other ways to recognize historically significant properties. In December 2017, the Metro Nashville Historical Commission recognized the significance of a local lesbian activist named Penny Campbell, adding a marker at her former home to the city's Historic Marker Program. A local LGBT activist who was instrumental in organizing the city's first pride parade, Campbell is also remembered as the lead plaintiff in a court case challenging the state's "homosexual acts" statute. Due to the efforts of Dr. Pippa Holloway, a professor of history at Middle Tennessee State University and Jessica Reeves, a member of the Metro Historical Commission, the city of Nashville dedicated its first marker to a queer rights activist. The commemoration of the Campbell house by the Metro Historical Commission serves as an example of the importance of local and regional designation programs in preserving the history of sexually variant and gender nonconforming Americans.[23]

Until recently, few lesbian, gay, bisexual, transgender, and queer-affiliated sites were recognized for their importance in American history. This is slowly changing as lawmakers, educators, and members of the public recognize the importance of queer stories and places in the larger narrative of American history. The designation of Stonewall National Monument by President Barack Obama in June 2016, for example, was a moment of triumph for LGBTQ Americans who witnessed part of queer history being federally recognized, honored, and protected as part of a larger movement for civil rights. Federal recognition of the importance of this place in American history is an important step in recognizing queer stories in the national narrative. Whether places of tragedy, triumph, celebration, or resistance, historic sites allow us to connect more deeply to our collective past. Recognizing and preserving LGBTQ history is also a collaborative effort between academics, civil servants, and members of the public. The three volumes in this series are a tangible example of the outcomes that can happen through such interdisciplinary efforts.

Over the past several years, the National Park Service has played a leading role in raising greater awareness of historic sites affiliated with LGBTQ history. As America's storyteller, the National Park Service identifies, preserves, and interprets the history of all U.S. citizens. Recently, the NPS and its programs, such as the National Register of Historic Places and National Historic Landmarks Program, have begun to care for and interpret more diverse historic sites that represent the broader spectrum of American experiences. The NPS is, by extension, addressing the underrepresentation of certain communities, including Latinos/Latinas, Asian Americans, Pacific Islanders, women, and LGBTQ communities.²⁴ *LGBTQ America: A Theme Study of Lesbian, Gay, Bisexual, Transgender, and Queer History,* released by the National Park Foundation and the National Park Service in 2016, is a prime example of the growing diversity represented within the National Park Service. Over twelve hundred pages in length and with contributions from dozens of authors, the study is intended to help historians, preservationists, and members of the public identify potential properties for nomination to the National Register of Historic Places and as National Historic Landmarks. The subsequent listings, designations, and amendments to existing listings resulting from the LGBTQ theme study further demonstrate the significance of LGBTQ sites to the overall American story.²⁵

At the time that *LGBTQ America* (the impetus for this book series) was released, I was a public history Ph.D. student completing my residency with the National Park Service's Cultural Resources Office of Interpretation and Education (the leading force behind the study's publication). Editor Megan E. Springate and I were invited by Berghahn Books to compose a book containing several chapters of *LGBTQ America.* As editor of the theme study, Megan's familiarity with the topic material and working relationship with the authors facilitated the conceptualization and execution of the series. To make the material more accessible to young professionals, community leaders, and members of the public, we created a series of activities for the practical application of topics and theories discussed in the chapters. With a background in civic engagement and public interpretation, I took on the challenge of creating activities to complement the content, with the target audience being college undergraduate and graduate students in fields relating to LGBTQ history, public history, and historic preservation. This project was meaningful not only as a way to guide people in the field; I was also grappling with how to identify myself as someone attracted to multiple genders. Accordingly, the project took on a special significance to me, and I was excited to have the opportunity to make the content accessible to a broader readership in a way that was deeply personal.

Megan and I were also eager to make the chapters of the LGBTQ theme study available in print (as the original is only accessible online) and to disseminate this information widely to a new generation of scholars. As we attempted to identify sections of the theme study to include in the book, we began to recognize the importance of all the chapters in depicting the LGBTQ experience in America. In *LGBTQ America,* the contributing authors addressed unique facets of queer communities and showed how affiliated historic sites are interconnected with the larger historical narrative. As a result, our book proposal to Berghahn Books was expanded to include a series of three volumes encompassing the themes of identity, community, and historic preservation.

The book series takes an all-encompassing approach to the study of queer history and culture. Due to their backgrounds as historians, public historians, preservationists, and community leaders, the authors bring different voices to the table. The series is also unique in offering an interactive element designed to engage undergraduate and graduate students. Each volume includes worksheets to prompt readers to think critically and immerse themselves in the subject matter. Each activity was intentionally crafted to allow faculty and educators the flexibility to tailor it to their course curriculum. Intended to be read as a series or individually, the books examine the history of LGBTQ communities in the United States, explore the complexities of LGBTQ identities, and provide guidance on how to identify, preserve, and interpret affiliated properties.

Katherine Crawford-Lackey is a Ph.D. candidate in public history at Middle Tennessee State University in Murfreesboro, Tennessee.

Notes

1. Dolores Hayden, *The Power of Place: Urban Landscapes as Public History,* (Cambridge, MA: MIT Press, 1995), xii.

2. Scholars such as architectural historian Dell Upton and American studies professor Bernard L. Herman examine the intentionality of the built landscape in influencing human behavior and perceptions. Their work reveals how landscapes and structures are designed to reinforce hierarchies of power. For more information about the topic, see Dell Upton, "White and Black Landscapes in Eighteenth-Century Virginia," in *Material Life in Amer-*

ica 1600-1860, ed. R. B. S. George (Boston: Northeastern University Press, 1988); and Bernard L. Herman, "The Embedded Landscapes of the Charleston Single House, 1780-1820," *Perspectives in Vernacular Architecture* 7 (1997): 41-57.

3. Historians including John D'Emilio, Estelle Freedman, and George Chauncey began exploring the history of gay Americans in the 1980s and 1990s. See, for example, John D'Emilio, *Sexual Politics, Sexual Communities: The Making of a Homosexual Minority in the United States, 1940-1970* (Chicago: University of Chicago Press, 1983); John D'Emilio, "Capitalism and Gay Identity," in *The Lesbian and Gay Studies Reader,* edited by Henry Abelove, Michele Aina Barale, and David M. Halperin (New York: Routledge, 1993); John D'Emilio and Estelle Freedman, *Intimate Matters: A History of Sexuality in America* (New York: Harper & Row, 1988); George Chauncey, *Gay New York: Gender, Urban Culture, and the Makings of the Gay Male World, 1890-1940* (New York: Basic Books, 1994).

4. Scholars have recently produced a range of studies on queer people living in various parts of North America, including John Howard's *Men Like That: A Southern Queer History* (Chicago: University of Chicago Press, 1999); Carol Mason's *Oklahoma: Lessons in Unqueering America* (Albany, NY: SUNY, 2015); and Colin R. Johnson's *Just Queer Folks: Gender and Sexuality in Rural America* (Philadelphia: Temple University Press, 2013).

5. Much of the existing queer scholarship ignores the diversity of LGBTQ people and experiences. In this book, the contributing authors explore different facets of queer identity, and attempt to address the diversity of LGBTQ communities by providing a broader understanding of how categories of difference impact daily life. For a more comprehensive analysis concerning the impact of race, gender, sexual orientation, and more on queer identities, see Megan E. Springate, "A Note about Intersectionality" (this volume).

6. Susan Ferentinos elaborates on how perceptions of sexual practice are contingent on time period and physical geography, which should be taken into consideration when interpreting LGBTQ history. She argues that scholars should not impose modern labels on queer people from the past as they would not necessarily have understood themselves in those terms. Susan Ferentinos, "Interpreting LGBTQ Historic Sites," in *Preservation and Place: Historic Preservation by and of LGBTQ Communities in the United States,* ed. Katherine Crawford-Lackey and Megan E. Springate (New York: Berghahn Books, 2019).

7. Lisa Bowleg, "When Black + Lesbian + Woman ≠ Black Lesbian Woman: The Methodological Challenges to Qualitative and Quantitative Intersectionality Research," Sex Roles 59 (2008): 312-25.

8. Loraine Hutchins, "Making Bisexual Visible" (this volume).

9. Susan Stryker, "Transgender History in the United States and the Places That Matter" (p. 89, this volume).

10. It should be noted that some gay individuals and communities still associate the term "queer" with very negative connotations due to the word's charged history. Authors in this study use this term to be more inclusive of identities that do not fit within lesbian, gay, bisexual, or transgender communities. Popular LGBT media outlets such as the *Advocate* and *Go Magazine* have published articles about the benefits and potential detriments of using this word given its historical context. Mark Segal, "The Problem with the Word 'Queer,'" *Advocate*, 11 February 2016, accessed 31 August 2018, https://www.advocate.com/commentary/2016/2/11/problem-word-queer; Dayna Troisi, "I'm A Lesbian and I'm Not Offended by the Word Queer," *Go Magazine*, 17 January 2018, accessed 31 August 2018, http://gomag.com/article/im-a-lesbian-and-im-not-offended-by-the-word-queer/.

11. John D'Emilio, *Sexual Politics, Sexual Communities*, 11.

12. Judith Jack Halberstam, *In a Queer Time and Place: Transgender Bodies, Subcultural Lives* (New York: New York University Press, 2005); Reina Lewis, "Review of *In a Queer Time and Place: Transgender Bodies, Subcultural Lives*, by Judith Halberstam; *In Your Face: 9 Sexual Studies* by Mandy Merck; *Lesbian Rule: Cultural Criticism and the Value of Desire* by Amy Villarejo," *Signs* 31, no. 3 (Spring 2006).

13. E. Patrick Johnson, "Introduction," in *No Tea, No Shade: New Writings in Black Queer Studies*, ed. E. Patrick Johnson (Durham, NC: Duke University Press, 2016).

14. Chauncey, *Gay New York*, 13.

15. Ibid., 20-21.

16. Ibid., 21.

17. Michel Foucault, *The History of Sexuality*, Vol. 1: *An Introduction* (New York: Vintage Press, 1990). Leisa Meyer and Helis Sikk, "Introduction to Lesbian, Gay, Bisexual, Transgender, and Queer (LGBTQ) History in the United States," in *LGBTQ America: A Theme Study of Lesbian, Gay, Bisexual, Transgender, and Queer History*, ed. Megan E. Springate (Washington, DC: National Park Foundation, 2016).

18. D'Emilio, *Sexual Politics, Sexual Communities*, 24.

19. Ibid., 108-18.

20. Michel-Rolph Trouillot, *Silencing the Past: Power and the Production of History* (Boston: Beacon Press, 1995), xix.

21. John H. Sprinkle Jr., *Crafting Preservation Criteria: The National Register of Historic Places and American Historic Preservation* (New York: Routledge, 2014), 1-4.

22. In the past, the National Register and National Historic Landmarks programs placed an emphasis on architecturally significant structures, and resulting nominations often ignored the human stories of those who lived and worked in these buildings. Additional challenges in nominating LGBTQ-affiliated properties arise when considering physical integrity. Current NPS bureau historian John H. Sprinkle Jr. gives an overview of requirements for

listing properties to these programs in his book *Crafting Historic Preservation* (previously cited), and he acknowledges that properties often lose integrity over time, especially those in urban areas. The National Register's "50 Year Rule" further complicates LGBTQ-affiliated nominations as the period of significance for many of the properties associated with queer history is relatively recent. Sprinkle, *Crafting Preservation Criteria.*

23. Chris St. Clair, "Metro Historical Commission Approves First Marker to Honor LGBT Struggle," Nashville Public Radio, 8 October 2017, accessed 27 August 2018, http://www.nashvillepublicradio.org/post/metro-historical-commission -approves-first-marker-honor-lgbt-struggle#stream/0.

24. Anne Mitchell Whisnant, Marla R. Miller, Gary B. Nash, and David Thelen, *Imperiled Promise: The State of History in the National Park Service* (Bloomington: Organization of American Historians, 2011).

25. The Pauli Murray Family Home (Durham, North Carolina) and Earl Hall (located on the campus of Columbia University) are examples of National Register listings and National Historic Landmark designations that have been recognized since the publication of the LGBTQ theme study. *LGBTQ America* has also led to the amendment of existing listings, including Whiskey Row, located in Louisville, KY. View the nominations: Pauli Murray Family Home, https://www.nps.gov/nhl/news/LC/fall2016/PauliMurrayFamilyHome.pdf; Earl Hall, http://www.nyclgbtsites.org/wp-content/uploads/2017/03/NY_NewYork County_EarlHall.pdf; and Kentucky's Whiskey Row, https://www.nps.gov/ nr/feature/places/pdfs/AD89000385_03_13_2017.pdf.

Bibliography

Bowleg, Lisa. "When Black + Lesbian + Woman ≠ Black Lesbian Woman: The Methodological Challenges to Qualitative and Quantitative Intersectionality Research." *Sex Roles* 59 (2008): 312–25.

Chauncey, George. *Gay New York: Gender, Urban Culture, and the Makings of the Gay Male World, 1890–1940.* New York: Basic Books, 1994.

D'Emilio, John. "Capitalism and Gay Identity," in *The Lesbian and Gay Studies Reader,* edited by Henry Abelove, Michele Aina Barale, and David M. Halperin, (New York: Routledge, 1993).

———. *Sexual Politics, Sexual Communities: The Making of a Homosexual Minority in the United States, 1940–1970.* Chicago: University of Chicago Press, 1983.

D'Emilio, John, and Estelle Freedman. *Intimate Matters: A History of Sexuality in America.* New York: Harper & Row, 1988.

Ferentinos, Susan. "Interpreting LGBTQ Historic Sites," in *Preservation and Place: Historic Preservation by and of LGBTQ Communities in the United States,* edited by Katherine Crawford-Lackey and Megan E. Springate (New York: Berghahn Books, 2019).

Foucault, Michel. *The History of Sexuality,* Vol. 1: *An Introduction.* New York: Vintage Press, 1990.

Halberstam, Judith Jack. *In a Queer Time and Place: Transgender Bodies, Subcultural Lives.* New York: New York University Press, 2005.

Hayden, Dolores. *The Power of Place: Urban Landscapes as Public History.* Cambridge, MA: MIT Press, 1995.

Herman, Bernard L. "The Embedded Landscapes of the Charleston Single House, 1780–1820." Perspectives in Vernacular Architecture 7 (1997): 41–57.

Howard, John. *Men Like That: A Southern Queer History.* Chicago: University of Chicago Press, 1999.

Hutchins, Loraine. "Making Bisexual Visible." In *Identities and Place: Changing Labels and Intersectional Communities of LGBTQ and Two-Spirit People in the United States,* edited by Katherine Crawford-Lackey and Megan E. Springate. New York: Berghahn Books, 2020.

Johnson, Colin R. *Just Queer Folks: Gender and Sexuality in Rural America.* Philadelphia: Temple University Press, 2013.

Johnson, E. Patrick. "Introduction." In *No Tea, No Shade: New Writings in Black Queer Studies,* edited by E. Patrick Johnson. Durham, NC: Duke University Press, 2016.

Lewis, Reina. "Review of *In a Queer Time and Place: Transgender Bodies, Subcultural Lives,* by Judith Halberstam; *In Your Face: 9 Sexual Studies* by Mandy Merck; *Lesbian Rule: Cultural Criticism and the Value of Desire* by Amy Villarejo," *Signs* 31, no. 3 (Spring 2006).

Mason, Carol. *Oklahoma: Lessons in Unqueering America.* Albany, NY: SUNY, 2015.

Meyer, Leisa, and Helis Sikk. "Introduction to Lesbian, Gay, Bisexual, Transgender, and Queer (LGBTQ) History in the United States." In *LGBTQ America: A Theme Study of Lesbian, Gay, Bisexual, Transgender, and Queer History,* edited by Megan E. Springate (Washington, DC: National Park Foundation, 2016).

Segal, Mark. "The Problem with the Word 'Queer.'" *The Advocate,* 11 February 2016. Accessed 31 August 2018. https://www.advocate.com/commentary/2016/2/11/problem-word-queer.

Springate, Megan E. "A Note on Intersectionality." In *Identities and Place: Changing Labels and Intersectional Communities of LGBTQ and Two-Spirit People in the United States,* edited by Katherine Crawford-Lackey and Megan E. Springate. New York: Berghahn Books, 2020.

Sprinkle, Jr., John H. *Crafting Preservation Criteria: The National Register of Historic Places and American Historic Preservation.* New York: Routledge, 2014.

St. Clair, Chris. "Metro Historical Commission Approves First Marker to Honor LGBT Struggle." Nashville Public Radio, 8 October 2017. Accessed 27 August 2018. http://www.nashvillepublicradio.org/post/metro-historical-commission-approves-first-marker-honor-lgbt-struggle#stream/0.

Stryker, Susan. "Transgender History in the United States and the Places That Matter." In *Identities and Place: Changing Labels and Intersectional Communities of LGBTQ and Two-Spirit People in the United States,* edited by

Katherine Crawford-Lackey and Megan E. Springate. New York: Berghahn Books, 2020.

Troisi, Dayna. "I'm A Lesbian and I'm Not Offended by the Word Queer." *Go Magazine,* 17 January 2018. Accessed 31 August 2018. http://gomag.com/article/im-a-lesbian-and-im-not-offended-by-the-word-queer/.

Trouillot, Michel-Rolph. *Silencing the Past: Power and the Production of History.* Boston: Beacon Press, 1995.

Upton, Dell. "White and Black Landscapes in Eighteenth-Century Virginia." In *Material Life in America 1600–1860,* edited by R. B. S. George. Boston: Northeastern University Press, 1988.

Whisnant, Anne Mitchell, Marla R. Miller, Gary B. Nash, and David Thelen. *Imperiled Promise: The State of History in the National Park Service.* Bloomington: Organization of American Historians, 2011.

National Register/National Historic Landmark Nominations:

Pauli Murray Family Home, National Historic Landmark Nomination, 2016, https://www.nps.gov/nhl/news/LC/fall2016/PauliMurrayFamilyHome.pdf.

Earl Hall, National Register of Historic Places Nomination, 2017, http://www.nyclgbtsites.org/wp-content/uploads/2017/03/NY_NewYorkCounty_EarlHall.pdf.

Kentucky's Whiskey Row, National Register of Historic Places Additional Documentation, 2017, https://www.nps.gov/nr/feature/places/pdfs/AD89000385_03_13_2017.pdf.

Acknowledgments

This book and the series it is part of are the product of the collaborative efforts of many individuals. Their dedication and support throughout this process has made this publication possible.

This series comes out of *LGBTQ America: A Theme Study of Lesbian, Gay, Bisexual, Transgender, and Queer History,* which was edited by Megan E. Springate for the National Park Foundation and the National Park Service (2016). We are grateful to the Gill Foundation for funding it, and to all of the National Park Service and National Park Foundation staff, scholars, community members, authors, peer reviewers, and production folks who made that project—and therefore also this one—possible. Many thanks to the authors and peer reviewers who worked with us on this volume for your thoughtful contributions. Your work is the heart of this book.

We would like to extend special thanks to Dr. Barbara J. Little at the National Park Service, who provided encouragement and guidance throughout this process, and to Dr. Caryn M. Berg, our editor at Berghahn Books, for suggesting this series and working with us to bring it to fruition.

We are grateful for the support and feedback of our colleagues in the Cultural Resources Office of Interpretation and Education and elsewhere in the Cultural Resources, Partnerships and Science Directorate at the National Park Service.

Of course, we could not have done this without the support of friends and colleagues. Katherine would like to thank Dr. Pippa Holloway and Dr. Carol Van West for reviewing her contributions, and her parents, Leo and Kathleen, for their continued support. She would also like to recognize her partner, Jonathan Eizyk, for reading (and re-reading) the prologues and activities. Megan is grateful for the support of her family and friends, including Chelsea Blackmore and Danielle Easter.

The views and conclusions contained in this volume are those of the authors and should not be interpreted as representing the opinions or policies of the U.S. Government. Mention of trade names or commercial products does not constitute their endorsement by the U.S. government.

CHAPTER 1

A Note about Intersectionality, LGBTQ Communities, History, and Place

Megan E. Springate

> There is no such thing as a single-issue struggle,
> because we do not live single-issue lives.
> —Audre Lorde

Intersectionality is the recognition that categories of difference (sometimes also referred to as axes of identity), including—but not limited to—race, ethnicity, gender, religion/creed, generation, geographic location, sexuality, age, ability/disability, and class, intersect to shape the experiences of individuals.[1] In other words, identity is multidimensional, and identities are not mutually exclusive but interdependent.[2] This means that oppression and prejudice (including racism, classism, transphobia, classism, homophobia, and sexism) also affect individuals and communities in multiple interdependent ways. LGBTQ is not a single community with a single history; indeed, each group represented by these letters (lesbian, gay, bisexual, transgender, and queer) is made up of multiple communities.[3] The axes of gender, generation, geographic location, ethnicity, and other factors play an important role in the history of LGBTQ America, shaping the various histories of LGBTQ communities across the nation and the places associated with them. For example, the experiences of rural LGBTQ individuals are different from those in urban areas; those of white, gay Latinos different from those of gay AfroLatino men; middle-class African American lesbians' lives differ from those of working-class African American lesbians and middle-class white lesbians. And of course, interwoven among all of these are the specific experiences and personalities of individual people.

The idea of intersectionality is not new; in her 1851 speech now known as "Ain't I a Woman," Sojourner Truth spoke about the intersections of being a woman, being Black, and having been enslaved.[4] In the 1960s and 1970s, Black and Chicana women articulated the intersectionality of their lives, forming Black feminist and Chicana feminist movements as their experiences as women of color were ignored, belittled, and/or erased by the largely white, middle-class women's movement that treated race and gender as mutually exclusive categories. In their lived experience, oppression as people of color, as women, and as women of color could not be untangled.[5] The term intersectionality was first used in print by Kimberlé Crenshaw in a law journal describing the problematic effects of a single-axis approach to antidiscrimination law, feminist theory, and antiracist politics.[6] Since then, intersectionality has become an important concept across many disciplines, including history, art and architectural history, anthropology, geography, sociology, psychology, and law.[7]

An understanding of intersectionality is important for place-based research and historic preservation because these axes of difference can affect the physical places associated with communities. They also affect the relationships that various individuals and communities have with places. People who own instead of rent their homes and commercial buildings are more likely to be able to stay in their neighborhoods as real estate prices increase—a result, for example, of gentrification. Using an intersectional approach that takes into account income disparities based on race, gender, and sexual orientation, it becomes clear that lesbians and transgender individuals (especially those of color), who tend to have lower incomes than others and therefore cannot afford to own their own homes, are forced out of neighborhoods more rapidly than middle-class gay white males, who tend to have more income that can be invested in purchasing buildings. Similarly, because lesbians (as women) have tended to have less disposable income than gay men, there have tended to be fewer lesbian clubs and bars. Instead, white women and women of color, as well as people of color, have tended to meet and socialize in private spaces.[8]

The meanings of places also differ across the various LGBTQ communities. For example, the Michigan Womyn's Music Festival was founded in 1976 as a women-only space and, until it ended in 2016, had been an important event in the history of women's land, women's music, and community-based organization. Founder Lisa Vogel recounts in a recent interview that from at least the late 1970s, the festival was described as being for "womyn-born-womyn," meaning "womyn who were born and survived girlhood and still identified as womyn."[9] In 1991, transgender women and their allies formed Camp Trans, a protest encampment just outside the festival grounds. They were protesting their exclusion from the festival. The Michigan Womyn's Music Festival has meant very different things to these different communities: some have experienced the place as one of inclusion and visibility, while others experienced oppression and exclusion.[10]

Intersectional analysis is one way to avoid causing epistemic violence (excluding people from how we understand and know the world). This violence affects individuals and communities by silencing their voices or rendering their experiences invisible.[11] The temptation to ignore those alternative voices in LGBTQ history is great: "Given the new opportunities available to *some* gays and lesbians," writes critical theorist Heather Love, "the temptation to forget—to forget the outrages and humiliations of gay and lesbian history and to ignore the ongoing suffering of those not borne up by the rising tide of gay normalization—is stronger than ever."[12] Those who fall outside the homonormative, mainstream gay rights movement and therefore its history—to varying degrees—include those living on low incomes, people with disabilities, people of color, the elderly, women, transgender and gender nonconforming people, drag kings and queens, bisexuals, those living in rural areas, and those whose sexual practices fall outside the realm of the socially acceptable, described by Gayle Rubin as the "charmed circle."[13] Especially alienated are those whose identities encompass more than one of these axes of exclusion.[14] Cynthia Levine-Rasky argues that a full understanding of these as axes of exclusion and oppression also requires that researchers pay attention to the intersectionality of whiteness and middle-class identity (and, by extension, other identities that are privileged in our society).[15] An intersectional reevaluation of the experiences of those groups that have been comparatively well represented (including gay, white, urban men) will also result in a more nuanced and accurate understanding of LGBTQ history and its role in American society

Also often excluded from mainstream narratives are parts of a person's or event's history that complicate our understanding or are considered uncomplimentary. Part of the purpose of doing LGBTQ history and historic preservation is to bring forward the LGBTQ aspects of history that have been silenced. However, some LGBTQ histories that are being brought forward leave out some of the less savory aspects of their subjects. A recent example is that of M. Carey Thomas, who was a long-term dean and then the second president of Bryn Mawr College (from 1894 to 1922). She was an activist for women's suffrage and was in long-

Figure 1.1. M. Carey Thomas standing on the Deanery porch and addressing students, 1905. Photo courtesy of the Photo Archives, Special Collections Department, Bryn Mawr College Library.

term relationships with women, including during her tenure at Bryn Mawr (Mamie Gwinn, followed by Mary Garrett, both of whom shared Thomas' residence, the Deanery, on campus; figure 1.1).[16] Like many white people in power at the time, Thomas was also racist and anti-Semitic, "openly and vigorously" advancing racism and anti-Semitism as part of her vision for Bryn Mawr. The college has begun struggling with this intersectional and complicated history in how it remembers Thomas's legacy.[17]

An intersectional approach to history provides a much more complete and nuanced understanding of our past. This includes the experiences and voices of those who are often silenced in dominant narratives that highlight the actions of those with privilege, including white, middle- and upper-class heterosexual men. One instance where an intersectional approach provided a more complete history is the inclusion of ethnicity and class in the study of women's rights. The dominant narrative of women's rights recognizes three "waves": the First Wave is described as spanning the years between 1848 (the First Convention for Women's Rights at Seneca Falls, New York) and 1920 (passage of the Nineteenth Amendment, granting women the right to vote); the Second Wave that emerged in the 1960s and 1970s as women worked toward ending gender discrimination in arenas including employment, medical care, and financial equity; and the Third Wave that began in the 1990s, which involved a more active and mainstream approach to intersectionality in the women's movement. This narrative of feminist waves is based predominantly on the experiences of white, middle-class women in advocating for women's rights and in reaping the benefits of their activism. For example, though women were granted the right to vote in 1920, Jim Crow laws in the southern states kept African American women (and men) from the voting booths until the passage of the Civil Rights Act of 1964. Many Native Americans of all genders were likewise denied voting rights, even after the passage of the Indian Citizenship Act of 1924, since it was up to states to decide who could vote. In 1962, Utah was the last state to allow Native Americans to vote.[18]

Recent scholarship that takes an intersectional approach to feminism recognizes that the women's movement did not vanish during the years following the passage of the Nineteenth Amendment.[19] Betty Friedan's book, *The Feminine Mystique*, is based on her observations of white, middle-class suburban housewives and her experiences as one of them, but does not mention her experiences as a journalist for leftist and labor union publications.[20] While her work is often credited with sparking the Second Wave of feminism, such an analysis ignores the experiences and gains of African American women and wage-earning women (and their white, middle-class allies) who had not stopped working toward feminist goals after suffrage.[21] In the years after 1920, women who had been focusing their efforts on suffrage shifted their attention to labor and social welfare legislation. Some women chose to work within the political party system or within the government itself, while others chose to work in private organizations or with labor organizers. Women who had been working within the labor and racial justice movements prior to the passage of the Nineteenth Amendment continued their work. This work culminated in the creation in 1961 of the President's Commission on the Status of Women and its 1963 report, *American Women: Report of the President's Commission on the Status of Women*, as well as the passage of the Civil Rights Act of 1964. These in turn laid the groundwork for the founding of the National Organization of Women (NOW) in 1966.[22] NOW (which included Betty Friedan, Shirley Chisholm, and Pauli Murray among its forty-nine founding members) was the organization that spearheaded the women's rights movement of the 1960s and 1970s.[23] This intersectional analysis, which includes working women and labor organizers as well as women working for racial justice, puts the lie to the idea of a Second Wave of feminism that is discontinuous from the reform movements of the early twentieth century and that has its roots in white, middle-class experience.

Missing from this intersectional analysis, however, is a consideration of LGBTQ contributions to the advancement of women's rights. This is consistent with the exclusion of LGBTQ people (or the exclusion of their LGBTQ identity) from American history more broadly. The result is an incomplete and oversimplified picture of U.S. history. More recent scholarship has included LGBTQ individuals and organizations such as Anna Howard Shaw, Pauli Murray, Carrie Chapman Catt, couples Esther Lape and Elizabeth Read, and Nancy Cook and Marion Dickerman in the history of the women's movement; Frances Kellor and Bayard Rustin in social reform movements; the Marine Cooks and Stewards Union, Howard Wallace and the Lesbian/Gay Labor Alliance, and Emily Blackwell in labor history.[24]

Working with Intersectionality

Intersectional analysis can be challenging to do. Several authors have presented different ways of working intersectionally. One is the inclusion of multiple narratives in interpretation. These serve to oppose dominant narratives and established power structures and as a way to enrich our understanding of the past by including multiple experiences and voices. Elsa Barkley Brown describes the Creole phenomenon of "gumbo ya-ya," where everyone talks at once, telling their stories in connection and in dialogue with one another, as a nonlinear approach to intersectionality and multivocality.[25] Applying a multivocal approach to understanding the past brings its own set of challenges, including the problem of unaccountable or competing narratives. Philosopher Alison Wylie advocates "integrity in scholarship" to evaluate and correct for competing narratives. This integrity includes being fair to the evidence and a methodological multivocality that incorporates multiple sources of information in support of interpretations.[26] These many voices may come from written documents, oral histories, and autoethnography, among others.[27] Gayatri Chakravorty Spivak talks about the use of "strategic essentialism," in which groups choose to foreground particular identities—a strategy that can also be used in analysis.[28] Chela Sandoval, Emma Pérez, and other authors also write about working intersectionally.[29] In the writing of LGBTQ history, some of these multiple sources of information may include rumor and willful silences where being out was too much of a risk.[30] Of such sources, historian John Howard writes, "This hearsay evidence—inadmissible in court, unacceptable to some historians—is essential to the recuperation of queer histories. The age-old squelching of our words and desires can be replicated when we adhere to ill-suited and unbending standards of historical methodology."[31] Below, I provide several examples of intersectional analysis in LGBTQ context.

Intersectional Analysis

Historian Judith Bennett demonstrates that "lesbian" (and by analogy other sexual identities) is an unstable and unfixed identity by describing the many different identities that it encompasses. These include "butch" (more masculine in appearance and behavior), "femme" (more feminine in appearance and behavior), "vanilla" (not sexually radical), and "sexually radical" (kinky or polyamorous), all of which are further influenced by age, ethnicity, and other axes of identity.[32] "If lesbian is not a stable entity now," she writes, there is "no reason to think it was stable in the past."[33] She also notes that the connection of sexuality to the act of having sex is problematic. We recognize that someone may identify as straight, gay, or bisexual without having had sex, or during periods of their lives where they are not sexually active. But what about studying people in the past, whose sexual activity remains uncertain? What about different definitions of what is considered sexual or erotic?[34] Bennett proposed the concept of "lesbian-like" for studying women in the past whose lives might have particularly offered opportunities for same-sex love, who resisted norms of feminine behavior based on heterosexual marriage, and who lived in circumstances that allowed them to nurture and support other women.[35] Other researchers have identified people as queer based on speculation, hearsay, and willful silences without "proof" that they were sexually active with others of the same gender. They argue, in part, that rumor carries meaning and that, regardless of their subjects' sexual behavior, they led queer, nonnormative lives.[36]

Butch and femme gender expressions among queer women have traditionally been associated with working-class people.[37] Despite this traditional association, a recent study suggests that the meaning of masculine gender presentation can vary by location. In urban areas, female masculinity is often associated with lesbian identity, while in some rural areas it is acceptable for women, regardless of their sexuality, to have a more masculine gender presentation.[38] The presence of LGBTQ people in rural areas has been largely overlooked, with much of the history focused on "the well-rehearsed triumvirate of . . . queer mythology: New York, Los Angeles, and San Francisco."[39] Regardless of gender presentation or location, "lesbians, suffering from the dual disqualification of being gay and female, have been repeatedly dispossessed of their history."[40] Additional "disqualifications," such as being a person of color or disabled, exacerbate the impacts.

Queer theorists such as Judith Jack Halberstam, Judith Butler, and Gayle Rubin provide frameworks for understanding not only how sexuality and gender interact to create multiple spectrums of identity, but also the possibility of (and ways of naming) more genders than male, female, and other.[41] Recent work by Freeman, Halberstam, and other authors describes how queer is more than just an expression of gender/sexual identity, arguing that the queer subculture works within ideas of space and time that are independent of those that structure the normative heterosexual lifestyle.[42] These shape how LGBTQ people experience and interact with space, place, and history.[43]

Often marginalized from mainstream narratives, LGBTQ people of color are often confronted by a "politics of respectability." They describe experiencing pressure to hide their sexuality or gender identity (or other identities) in order to appear respectable within their community and to be respectable representatives of their community to the dominant (white) culture.[44] This politics of respectability is not limited to expressions of sexuality or gender. Evelyn Higginbotham describes it within the context of African American experience, but other people of color, including those in the Latinx communities, also describe the effects of respectability politics.[45] Some LGBTQ people feel pressure, harassment, and violence both from within their communities and from without—pressure to be respectable as a means of advancing acceptance and LGBTQ rights. This has been associated with increased rates of depression, anxiety, and even suicide among LGBTQ populations.[46] Straight, white, middle-class people, by contrast, generally do not have to contend with accusations or feelings of disappointing their communities because heterosexual, middle-class, white privilege means that any vi-

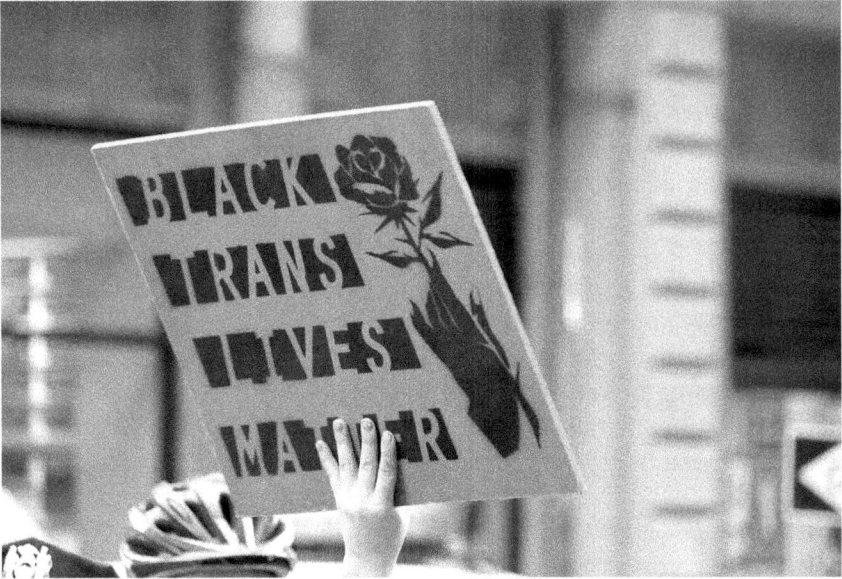

Figure 1.2. Black Trans Lives Matter sign, May Day demonstrations, New York City, 2017. Photo courtesy of Alec Perkins (CC BY-2.0; https://www.flickr.com/photos/alecperkins/34045294240/).

olation of social norms is an individual act and not representative of community identity.[47] Black Lives Matter (BLM) was founded by three queer women of color (Alicia Garza, Patrisse Cullors, and Opal Tometi) in response to violence targeted against African Americans. Intersectional by design, BLM pushes against violence (physical, epistemic, and/or by exclusion) directed towards all Black people, including those who are LGBTQ. This has brought into sharp relief many of the divisions that persist among and between LGBTQ communities. In 2015, in response to an unprecedented murder rate of transgender people, particularly transgender women of color, BLM and Trans Lives Matter worked together, insisting that #BlackTransLivesMatter (figure 1.2).[48]

Within the Latinx community, expressions of gender (masculinity and femininity) have been shaped historically by unique traditions, religious influences, and laws. Gender norms emphasize *macho* masculinity for men and *Marianismo* femininity for women, serving as the basis for heterosexuality and the family as the central social structure. *Macho* is an expression of Latino heterosexual masculinity: an often exaggerated sense of masculine pride associated with strength, sexual potency and prowess, and ideals of chivalry. In traditional Latinx thinking, most gay men are considered insufficiently *macho*. In contrast, *Marianismo* is characterized by women who are modest, virtuous, and sexually abstinent until heterosexual marriage, after which they are faithful and subordinate to their husbands. The *mujer passiva* (passive woman) or *la mujer abnegada* (self-denying woman) sacrifices her own individualism for the benefit of her (heterosexual) family.[49] Individuals who express their gender and sexuality outside these cultural gender roles risk censure and ostracism from their family, which is central to Latinx experience.[50]

In much of the mainstream LGBTQ history, Latinx people have been found largely at the margins or invisible. In part, this has been because many chose to remain closeted and to protect their status in their families and communities. Others stayed away from the predominantly white, mainstream gay rights movement because they felt marginalized or felt the weight of widespread anti-Latinx sentiment.[51] LGBTQ Latinx people are becoming increasingly visible both because homosexuality is slowly becoming more acceptable in their communities and because they are becoming more politically active overall.[52]

Examples of how the emphasis on respectability for African Americans plays out include the experiences of middle-class Black lesbians and queer gospel singers. Researchers describe Black lesbians navigating their identities in such a way that they retain racial group commitments to be seen to be "people of good character" while simultaneously being autonomous sexual selves.[53] Gospel singers within the Black church likewise have navigated their identities to be both godly (of good character) and to express their sexuality.

Contemporary gospel music had its beginnings in Chicago in the 1920s, blurring the lines between secular rhythms and sacred texts. With this melding of forms, "gospel provided a space for those who were not necessarily accepted around the 'welcome table'—namely sexual and gender nonconformists—to participate in the musical form's continued growth and innovation."[54] In the culture of silence around sexuality in general and homosexuality in particular within Black churches, and where homosexuality was seen to violate the "God-given order of things," many queers remained closeted or neither confirmed nor denied their sexuality. This secrecy was crucial: without it, one could lose both their livelihood and their acceptance in their "first family," the church.[55] Church choirs, argues historian E. Patrick Johnson, served as "nurturing sites" for the creative expression of effeminate boys who otherwise may have been ostracized. "Church sissies" and "church butches" found each other in choirs, and it was not uncommon for queer singers and musicians to use conventions, including the National Baptist Convention, as opportunities to socialize with each other.[56] While homosexuality was considered an abomination and preached against from the pulpit, parishioners often looked the other way for talented artists. There seemed to be no such opprobrium regarding gender nonconformity: "How else," asks Johnson, "could one explain the number of flamboyant singers such as Little Richard, who grew up and returned to the church, whose sexuality seems to have never been an issue?"[57]

What are the implications of an intersectional approach to LGBTQ history and heritage, particularly in the context of the National Register of Historic Places and National Historic Landmarks programs? By recognizing that there are many LGBTQ communities and histories formed around and influenced by various aspects of identity, we can ensure that the richness and complexities of these multiple voices—including ones often silenced or marginalized—can be represented. An intersectional approach also allows the recognition and evaluation of historic properties in context.[58] For instance, the interiors of bars and clubs have often been extensively remodeled and may no longer retain their historic integrity.[59] This is, however, the nature of clubs, which often changed hands or were renovated to either retain their current clientele or to attract a different one (like a different segment of the LGBTQ community or a more heterosexual patronage) in order to remain profitable. Integrity, then, may be evaluated differently for an LGBTQ bar than for a residence. Recognizing that lesbians historically have had fewer bars and clubs for socializing encourages us to look elsewhere for women's social spaces. Intersectionality also allows us to broaden our thinking about what the division of social space along axes including binary gender (male-female), ethnicity, and sexuality (gay-straight) means and has meant for those whose identities include being trans and/or bisexual and/or of a particular ethnicity (white, African American, Latinx, Asian American, American Indian, etc.) and to consider these effects in our analysis. As well as providing a more nuanced and complete approach to documenting LGBTQ sites, an intersectional approach also connects LGBTQ history to broader patterns in American history, including Civil Rights, women's history, and labor history, to name just a few. Understanding intersectional and complex identities and histories—both community and individual—also opens space for us to see our imperfect selves as having the potential to be agents of change.

Dr. Megan E. Springate is the National Coordinator for the National Park Service 19th Amendment Centennial Commemoration and editor of *LGBTQ America: A Theme Study of Lesbian, Gay, Bisexual, Transgender, and Queer History* (2016).

Notes

1. The epigraph is from Audre Lorde, "Learning from the 60s," in *Sister Outsider: Essays & Speeches by Audre Lorde* (Berkeley, CA: Crossing Press, 2007), 138.
2. Lisa Bowleg, "When Black + Lesbian + Woman ≠ Black Lesbian Woman: The Methodological Challenges to Qualitative and Quantitative Intersectionality Research," *Sex Roles* 59 (2008): 312–25.
3. Judith M. Bennett, "'Lesbian-Like' and the Social History of Lesbianisms," *Journal of the History of Sexuality* 9 (2000): 1–24; Trina Grillo, "Anti-Essentialism and Intersectionality: Tools to Dismantle the Master's House," *Berkeley Women's Law Journal* 10 (1995): 16–30.
4. Truth spoke at the Women's Convention at the Old Stone Church, corner of North High and Perkins Streets, Akron, Ohio, on 29 May 1851 (now demolished). Various versions of the speech exist, including several published from memory by Frances Dana Barker Gage, which include the phrase "Ain't I a Woman." The earliest published version, recalled by Marius Robinson, does not include this phrase. See Corona Brazina, *Sojourner Truth's "Ain't I a Woman?" Speech: A Primary Source Investigation* (New York: RosenCentral Primary Source, 2005); Kay Siebler, "Teaching the Politics of Sojourner Truth's 'Ain't I a Woman?'" *Pedagogy* 10, no. 3 (Fall 2010): 511–33.
5. Patricia Hill Collins and Sirma Bilge, *Intersectionality* (Malden, MA: Polity Press, 2016), 63–87. See, for example, Alma M. Garcia, "The Development of Chicana Feminist Discourse, 1870-1980," *Gender and Society* 3, no. 2 (1989): 217-38; Alma M. Garcia, *Chicana Feminist Thought: The Basic Historical Writings* (New York: Routledge, 1997); Combahee River Collective, "A Black Feminist Statement [1977]." In *The Second Wave: A Reader in Feminist Theory*, ed. Linda Nicholson, 63–70 (New York: Routledge, 1997). See also Cherrie Moraga and Gloria Anzaldua, *This Bridge Called My Back: Writings by Radical Women of Color* (Massachusetts: Persephone Press, 1981).
6. Kimberlé Crenshaw, "Demarginalizing the Intersection of Race and Sex: A Black Feminist Critique of Antidiscrimination Doctrine, Feminist Theory and Antiracist Politics," *University of Chicago Legal Forum* (1989): 139–67.
7. See, for example, Bowleg, "When Black + Lesbian + Woman ≠ Black Lesbian Woman"; Grillo, "Anti-Essentialism and Intersectionality"; Mike C. Parent, Cirleen DeBlaere, and Bonnie Moradi, "Approaches to Research on Intersectionality: Perspectives on Gender, LGBT, and Racial/Ethnic Identities," *Sex Roles* 68 (2013): 639–45; Gill Valentine, "Theorizing and Researching Intersectionality: A Challenge for Feminist Geography," *The Professional Geographer* 59, no. 1 (2007): 10–21; and Leah R. Warner and Stephanie A. Shields,

"The Intersections of Sexuality, Gender, and Race: Identity Research at the Crossroads," *Sex Roles* 68 (2013): 803–10.

8. See, for example, Elizabeth Lapovsky Kennedy and Madeline D. Davis, *Boots of Leather, Slippers of Gold: The History of a Lesbian Community* (New York: Routledge, 1993); see also the other chapters in this volume.

9. Jocelyn Macdonald, "Setting the Record Straight about MichFest," *After-Ellen*, 24 October 2018, https://www.afterellen.com/general-news/565301-setting-the-record-straight-about-michfest. See also Susan Stryker, "Transgender History in the United States and the Places That Matter" (this volume); and Katherine Schweighofer, "LGBTQ Sport and Leisure," in *LGBTQ America: A Theme Study of Lesbian, Gay, Bisexual, Transgender, and Queer History*, ed. Megan E. Springate (Washington, DC: National Park Foundation and National Park Service, 2016), https://www.nps.gov/articles/lgbtqtheme-sport.htm.

10. Compare, for example, Michigan Womyn's Music Festival Community with Sara St. Martin Lynne, ed., *Voices from the Land: A Collective Memoir*, Kindle edition, 2015; and Cristan Williams, "Michigan Womyn's Music Festival," *TransAdvocate*, 2013, http://transadvocate.com/michigan-womyns-music-festival_n_8943.htm.

11. See, for example, Sabrina Alimahomed, "Thinking Outside the Rainbow: Women of Color Redefining Queer Politics and Identity," *Social Identities* 16, no. 2 (2010): 151–68; Amy L. Brandzel, "Haunted by Citizenship: White-normative Citizen-Subjects and the Uses of History in Women's Studies," *Feminist Studies* 37, no. 3 (2011): 503–33.

12. Heather Love, *Feeling Backward: Loss and the Politics of Queer History* (Cambridge, MA: Harvard University Press, 2007), xiv; see also Elizabeth Freeman, *Time Binds: Queer Temporalities, Queer Histories* (Durham, NC: Duke University Press, 2010).

13. Gayle S. Rubin, "Thinking Sex: Notes for a Radical Theory of the Politics of Sexuality," in *Culture, Society and Sexuality: A Reader*, 2nd ed., ed. Richard Parker and Peter Aggleton (New York: Routledge, 1984), 143–78. Homonormativity is a term that encompasses the intersection of issues including white privilege, ableism, capitalism, classism, sexism, and transmisogyny that excludes those who do not fit the resulting norms from consideration. See Laura Kacere, "Homonormativity 101: What It Is and How It's Hurting Our Movement," *Everyday Feminism*, 24 January 2015, https://everydayfeminism.com/2015/01/homonormativity-101/.

14. See, for example, Alimahomed, "Thinking Outside the Rainbow"; Lou Chibbaro Jr., "Special Report: Poverty in the LGBT Community," *Washington Blade*, 12 February 2014, http://www.washingtonblade.com/2014/02/12/special-report-poverty-lgbt-community; Eli Clare, *Exile & Pride: Disability, Queerness, and Liberation* (Cambridge, MA: South End Press, 1999); Petra L. Doan, "The Tyranny of Gendered Spaces: Reflections from Beyond the Gender Dichotomy," *Gender, Place & Culture: A Journal of Feminist*

Geography 17, no. 5 (2010): 635–54; Heron Greenesmith, "Drawing Bisexuality Back into the Picture: How Bisexuality Fits into LGBT Legal Strategy Ten Years after Bisexual Erasure," *Cardozo Journal of Law & Gender* 17, no. 65 (2010): 65–80; Daniel Hirsch, "R-Rated and Ephemeral: Spinning LGBT History," *MissionLocal*, 18 July 2014, http://missionlocal.org/2014/07/r-rated-and-ephemeral-spinning-lgbt-history; E. Patrick Johnson, "Gays and Gospel: A Queer History of Sacred Music," in *Out in Chicago: LGBT History at the Crossroads*, ed. Jill Austin and Jennifer Brier (Chicago: Chicago History Museum, 2011), 109–26; Emily Kazyak, "Midwest or Lesbian? Gender, Rurality, and Sexuality," *Gender & Society* 26, no. 6 (2012): 825–48; Love, *Feeling Backward*; Jeff Maskovsky, "Do We All 'Reek of the Commodity'? Consumption and the Erasure of Poverty in Lesbian and Gay Studies," in *Out in Theory: The Emergence of Lesbian and Gay Anthropology*, ed. Ellen Lewin and William L. Leap (Urbana: University of Illinois Press, 2002), 264–86; Doug Meyer, "An Intersectional Analysis of Lesbian, Gay, Bisexual, and Transgender (LGBT) People's Evaluations of Anti-Queer Violence," *Gender & Society* 26, no. 6 (2012): 849–73; Mignon R. Moore, *Invisible Families: Gay Identities, Relationships, and Motherhood among Black Women* (Berkeley: University of California Press, 2011); Mignon R. Moore, "Intersectionality and the Study of Black, Sexual Minority Women," *Gender & Society* 26, no. 1 (2012): 33–39; Rubin, "Thinking Sex"; Gayle S. Rubin, *Deviations: A Gayle Rubin Reader* (Durham, NC: Duke University Press, 2011); Stephanie A. Shields, "Gender: An Intersectionality Perspective," *Sex Roles* 59 (2008): 301-11; Megan Sinnott, "Public Sex: The Geography of Female Homoeroticism and the (In)Visibility of Female Sexualities," in *Out in Public: Reinventing Lesbian/Gay Anthropology in a Globalizing World*, ed. Ellen Lewin and William L. Leap (Malden, MA: Wiley-Blackwell, 2009), 225–39; Urvashi Vaid, *Irresistible Revolution: Confronting Race, Class and the Assumptions of LGBT Politics* (New York: Magnus Books, 2012); and Kathi Wolfe, "Special Report in Their Own Words: Elders Facing Poverty, Ageism," *Washington Blade*, 27 March 2014, http://www.washingtonblade.com/2014/03/27/special-report-words-elders-facing-poverty-ageism.

15. Cynthia Levine-Rasky, "Intersectionality Theory Applied to Whiteness and Middle-Classness," *Social Identities* 17, no. 2 (2011): 239–53.

16. Lillian Faderman, *Odd Girls and Twilight Lovers: A History of Lesbian Life in Twentieth-Century America* (New York: Columbia University Press, 1991), 26. From 1885 until 1933, Thomas lived in "the Deanery" on campus, Bryn Mawr, Pennsylvania. The Deanery was demolished in 1968 for the construction of the Canaday Library.

17. Susan Snyder, "Bryn Mawr Confronts Racist Views of Former Leader," *Inquirer* (Philadelphia), 24 August 2017, http://www.philly.com/philly/education/bryn-mawr-confronts-racist-views-of-former-leader-20170824.html; Kim Cassidy, "Message from President Cassidy: Grappling with Bryn

Mawr's Histories," Bryn Mawr College, 24 August 2017, https://www.brynmawr
.edu/news/message-president-cassidy-grappling-bryn-mawr-s-histories.

18. Library of Congress, "Voting Rights for Native Americans," *Elections . . . the
American Way,* Library of Congress, n.d., https://www.loc.gov/teachers/
classroommaterials/presentationsandactivities/presentations/elections/
voting-rights-native-americans.html.

19. See, for example, Nancy A. Hewitt, introduction to *No Permanent Waves:
Recasting Histories of U.S. Feminism* (New Brunswick, NJ: Rutgers Univer-
sity Press, 2010), 2–14; Robyn Muncy, *Creating a Female Dominion in Amer-
ican Reform, 1890-1935* (New York: Oxford University Press, 1991); Becky
Thompson, "Multiracial Feminism: Recasting the Chronology of Second
Wave Feminism," in Hewitt, *No Permanent Waves,* 39–60.

20. Betty Friedan, *The Feminine Mystique* (New York: W. W. Norton, 1963); Dan-
iel Horowitz, *Betty Friedan and the Making of* The Feminine Mystique: *The
American Left, the Cold War and Modern Feminism* (Amherst: University of
Massachusetts Press, 2000).

21. See, for example, Nancy Felice Gabin, *Feminism in the Labor Movement:
Women and the United Auto Workers, 1935–1975* (Ithaca, NY: Cornell University Press, 1990); Annelise Orleck, *Common Sense & a Little Fire: Women
and Working-Class Politics in the United States, 1900–1965* (Chapel Hill:
University of North Carolina Press, 1995); Deborah Gray White, *Too Heavy
a Load: Black Women in Defense of Themselves 1894–1994* (New York: W.
W. Norton, 1999); and Kate Weigand, *Red Feminism: American Communism
and the Making of Women's Liberation* (Baltimore: Johns Hopkins University
Press, 2001).

22. Dorothy Sue Cobble, "Labor Feminists and President Kennedy's Commission on Women," in Hewitt, *No Permanent Waves,* 144–67.

23. In 1968, Shirley Chisholm became the first Black woman elected to the U.S.
Congress, and in 1972 became the first Black candidate to be nominated
by a major party for president of the United States. This was also the first
time that a woman had run for the Democratic Party's nomination to run
for president. Pauli Murray, who was African American, had a long history
of civil rights activism. She coined the term "Jane Crow" to describe how
segregation intersected with sexism in the Jim Crow United States. She
struggled throughout her life with her sexual and gender identity. The Pauli
Murray Childhood Home, 906 Carroll Street, Durham, North Carolina, was
designated a National Historic Landmark on 23 December 2016.

24. See, for example, Lillian Faderman, *To Believe in Women: What Lesbians
Have Done for America* (Boston: Houghton Mifflin, 1999); Miriam Frank,
Out in the Union: A Labor History of Queer America (Philadelphia: Temple
University Press, 2014); and Wendell Ricketts, *Blue, Too: More Writing by
(for or about) Working-Class Queers* (FourCats Press, 2014); Allan Bérubé,
"Queer Work and Labor History," in *My Desire for History,* ed. John D'Emilio

and Estelle Freedman (Chapel Hill: University of North Carolina Press, 2011), 259–69; Bérubé, "No Race-Baiting, Red-Baiting, or Queer-Baiting! The Marine Cooks and Stewards Union from the Depression to the Cold War," in *My Desire for History*, 294–320; Kitty Krupat and Patrick McCreery, *Out At Work: Building a Gay-Labor Alliance* (Minneapolis: University of Minnesota Press, 2001). Anna Howard Shaw and her partner, Lucy Anthony (niece of Susan B. Anthony), lived together in Moylan, Pennsylvania; Carrie Chapman Catt and her partner, Mary Hay, lived at Juniper Ledge, Briarcliff Manor, New York, during Catt's most influential years, 1919–1928. Juniper Ledge was added to the NRHP on 4 May 2006; Esther Lape and Elizabeth Read shared an apartment on East Eleventh Street, New York City, New York, in a building they owned. They rented an apartment in the building to Eleanor Roosevelt. The pair also had a summer home called Salt Meadow, where they entertained Eleanor Roosevelt, at 733 Old Clinton Road, Westbrook, Connecticut (donated to the U.S. Fish and Wildlife Service on 20 July 1972, forming the core of the Stewart B. McKinney National Wildlife Refuge); Marion Dickerman and Nancy Cook lived at an apartment on West Twelfth Street, New York City, New York; Frances Kellor lived with her partner, Mary Dreier, near the Museum of Modern Art, New York City, New York; Bayard Rustin's apartment in New York City was added to the NRHP on 8 March 2016. Dr. Emily Blackwell was the third woman to earn a medical degree in the United States; in 1857, she cofounded the New York Infirmary for Indigent Women and Children at East Seventh Street near Tompkins Square Park (an expansion of the New York Dispensary for Poor Women and Children founded by her sister, Dr. Elizabeth Blackwell, in 1853). When it opened in 1868, Emily was on the faculty of the Woman's Medical College of the New York Infirmary founded by her sister at 126 Second Avenue, New York City, New York. Emily became the director of the college when Elizabeth moved to England. From 1883, Dr. Emily Blackwell lived with her partner, Dr. Elizabeth Cushier.

25. Elsa Barkley Brown, "'What Has Happened Here': The Politics of Difference in Women's History and Feminist Politics," *Feminist Studies* 18, no. 2 (1992): 295–312.

26. Alison Wylie, "The Integrity of Narratives: Deliberative Practice, Pluralism, and Multivocality," in *Evaluating Multiple Narratives: Beyond Nationalist, Colonialist, Imperialist Archaeologies,* ed. Junko Habu, Clare Fawcett, and John M. Matsunaga (New York: Springer, 2008), 201–12.

27. Nan Alamilla Boyd and Horacio Roque Ramirez, eds., *Bodies of Evidence: The Practice of Queer Oral History* (New York: Oxford University Press, 2012); Doan, "The Tyranny of Gendered Spaces."

28. Gayatri Chakravorty Spivak, "Subaltern Studies: Deconstructing Historiography," in *The Spivak Reader: Selected Works of Gayatri Chakravorty Spivak,* ed. Donna Landry and Gerald M. MacLean (New York: Routledge, 1996), 216.

29. Emma Pérez, *The Decolonial Imaginary: Writing Chicanas into History* (Bloomington: University of Indiana Press, 1999); Chela Sandoval, *Methodology of the Oppressed* (Minneapolis: University of Minnesota Press, 2000).
30. Johnson, "Gays and Gospel," 116.
31. John Howard, *Men Like That: A Southern Queer History* (Chicago: University of Chicago Press, 1999), 5.
32. Bennett, "Lesbian-Like," 10-11.
33. Ibid., 13.
34. Barbara L. Voss, "Looking for Gender, Finding Sexuality: A Queer Politic of Archaeology, Fifteen Years Later," in *Que(e)rying Archaeology: Proceedings of the Thirty-Seventh Annual Chacmool Conference, University of Calgary,* ed. Susan Terendy, Natasha Lyons, and Michelle Janse-Smekal (Calgary: Archaeological Association of the University of Calgary, 2009), 32.
35. Bennett, "Lesbian-Like," 9–10, 14; see also Judith M. Bennett, *History Matters: Patriarchy and the Challenge of Feminism* (Philadelphia: Pennsylvania University Press, 2006).
36. Victoria Bissell Brown, "Queer or Not: What Jane Addams Teaches Us about Not Knowing," in Austin and Brier, *Out in Chicago,* 63–76; Howard, *Men Like That;* Johnson, "Gays and Gospel."
37. Kennedy and Davis, *Boots of Leather, Slippers of Gold;* Esther Newton, "Beyond Freud, Ken, and Barbie," in *Margaret Mead Made Me Gay: Personal Essays, Public Ideas* (Durham, NC: Duke University Press, 2000), 189–94, reprint of "Closing the Gender Gap," originally published in 1986 in *The Women's Review of Books;* Esther Newton, "My Butch Career," in *Margaret Mead Made Me Gay,* 195–212 (originally read at the David R. Kessler Lecture, 6 December 1996, at the Center for Lesbian and Gay Studies at the Graduate Center of the City University of New York).
38. Kazyak, "Midwest or Lesbian?"
39. Lawrence La Fountain-Stokes, Lourdes Torres, and Ramon H. Rivera-Servera, "Toward an Archive of Latina/o Queer Chicago: Arts, Politics, and Social Performance," in Austin and Brier, *Out in Chicago,* 127.
40. Gayle Rubin (1976) quoted in Elizabeth L. Kennedy, "'These Natives Can Speak for Themselves': The Development of Gay and Lesbian Studies in Anthropology," in Lewin and Leap, *Out in Theory: The Emergence of Lesbian and Gay Anthropology,* 95.
41. Judith Halberstam, *Female Masculinity* (Durham, NC: Duke University Press, 1998); Judith Butler, *Gender Trouble* (New York: Routledge, 1989); and Gayle Rubin, "The Traffic in Women: Notes on the 'Political Economy' of Sex," in *Toward an Anthropology of Women,* ed. Rayna Reiter (New York: Monthly Review Press, 1975).
42. Freeman, *Time Binds;* and Jack Halberstam, *In a Queer Time and Place: Transgender Bodies, Subcultural Lives* (New York: New York University Press, 2010).

43. See, for example, Doan, "The Tyranny of Gendered Spaces" for a discussion of how being transgender shapes her experience of places, public and private.

44. Alimahomed, "Thinking Outside the Rainbow"; Meyer, "An Intersectional Analysis," 861; and Moore, "Intersectionality and the Study of Black, Sexual Minority Women."

45. Evelyn Brooks Higginbotham, *Righteous Discontent: The Women's Movement in the Black Baptist Church, 1880–1920* (Cambridge, MA: Harvard University Press, 1993); see also Deena J. Gonzalez and Ellie D. Hernandez. "Latina/o Gender and Sexuality" (this volume); and Meyer, "An Intersectional Analysis," 853.

46. Overall, LGBTQ individuals are two and a half times more likely to experience depression, anxiety, and substance abuse than heterosexual people. An intersectional analysis gives a much more nuanced picture. For example, while 2.3 percent of heterosexual people are reported to have considered attempting suicide, that number jumps to 4.4 percent for gay or lesbian individuals; to 7.4 percent for those who identify as bisexual, and 30.8 percent for transgender folks. Transgender people of color are at an increased risk of suicide attempts than white transgender folks. American Psychiatric Association, "Mental Health Disparities: LGBTQ," American Psychiatric Association, 2017, https://www.psychiatry.org/File%20Library/Psychiatrists/ Cultural-Competency/Mental-Health-Disparities/Mental-Health-Facts-for-LGBTQ.pdf.

47. Grillo, "Anti-Essentialism and Intersectionality"; Meyer, "An Intersectional Analysis," 853; and Moore, "Intersectionality and the Study of Black, Sexual Minority Women," 37.

48. See, for example, Janaya Khan, "Exclusive: Black Lives Matter Toronto Co-Founder Responds to Pride Action Criticism," *Now*, 6 July 2016, https:// nowtoronto.com/news/pride-2016/exclusive-black-lives-matter-pride-action-criticism/; INPAQ, "Queerness—On The Frontlines of #BlackLivesMatter (MSNBC)," *LGBT Update*, 23 February 2015, http://www.thelgbtupdate .com/queerness-on-the-frontlines-of-blacklivesmatter-msnbc; Esperanza Garcia and Ty Brooks, "Op-ed: Why Black Lives Should Matter to All LGBT People," *Advocate*, 2 February 2015, http://www.advocate.com/commen tary/2015/02/02/op-ed-why-black-lives-should-matter-all-lgbt-people; Cleis Abeni, "Trans Lives Matters and Black Lives Matters Join Forces for Justice," *Advocate*, 10 September 2015, http://www.advocate.com/2015/9/10/ trans-lives-matters-and-black-lives-matters-join-forces-justice.

49. See Gonzalez and Hernandez, "Latina/o Gender and Sexuality."

50. Ibid.

51. Alimahomed, "Thinking Outside the Rainbow"; Gonzalez and Hernandez. "Latina/o Gender and Sexuality."

52. Gonzalez and Hernandez, "Latina/o Gender and Sexuality"; Uriel Quesada, Letitia Gomez, and Salvador Vidal-Ortiz, *Queer Brown Voices: Personal Narratives of Latina/o LGBT Activism* (Austin: University of Texas Press, 2015).

53. Moore, "Intersectionality and the Study of Black, Sexual Minority Women," 37.
54. Johnson, "Gays and Gospel," 110.
55. Johnson, "Gays and Gospel."
56. Ibid.
57. Ibid., 117.
58. For a discussion of this in the context of African American sites, see Kerri S. Barile, "Race, the National Register, and Cultural Resource Management: Creating an Historic Context for Postbellum Sites," *Historical Archaeology* 38, no. 1 (2004): 90–100.
59. Seven aspects are considered when evaluating integrity in the context of the National Register of Historic Places (NRHP) and National Historic Landmark (NHL) programs. These seven aspects are location, design, setting, materials, workmanship, feeling, and association. The evaluation of integrity is always a variable process, and guidance provided by the National Park Service for their NRHP and NHL programs is always applied on a case-by-case basis. See Megan E. Springate and Caridad de la Vega, "Nominating LGBTQ Places to the National Register of Historic Places and as National Historic Landmarks: An Introduction," in *LGBTQ America: A Lesbian, Gay, Bisexual, Transgender, and Queer History* (Washington, DC: National Park Foundation and National Park Service, 2016), https://www.nps.gov/articles/lgbtqtheme-nominating.htm.

Bibliography

Abeni, Cleis. "Trans Lives Matters and Black Lives Matters Join Forces for Justice." *Advocate*, 10 September 2015. http://www.advocate.com/2015/9/10/trans-lives-matters-and-black-lives-matters-join-forces-justice.

Alimahomed, Sabrina. "Thinking Outside the Rainbow: Women of Color Redefining Queer Politics and Identity." *Social Identities* 16, no. 2 (2010): 151–68.

American Psychiatric Association, "Mental Health Disparities: LGBTQ." American Psychiatric Association, 2017. https://www.psychiatry.org/File percent20Library/Psychiatrists/Cultural-Competency/Mental-Health-Disparities/Mental-Health-Facts-for-LGBTQ.pdf

Barile, Kerri S. "Race, the National Register, and Cultural Resource Management: Creating an Historic Context for Postbellum Sites." *Historical Archaeology* 38, no. 1 (2004): 90–100.

Bennett, Judith M. *History Matters: Patriarchy and the Challenge of Feminism.* Philadelphia: Pennsylvania University Press. 2006.

———. "'Lesbian-Like' and the Social History of Lesbianisms." *Journal of the History of Sexuality* 9 (2000): 1–24.

Bérubé, Allan. "No Race-Baiting, Red-Baiting, or Queer-Baiting! The Marine Cooks and Stewards Union from the Depression to the Cold War." In *My*

Desire for History, edited by John D'Emilio and Estelle Freedman, 294–320. Chapel Hill: University of North Carolina Press, 2011.

———. "Queer Work and Labor History." In *My Desire for History*, edited by John D'Emilio and Estelle Freedman, 259–69. Chapel Hill: University of North Carolina Press, 2011.

Bowleg, Lisa. "When Black + Lesbian + Woman ≠ Black Lesbian Woman: The Methodological Challenges to Qualitative and Quantitative Intersectionality Research." *Sex Roles* 59 (2008): 312–25.

Boyd, Nan Alamilla, and Horacio Roque Ramirez, eds. *Bodies of Evidence: The Practice of Queer Oral History*. New York: Oxford University Press, 2012.

Brandzel, Amy L. "Haunted by Citizenship: Whitenormative Citizen-Subjects and the Uses of History in Women's Studies." *Feminist Studies* 37, no. 3 (2011): 503–33.

Brazina, Corona. *Sojourner Truth's "Ain't I a woman?" Speech: A Primary Source Investigation*. New York: RosenCentral Primary Source, 2005.

Brown, Elsa Barkley. "What Has Happened Here: The Politics of Difference in Women's History and Feminist Politics." *Feminist Studies* 18, no. 2 (1992): 295–312.

Brown, Victoria Bissell. "Queer or Not: What Jane Addams Teaches Us about Not Knowing." In *Out in Chicago: LGBT History at the Crossroads*, edited by Jill Austin and Jennifer Brier, 63–76. Chicago: Chicago History Museum, 2011.

Butler, Judith. *Gender Trouble*. New York: Routledge, 1989.

Cassidy, Kim. "Message from President Cassidy: Grappling with Bryn Mawr's Histories." Bryn Mawr College, 24 August 2017. https://www.brynmawr.edu/news/message-president-cassidy-grappling-bryn-mawr-s-histories.

Chibbaro, Lou, Jr. "Special Report: Poverty in the LGBT Community." *Washington Blade*, 12 February 2014. http://www.washingtonblade.com/2014/02/12/special-report-poverty-lgbt-community.

Clare, Eli. *Exile & Pride: Disability, Queerness, and Liberation*. Cambridge, MA: South End Press, 1999.

Cobble, Dorothy Sue. "Labor Feminists and President Kennedy's Commission on Women." In *No Permanent Waves: Recasting Histories of U.S. Feminism*, edited by Nancy A. Hewitt, 144–67. New Brunswick, NJ: Rutgers University Press, 2010.

Collins, Patricia Hill, and Sirma Bilge. *Intersectionality*. Malden, MA: Polity Press, 2016.

Combahee River Collective. "A Black Feminist Statement [1977]." In *The Second Wave: A Reader in Feminist Theory*, edited by Linda Nicholson, 63–70. New York: Routledge, 1997.

Crenshaw, Kimberlé. "Demarginalizing the Intersection of Race and Sex: A Black Feminist Critique of Antidiscrimination Doctrine, Feminist Theory and Antiracist Politics." *University of Chicago Legal Forum* (1989): 139–67.

Doan, Petra L. "The Tyranny of Gendered Spaces: Reflections from Beyond the Gender Dichotomy." *Gender, Place & Culture: A Journal of Feminist Geography* 17, no. 5 (2010): 635–54.

Faderman, Lillian. *Odd Girls and Twilight Lovers: A History of Lesbian Life in Twentieth-Century America.* New York: Columbia University Press, 1991.

———. *To Believe in Women: What Lesbians Have Done for America.* Boston: Houghton Mifflin, 1999.

Frank, Miriam. *Out in the Union: A Labor History of Queer America.* Philadelphia: Temple University Press, 2014.

Freeman, Elizabeth. *Time Binds: Queer Temporalities, Queer Histories.* Durham, NC: Duke University Press, 2010.

Friedan, Betty. *The Feminine Mystique.* New York: W. W. Norton, 1963.

Gabin, Nancy Felice. *Feminism in the Labor Movement: Women and the United Auto Workers, 1935–1975.* Ithaca, NY: Cornell University Press, 1990.

Garcia, Alma M. *Chicana Feminist Thought: The Basic Historical Writings.* New York: Routledge, 1997.

———. "The Development of Chicana Feminist Discourse, 1870–1980." *Gender and Society* 3, no. 2 (1989): 217–38.

Garcia, Esperanza, and Ty Brooks. "Op-Ed: Why Black Lives Should Matter to All LGBT People." *Advocate,* 2 February 2015. http://www.advocate.com/commentary/2015/02/02/op-ed-why-black-lives-should-matter-all-lgbt-people.

Gonzalez, Deena J., and Ellie D. Hernandez. "Latina/o Gender and Sexuality." In *Identities and Place: Changing Labels and Intersectional Communities of LGBTQ and Two-Spirit People in the United States,* edited by Katherine Crawford-Lackey and Megan E. Springate. New York: Berghahn Books, 2020.

Greenesmith, Heron. "Drawing Bisexuality Back into the Picture: How Bisexuality Fits into LGBT Legal Strategy Ten Years after Bisexual Erasure." *Cardozo Journal of Law & Gender* 17, no. 65 (2010): 65–80.

Grillo, Trina. "Anti-Essentialism and Intersectionality: Tools to Dismantle the Master's House." *Berkeley Women's Law Journal* 10 (1995): 16–30.

Halberstam, Jack (Judith). *In a Queer Time and Place: Transgender Bodies, Subcultural Lives.* New York: New York University Press, 2010.

Halberstam, Judith (Jack). *Female Masculinity.* Durham, NC: Duke University Press, 1998.

Hewitt, Nancy A. "Introduction." In *No Permanent Waves: Recasting Histories of U.S. Feminism,* edited by Nancy A. Hewitt, 2–14. New Brunswick, NJ: Rutgers University Press, 2010.

Higginbotham, Evelyn Brooks. *Righteous Discontent: The Women's Movement in the Black Baptist Church, 1880–1920.* Cambridge, MA: Harvard University Press, 1993.

Hirsch, Daniel. "R-Rated and Ephemeral: Spinning LGBT History." *Mission-Local.* 18 July 2014. http://missionlocal.org/2014/07/r-rated-and-ephemeral-spinning-lgbt-history.

Horowitz, Daniel. *Betty Friedan and the Making of* The Feminine Mystique: *The American Left, the Cold War and Modern Feminism.* Amherst: University of Massachusetts Press, 2000.

Howard, John. *Men Like That: A Southern Queer History.* Chicago: University of Chicago Press, 1999.

INPAQ. "Queerness—On the Frontlines of #BlackLivesMatter (MSNBC)." *LGBT Update*, 23 February 2015. http://www.thelgbtupdate.com/queerness-on-the-frontlines-of-blacklivesmatter-msnbc.

Johnson, E. Patrick. "Gays and Gospel: A Queer History of Sacred Music." In *Out in Chicago: LGBT History at the Crossroads*, edited by Jill Austin and Jennifer Brier, 109–26. Chicago: Chicago History Museum, 2011.

Kacere, Laura. "Homonormativity 101: What It Is and How It's Hurting Our Movement." *Everyday Feminism*, 24 January 2015. https://everydayfeminism.com/2015/01/homonormativity-101/.

Kahn, Janaya. "Exclusive: Black Lives Matter Toronto Co-Founder Responds to Pride Action Criticism." *Now*, 6 July 2016. https://nowtoronto.com/news/pride-2016/exclusive-black-lives-matter-pride-action-criticism/.

Kazyak, Emily. "Midwest or Lesbian? Gender, Rurality, and Sexuality." *Gender & Society* 26, no. 6 (2012): 825–48.

Kennedy, Elizabeth L. "These Natives Can Speak for Themselves: The Development of Gay and Lesbian Studies in Anthropology." In *Out in Theory: The Emergence of Lesbian and Gay Anthropology*, edited by Ellen Lewin and William L. Leap, 93–109. Urbana: University of Illinois Press, 2002.

Kennedy, Elizabeth Lapovsky, and Madeline D. Davis. *Boots of Leather, Slippers of Gold: The History of a Lesbian Community.* New York: Routledge, 1993.

Krupat, Kitty, and Patrick McCreery. *Out At Work: Building a Gay-Labor Alliance.* Minneapolis: University of Minnesota Press, 2001.

La Fountain-Stokes, Lawrence, Lourdes Torres, and Ramon H. Rivera-Servera. "Toward an Archive of Latina/o Queer Chicago: Arts, Politics, and Social Performance." In *Out in Chicago: LGBT History at the Crossroads,* edited by Jill Austin and Jennifer Brier, 127–53. Chicago: Chicago History Museum, 2011.

Levine-Rasky, Cynthia. "Intersectionality Theory Applied to Whiteness and Middle-Classness." *Social Identities* 17, no. 2 (2011): 239–53.

Library of Congress. "Voting Rights for Native Americans." *Elections . . . the American Way.* Library of Congress, n.d. https://www.loc.gov/teachers/classroommaterials/presentationsandactivities/presentations/elections/voting-rights-native-americans.html.

Lorde, Audre. "Learning from the 60s." In *Sister Outsider: Essays & Speeches by Audre Lorde.* Berkeley, CA: Crossing Press, 2007.

Love, Heather. *Feeling Backward: Loss and the Politics of Queer History.* Cambridge, MA: Harvard University Press, 2007.

Maskovsky, Jeff. "Do We All 'Reek of the Commodity'? Consumption and the Erasure of Poverty in Lesbian and Gay Studies." In *Out in Theory: The Emergence of Lesbian and Gay Anthropology*, edited by Ellen Lewin and William L. Leam, 264–86. Urbana: University of Illinois Press, 2002.

Meyer, Doug. "An Intersectional Analysis of Lesbian, Gay, Bisexual, and Transgender (LGBT) People's Evaluations of Anti-Queer Violence." *Gender & Society* 26, no. 6 (2012): 849–73.

Michigan Womyn's Music Festival Community, with Sara St. Martin Lynne, ed. *Voices from the Land: A Collective Memoir.* Kindle edition, 2015.

Moore, Mignon R. "Intersectionality and the Study of Black, Sexual Minority Women." *Gender & Society* 26, no. 1 (2012): 33–39.

———. *Invisible Families: Gay Identities, Relationships, and Motherhood among Black Women.* Berkeley: University of California Press, 2011.

Moraga, Cherrie, and Gloria Anzaldua, eds. *This Bridge Called My Back: Writings by Radical Women of Color.* Massachusetts: Persephone Press, 1981.

Muncy, Robyn. *Creating a Female Dominion in American Reform, 1890–1935.* New York: Oxford University Press, 1991.

Newton, Esther. "Beyond Freud, Ken, and Barbie." In *Margaret Mead Made Me Gay: Personal Essays, Public Ideas*, edited by Esther Newton, 189–94. Durham, NC: Duke University Press, 2000 [1986].

———. "My Butch Career." In *Margaret Mead Made Me Gay: Personal Essays, Public Ideas,* edited by Esther Newton, 195–212. Durham, NC: Duke University Press, 2000 [1996].

Orleck, Annelise. *Common Sense & a Little Fire: Women and Working-Class Politics in the United States, 1900–1965.* Chapel Hill: University of North Carolina Press, 1995.

Parent, Mike C., Cirleen DeBlaere, and Bonnie Moradi. "Approaches to Research on Intersectionality: Perspectives on Gender, LGBT, and Racial/Ethnic Identities." *Sex Roles* 68 (2013): 639–45.

Perez, Emma. *The Decolonial Imaginary: Writing Chicanas into History.* Bloomington: University of Indiana Press, 1999.

Quesada, Uriel, Letitia Gomez, and Salvador Vidal-Ortiz. *Queer Brown Voices: Personal Narratives of Latina/o LGBT Activism.* Austin: University of Texas Press, 2015.

Ricketts, Wendell. *Blue, Too: More Writing by (for or about) Working-Class Queers.* FourCats Press, 2014.

Rubin, Gayle S. *Deviations: A Gayle Rubin Reader.* Durham, NC: Duke University Press, 2011.

———. "Thinking Sex: Notes for a Radical Theory of the Politics of Sexuality." In *Culture, Society and Sexuality: A Reader*, 2nd ed., edited by Richard Parker and Peter Aggleton, 143–78. New York: Routledge, 1984.

———. "The Traffic in Women: Notes on the 'Political Economy' of Sex." In *Toward an Anthropology of Women,* edited by Rayna Reiter. New York: Monthly Review Press, 1975.

Sandoval, Chela. *Methodology of the Oppressed.* Minneapolis: University of Minnesota Press, 2000.

Schweighofer, Katherine. "LGBTQ Sport and Leisure." In *LGBTQ America: A Theme Study of Lesbian, Gay, Bisexual, Transgender, and Queer History*, edited by Megan E. Springate. Washington, DC: National Park Foundation and National Park Service, 2016. https://www.nps.gov/articles/lgbtqtheme-sport.htm.

Shields, Stephanie A. "Gender: An Intersectionality Perspective." *Sex Roles* 59 (2008): 301–11.

Siebler, Kay. "Teaching the Politics of Sojourner Truth's 'Ain't I a Woman?'" *Pedagogy* 10, no. 3 (Fall 2010): 511–33.

Sinnott, Megan. "Public Sex: The Geography of Female Homoeroticism and the (In)Visibility of Female Sexualities." In *Out in Public: Reinventing Lesbian/Gay Anthropology in a Globalizing World,* edited by Ellen Lewin and William L. Leap, 225–39. Malden, MA: Wiley-Blackwell, 2009.

Snyder, Susan. "Bryn Mawr Confronts Racist Views of Former Leader," *Inquirer* (Philadelphia), 24 August 2017. http://www.philly.com/philly/education/bryn-mawr-confronts-racist-views-of-former-leader-20170824.html.

Spivak, Gayatri Chakravorty. "Subaltern Studies: Deconstructing Historiography." In *The Spivak Reader: Selected Works of Gayatri Chakravorty Spivak*, edited by Donna Landry and Gerald M. MacLean, 216. New York: Routledge, 1996.

Springate, Megan E., and Caridad de la Vega. "Nominating LGBTQ Places to the National Register of Historic Places and as National Historic Landmarks: An Introduction." In *LGBTQ America: A Lesbian, Gay, Bisexual, Transgender, and Queer History.* Washington, DC: National Park Foundation and National Park Service, 2016. https://www.nps.gov/articles/lgbtqtheme-nominating.htm.

Stryker, Susan. "Transgender History in the United States and the Places That Matter." In *Identities and Place: Changing Labels and Intersectional Communities of LGBTQ and Two-Spirit People in the United States,* edited by Katherine Crawford-Lackey and Megan E. Springate. New York: Berghahn Books, 2020.

Thompson, Becky. "Multiracial Feminism: Recasting the Chronology of Second Wave Feminism." In *No Permanent Waves: Recasting Histories of U.S. Feminism,* edited by Nancy A. Hewitt, 39–60. New Brunswick, NJ: Rutgers University Press, 2010.

Vaid, Urvashi. *Irresistible Revolution: Confronting Race, Class and the Assumptions of LGBT Politics.* New York: Magnus Books, 2012.

Valentine, Gill. "Theorizing and Researching Intersectionality: A Challenge for Feminist Geography." *Professional Geographer* 59, no. 1 (2007): 10–21.

Voss, Barbara L. "Looking for Gender, Finding Sexuality: A Queer Politic of Archaeology, Fifteen Years Later." In *Que(e)rying Archaeology: Proceedings of the Thirty-Seventh Annual Chacmool Conference, University of Calgary,* edited by Susan Terendy, Natasha Lyons, and Michelle Janse-Smekal, 29–39. Calgary: Archaeological Association of the University of Calgary, 2009.

Warner, Leah R., and Stephanie A. Shields. "The Intersections of Sexuality, Gender, and Race: Identity Research at the Crossroads." *Sex Roles* 68 (2013): 803–10.

Weigand, Kate. *Red Feminism: American Communism and the Making of Women's Liberation*. Baltimore: Johns Hopkins University Press, 2001.

White, Deborah Gray. *Too Heavy a Load: Black Women in Defense of Themselves 1894–1994*. New York: W. W. Norton, 1999.

Williams, Cristan. "Michigan Womyn's Music Festival." *TransAdvocate*, 2013. http://transadvocate.com/michigan-womyns-music-festival_n_8943.htm.

Wolfe, Kathi. "Special Report in Their Own Words: Elders Facing Poverty, Ageism." *Washington Blade*, 27 March 2014. http://www.washingtonblade.com/2014/03/27/special-report-words-elders-facing-poverty-ageism.

Wylie, Alison. "The Integrity of Narratives: Deliberative Practice, Pluralism, and Multivocality." In *Evaluating Multiple Narratives: Beyond Nationalist, Colonialist, Imperialist Archaeologies*, edited by Junko Habu, Clare Fawcett, and John M. Matsunaga, 201–12. New York: Springer, 2008.

CHAPTER 2

Making Bisexuals Visible

Loraine Hutchins

Introduction

Everyone is not *either gay or straight*. This mistaken assumption lies behind most ordinary daily conversations about with whom and how people create their families, identities, and love lives, but it is often not the whole truth. Bisexual people's experiences are hidden in plain view, perhaps not visible, sometimes revealed.

This chapter is about that paradox: how we see what has been unseen, and become more conscious of those who love others of more than one gender, until we recognize that these relationships and realities are more common than is usually acknowledged and have always been a part of history, visible or not.

If they think about it, most English teachers are aware, for instance, that the writing of Walt Whitman, the well-loved U.S. civil war nurse who changed the form of poetry from rhyming verse to lush free-form praise songs, celebrated the beauty of both women and men in his works, as did poet Edna St. Vincent Millay.[1] Students, however, are rarely taught these parts of their biographies.[2] When studying nineteenth-century U.S. political history, many pupils discover the story of social justice organizer Emma Goldman, but only a few textbooks record her significant relationships with both women and men during her lifetime or the fact that she was a very outspoken advocate for gay and lesbian rights.[3] It is now pretty well established that First Lady Eleanor Roosevelt had a long-term relationship with journalist Lorena Hickok, who even had a special guest room at the White House.[4] People now know that CNN anchor Anderson Cooper is gay, because he's spoken openly about it over the past few years. But what he and his mother, Gloria Vanderbilt, have only recently revealed publically is that her mother—his grandmother—had at least one relationship with a woman back in the 1920s.[5]

Similar stories circulate about other U.S. public figures, such as famous musician Leonard Bernstein.[6] Contemporary artists such as Margaret Cho and Alan Cumming, usually described as gay OR straight (but not both), insist that their lives are just not that simple.[7] "Some days I feel like I have a foot in both worlds, yet never really belonging to either," says Oregon's Governor Kate Brown, the country's first out bisexual governor, speaking openly about how hard it is being a public bisexual role model, in government or anywhere.[8] Hundreds of these stories wait to be uncovered or have been uncovered and then covered up again. An organized U.S. bisexual rights and liberation movement keeps bringing stories like these to light, insisting on the importance of bisexual role models for everyone.

The acronym LGBTQ—lesbian, gay, bisexual, transgender, queer—encompasses an inclusive, diverse coalition of sexual orientations and gender identities, and out bisexual people, whatever name they have called themselves or been called, have been a key part of making these changes happen from the start.[9] However, when we open the book on the modern gay liberation movement in this country, its bisexual roots are often ignored. Though Sylvia Rivera, one of the key mobilizers of the resistance against the police crackdown at the Stonewall bar in New York City in June 1969, for instance, is often identified as a gay and/or transgender person, what is not as widely acknowledged is that Rivera openly related intimately to more than one gender and was open about loving women as well as men.[10] So why not say that and teach that? Why keep part of Rivera's—and all these others'—identities silent? The list of famous U.S. bisexuals is long, and growing, but as we reconstruct the history, where do we find the places they lived and loved?[11] Where do we find the big events that mark accomplishments for bisexual rights and liberation in the United States during the past fifty years? That is what this chapter brings to light.

Though much has been said about the limits of the binary (either/or) view of assuming everyone is gay OR straight, much has yet to be uncovered and understood. A great many people of all ages have the capacity to be bisexual. Many may know privately that they are. Many still are not open about it, for various reasons. However, there is a huge change in visibility that has been building over the past fifty years. New studies show that the majority of teens in the United States and in some other Western countries now recognize themselves as *nonheterosexual*.[12] They are comfortable being openly attracted to more than one gender, whether they act on it or not. This is a huge shift that U.S. culture is still adjusting to, to say the least.

This chapter is dedicated to this next generation, and to everyone older who wants to better understand that bisexuality is not a "new" identity at all, by whatever names it goes by. Bisexualities and other nonbinary ways of viewing attraction are merely coming out more into the open. It behooves us to be more informed about how this is happening. Chronological timelines of bisexual U.S. history are available elsewhere.[13] This chapter offers a selection of the emblematic stories, the people, and places where important bisexual events have happened in the United States, particularly over the past half century. First some basic definitions and historic research background for those interested.

Defining Bi Identity; the History of Being Bi

Bisexuality is simply the capacity to be attracted to and love more than one gender. Alfred Kinsey, the father of sexuality research in the United States was himself someone who had relations with men as well as women. In the 1930s through 1950s when U.S. sexuality research was mostly nonexistent, Kinsey and his team surveyed thousands of people about their sexual experiences.[14] Out of this work he developed the Kinsey Scale, which charted a range of sexual orientations or attractions, all the way from exclusively attracted to a different sex than oneself (usually marked as zero) to exclusively attracted to one's own sex (marked as six), with five gradations or degrees in between.[15] Kinsey didn't label people or ask them how they identified; he merely cataloged their behaviors and experiences. What he found was that a lot of people who would regard themselves, and be regarded, as heterosexual (near the zero end of the scale), in fact had significant same-sex experience, and that a number of people who were primarily attracted to their own sex (toward the six end of the scale) had also sometimes had significant relations with a sex different than their own. But the human mind tends to sort things into easy binaries; black/white, hot/cold, up/down. And so the categories gay and straight oversimplify and distort the natural range of people's attractions, causing the vast and populated middle grounds to be minimized and disappear.

To complicate things even further, a lot of the post-Kinsey researchers tended to lump lesbians, gays, and bisexuals together when doing studies about nonheterosexual people, so it was difficult, for a long time, to get good information on how many people have attractions for, and relationships with, more than one gender—that is, how many people are bisexual in the broadest sense.[16] And, even when studies did try to collect that kind of data, there were/are often discrepancies between which study counts only people who openly identify with the label "bisexual" (which is still a fairly small group, partly due to the stigma of being labeled such) versus the much larger group of people who have had sexual experiences with more than one gender/sex but don't openly identify as members of a community or movement for bisexual rights and liberation (or a gay or lesbian rights movement either, for that matter). Still, as mentioned above about the teens surveyed, things have changed a lot in the past several decades, with more people now identifying as other than straight—and even other than homosexual. Marriage equality has changed things tremendously. Even while conservative backlash aims to limit and roll back the rights of lesbian, gay, bisexual, transgender, and queer people as well as of other sexual minorities, there also continues to be forward motion and inclusionary measures building toward making our society more accepting of a diversity of sexualities and sexual identities.

Erasure's Roots in Research (and Organizing)

It is no exaggeration to say that bisexuality's existence, prevalence, and significance in United States history has been erased and discounted, repeatedly made invisible, even after it has surfaced, again and again and again. The reasons for this have been explored by some authors, but generally go beyond the scope of this chapter.[17] To briefly summarize the phenomena here, it is important to say that the foundational concepts of sexuality research over the past century and a half of its existence have tended far too much to frame human behaviors in a binary way that dismisses and/or eclipses attraction to any one sex/gender in favor of ignoring or discounting the other(s).[18] Beginning with sexuality researchers in nineteenth-century Europe, the same assumptions that have stigmatized homosexuality as a lesser-than and inferior orientation have also reinforced the heterosexual/homosexual binary-only frame. In other words, the nineteenth-century white European males who were the first sexologists based their research on key binary assumptions that heterosexuality was the "opposite" of being attracted to one's own sex, and that it was also superior to same-sex attractions. Underlying these assumptions was the belief that people are *either* heterosexual or homosexual, and that being bisexual and attracted to more than one gender is neither legitimate nor real.[19] Of course this framework was invented by heterosexuals to differentiate themselves from homosexuals, neither of which category really exists outside the human mind. As Kate Millet wrote, "Homosexuality was invented by a straight world dealing with its own bisexuality."[20]

During the first few decades of LGBTQ studies, bisexual erasure was, and still is, common.[21] The "B" has been included mostly in name only, and often events and organizations that are labeled with the inclusive acronym are not really inclusive in the processes of reporting and pedagogy that play out. For example, while English departments, psychology departments, sociology departments, history departments, and others have opened up to including positive examples of gay and lesbian life and accomplishments and to formalizing them via scholarly journals, textbooks, academic conferences, and curricula at undergraduate and graduate levels, the stories that follow here in this chapter have almost never been included as part of these narratives. They still, for the most part, are not. You will read two examples under the Resistance and Protest heading, and more under other headings below.

Continuing to assert one's bisexuality in the face of this denial, dismissal, and erasure takes tremendous strength of will and sometimes just sheer cussedness or stubbornness—attributes that are often seen to be anathema to those who want to fit in and be well liked by others. And yet, bisexuals have been a part of many social movements, including what is now called the LGBTQ one. This activism has not been without cost, nor without almost constant censorship, even from within and without the bisexual movement. This biphobia, both internalized and from external sources, has resulted in the achievements and events related to bisexual identities being erased or excluded from the record. Repeated efforts are needed to put bisexuality and bisexual history back in, over and over again.

Important Events and Places in U.S. Bisexual History

Although there were individual bisexual support groups in various cities during the 1970s and 1980s—including BiPOL, the first bisexual political organization that formed in San Francisco in 1983—it took until the late 1980s for a national bisexual networking capacity to form.[22] During the mid-1980s, U.S. bisexual social groups and political action groups, not only on both coasts, but also in the Midwest, the Northwest, and the Southeast, began to communicate with each other. The official start of the U.S. bisexual movement and the launch of BiNET USA is often marked as the day in October 1987 when about eighty bisexual activists from around the country who had come for the second national

March on Washington for Lesbian and Gay Rights gathered to form the first ever bisexual contingent at a national march. But years of preparation and cross-country organizing went into making that contingent possible. People brought homemade bisexual pride signs. Some wore T-shirts bearing a bisexual symbol of overlapping pink and blue triangles making a purple triangle in the middle. Everyone marveled to see each other, finally, assembled in a suite at the Mayflower Hotel, a few blocks north of the White House.[23] Before they joined the line of the march farther south, they distributed copies of a flyer to give out to others along the route. The flyer, "Are We Ready for a National Bisexual Network?," included BiPOL's address that people could write to in order to keep in touch with national organizing efforts.[24] Some of these same bisexual leaders had been active with the March on Washington's national organizing committee during the previous year, including San Francisco BiPOL organizer Lani Ka'ahumanu. Her piece in the march's civil disobedience handbook, "The Bisexual Movement, Are We Visible Yet?," was a first of its kind in national gay/lesbian publications of the day.[25] While the 1987 March weekend marks the beginning of national bisexual organizing, bisexual activists have been involved in the LGBTQ movement from its very beginnings.

For those interested, a number of bi history timelines chronicling important meetings and occurrences from the 1960s on are available online.[26] These helpful resources—particularly on health and political organizing topics—provide useful touchstones. What follows are examples of bisexual history being reclaimed. A number of archives concentrating on bisexual history are now also available, most notably the Bisexual Resource Center's collection in Boston, the University of Minnesota's Tretter Collection, the collection at the James C. Hormel LGBTQIA Center at the San Francisco Public Library, and the bisexual materials that are part of the San Francisco GLBT Historic Society Archives.[27]

Sites of Resistance and Protest

Were bisexuals at Stonewall? Yes, of course. Those attracted to more than one gender, like Sylvia Rivera, one of the first transgender activists, and Brenda Howard, a multi-issue social justice activist, were part of an organized response to police violence directed against sexual minorities during the days of the Stonewall uprising in New York City in June 1969, and a part of the one-year anniversary commemorative event, later recognized as Pride Day.[28] Howard, now known as "the Mother of

Pride" for her work coordinating the first rally the year after Stonewall, was an antiwar activist who chaired the Gay Activists Alliance Speakers Bureau and was one of the first members of the Gay Liberation Front in New York City.[29] She helped steer the city's gay rights law through the city council in 1986, worked with ACT UP and Queer Nation, and helped found the New York Area Bisexual Network, along with its Bisexual Political Action Campaign (BiPAC) and many other groups. She served as a regional representative in the national organizing that mobilized the 1993 March on Washington for Lesbian, Gay and Bi Equal Rights and Liberation in Washington, D.C., and served in 1994 as female cochair of the leather contingent of the Stonewall 25 march held 26 June 1994 in New York City. She was also instrumental in organizing the Third International Bisexual Conference held on 25 June, the day before Stonewall 25, at Bayard Rustin High School.[30]

Though often described as gay in historic accounts, Alan Rockway, one of the key organizers of the Florida orange juice boycott against Save Our Children's Anita Bryant, was an out bisexual psychologist.[31] He went on to do bisexual political organizing with BiPOL in San Francisco, including helping organize the first Bisexual Rights Rally and protest during the 1984 Democratic Convention.[32] In 1976 Rockway created and taught the first college-level course on bisexuality, "Psychological Views of Bisexual Behavior," offered at Sonoma State College in California.[33] In 2007, Alliant International University named their center for LGBTQ research and public policy after Rockway.[34]

Bisexuals are resilient, surviving in a world that repeatedly erases and elides their existence. Left out of the names of organizations and marches, excluded from studies and efforts purporting to represent all same-sex loving people, they persist, resist, and continue to assert who they are. For example, in 1991, Princeton and Rutgers Universities cohosted the fifth annual Lesbian and Gay Studies Conference at the Rutgers campus in New Brunswick, New Jersey. Although organizers at the 1990 conference held at Harvard University had added bi into the title the year before, the word "bisexual" was taken back out of the name of the conference when it was held in New Jersey. Likewise, although a number of papers on bisexuality were presented at the 1991 New Jersey conference, the resulting anthology, *Negotiating Lesbian and Gay Subjects*, contained none of them.[35] No conference was held during 1992 or 1993, but this foundational effort in LGBTQ studies resulted in one last November 1994 conference at the University of Iowa, Iowa City. As a result of bisexual advocacy and resistance over being "written in and out" of earlier gatherings, the 1994 conference was dubbed "InQueery/ InTheory/InDeed: The Sixth North American Lesbian, Gay and Bisexual Studies Conference." The Iowa City conference included programming on bisexual and transgender issues as well as gay and lesbian ones, and produced a book based on conference proceedings.[36] Another example happened in Northampton, Massachusetts, where the public parks and town square became a parallel site of resistance in response to this exclusionary "Now You See Us, Now You Don't" mentality. As has been partially related in Hemmings's *Bisexual Spaces: A Geography of Sexuality and Gender,* this small western Massachusetts town used a bi-inclusive title for its annual Pride celebration one year, and then erased the bisexual part of the name the next.[37]

Is resistance "futile," as the Star Trek Borg would tell us, or is it "fertile," as indomitable resisters of all types assert? Many bisexuals long known for refusing-to-choose (sides in a war not of their making) answer "it's both"—"futile" in the sense of being monumentally discouraging to continually insist on one's right to belong and exist, and inspirationally "fertile" in the sense that hope beyond simplistic binaries springs eternal in nongendered human breasts.

Many, many small towns and big city communities around the country have their own specific tales of bi inclusion/exclusion—instances where bisexuals were included in groups' titles, marches and other events, and then excluded again, sometimes repeatedly, even up to this day in time. There have been bisexual grand marshals who were honored and helped lead Pride parades, and also many times when they could/should have been, and were not. For example, it was not until 1986, when BiPOL's Autumn Courtney was elected cochair of San Francisco's Lesbian Gay Freedom Day Pride Parade Committee, the first time that an openly bisexual person was chosen to hold this sort of position in the United States.[38]

Another kind of protest has been individual and small group actions, sometimes involving civil disobedience, to try and draw attention to their cause. One such example was the action of Dr. Elias Farajajé-Jones, an African American bisexual professor at Howard University School of Divinity, who staged a sit-in at the Washington, D.C., mayor's office in 1991 to protest inaction of the D.C. government regarding the release of HIV/AIDS funding.[39] The exact date of this protest has been lost, and Farajajé himself died in early 2016. This protest is particularly poignant as his own lover was dying of AIDS in Washington, D.C.'s Veterans Administration Hospital at the time.

As the above stories show, there is a lot of hidden history about the dynamics of coalition organizing—what gets put in a group's platform or a campaign's demands or a march's platform, and what gets left out or voted down.[40] It is always informative to ask your local college or place of worship or activist group what kind of naming battles went on, and/or are still going on, and what people think it means, what kinds of messages are sent by the ways we use language: who is represented and who is not, present absences, absent presences, whose lives matter, here, there, anywhere.[41]

Building Bisexual Communities— Local, Global, and Everything in Between

The first thing to understand about the concept of bisexual communities is that they do not stand alone, apart from other demographic groups. That's not how bisexuality works. Bisexuals partner and have children with those who are not bisexual, and work within and among and apart from and alongside many different kinds of interest groups. Bisexual leaders and activists in the past were well known for saying that "there is no point in organizing a separate bisexual political movement" because the issues of loving more than one gender are woven into more than one community, so the point has been to organize across communities and among them, not apart from them. Like others, bisexual activists do not work only to build bisexual-specific organizations or for bisexual rights, but work as out bisexuals in many movements that, ideally, network with each other. It means there are bisexually-identified people organizing within electoral politics and political parties, within LGBTQ organizations, within the labor movement, the civil rights movement, the women's movement, the environmental movement, and more, making the intersectional connections between bisexual issues and other issues whenever platforms, campaigns, and protest demands are formulated.

Still, when trying to trace more precisely the beginnings of bisexual-focused community efforts, we often start by looking back at the "firsts" in LGBTQ history, those that have been commemorated in the LGBTQ history books and textbooks, and also those that have sometimes been left out. Recognized as the first homophile organization in the United States, the Society for Human Rights was founded by Henry Gerber and others, including an African American clergyman named John T. Graves (who is listed as president on the incorporation papers), in Chicago, Illinois, in 1924. The group, which operated out of Gerber's flat in a rooming house, limited membership to gay men only, explicitly excluding bisexuals. Unknown to the organizers, the society's vice president, Al Weininger, was married. His wife reported the organization to a social worker in 1925, resulting in a police raid of Gerber's quarters. The organization's records and typewriter were seized and not returned, effectively ending the society's existence.[42]

Using "gay" in the most expansive, inclusive sense possible, there have been lasting gay support and social groups on college campuses and in individual communities for over sixty years.[43] Some histories tell the story about how students in the late 1980s and early 1990s agitated to change the names of their groups to be more inclusive, often adding "lesbian" and "bisexual," and then "transgender" and "queer," to their names. But what is not generally known, taught, or told, is that the very first U.S. gay student group was started by a bisexual man.

The Student Homophile League at Columbia University was started in 1966, several years before Stonewall.[44] The founder was student Stephen Donaldson (birth name Robert Martin), perhaps better known as Donny the Punk. Donny led a short, illustrious life, having affairs with famous gay and lesbian political leaders and organizing for bisexual rights among everyone from nonviolent Quakers to convicted felons. He was one of the very first anti-prison-rape activists and died of AIDS much too young. Today, meetings of the Columbia Queer Alliance are held in a special room dedicated to Donaldson's memory. With Donaldson's support, activists on other campuses formed similar groups, laying the groundwork for what became the gay liberation movement in the late 1960s and early 1970s.[45]

This is but one example of what historian Genny Beemyn has characterized as the pattern of many LGBTQ groups being started by, and continuing to be run by, bisexual people, whether they are out and recognized as bisexual or not. Other LGBTQ youth groups have also been started by bisexuals. In Miami in 1977, Alexei Guren, a young Cuban American bisexual activist, organized the Gay Teen Task Force, an LGBTQ youth group that met monthly at the offices of the *Weekly News*. In 1982, it moved to the Institute of Sexism and Sexuality at Miami Dade College, where it often hosted up to fifty LGBTQ youth at the meetings. In 1996, the group incorporated and renamed itself Pridelines; it continues to provide a number of programs and services for the LGBTQ youth of Miami.[46] In 1975, Carol Queen—a young woman growing up in rural Oregon—cofounded Growing Alternative Youth (GAYouth) in Eugene, Oregon. When founded, it was only the third LGBTQ youth support/

social group in the nation. It later affiliated itself with the Metropolitan Community Church of Eugene.

Grassroots bisexual social and support groups were the pre-internet way of organizing the bisexual community and movement. There are hundreds unmentioned here. They continue, with the assistance of social media, to foster community ties and to serve as entry points for helping people identify openly as bi and to find resources, and for those interested in getting involved with activist and advocacy work on behalf of LGBTQ issues as well as those specific to bisexuality. Some long-lasting examples include BiFriendly in San Francisco, Biversity in Boston, and the many bi brunches and munches that spring up and die down and spring up again in communities across the country.

Leisure

What is *leisure* to a community under oppression? It might seem like an impossible luxury, a distraction from the necessary work. Then again, leisure is all the more necessary and life-giving to people in crisis and under stress. During the 1980s and 1990s (and often still today), bisexuals were vilified as being the disease vectors who "spread AIDS to the general population," as if they themselves were not part of society.[47] In reality, bisexual health workers and activists designed and developed some of the first city, county, state, and federally supported safer sex protocols now in use around the country. In San Francisco, bisexual activists David Lourea and Cynthia Slater worked to prevent the spread of HIV/AIDS before they themselves died of the disease. As early as 1981, they were providing safer-sex education in the city's bathhouses and BDSM clubs, and by 1983, Lourea had been appointed to San Francisco Mayor Dianne Feinstein's AIDS Education Advisory Committee. In 1984, he convinced the city's public health department to include bisexual men in its weekly "New AIDS Cases and Mortality Statistics" reports, a model later adopted by other public health departments across the country. Slater started the first Women's HIV/AIDS Information Switchboard in San Francisco in 1985.[48]

Other bisexuals have made important contributions to HIV/AIDS prevention, including Rob Yaeger at the Minneapolis AIDS Project and Alexei Guren, who, as well as founding Pridelines, was involved with the 1983 founding of the Health Crisis Network in Miami, Florida, which did outreach and advocacy for Latino married men who have sex with men. From 1992 to 1994, Lani Ka'ahumanu was project coordinator at

Lyon-Martin Women's Health Services in San Francisco for an American Foundation for AIDS research grant—the first grant in the United States targeting young high-risk lesbian and bisexual women for HIV/AIDS prevention and education research.[49]

Safer sex education is a topic of science and organizing, not a topic of leisure. But it relates to leisure because in the time of HIV/AIDS, the prevention of sexually transmitted diseases became a matter of life or death. These safer sex protocols were most efficiently, effectively, and popularly taught at public baths, at leather bars and sex parties, and at workshops during conferences where explicit demonstrations and conversations could be had without fear of condemnation or retribution. These often transient places can never be fully cataloged.

One of the modern-day inheritors of these traditions was the Center for Sex and Culture founded in 2000 by bisexual activists Carol Queen (who also cofounded GAYouth, described above) and Robert Lawrence.[50] The Center for Sex and Culture hosted many bisexual-focused and bi-friendly events for the larger San Francisco community and maintained an archive of sexuality research. In New England, long-time bisexual activist and author Wayne Bryant founded Bi Camp, a popular summertime leisure activity that ran from 1994–2009.[51] Each winter, announcements and flyers were mailed out encouraging people to get their camping gear together, to start thinking about potluck campfire recipes, and to make packing lists of musical instruments, games, and sports equipment to bring along. Bi Camp started at a campground in Vermont's Green Mountain National Forest, and moved after five years to Indian Hollow Campground owned by the Army Corps of Engineers in Chesterfield, Massachusetts.[52] The camp hosted anywhere from twenty-five to eighty campers each year, including bisexual people, their families, and friends. It inspired a video Bryant made, and a sing-along, multi-versed song by Philadelphian Moss Stern, called "Bi Camp."

Organizing Every Which Way

Bisexuals helped organize the first national marches for the rights of sexual minorities in the United States, as well as similarly oriented local community events, and have been part of Pride parades since the beginning. They have helped organize LGBTQ events as well as bisexual-specific ones, locally, nationally, and globally, for many years, recognized or not.

Bill Beasley, a bisexual man who was also involved in the Black civil rights movement, helped lead the first Los Angeles Pride parade down Hollywood Boulevard in 1970, and went on to serve on the board of San Francisco Pride and become an active member of the Bay Area Bisexual Network.[53] A. Billy S. Jones (now Jones-Hennin), an African American activist and author, served as operations coordinator for the first National March on Washington for Lesbian and Gay rights on 14 October 1979.[54] The event featured a march down Washington, D.C.'s Pennsylvania Avenue to the National Mall, where a program of speeches and musical entertainment occurred. Illustrating the kind of bicoastal organizing of the time, Jones had been active in San Francisco's Bisexual Center before moving to the Washington, D.C., area.[55] During the weekend of the 1979 march, Jones also served as one of the key conveners of the Third World Lesbian Gay Conference held at the Harambee House Hotel.[56] It was at this conference that ties among many Black LGBTQ communities and LGBTQ communities of other people of color were strengthened. Audre Lorde, who was just beginning to come out as a lesbian poet and leader, spoke at that conference, as did many others. In the year following that conference, Jones and the National Coalition of Black Lesbians and Gays brought the first ever people of color delegation to meet with President Carter's White House staff. This delegation was organized because an all-white gay delegation had arranged a meeting with the White House a year earlier. Thirty-three years later, on a cool 2013 September morning, Jones and many other bisexual activists and leaders returned to the White House to talk with administration officials about bisexual policy issues for the first time.[57]

The bisexual movement in the United States has been built on conferences that knit and weave and sew the experiences of local communities together and make joint actions across state, and even national, borders possible. One of the earliest recorded meetings on bisexuality took place at a gathering of Quakers (Friends) in upstate New York in the early 1970s. Bisexual activist Stephen Donaldson—the same man who founded the first gay student group in the United States—told the *Advocate* that he had organized an impromptu workshop on bisexuality at the 1972 Friends General Conference in Ithaca, New York.[58] Donaldson, whose birth name was Robert Martin, said the workshop involved over one hundred participants and overflowed into several different meeting rooms over two days, resulting in what has become known as the Ithaca Statement on Bisexuality, which may have been the first public statement on bisexuality by a religious or political group.

Figure 2.1. Participants of the first ever National Conference on Bisexuality sit on the steps of Mission High School, San Francisco, California, June 1990. Photo courtesy of Efrain John Gozalez, Hellfire Press Archive (gonzo@ hellfirepress.com).

From the 1970s, one bisexual man, Dr. Fritz Klein, has helped perhaps more than anyone else to facilitate bisexual networking and conferences. Dr. Klein was a psychiatrist who did early research and publishing on bisexuality. He also traveled widely, especially in the 1980s and 1990s, connecting bisexual communities around the world with each other, and helping to start international bisexual conferences in London, Amsterdam, Toronto, and Vancouver. Klein himself was bicoastal, living for a long time in New York City and then moving to San Diego. He started the first peer-reviewed scholarly journal on bisexuality, the *Journal of Bisexuality*. Klein founded the American Institute of Bisexuality in 1998 to encourage research and education about bisexuality. He served as chairman of the board until his death in 2006.[59]

One of the most catalyzing and foundational conferences of the U.S. bisexual movement took place in June 1990 at San Francisco's Mission High School (figure 2.1).[60] The conference was the result of outreach done during the 1987 March on Washington for Lesbian and Gay Rights mentioned earlier, and drew over 450 people from twenty U.S. states and five countries. The school is located directly across from Dolores Park in the Mission District, and, in the beautiful weather that weekend, many conference goers took their conversations out onto the grass across the street and created impromptu workshops on the balconies

Figure 2.2. Photograph of Eleanor Roosevelt and Cliff Arnesen at Val-Kill, Hyde Park, New York, 18 July 1959. Mrs. Roosevelt was Chair of the Wiltwyck School for Boys; she held an annual picnic at Val-Kill for the one hundred boys of the predominantly African American school located in Esopus, New York. Photo copyright Clifton Francis Arnesen Jr.

and in the courtyard of the old school. It was at this conference that Bi-Net USA, the oldest national bisexual organization in the United States, was inaugurated.[61] Other regional bisexual organizing conferences have been held, including Washington, D.C.'s Embracing Diversities Conference in fall 1991; the BECAUSE Conference, which has been annually convening in the Midwest since 1992; and the Transcending Boundaries Conference, created to bring the bisexual and transgender communities together, which has taken place since 2001 around New England.[62]

Much has changed in the way municipal, state, and federal laws deal with same-sex relationships over the years, yet in some ways much remains to be done. Years before bisexual people, along with their lesbian, gay, and queer siblings, became active in marriage equality efforts, bisexuals were also active in organizing for veterans' rights and for the rights of those in the military. One of the most prominent was Cliff Arnesen, who was dishonorably discharged from the military for being bisexual (figure 2.2). Afterwards, he went on to become an activist for all LGBTQ people in the military and was the first LGBTQ veteran to testify before a congressional subcommittee about the health needs and rights of his fellow service members.[63]

In 2013, a group of activists at the Lavender Law Conference, hosted by the National LGBT Bar Association, formed BiLaw, the first national organization of bisexual-identified lawyers, law professors, law students, and their allies.[64] In 2015, the Lavender Law Conference programmed its first panel on issues of bisexual jurisprudence, bisexuality, and the law.

Protesting among Our Own

As mentioned earlier, a lot of the hard work of bisexual organizing occurs within nonbisexual organizations. These may not be openly welcoming to people with bisexual identities but may include many closeted bisexuals among them, whether passing as heterosexual, lesbian/gay, or both. More explicitly, the work of dismantling bisexual erasure and invisibility is constant. It takes place not only in the energizing bisexual conferences and meetings held around the country, but also within professional organizations like the National LGBT Bar Association (mentioned above) and professional organizations such as the American Library Association, the American Psychological Association, the National Association of Social Workers, the National Women's Studies Association, the American Historical Association, and more. When LGBTQ caucuses are formed within these groups and when gay/lesbian specific presentations and panels are scheduled at annual conferences, bisexual topics are often left out. This, alas, is almost as likely to occur within gay- and lesbian-oriented organizations as it is within those more in the mainstream. For example, in 1989, the Hetrick-Martin Institute, a nonprofit organization serving the needs of LGBTQ youth, advertised a workshop to be held at their Harvey Milk High School.[65] The workshop was called, "Bisexual Men: Fact or Fiction?" In response to the workshop title, which challenged the very existence of bisexual men, BiPAC New York, a bisexual political action group, protested. In response, institute staff agreed to withdraw the workshop from their curriculum. This is but one example of instances like it around the country.

On a national basis, many national LGBTQ gatherings have been sites of protests focused on bisexual rights. Two historic examples from the early 1990s concern bisexual activists and the National LGBTQ Task Force—then known as the National Gay and Lesbian Task Force.[66] The Task Force began its historic annual Creating Change conferences in Washington, D.C., in 1988, the year after the 1987 March on Washington for Lesbian and Gay Rights. Since then, Creating Change has become the largest annual gathering of LGBTQ activists and leaders in the United States, and bisexuals have been there from the beginning, often fighting for recognition and space on the program, sometimes recognized and sometimes not. In November 1991, Creating Change drew almost one thousand participants to Alexandria, Virginia.[67] For the first time at Creating Change, bisexual activists held a workshop for gay and lesbian leaders to talk with bisexual activists about tensions between the groups.

Creating Change returned to the D.C. area again in November 1996, when two thousand people convened, again in Alexandria, Virginia.[68] In the intervening years, the bisexual community had continued to hold separate women's and men's dialogues across orientation lines at each annual Creating Change, initiating and fostering difficult communication between those who identified as gay or lesbian and those who identified as bisexual. Things came to a head at the 1996 conference when the number of discriminatory acts and remarks against bisexuals and transgender people reached such a peak that a Bi/Trans Action at the main plenary on Saturday morning was planned. Before the keynote speeches began, activists took to the stage recounting examples of biphobic and transphobic offenses committed against them during that weekend conference. They asked everyone in the room who identified as bi and/or transgender, and/or who was an ally, to stand up and be counted and to vow to confront biphobic and transphobic actions and attitudes in the future. Although the Bi/Trans Action was not included in the Gay and Lesbian Task Force press release following the conference, they did note that the first significant conversation between bisexual and transgender activists and members of the administration had occurred that weekend:

> Representatives of the bisexual and transgender community held a first-ever meeting at the Conference with a White House representative to discuss discrimination, violence, ENDA, bi and trans visibility and inclusivity in the Administration and other issues. Richard Socarides, outgoing White House liaison to the g/l/b/t community, met with the bi and transgender leaders to hear their concerns in a meeting that was described as productive and promising.[69]

That meeting laid the groundwork for White House meetings that would take place in the new century.

Political Activism as Celebration

Sometimes political victories are the cause for much celebration and, in fact, inspire sites of rejoicing and festivities in and of themselves. Such was the case with the 1993 March on Washington for Lesbian, Gay and Bi Equal Rights and Liberation the last weekend in April. The 1993 march was the third of a total of five marches held on Washington for LGBTQ rights and, in many ways, the most grassroots and inclusive of all of them. The "bi" word was included, after much debate, in the title of the march for the first time, and a bisexual speaker, Lani Ka'ahumanu, was invited to speak from the main stage on the National Mall for the first time as well.[70] Bisexual activists converged on Washington, D.C., a week before the march to staff an impromptu bisexual coordinating center located in donated office space in the Dupont Circle neighborhood. They camped out in the homes of local bisexual activists in the Mt. Pleasant, Adams Morgan, and Takoma neighborhoods; organized the Second National Conference Celebrating Bisexuality that took place two days before the march; and held a national meeting of BiNet USA, followed by a Bi Dance at George Washington University's Marvin Center, the night before.[71] The march itself had been organized with 50/50 gender/racial parity, meaning that there were many more women and people of color involved in leadership roles determining the platform demands of the march as well as traveling to Washington, D.C., as participants.

First observed in 1999, Celebrate Bisexuality Day was started by three BiNet USA activists, Wendy Curry from Maine, Michael Page from Florida, and Gigi Raven Wilbur from Texas. It has been celebrated in small towns, large cities, and internationally, on the internet and at many events, usually around 23 September, the date of the first event. A 2013 White House meeting between federal officials and bisexual activists to discuss bisexual issues was scheduled for 23 September in recognition of the day.[72] Since 2013, BiNet USA working in coalition with other bisexual and LGBTQ organizations, has expanded Celebrate Bisexuality Day to cover a whole week. The Bisexual Resource Center in Boston has also designated the month of March as Bisexual Health Awareness Month, focusing on raising awareness about bisexual health issues, nationally and locally.

Two years later, many of the same leaders who had been at the 2013 meeting returned that same week in September to meet again with representatives from federal offices to discuss bisexual concerns. When leaving the meeting, many participants pulled bisexual pride flags out of their backpacks and briefcases and created an impromptu celebration in front of the White House.

Conclusion

People whose lives encompass loving more than one gender, whether or not they openly identify themselves as bisexual—or even queer or gay or lesbian, or any other label that describes a sexual minority—continue to exist, to make families and communities, and to organize, among themselves and with others, for better acceptance and understanding. Did bisexuals help build the United States of America? Absolutely. Have we discovered all the places they have lived and worked and loved and where they continue to do so? Not a chance. And that is beautiful. Discovering more of the history, seeing them clearly, are the next steps.

Dr. Loraine Hutchins is an author and adjunct professor at Montgomery College in Maryland.

Notes

1. Walt Whitman nursed injured American Civil War soldiers at the Old Patent Office Building at F and Seventh Streets NW, Washington, D.C. Now home to the National Portrait Gallery, this building was listed on the NRHP on 15

October 1966 and designated an NHL on 12 January 1965. Whitman spent the last years of his life at his home, 330 Dr. Martin Luther King Jr. Boulevard (formerly Mickle Street), Camden, New Jersey (listed on the NRHP on 15 October 1966; designated an NHL on 29 December 1962). It was here that, just before his death, he finished his final edits to *Leaves of Grass*. In 1923, Edna St. Vincent Millay was the first woman to win the Pulitzer Prize for poetry. In 1924, she and a group of friends founded the Cherry Lane Theatre, 38 Commerce Street, New York City. While the original group disbanded in 1926, Cherry Lane is the longest continuously-operating off-Broadway theater in New York City, and has a long history of producing LGBTQ-themed plays. Millay's home, Steepletop, in Austerlitz, New York, was listed on the NRHP and designated an NHL on 11 November 1971. She lived in the house from 1925 through 1950.

2. "The discussion of Whitman's sexual orientation will probably continue in spite of whatever evidence emerges." From Jerome Loving, *Walt Whitman: The Song of Himself* (Berkeley: University of California Press, 1999), 19. Millay had relationships with both women and men. In 1923, she married Eugen Boissevain. Married for twenty-six years, Millay and Boissevain had an open marriage and "acted like two bachelors." See "Edna St. Vincent Millay," Academy of American Poets website, https://www.poets.org/poetsorg/poet/edna-st-vincent-millay.

3. Michael Bronski, *A Queer History of the United States* (Boston: Beacon Press, 2011), 146.

4. Ibid., 150.

5. Hank Stuever, "Gloria Vanderbilt and Anderson Cooper: Sorting through Family Hurt and History," *Washington Post,* 8 April 2016.

6. "That Bernstein was bisexual was no secret in his later years, and he has been outed (snarkily, awkwardly, gleefully) since his death. Here he outs himself, through frank exchanges with his new wife, Felicia Montealegre, with whom he formed an unspoken covenant: He could have affairs with men, he could lead his 'double life,' as long as he was reasonably discreet." From John Rockwell, "Maestro: The Leonard Bernstein Letters," *New York Times Sunday Book Review,* 13 December 2013.

7. Margaret Cho, "Queer," *Huffpost Queer Voices,* 3 October 2011, http://www.huffingtonpost.com/margaret-cho/queer_b_984123.html; Adam Sandel, "Alan Cumming Is Bisexual—And You Might Be Too," *Advocate,* 30 March 2015, http://www.advocate.com/bisexuality/2015/03/30/alan-cumming-bisexual-and-you-might-be-too.

8. "She wrote in 'Out and Elected in the USA,' an online collection of essays by LGBTQ elected officials, that some of her gay friends called her 'half-queer.' Straight friends were convinced she couldn't make up her mind." See Associated Press, "Gov. Kate Brown veers from typical graduation speech to talk about her sexuality," *Oregonian,* 20 May 2016, http://www.oregonlive.com/politics/index.ssf/2016/05/gov_kate_brown_veers_from_typi.html.

9. There is very little research on how the acronym emerged and why it is so well-used now. Careful inspection of historic references shows that it started with groups with "gay" in their title adding "lesbian" first, and then many student groups in the 1980s adding bisexual and transgender into their groups' titles. The first acronym showed the G first, and the L started leading as women's leadership and positions came more forward. During the mid-1990s in the United States, the acronym became more used and is now seen as the reference point. Note: "Q" is often now added onto the LGBT term because it denotes "Queer" and because people argue that it is a more contemporary representation of sexual minorities' identities/labels. However, older and more conservative people still resist embracing the Q-word as a part of how they identify, so the debate continues. The National Gay and Lesbian Taskforce, for instance, debated changing their name for many years for exactly this reason, and finally changed it several years ago, adding the LGBTQ acronym.

10. Sylvia Rivera was assigned male at birth and claimed her female identity at age ten, when she changed her name from Ray to Sylvia. Sylvia Rivera, "Queens in Exile: The Forgotten Ones," in *Street Transvestite Action Revolutionaries: Survival, Revolt, and Queer Antagonist Struggle* (N.p.: Untorelli Press, 2013).

11. Nicole Kristal and Mike Szymanski, *The Bisexuals Guide to the Universe: Quips, Tips, and Lists for Those Who Go Both Ways* (New York: Alyson Publications, 2006), has a list of famous bisexuals, as do a number of websites like the October LGBT History Month site at http://www.lgbthistorymonth.com.

12. Matthew Rodriguez, "Queer Teens Are Now the Majority: Goodbye Straight People," *Mic,* 12 March 2016, citing a report from the J. Walter Thompson Innovation Group that found only 48 percent of teens identify as completely heterosexual on the Kinsey scale, a smaller percentage than any previous generations surveyed; see http://mic.com/articles/137713/queer-teens-are-now-the-majority-goodbye-straight-people. See also Shabab Ahmed Mirza, "Disaggregating the Data for Bisexual People," Center for American Progress, 24 September 2018, https://www.americanprogress.org/issues/lgbt/reports/2018/09/24/458472/disaggregating-data-bisexual-people/.

13. For bisexual history timelines, see, for example, Lani Ka'ahumanu, "Timeline: The Bisexual Health Movement in the U.S.," BiNet USA website, n.d., http://binetusa.org/bihealth.html; "A Brief History of the Bisexual Movement," BiNet USA website, n.d., http://www.binetusa.org/bi-history; and "The Bisexual History of HIV/AIDS, In Photos," LGBT HealthLink website, 29 January 2015, https://blog.lgbthealthlink.org/2015/01/29/the-bisexual-history-of-hivaids-in-photos.

14. From 1927 through 1956, Alfred Kinsey and his family lived in a home he designed in a neighborhood just south of the University of Indiana. It is a contributing element to the Vinegar Hill Historic District, listed on the

NRHP on 17 June 2005. The Kinsey Institute for Research in Sex, Gender, and Reproduction is currently located in Morrison Hall, University of Indiana, Bloomington. See Alfred C. Kinsey, Wardell B. Pomeroy, and Clyde E. Martin, *Sexual Behavior in the Human Male* (Philadelphia: W. B. Saunders Co., 1948), 651, Table 147. Also see Ron J. Suresha, ed., *Bisexual Perspectives on the Life and Work of Alfred C. Kinsey* (London: Routledge, 2010).

15. Kinsey also recognized that some individuals were asexual, or not sexually attracted to other people, regardless of gender. He placed these individuals in a category he labeled "X" that was separate from the Kinsey scale.

16. See Lani Ka'ahumanu and Loraine Hutchins, eds., *Bi Any Other Name: Bisexual People Speak Out,* 25th anniversary edition (New York: Riverdale Avenue Books, [1991] 2015), 38–47, psychology overview section.

17. The interested reader is referred to texts such as sociologist Paula Rust's works; legal scholars Ruth Colker's and Kenji Yoshino's classic studies on bisexual labeling, politics, and erasure; historians Stephen Angelides's and Clare Hemmings's books; and Lindasusan Ulrich's groundbreaking report to the San Francisco Human Rights Commission. See Loraine Hutchins, "Let's Not Bijack Another Century," in *The Routledge History of Queer America,* ed. Don Romesburg (London: Routledge, 2018). See also Bisexual.org, "Legally Bi: A Brief History of Bi Erasure in LGBT Political Discourse," 11 August 2018, https://bisexual.org/legally-bi-a-brief-history-of-bi-erasure-in-lgbt-political-discourse/.

18. "Other(s)" includes the plural since there are many who now argue there are more than two genders, that gender is not inherently binary, that binary, either/or, male/female genders are a culturally specific phenomena and an oversimplification of the vastly more complex reality of how humans understand and express themselves.

19. Stephen Angelides, *A History of Bisexuality* (Chicago: University of Chicago Press, 2001).

20. Kate Millet, *Flying* (Champaign: University of Illinois Press, 2000), 97.

21. The first decades of LGBTQ studies are considered here to be the mid-1970s to the mid-1990s, beginning with the release of the first edition of Jonathan Ned Katz's groundbreaking work, *Gay American History: Lesbians and Gay Men in the U.S.A.* (New York: Avon Books, 1978).

22. BiPOL was founded in San Francisco by Autumn Courtney, Lani Ka'ahumanu, Arlene Krantz, David Lourea, Bill Mack, Alan Rockway, and Maggi Rubenstein. See Lani Ka'ahumanu, "Timeline"; Alan Soble, ed., *Sex from Plato to Paglia: A Philosophical Encyclopedia* (New York: Greenwood Publishing Group, 2006), 115.

23. The Mayflower Hotel, 1127 Connecticut Avenue NW, Washington, D.C., was listed on the NRHP on 14 November 1983.

24. The address given for BiPOL was 584 Castro Street, San Francisco, California.

25. The Civil Disobedience Handbook guided people through a day of nonviolent protest at the United States Supreme Court, in response to the Bowers

v. Hardwick decision upholding Georgia's sodomy law criminalizing oral and anal sex in private between consenting same-sex adults. This decision was later overturned by the court's Lawrence v. Texas decision. The civil disobedience actions accompanying the 1987 march weekend occurred the day after the long march down Pennsylvania Avenue to the U.S. Capitol Building.

26. For bisexual history timelines, see websites included in note 13.

27. The Bisexual Resource Center's collection is housed at Northeastern University's Snell Library, 360 Huntington Avenue, Boston, Massachusetts. The Jean-Nickolaus Tretter Collection in Gay, Lesbian, Bisexual and Transgender Studies is at the University of Minnesota's Andersen Library, 222 Twenty-First Avenue South, Minneapolis, Minnesota. The James C. Hormel LGBTQIA Center (formerly the James C. Hormel Gay and Lesbian Center) is located at the San Francisco Public Library, 100 Larkin Street, San Francisco (part of the Civic Center Historic District, added to the NRHP on 10 October 1978 and designated an NHL on 27 February 1987). The GLBT Historical Society Archives are at 989 Market Street, San Francisco, California.

28. "Brenda Howard," LGBT History Month website, n.d., http://lgbthistory-month.com/brenda-howard?tab=biography; Jade Salazar, "LGBTQ History #18: Sylvia Rivera: Transgender Activist and Stonewall Legend," *Tagg Magazine*, 29 October 2014, http://taggmagazine.com/community/sylvia-rivera-transgender-activist-stonewall-legend; Stonewall, 51–53 Christopher Street, New York City, New York, was listed on the NRHP on 28 June 1999, designated an NHL on 16 February 2000, and declared Stonewall National Monument (an NPS unit) on 24 June 2016.

29. Eliel Cruz, "Remembering Brenda: An Ode to the 'Mother of Pride,'" *Advocate*, 17 June 2014, http://www.advocate.com/bisexuality/2014/06/17/remembering-brenda-ode-%E2%80%98mother-pride%E2%80%99.

30. The Bayard Rustin High School, named after the famous gay civil rights leader who was chief architect of the 1963 March on Washington for Jobs and Freedom, is now called the Bayard Rustin Educational Complex. It is located at 351 West Eighteenth Street, New York City, New York.

31. This early homophobic campaign, the precursor of today's anti-LGBT initiatives, was called "Save Our Children." It started in Florida in the 1970s and spread to other cities and states, and was championed by singer and Florida Citrus Commission spokesperson Anita Bryant. See "Foes of Anita Bryant Successful in Getting New Gay Law on Ballot," *Akron Beacon Journal* (Akron, Ohio), 5 October 1978, 37.

32. The 1984 Democratic Party Convention was held July 16–19 in the Moscone Center, San Francisco's convention center, built in 1981 in the South of Market area. It was named after San Francisco Mayor George Moscone, who had been assassinated, along with Supervisor Harvey Milk, in 1978. The Moscone Center currently consists of Moscone North, Moscone South, and Moscone West; Moscone South is the original structure built in 1981.

Rockway worked with San Francisco bisexual activist Lani Ka'ahumanu and others in BiPOL, a political action group, to create bisexual visibility actions around the convention, including securing a permit from the city for a protest stage for the first Bisexual Rights Rally in a parking lot across from the Moscone Center. The parking lot at 730 Howard Street is now occupied by Moscone Center North. Bisexuals had been explicitly told by organizers that they were not welcome in the National March for Lesbian and Gay Rights that took place from Castro and Market Streets to the Moscone Center during the convention.

33. In some historic records, Susan Carlton's 1990 course on bisexuality at the University of California, Berkeley, is listed as the first college-level course taught on bisexuality. In fact, Rockway originated the first course a decade and a half earlier. Others have followed suit in various LGBTQ university programs, but stand-alone courses that focus solely on bisexual issues are still rare forty years later. Sonoma State College (since 1978, Sonoma State University) is located at 1801 East Cotati Avenue, Rhonert Park, California.

34. The Rockway Institute is part of the California School of Professional Psychology, Alliant International University, One Beach Street, San Francisco, California. http://www.alliant.edu/cspp/about-cspp/cspp-research-institutes/rockway-institute/index.php

35. Brett Beemyn and Michele Eliason, eds., *Queer Studies: A Lesbian, Gay, Bisexual and Transgender Anthology* (New York: New York University Press, 1996), 1–2; Monica Dorenkamp and Richard Henke, eds., *Negotiating Lesbian and Gay Subjects* (London: Routledge, 1994.)

36. Beemyn and Eliason, *Queer Studies.*

37. Clare Hemmings, *Bisexual Spaces: A Geography of Sexuality and Gender* (New York: Routledge, 2002). See pages 62–75 for photo reproductions of posters used for various years of the marches in Northampton, illustrating bi inclusion and exclusion. Since at least the late 1970s/early 1980s, Northampton, Massachusetts, has been recognized as home to a large number of lesbians; in the early 1990s, it was dubbed "Lesbianville, U.S.A." by the mainstream media. See Julia Penelope, "Lesbianville, U.S.A.?" *Off Our Backs* 23, no. 9 (October 1993): 8, 16–17.

38. For more of these kinds of bisexual historic political facts, see BiNet USA, "A Brief History of the Bisexual Movement."

39. The Office of the Mayor is located at 1350 Pennsylvania Avenue NW, Washington, D.C. Howard University, an historically black university, has its divinity school at 2900 Van Ness Street NW, Washington, D.C. Dr. Farajajé-Jones became a Sufi scholar and later changed his name to Ibrahim Farajajé. He developed a department of Islam Studies at Starr King School for the Ministry in Berkeley, California, where he served as provost for many years before his death in February 2016. Starr King School for the Ministry is located at 2441 Le Conte Avenue, Berkeley, California.

40. See, for example, the updated introduction, Lani Ka'ahumanu and Loraine Hutchins, "Introduction: Still about Naming after All These Years," in Ka'ahumanu and Hutchins, *Bi Any Other Name,* 1–21.

41. For example, regarding organizations on college campuses, see Brett Beemyn, "The Silence is Broken: A History of the First Lesbian, Gay and Bisexual College Student Groups," *Journal of the History of Sexuality* 12, no. 2 (April 2003), 205–23.

42. The Henry Gerber Residence in the Old Town Triangle neighborhood of Chicago, Illinois, was designated an NHL on 19 June, 2015. Vern L. Bullough, *Before Stonewall: Activists for Gay and Lesbian Rights in Historical Context* (New York: Harrington Park Press, 2002), 27; John Loughery, *The Other Side of Science—Men's Lives and Gay Identities: A Twentieth-Century History* (New York: Henry Holt and Co., 1998), 54.

43. The Mattachine Society was founded in Los Angeles, California, in 1950; the Daughters of Bilitis formed in 1955 in San Francisco, California. Both of these homophile organizations lasted in various forms for many years.

44. Brett Beemyn, "Bisexuality, Bisexuals and Bisexual Movements," in *Encyclopedia of LGBT History in America,* vol. 1, ed. Marc Stein (New York: Charles Scribner's Sons, 2003), 141–45. The Student Homophile League met in a room at Earl Hall, 2980 Broadway, New York City, New York. Earl Hall was added to the National Register of Historic Places for its association with the Student Homophile League on 12 March 2018.

45. Meetings are held in the basement of Columbia University's Furnald Hall, Broadway and 116th Street, New York City, New York.

46. Offices of the *Weekly News* were located at 901 NE Seventy-Ninth Street, Miami, Florida. The Institute of Sexism and Sexuality is located at the Wolfson Campus of Miami Dade College, 300 NE Second Avenue, Miami, Florida. Pridelines Youth Services currently has offices at 9526 NE Second Avenue, Miami, Florida.

47. See, for example, Martin S. Weinberg, Colin J. Williams, and Douglas W. Pryor, *Dual Attraction: Understanding Bisexuality* (New York: Oxford University Press, 1995), 205.

48. Lourea also worked professionally with LGBTQ and HIV/AIDS communities, and published articles including "HIV Prevention: A Dramaturgical Analysis and Practical Guide to Creating Safer Sex Interventions" (with Clark L. Taylor), in *Bisexualities: Theory and Research,* ed. Dr. Fritz Klein and Timothy J. Wolf (New York: Haworth Press, 1985). Also see Clark L. Taylor and David Lourea, "HIV Prevention: A Dramaturgical Analysis and Practical Guide to Creating Safer Sex Interventions." *Medical Anthropology* 14, no. 2–4 (1992): 243–84. Lourea died in 1992; Slater in 1989.

49. In 1998, Heath Crisis Network merged with the Community Research Initiative to form Care Resource, South Florida's oldest and largest HIV/AIDS service organization. They currently have four locations in Miami, Fort Lauderdale, and Miami Beach, Florida, see "About," Care Resource website,

http://www.careresource.org/about. For more information on bisexual in-volvement in health, see Lani Ka'ahumanu, "Timeline"; see also Katie Batza, "LGBTQ Experiences and Health," in *Communities and Place: A Thematic Approach to the Histories of LGBTQ Communities in the United States,* ed. Katherine Crawford-Lackey and Megan E. Springate (New York: Berghahn Books, 2020) and Julio Capó Jr., "Locating Miami's Queer History," in Craw-ford-Lackey and Springate, *Communities and Place.* The Minneapolis AIDS Project is located at 1400 Park Avenue, Minneapolis, Minnesota; Lyon-Martin Women's Health Services is at 1748 Market Street, San Francisco, California.

50. The Center for Sex and Culture was located at 1349 Mission Street, San Francisco, California. They strove to promote creativity, information, and healthy sexual knowledge, see "Mission and Vision," Center for Sex and Cul-ture website, http://www.sexandculture.org/mission. Faced with unsustain-able rent increases, the Center for Sex and Culture closed on 25 January 2019. Their library and collections have been sent to several repositories and archives, including Harvard University, Cambridge, Massachusetts; Cornell University, Ithaca, New York; the GLBT Historical Society, San Fran-cisco, California; the San Francisco Library's Hormel LGBTQIA Center; the One Archives Foundation, Los Angeles, California; and the Carter/Johnson Library and Collection, Newburgh, Indiana. Joe Kukura, "Culture for Sex and Culture Moving Out of Its Space," *SF Weekly,* 25 January 2019. http://www.sfweekly.com/news/center-for-sex-and-culture-moving-out-of-its-space/.

51. Bryant was the author of the first book ever to critique films from a bi-sexual point of view, *Bisexual Characters in Film: From Anais to Zee,* Ha-worth Gay & Lesbian Studies (New York: Haworth Press, 1997). He served on the board of the Bisexual Resource Center, 29 Stanhope Street, Boston, Massachusetts, and was an organizer of the Fifth International Conference on Bisexuality, which drew nine hundred attendees to Harvard University, Cambridge, Massachusetts, on 3–5 April 1998.

52. Green Mountain National Forest is located near Rutland, Vermont. Part of the U.S. Forest Service, it was established on 25 April 1932.

53. The Bay Area Bisexual Network met at the San Francisco LGBT Community Center, 1800 Market Street, San Francisco, California.

54. Wanting more support as a bisexual man with a wife and family and not finding it in existing groups, in 1978 Jones founded the Gay Married Men Association (GAMMA) of Washington, D.C., which has been meeting con-tinuously ever since. They currently meet at Saint Thomas' Parish Episcopal Church, 1772 Church Street NW, Washington, D.C. There are now several GAMMA groups meeting across the country. See GAMMA-DC website, http://www.gammaindc.org.

55. The San Francisco Bisexual Center was located on Hayes Street just north of the Golden Gate Park panhandle, in the bottom flat of a two-flat building that is now a residence. The San Francisco Bisexual Center was founded by Maggi Rubenstein and Harriet Levi. Before it closed in 1984, it provided a

newsletter, support groups, counseling, social activities, and a presence in Pride marches, and was internationally renowned.

56. The Harambee House Hotel was located on the 2200 block of Georgia Avenue NW, Washington, D.C., near the Howard University campus. It opened in 1978. In 1981, Howard University purchased the Harambee House Hotel from the federal Economic Development Administration. Profitable in the 1980s, Howard University operated the hotel until 1995, when they closed it after continued financial losses. See Ronald Roach, "The Promise and the Peril: African American Colleges and Universities' Hotel and Conference Center Ownership," *Diverse: Issues in Higher Education,* 5 July 2007, http://diverseeducation.com/article/8075.

57. Bisexual leaders met twice with Obama Administration officials for roundtable consultations focused on the specific needs of bisexual people regarding health, education, employment, and immigration, among others. See Amy Andre, "Obama Administration Invites Bisexual Leaders to the White House," *Huffpost Queer Voices,* 27 August 2013, http://www.huffingtonpost.com/amy-andre/obama-bisexual-leaders_b_3819857.html; Faith Cheltenham, "BiNet USA in the White House Photo Blast #whatbilookslike," BiNet USA's blog, 4 September 2014, http://binetusa.blogspot.com/2014/09/binet-usa-in-white-house-photo-blast.html.

58. While efforts to find records of this meeting in Friends' archives have been unsuccessful, there are mentions of it in the 8 August 1972 *Advocate* article and in a number of anthologies chronicling bisexual history. Stephen Donaldson, "The Bisexual Movement's Beginnings in the '70s: A Personal Retrospective," in *Bisexual Politics: Theories, Queries, & Visions,* ed. Naomi Tucker (New York: Harrington Park Press, 1995), 31–45; Robert Martin, "Quakers 'Come Out' at Conference," *Advocate,* 2 August 1972, 8. The Friends General Conference took place in June 1972 at Ithaca College, 953 Danby Road, Ithaca, New York.

59. The American Institute of Bisexuality was located at 8265 West Sunset Boulevard, West Hollywood, California. Fritz Klein also developed a variation of the Kinsey Scale called the Klein Sexual Orientation Grid, which built upon Kinsey's zero to six scale. His book, *The Bisexual Option: A Concept of One-Hundred Percent Intimacy,* was one of the first studies that did not pathologize bisexuality, and that gave the identity legitimacy. See "About Fritz Klein," American Institute of Bisexuality website, http://www.americaninstituteofbisexuality.org/fritz-klein. Klein lived with his partner, Tom Reise, in the Emerald Hills neighborhood of San Diego, California, from 1995 until his death in 2006.

60. The Mission High School is located at 3750 Eighteenth Street, San Francisco, California.

61. BiNet USA facilitates communication and networking among bisexual communities, promotes bisexual visibility, and distributes educational in-

formation about bisexuality, see BiNet USA website, http://www.binetusa .org.

62. Embracing Diversities was sponsored by AMBi, Washington D.C.'s bisexual political action group at the time, and was held at St. Thomas' Parish Episcopal Church, 1772 Church Street NW, Washington, D.C. The BECAUSE conference is usually held on the University of Minnesota campus in Minneapolis.

63. Ka'ahumanu and Hutchins, *Bi Any Other Name.*

64. The Lavender Law Conference that year was held at the San Francisco Marriott Marquis Hotel, 55 Fourth Street, San Francisco, California.

65. Harvey Milk High School was founded in 1985 by the Hetrick-Martin Institute to provide a safe place for LGBTQ youth to get an education (threats and instances of violence, bullying, and harassment affect the ability of many LGBTQ youth from succeeding in school). It is located at 2–10 Astor Place, New York City, New York. The Hetrick-Martin Institute operated the school until 2002, when it became a fully accredited public school under the jurisdiction of the New York City Department of Education.

66. The National LGBTQ Task Force was founded in 1973 as the National Gay Task Force; they changed their name to the National Gay and Lesbian Task Force in 1985, and to the current name that includes bisexuals, transgender people, and queer/questioning people in October 2014. Lani Ka'ahumanu was the first openly bisexual person to serve on the board of the National Gay and Lesbian Task Force, completing her term in 2000. The National LGBTQ Task Force headquarters are located at 1325 Massachusetts Avenue NW, Washington, D.C.

67. The 1991 Creating Change Conference was held at the Best Western Old Colony Inn, 1101 North Washington Street, Alexandria, Virginia.

68. The 1996 Creating Change Conference was held at the Radisson Plaza Hotel at Mark Center, 5000 Seminary Road, near the Crystal City neighborhood of Alexandria, Virginia. In 1999, Hilton Hotels and Resorts bought the hotel; it is now the Hilton Alexandria Mark Center.

69. "Creating Change Wrap-up," National Gay and Lesbian Task Force Press Release, 19 November 1996, http://www.qrd.org/qrd/orgs/NGLTF/1996/ creating.change.wrap-up-11.19.96. Richard Socarides, ironically, is an out gay man who is the son of Charles Socarides, a psychiatrist who worked to "treat" homosexuality beginning in the 1960s and, in 1992, helped found an organization offering conversion therapy to change the sexual orientation of people with same-sex attraction. See "Deaths: Socarides, Charles William, MD," *New York Times,* 27 December 2005, http://query.nytimes .com/gst/fullpage.html?res=9B0DEED91230F934A15751C1A9639C8B63. Use of conversion therapy on minors is currently banned in several states. It is considered unethical by the American Psychiatric Association.

70. The National Mall was added to the NRHP on 15 October 1966. It is part of the National Mall and Memorial Parks NPS unit.

71. The Second National Conference Celebrating Bisexuality—organized by BiNet USA, the Bisexual Resource Center, and the Washington, D.C., organization Alliance of Multicultural Bisexuals (AMBi)—was held at American University's Ward Circle Building, 3590 Nebraska Avenue NW, Washington, D.C. The Bi Dance was held at George Washington University's Cloyd Heck Marvin Center, 800 Twenty-First Street NW, Washington, D.C.

72. The informal meeting took place in the Indian Treaty Room of the Eisenhower Executive Office Building (then the Old Executive Office Building) at Pennsylvania Avenue NW and Seventeenth Street NW, Washington, D.C. The building was added to the NRHP on 4 June 1969 and designated an NHL on 11 November 1971.

Bibliography

Academy of American Poets. "Edna St. Vincent Millay." Academy of American Poets website. https://www.poets.org/poetsorg/poet/edna-st-vincent-millay.

Akron Beacon Journal. "Foes of Anita Bryant Successful in Getting New Gay Law on Ballot." *Akron Beacon Journal,* 5 October 1978.

American Institute of Bisexuality. "About Fritz Klein." American Institute of Bisexuality, http://www.americaninstituteofbisexuality.org/fritz-klein.

Andre, Amy. "Obama Administration Invites Bisexual Leaders to the White House." *Huffpost Queer Voices,* 27 August 2013. http://www.huffingtonpost.com/amy-andre/obama-bisexual-leaders_b_3819857.html.

Angelides, Stephen. *A History of Bisexuality.* Chicago: University of Chicago Press, 2001.

Associated Press. "Gov. Kate Brown Veers from Typical Graduation Speech to Talk about Her Sexuality." *Oregonian,* 20 May 2016. http://www.oregonlive.com/politics/index.ssf/2016/05/gov_kate_brown_veers_from_typi.html.

Batza, Katie. "LGBTQ Experiences and Health." In *Communities and Place: A Thematic Approach to the Histories of LGBTQ Communities in the United States,* edited by Katherine Crawford-Lackey and Megan E. Springate. New York: Berghahn Books, 2020.

Beemyn, Brett. "The Silence is Broken: A History of the First Lesbian, Gay and Bisexual College Student Groups." *Journal of the History of Sexuality* 12, no. 2 (April 2003): 205–23.

———. "Bisexuality, Bisexuals and Bisexual Movements." In *Encyclopedia of LGBT History in America,* vol. 1, edited by Marc Stein, 141–45. New York: Charles Scribner's Sons, 2003.

Beemyn, Brett, and Michele Eliason, eds. *Queer Studies: A Lesbian, Gay, Bisexual and Transgender Anthology.* New York: New York University Press, 1996.

BiNet USA. "A Brief History of the Bisexual Movement." BiNet USA, n.d. http://www.binetusa.org/bi-history and http://www.binetusa.org/bihistory2.html.

Bisexual.org. "Legally Bi: A Brief History of Bi Erasure in LGBT Political Dis
course." Bisexual.org, 11 August 2018. https://bisexual.org/legally-bi-a-brief-
history-of-bi-erasure-in-lgbt-political-discourse/.

Bronski, Michael. *A Queer History of the United States.* Boston: Beacon Press, 2011.

Bryant, Wayne. *Bisexual Characters in Film: From Anais to Zee.* New York:
Haworth Press, 1997.

Bullough, Vern L. *Before Stonewall: Activists for Gay and Lesbian Rights in
Historical Context.* New York: Harrington Park Press, 2002.

Capó, Julio, Jr. "Locating Miami's Queer History." In *Communities and Place: A
Thematic Approach to the Histories of LGBTQ Communities in the United
States,* edited by Katherine Crawford-Lackey and Megan E. Springate. New
York: Berghahn Books, 2020.

Care Resource. "About." Care Resource, n.d. http://www.careresource.org/about/.

Center for Sex and Culture. "Mission and Vision." Center for Sex and Culture, n.d.
http://www.sexandculture.org/mission.

Cheltenham, Faith. "BiNet USA in the White House Photo Blast #whatbilookslike."
BiNet USA's blog, 4 September 2014. http://binetusa.blogspot.com/2014/09/
binet-usa-in-white-house-photo-blast.html.

Cho, Margaret. "Queer." *Huffpost Queer Voices,* 3 October 2011. http://www
.huffingtonpost.com/margaret-cho/queer_b_984123.html.

Cruz, Eliel. "Remembering Brenda: An Ode to the 'Mother of Pride.'" *Advocate,*
17 June 2014. http://www.advocate.com/bisexuality/2014/06/17/remember
ing-brenda-ode-%E2%80%98mother-pride%E2%80%99.

Donaldson, Stephen. "The Bisexual Movement's Beginnings in the '70s: A
Personal Retrospective." In *Bisexual Politics: Theories, Queries, & Visions,*
edited by Naomi Tucker, 31–45. New York: Harrington Park Press, 1995.

Dorenkamp, Monica, and Richard Henke, eds. *Negotiating Lesbian and Gay
Subjects.* London: Routledge, 1994.

Hemmings, Clare. *Bisexual Spaces: A Geography of Sexuality and Gender.* New
York: Routledge, 2002.

Hutchins, Loraine. "Let's Not Bijack Another Century." In *The Routledge History
of Queer America,* edited by Don Romesburg. London: Routledge, 2018.

Ka'ahumanu, Lani. "Timeline: The Bisexual Health Movement in the U.S." BiNet
USA, n.d. http://binetusa.org/bihealth.html.

Ka'ahumanu, Lani, and Loraine Hutchins. "Introduction: Still about Naming after
All These Years." In *Bi Any Other Name: Bisexual People Speak Out,* 25th
anniversary edition, edited by Lani Ka'ahumanu and Loraine Hutchins,
1–22. New York: Riverdale Avenue Books, (1991) 2015.

———, eds. *Bi Any Other Name: Bisexual People Speak Out.* 25th anniversary
edition. New York: Riverdale Avenue Books, (1991) 2015.

Katz, Jonathan Ned. *Gay American History: Lesbians and Gay Men in the U.S.A.*
New York: Avon Books, 1978.

Kinsey, Alfred C., Wardell B. Pomeroy, and Clyde E. Martin. *Sexual Behavior in the
Human Male.* Philadelphia: W. B. Saunders, 1948.

Klein, Fritz. *The Bisexual Option: A Concept of One-Hundred Percent Intimacy.* New York: Arbor House, 1978.

Klein, Fritz, and Timothy J. Wolf, eds. *Bisexualities: Theory and Research.* New York: Haworth Press, 1985.

Kristal, Nicole, and Mike Szymanski. *The Bisexuals Guide to the Universe: Quips, Tips, and Lists for Those Who Go Both Ways.* New York: Alyson Publications, 2006.

Kukura, Joe. "Center for Sex and Culture Moving Out of Its Space." *SF Weekly,* January 25, 2019. http://www.sfweekly.com/news/center-for-sex-and-culture-moving-out-of-its-space/.

LGBT HealthLink. "The Bisexual History of HIV/AIDS, In Photos." LGBT HealthLink website, 29 January 2015. https://blog.lgbthealthlink.org/2015/01/29/the-bisexual-history-of-hivaids-in-photos.

LGBT History Month. "Brenda Howard." LGBT History Month website, n.d. http://lgbthistorymonth.com/brenda-howard?tab=biography.

Loughery, John. *The Other Side of Science—Men's Lives and Gay Identities: A Twentieth-Century History.* New York: Henry Holt and Co., 1998.

Loving, Jerome. *Walt Whitman: The Song of Himself.* Berkeley: University of California Press, 1999.

Martin, Robert. "Quakers 'Come Out' at Conference." *Advocate,* 2 August 1972.

Millet, Kate. *Flying.* Champaign: University of Illinois Press, 2000.

Mirza, Shabab Ahmed. "Disaggregating the Data for Bisexual People," Center for American Progress, 24 September 2018. https://www.americanprogress.org/issues/lgbt/reports/2018/09/24/458472/disaggregating-data-bisexual-people/.

National Gay and Lesbian Task Force. "Creating Change Wrap-up." National Gay and Lesbian Task Force Press Release, 19 November 1996. http://www.qrd.org/qrd/orgs/NGLTF/1996/creating.change.wrap-up-11.19.96.

New York Times. "Deaths: Socarides, Charles William, MD." *New York Times,* 27 December 2005. http://query.nytimes.com/gst/fullpage.html?res=9B0DEED91230F934A15751C1A9639C8B63.

Panama City News-Herald. "Nation's Press." *Panama City News-Herald,* 16 December 1977.

Penelope, Julia. "Lesbianville, U.S.A.?" *Off Our Backs* 23, no. 9 (October 1993): 8, 16–17.

Rivera, Sylvia. "Queens in Exile: The Forgotten Ones." In *Street Transvestite Action Revolutionaries: Survival, Revolt, and Queer Antagonist Struggle.* N.p.: Untorelli Press, 2013.

Roach, Ronald. "The Promise and the Peril: African American Colleges and Universities' Hotel and Conference Center Ownership." *Diverse: Issues in Higher Education,* 5 July 2007. http://diverseeducation.com/article/8075.

Rockwell, John. "Maestro: The Leonard Bernstein Letters." *New York Times Sunday Book Review,* 13 December 2013.

Rodriguez, Matthew. "Queer Teens Are Now the Majority: Goodbye Straight People." *Mic,* 12 March 2016. http://mic.com/articles/137713/queer-teens-are-now-the-majority-goodbye-straight-people.

Salazar, Jade. "LGBTQ History #18: Sylvia Rivera: Transgender Activist and Stonewall Legend." *Tagg Magazine,* 29 October 2014. http://taggmagazine.com/community/sylvia-rivera-transgender-activist-stonewall-legend.

Sandel, Adam. "Alan Cummings is Bisexual—And You Might Be Too." *Advocate,* 30 March 2015.

Soble, Alan, ed. *Sex from Plato to Paglia: A Philosophical Encyclopedia.* New York: Greenwood Publishing Group, 2006.

Stuever, Hank. "Gloria Vanderbilt and Anderson Cooper: Sorting through Family Hurt and History." *Washington Post,* 8 April 2016.

Suresha, Ron J., ed. *Bisexual Perspectives on the Life and Work of Alfred C. Kinsey.* London: Routledge, 2010.

Taylor, Clark L., and David Lourea. "HIV Prevention: A Dramaturgical Analysis and Practical Guide to Creating Safe Sex Interventions." *Medical Anthropology* 14, no. 2–4 (1992): 243–84.

Weinberg, Martin S., Colin J. Williams, and Douglas W. Pryor. *Dual Attraction: Understanding Bisexuality.* New York: Oxford University Press, 1995.

CHAPTER 3

Sexual and Gender Diversity in Native America and the Pacific Islands

Will Roscoe

Introduction: Two Spirits in Native Tradition— Roles, Genders, and Identities

In the summer of 1564, René Goulaine de Laudonnière arrived in Florida to assert French claims to the region, homeland of the village-dwelling Timucua people.[1] Landing on the banks of the St. John River, he led a party into the dense Florida woodlands to find a suitable site to establish a fort. After a long day of forced marching, the party was exhausted and far from its destination. What happened next is recorded in Laudonnière's report:

> We met an Indian woman of tall stature, which also was an Hermaphrodite, who came before us with a great vessell full of cleere fountaine water, wherwith she greatly refreshed us. For we were exceeding faint by reason of the ardent heate which molested us as we passed through those high woods. And I beleeve that without the succour of that Indian Hermaphrodite . . . we had taken up our lodging all night in the wood.[2]

Later he encountered another "hermaphrodite" serving as an emissary of a Timucuan king.

The artist Jacques Le Moyne, who accompanied the expedition, painted two pictures of these "hermaphrodites," published as engravings in 1591. One depicts four long-haired men carrying corpses on stretchers, while two others carry sick or injured persons on their backs.

According to Le Moyne, because they were strong, hermaphrodites accompanied warriors to battle, carrying provisions and tending to the injured.[3]

The multiplicity of gender and sexuality among native peoples was noted as early as 1540 along the Colorado River by Alarcón, in the 1770s in Hawaii by Cook's third expedition, and in the same decade by Russian explorers in Alaska.[4] Sadly, the gestures of friendship made by the Timucuan hermaphrodite and others in these early encounters were typically met with condemnation and violence—epitomized by the grizzly episode in 1513 when Vasco Núñez de Balboa had forty two spirits in Panama thrown to his dogs.[5]

The term hermaphrodite was often used by Europeans to describe native people they encountered who appeared to be crossing or mixing genders. In fact, the striking individual that gave Laudonnière "succour" represents a tradition with no counterpart in European societies—social roles and belief systems in which gender is not limited to "man" and "woman," and sexuality is not constrained to relationships between "opposite" genders defined by anatomical sex. Europeans had no single term for these multidimensional identities—and, indeed, the sheer diversity of Native American and Pacific Island cultures makes the use of any umbrella term problematic.

One finds an array of terminology in Euro-American accounts. To describe what appeared to be a mixing of genders, some of the earliest explorers evoked the figure of Hermaphroditos from Greco-Roman mythology. In Renaissance Europe, "hermaphrodite" could indicate intersexuality, androgyny, or homosexuality. Others singled out what they saw as the sexuality of the males they observed and deemed them "sodomites"—men who committed an abominable act. Throughout the contact period, the terminology used by Euro-Americans alternated between this dichotomy of gender and sexuality. As a Spanish explorer of California in 1775 wrote, "I inferred they must be hermaphrodites, but from what I learned later I understood that they were sodomites."[6]

The word "berdache" was introduced in North America by French-speaking fur traders and missionaries in the 1690s to describe two spirits they observed among the Illinois.[7] At the time, variations of the word were current in several western European languages. "Berdache" had a range of meanings but typically referred to a younger, non-masculine males who engaged in homosexual relations. In Canada and the Mississippi Valley it became an intercultural or "frontier" term used by both French speakers and Native Americans in reference to a status common among many tribes.[8] From the Mississippi Valley, traders and voyageurs carried the term into the Plains, Rocky Mountain, and Pacific Northwest regions.[9] In some instances, it was used as a personal name.[10] When anthropologists heard it spoken by both whites and natives, they recorded it using various spellings—"bardache," "berdashe," "bird-ash," "bredache," and so forth—and identified it merely as French-Canadian in origin, unaware of its longer history in European, Arabic, and Persian languages.[11]

In the twentieth century, "berdache" became the standard anthropological term for alternative gender roles among Native Americans. By the 1980s, however, its inappropriateness, as articulated by scholars and community members, led to a search for new terminology. "Two spirit" was coined at a gathering of Native American and First Nations people in 1990 and embraced for its connotations of balancing or combining male and female qualities.[12] In 1993, a conference sponsored by the Wenner-Gren Foundation brought together anthropologists, native scholars, and community members who adopted a formal statement endorsing its use.[13] Today, "two spirit" (also "two-spirit" and sometimes "two-spirited") is widely used in reference to both male-bodied and female-bodied native people who mix, cross, or combine the standard roles of men and women.[14]

Two-spirit males have been documented in at least 155 tribes; in about a third of these a recognized status for females who adopted a masculine lifestyle existed as well.[15] Each tribal language has its own terms for such individuals, and each term represents distinct beliefs, traditions, and social customs. In Crow, a male two spirit is called *boté*; in Lakota, *winkte*; in Zuni, *lhamana*; in Navajo, *nádleehí*.[16] Terms for a female two spirit include *hwame:* in Mohave, *hetaneman* in Cheyenne (figure 3.1), and *tayagigux'* in Aleut. Sometimes the same word was used for both male and female two spirits: *tw!inna'ek* in Klamath, *t'übás* in Northern Paiute, and *tangowaip* in western Shoshone. Some of these terms can be translated as "man-woman" but many cannot. *Nádleehí*, for example, literally means "one who is changing."[17]

These terms, which distinguish two spirits from men and women, have led anthropologists, historians, and archeologists to describe two-spirit roles as alternative or multiple genders.[18] Although Western cultures assume only two genders are "natural" based on anatomical sex, many native societies are capable of accommodating three, four, and possibly more genders, or having a gender system characterized by fluidity, transformation, and individual variation.

Typically, male and female two spirits were identified in childhood based on a preference for activities of the "opposite" sex. In some tribes,

Figure 3.1. Cheyenne *hetaneman*, or female two spirit, in battle wearing a man's breechcloth. Ledger-book drawing attributed to Yellow Nose, ca. 1889. Image courtesy of the National Anthropological Archives, Smithsonian Institution (MS 166,032, 08709000).

entry into two-spirit status was marked ceremonially. Shoshone, Ute, Kitanemuk, and Pima-Papago families staged a ritual test in which a boy was placed in a circle of brush with a bow and a basket (men's and women's objects, respectively). The brush was set on fire, and whichever object the boy picked up as he ran out determined his identity: if he took the basket he would be two spirit.

The occupations Le Moyne attributed to Timucuan "hermaphrodites"—conducting burial rites, caring for the ill, assisting on war parties, serving as intermediaries—were common to male two spirits in many parts of North America. Perhaps the trait most often attributed to them was skill in crafts typically made by women. As Ruth Benedict noted, "The Dakota had a saying, 'fine possessions like a berdache's,' and it was the epitome of praise for any woman's household possessions."[19]

Among Plains tribes, male two spirits excelled in working with hides, which were used to make everything from clothing to shelter; in California they were basket-makers; in the Southwest, weavers and potters.

In many instances, male and female two spirits were medicine people, healers, shamans, and ceremonial leaders. Although these roles were not specific to two spirits, certain ceremonial functions were. Cheyenne *he'emaneo* and Mohave *alyha:* directed their tribes' victory dances, while Crow and Hidatsa two spirits selected the tree used for construction of Sun Dance lodges. In the late nineteenth century, a Mohave female two spirit, or *hwame:*, was widely recognized as a powerful shaman able to cure venereal disease. Among Plains tribes, dreams and visions of female deities or the moon served to confirm male two-spirit identity and convey distinct abilities. Some *winkte* were seers who could locate enemies at great distances, predict the weather, and foretell future events. Among the Pueblo Indians, two-spirit status was sanctioned by myths and portrayed in masked dances representing mythological figures.

Instances of a named status for females who routinely engaged in men's activities such as hunting and warfare come predominantly from tribes west of the Rocky Mountains; but absence of evidence is not necessarily evidence of absence. The lives of native women have been overlooked in general and obscured by Euro-American sexual and racial stereotypes. Taking a broader view reveals that women throughout North America and the Pacific Islands often engaged in male pursuits, from hunting and warfare to tribal leadership, without necessarily acquiring a different gender identity. Some of these women deserve recognition as leaders in the Native American resistance to European settlement. Weetamoo, a chief of the Pocasset, led a force of more than three hundred warriors against the English during King Philip's war, and the Apache warrior woman Lozen fought alongside Geronimo until his final surrender in 1886.[20]

Two spirits typically formed relationships with non-two-spirit individuals of the same sex, which were viewed within their own cultures as equivalent to those between men and women, that is, between different genders, while Euro-Americans viewed them as homosexual. In the 1930s, a Navajo elder told Willard Hill, "If they marry men, it is just like two men working together."[21] In the early nineteenth century, the Crow leader Woman Chief married four women following her successes in battle. Some two spirits had relations with both men and women, and sometimes heterosexually married men and women became two spirits on the basis of dreams or visions. (The one sexual pattern not attested is that of two spirits in sexual relationships with each other.)

Sexual and Gender Diversity in Native Hawaii

In native Hawaii, males who preferred the work of women and formed relationships with other men were called *māhū*, a status present in several Polynesian societies.[22] Christian missionaries and travelers, in their zeal to suppress what they considered immoral practices, recorded little about *māhū*, but a vibrant oral tradition credits them with a variety of significant roles, from healing to caretaking, naming infants, and above all teaching and leading the hula dance.[23]

Distinct from *māhū* were men who formed *aikāne* relationships. This term is often translated as "friend" or "lover," but in the Hawaiian language it has a distinctly sexual connotation. A member of the Cook expedition of 1776–1780 wrote, "It is a disagreeable circumstance to the historian that truth obliges him to inform the world of a custom among them contrary to nature, and odious to a delicate mind. . . .The custom alluded to is that of sodomy, which is very prevalent if not universal among the chiefs."[24] *Aikāne* relationships were often between older and younger or higher- and lower-status men, but they could occur between men of similar age and status, and in traditional stories the goddess Hi'iaka has an *aikāne*.[25] Most men with *aikāne* were bisexual and married women as well. One of the legendary hero-kings of Hawaiian mythology, Kepakailiula, has an *aikāne*, and with him performs some of his most spectacular feats.[26]

The Cook expedition had several encounters with *aikāne* of Hawaiian chiefs. In January 1779, after making landfall at Kealakekua Bay on the island of Hawaii, Palea, an *aikāne* of the chief Kalani'opu'u, appeared as an emissary.[27] His negotiations with one of Cook's officers resulted in the chief's ceremonial visit soon after. But a month later, when Cook returned, Palea had been replaced by a rival. The embittered former *aikāne* was implicated in the theft of one of Cook's boats, resulting in the hostilities that led to the explorer's death.[28]

Two Spirits Today: Renewal and Change

"Before Alcatraz," recalled Mohawk poet Maurice Kenny, referring to the occupation of the island by Indian activists in 1969, "it was just about impossible to stand up and say who you were. If you had a job you'd get fired. Your family might disown you. You certainly would be ridiculed."[29] Kenny's 1976 essay, "Tinselled Bucks: An Historical Study of Indian Homosexuality," and Paula Gunn Allen's 1981 article, "Beloved Women: Lesbians in American Indian Cultures," marked the beginning of renewed awareness of two-spirit traditions.[30]

In 1975, Barbara Cameron (Lakota) and Randy Burns (Northern Paiute) founded Gay American Indians in San Francisco.[31] In addition to providing advocacy and social services, the group published *Living the Spirit: A Gay American Indian Anthology* in 1988. Several contributors have since played prominent roles in fostering cultural renewal and political activism among two-spirit/LGBTQ native people, including Richard LaFortune (Anguksuar), who launched the Two Spirit Press Room in 2005, and the writers Beth Brant, Chrystos, Anne Waters, and Janice Gould.[32] In 1988, a conference organized by American Indian Gay and Lesbians in Minneapolis inaugurated a tradition of annual gatherings.[33] By the 1990s, LGBTQ native organizations had appeared throughout the country, often in response to the need for services created by the HIV/AIDS epidemic.

Many who identify as two spirits today are active in intertribal powwow networks. In 2015, the Bay Area American Indian Two-Spirit Powwow drew more than two thousand attendees.[34] Comments from participants reveal the broad range of identities and beliefs encompassed by the term "two spirit" today. One dancer explained that "two spirit means being born with a male and a female spirit," while for another the term is "more of a historical reminder that before colonization all of our tribes had multiple genders."[35]

In Hawaii, a wide range of individuals, male and female, are reclaiming the *māhū* role. Some, like Hina Wong-Kalu, are *kumu*, or teachers (figure 3.2).[36] As one contemporary *māhū* explains,

> The American Indians have a really nice way of putting it. They say "two-spirited." So I like to borrow that and apply it to *māhū*, and have it mean "two-spirited" . . . . Because *māhū* could mean a guy who likes a guy, but is somewhat soft, and likes to have relations with the same sex. Or it could be like us [transgender]. And many, many others. So, if you're anywhere within that two-spirited realm, the word *māhū* could apply to you. People like this have an aura . . . they give off both man and woman.[37]

The recovery of two-spirit history by historians and anthropologists, both Indian and white, in the 1980s and the vibrant emergence of two-spirit identity in Native communities and cultural life in the 1990s and 2000s were an impetus for a remarkable efflorescence of gender expression and identities in American society today. It would seem that

Figure 3.2. Hina Wong-Kalu, Hawaiian *kumu* and *māhū*. Kumu Hina photograph by Kai Markell. Copyright Qwaves, LLC (http://kumuhina.com).

when individuals are free to express their authentic experience of gender, amazing diversity appears. Today, this includes not only transgender identities, but identities defined as being nonbinary or genderqueer or bigender or genderfluid, and individuals who prefer to be referred to not as "he" or "she," but as "they" or "hir" and other alternative pronouns. A third or nonbinary gender status is now legally recognized in several countries, including Australia, and tentatively in the United States in recent legal rulings.[38]

The Landscape of Two-Spirit History

In Waikīkī, Hawaii, tucked between the tourist hotels lining Kalakaua Avenue, four worn boulders embedded upon a stone platform attest to the endurance of *māhū* traditions in Hawaiian history.[39] According to markers in English and Hawaiian, the stones were erected as monuments in the early sixteenth century at the direction of four powerful healers from Tahiti.[40] In Hawaiian historical accounts, these healers performed miraculous cures throughout the Hawaiian Islands. To commemorate their deeds, they had these stones placed at Waikiki, transferring their *mana,* or spiritual power, to them before they returned to their home-land. The stones were named for these four priests, the most important of whom was Kapaemahu.

The element "mahu" in this name is the only trace in this account of the true significance of the stones. Supplementing written sources with oral tradition, Andrew Matzner gives a fuller telling of their history. The four priests were all *māhū*—"hermaphrodites" in the earliest sources. They had both male and female appearance and manners, and this quality was the source of their powers. Today, hundreds of tourists pass by the site every day, but, as Matzner notes, "the transgendered aspect at its core remains deeply buried, like a piece of history deemed unfit for consumption."[41]

For centuries the stones remained in place and were credited with healing the sick and protecting seagoers. When Archibald Cleghorn acquired the site in 1872, the stones had naturally settled into the sand. Cleghorn had them unearthed and placed in a prominent setting on his estate; his wife, Princess Likelike, and her daughter prayed to them whenever they went swimming. Following Cleghorn's death, the stones underwent a variety of ignominies: the Moana Hotel was built behind them; in the 1920s, they were buried beneath a bowling alley.[42]

By the standards of many preservationists, historical significance is a function of what humans attribute to places and structures. The disappearance of the stones in the sands of Waikiki Beach represents an interruption in their use that compromises their historical integrity. But for native people, as Luan Fauteck Makes Marks notes, "the Land inheres as sacred—beyond human perception and conception, beyond our capacities for belief and imagination—in and of itself."[43] This is especially true for sacred places. As Christopher H. Peters of the Seventh Generation Fund says, "If there were no humans on earth, they would still be sacred."[44]

Recovered in the 1960s, the Stones of Kapaemāhū, as they are known today, were relocated to their present site in 1980; in 1997, they were re-dedicated in a ceremony led by the Hawaiian leader Papa Henry Auwe. And as the leis strewn upon the wrought iron fence that surrounds them today attest, for Hawaiian people the influence of the stones in their lives, that is, their spiritual power, has never been interrupted.

The historical landscape of the United States has many places that tell the history of two-spirit people. Several are already listed in the National Register of History Places and as National Historical Landmarks, and others, like the Stones of Kapaemāhū, deserve such recognition. Equally important, the stories of two spirits need to be added to the public interpretation of these places and to the broader narratives of American history.[45]

Two Spirits in the History of the United States

In the long history of contact between native and Euro-American peoples, two spirits have had important roles, and their stories are linked to many places and sites. Qánqon-kámek-klaúlha (Kutenai), Ohchiish (Crow), We'wha (Zuni), and Hastíín Klah (Navajo) were each remarkable individuals who lived complex lives against the backdrop of unfolding conflict and rapid change.

Qánqon-kámek-klaúlha (ca. 1790s–1837)

One of the most fascinating, if ultimately mysterious, female two spirits, was the Kutenai known as Qánqon-kámek-klaúlha, Sitting-in-the-Water-Grizzly, or simply Qánqon. Born around 1790 along the lower Kootenai River near the border of Idaho and British Columbia, her tribe occupied a strategic region of the Northwest, the site of fierce competition between Canadian, British, and American fur traders.

According to Kutenai elders interviewed in the 1930s, Qánqon's original name was Qúqunok patke (One-Standing-Lodge-Pole-Woman).[46] Undistinguished as a child, she grew up to be large and strong. The earliest written reference to her is in the journals of David Thompson of the North West Company, who crossed the Rocky Mountains and established a trading post near the headwaters of the Columbia River. During the winter of 1808–1809, one of his men returned from a trading expedition accompanied by a Kutenai wife. According to Thompson, her "conduct was then so loose that I had to request him to send her away to her friends."[47]

When the Kutenai woman rejoined her people sometime later she told a fantastic tale. Her white husband had "operated" on her and transformed her into a man; she now called herself Kaúxuma núpika, Gone-to-the-Spirits (which suggests she had undergone a shamanic spiritual experience involving a journey to the spirit world). "We Indians," she said, "did not believe that white people possessed such power from the supernaturals. I can tell you that they do, greater power than we have." As a result of her transformation, Gone-to-the-Spirits had acquired supernatural power.[48]

She began dressing in men's clothes and courting women (and according to Kutenai reports, she fashioned a leather dildo for sexual encounters), and she joined hunting and war parties. The Kutenai called such women *títqattek,* which has been translated as "pretending to be a man."[49] After her first war party, she adopted the name Qánqon Kámek Klaúlha, Sitting-in-the-Water-Grizzly.

Given these accounts and others, Qánqon is best understand in contemporary terms as a transgender male—that is, an individual born female but whose gender identity was that of a man. Honoring her identity, I will refer to Qánqon hereafter with male pronouns.

In April 1811, the Americans established the trading post of Astoria at the mouth of the Columbia River.[50] Simultaneously, David Thompson was making his way down the river from the Rocky Mountains. Unbeknownst to him, two Kutenai Indians were traveling ahead of his party and reached Astoria some weeks before him. The Americans believed them to be a man and a woman; in fact, they were the two-spirit Qánqon and his wife. They had with them a letter addressed to a trading post in British Columbia, and they claimed, somewhat dubiously, to have become lost while attempting to deliver it.[51]

When David Thompson arrived at Fort Astoria in July, he recognized Qánqon as the Indian woman once married to his servant. The Americans were unfazed. Qánqon's glowing description of the interior and the maps he drew for them convinced them to organize an exploring party to compete with Thompson. In late June 1811, two parties left Astoria—the Americans, guided by Qánqon and his wife, and Thompson.[52]

One of the Astorians described the Kutenai couple as "bold adventurous amazons . . . . They sometimes shot ahead, and at other times loitered behind, as suited their plans. The stories they gave out among the unsuspecting and credulous natives as they passed were well calculated to astonish as well as to attract attention."[53] In fact, Qánqon was delivering prophesies of an impending world transformation. Two giants, he claimed, were coming who would overturn the ground and bury villages. These prophecies were consistent with stories that had been spreading among natives throughout the Northwest for a generation, told by individuals who had "died," traveled to the land of the dead, and returned to life. But Qánqon also claimed that "the great white chief" had sent him to announce that white men were bringing the Indians wonderful presents. And so, as Qánqon and his wife returned upstream from Astoria traveling with the Americans, they were eagerly greeted at villages all along the Columbia River and given generous gifts.

Eventually, they led the Americans to the confluence of the Columbia and Okanogan rivers, where the Astorians established Fort Okanogan.[54]

Stories of Qánqon spread throughout the Northwest. The explorer John Franklin learned of his prophecies and adventures in 1827 while traveling in northern Canada. "Many young men," he learned, "put themselves under her [sic] command.... and at length she became the principle leader of the tribe, under the designation of 'Manlike Woman.'"[55] In the early twentieth century, Kutenai elders remembered Qánqon as a shaman, who on one occasion cured a chief.[56] In the 1930s, the anthropologist Leslie Spier linked Qánqon's prophecies to the origins of the Prophet Dance, a religious movement that eventually spread across the entire Pacific Northwest and, in turn, gave rise to the Ghost Dance among the Northern Paiute in the early 1890s.[57]

In 1825, Qánqon appeared at Flathead Post in western Montana accompanying a Kutenai chief, a status he seems to have shared.[58] The trader John Work described him as a "leading character among them" and called him "Bundosh"—a variation of the word "berdache." Fluent in the Flathead language, Qánqon served as an interpreter.

In 1837, he appeared at another key moment in Northwest history, when William Gray, who had helped establish the Whitman Mission at Walla Walla, Washington, was traveling with a Hudson's Bay Company trading party and a group of Flathead Indians through western Montana.[59] In the Big Hole Valley, the party encountered hostile Blackfoot Indians, and the Flathead killed several of them. As the Flathead were celebrating their victory, three unknown Indians appeared—two Blackfoot and a "woman," whom Gray later identifies as "Bowdash." (Perhaps Qánqon was on this occasion dressed as a woman to pass more easily between hostile camps.) They were seeking a truce, with Qánqon serving as an interpreter.

Gray was able to safely resume his journey. A few days later he noted in his journal, "We have been told that the Black Feet have killed the Kootenie woman, or Bowdash, as she is called. She has hitherto been permitted to go from all the camps, without molestation, to carry any message given her to either camp."[60]

In 1916, a Flathead elder recalled his childhood memories of the Kutenai two spirit. Using the pronoun "she," he noted that "Bundosh" was a strong woman and a great prophet. During the time she was a warrior, she had called herself Ignace Onton, but later in life she became a peace messenger. She was killed by the Blackfeet in 1837 because they discovered that she had helped the Flatheads escape them.[61]

Qánqon was not the only Native female who crossed genders and cultures in the early nineteenth century. Running Eagle, a Blackfoot, joined nine raids and counted coup three times; Kuilix, a Pend d'Oreille woman who wore a bright-red, British-made coat, emblematic of chiefly status, was observed leading men into battle by the Jesuit missionaries Pierre-Jean De Smet and Nicholas Point; and Woman Chief, of the Crow, led war parties, killed a grizzly bear single-handedly, and had four wives.[62]

We'wha (ca. 1849–1896)

Gender diversity among the Zuni Indians of western New Mexico can be traced from prehistoric times. At the site of Hawikku, near present-day Zuni, archeologists found males buried with objects typically associated with women—a ball of clay and baskets—and in one case a woman buried wearing both a dress and a man's dance kilt.[63]

In 1879, the first expedition of the government's newly founded Bureau of Ethnology arrived at the remote village of Zuni. Led by James Stevenson, accompanied by his wife Matilda Coxe Stevenson, the expedition was charged with collecting artifacts and recording the customs of a people considered to be both ancient and on the verge of extinction. They encountered a striking individual working for the local missionaries. We'wha, Matilda Stevenson noted, "was the most intelligent person in the pueblo," with an extensive knowledge of Zuni history and culture, and therefore an excellent informant for anthropological research. But there was something unusual about We'wha. "She" was one of the tallest members of the tribe, male or female, and in Stevenson's opinion, "certainly the strongest, both mentally and physically."[64] Nonetheless, many years passed before Stevenson discovered the truth: We'wha was male. His identity in Zuni culture was that of a *lhamana* or third-gender male.

The *lhamana* role entailed complex interweavings of men's and women's traits and activities. Born around 1849, We'wha demonstrated a talent for women's work at an early age and learned pottery making from female relatives. But We'wha also excelled in weaving, which was usually done by men, and in a census made in 1881 is listed as a farmer, another male role. We'wha was also a member of the men's kachina society, responsible for performing masked dances.

Matilda Stevenson formed an enduring friendship with the Zuni *lhamana*. In 1886, she brought We'wha to live with her and James for six months in Washington, D.C. We'wha called on President Cleveland and other political leaders and circulated in Washington society (figure 3.3).[65]

Figure 3.3. We'wha in ceremonial dress. Photograph by John K. Hillers, Washington, D.C., 1886. Courtesy of the U.S. National Archives and Records Administration (NAI 523798).

All believed that We'wha was a woman. We'wha assisted Stevenson with her ethnographic research and posed for a series of photographs documenting Zuni weaving at the Smithsonian Institution and on the National Mall—one of the first uses of photography for this purpose.[66] In fact, We'wha may be one of the first Native American artists to have signed their work—two pots in the collections of the American Museum of Natural History bear a crude signature with a version of that name.[67]

In 1892, six years after traveling to D.C., We'wha was arrested for striking an American soldier who was attempting to arrest the Zuni governor. A contingent of heavily armed troops from Fort Wingate was dispatched to the pueblo, and a raucous confrontation ensued. In the aftermath, key Zuni leaders, including We'wha, were imprisoned at Fort Wingate for a month.[68]

Stevenson was present at We'wha's death in 1896:

> We'wha asked the writer to come close and in a feeble voice she said, in English: "Mother, I am going to the other world . . . . Tell all my friends in Washington good-by. Tell President Cleveland, my friend, good-by. Mother, love all my people; protect them; they are your children; you are their mother."[69]

We'wha's death, Stevenson reported, elicited "universal regret and distress."[70] When tribal authorities tried a Zuni woman for having caused We'wha's death by witchcraft, soldiers were again dispatched from Fort Wingate and occupied the village for five months. Zunis remember these traumatic events vividly to the present day.[71]

We'wha is perhaps the best-known Native American two spirit, as attested by the bronze plaque installed in 2017 as part of San Francisco's Rainbow Honor Walk. It reads, "We'wha (1849–1896)—Respected Zuni *lhamana*, or two spirit, accomplished potter, weaver, and cultural ambassador of the Zuni nation."

Ohchiish (1854–1929)

On 17 June 1876, General George Crook was leading one of three army columns in southern Montana bearing down upon the hostile Lakota Sioux and Cheyenne Indians amassed under Sitting Bull, when he decided to bivouac along the Rosebud River.[72] As he sat down to play a game of cards with his officers, the Sioux and their allies, the Cheyenne, attacked. Crook barely avoided Custer's fate, whose forces were wiped out ten days later at the Battle of the Little Big Horn. In the initial fray, Crook's command was nearly overwhelmed, and only the intervention of Crow warriors, who had joined his forces to fight their traditional enemies, saved his position. Among these was the *boté* Ohchiish, a shorted form of Ohchikapdaapesh, or Finds-Them-and-Kills-Them.[73]

Born in 1854, Ohchiish had shown interest in women's work from an early age and as an adult dressed as a woman. He enjoyed a reputation for skilled leatherwork and beading, and was credited with making the largest tipi known in the tribe, the lodge of Chief Iron Bull. Years later, a Crow woman named Pretty Shield recalled what happened that day on the Rosebud:

> Yes, a Crow woman fought with Three-stars [Crook] on the Rosebud, two of them did, for that matter; but one of them was neither a man nor a woman. She looked like a man, and yet she wore woman's clothing; and she had the heart of a woman. Besides, she did a woman's work. Her name was Finds-them-and-kills-them . . . .
>
> The other woman . . . was a wild one who had no man of her own. She was both bad and brave, this one. Her name was The-other-magpie; and she was pretty . . . .
>
> During the fight on the Rosebud both these women did brave deeds. When Bull-snake fell from his horse, badly wounded, Finds-them-and-kills-them dashed up to him, got down from her horse, and stood over him, shooting at the Lacota as rapidly as she could load her gun and fire. The-other-magpie rode round and round them, singing her war-song and waving her coup-stick, the only weapon she had.
>
> When the Lacota, seeing Bull-snake on the ground, charged to take his scalp, The-other-magpie rode straight at them, waving her coup-stick. Her medicine was so strong that the Lacota turned and rode away; and Bull-snake was saved.
>
> Both these women expected death that day. Finds-them-and-kills-them, afraid to have the Lacota find her dead with woman-clothing on her, changed them to a man's before the fighting commenced, so that if killed the Lacota would not laugh at her, lying there with a woman's clothes on her. She did not want the Lacota to believe that she was a Crow man hiding in a woman's dress, you see.[74]

Fighting together, Ohchiish and The-Other-Magpie killed a Lakota warrior and returned to camp bearing his scalp.

In the years that followed, the Crow faced growing pressure to abandon their traditional culture. *Boté*, including Ohchiish, were singled out by government agents, school teachers, and missionaries. One agent attempted to suppress the role altogether. According to tribal historian Joe Medicine Crow, "The agent incarcered the *badés*, cut off their hair, made them wear men's clothing. He forced them to do manual labor, planting these trees that you see here on the BIA [Bureau of Indian Affairs] grounds. The people were so upset with this that Chief Pretty Eagle came into Crow Agency, and told [the agent] to leave the reservation."[75]

In the end, none of this seemed to affect Ohchiish. In 1919, retired army general Hugh Scott interviewed "Woman Jim," as he was known among the local whites. Using Plains Indian sign language, Ohchiish recalled the day he fought on the Rosebud. An officer, Colonel Guy Henry, had been shot in the face, and while being carried on a travois was dropped into a mud hole. Ohchiish had pulled him up, and he remembered how the gallant officer laughed at his predicament. According to another eyewitness, when Henry was asked how he felt, he replied, "Bully! Never felt better in my life. Everybody is so kind."[76]

Hastíin Klah (1867–1937)

In November 1937, a group of Anglo-Americans and Navajo Indians gathered on a hilltop above Santa Fe to inaugurate a unique institution, the Museum of Navajo Ceremonial Art. Built at the expense of the Boston heiress Mary Cabot Wheelwright, the museum was to be devoted to the preservation of the art and culture of the Navajo Nation. Today, the Wheelwright Museum of the American Indian continues to occupy the same striking structure dedicated that day—a large-scale recreation of the traditional Navajo house, the eight-sided hogan.[77] It was the result of collaboration between two remarkable individuals, Wheelwright and perhaps the most influential two spirit in American history, the Navajo *nádleehí,* Hastíin Klah.

Klah was born in 1867 in western New Mexico. He showed interest in religion at an early age, and by the time he was ten he had learned his first ceremony.[78] This required memorizing long chants, mastering complex ceremonial procedures, and creating sandpaintings using ground stones and other materials to depict mythological scenes. Klah's *nádleeh* status was confirmed when he was a teenager after recovering from a near-fatal accident. According to his friend Francis Newcomb, he had entered a "very special category":

> The Navahos believed him to be honored by the gods and to possess unusual mental capacity combining both male and female attributes. He was expected to master all the knowledge, skill, and leadership of a man and also all of the skills, ability, and intuition of a woman. Klah during his lifetime lived up to these expectations in every way.[79]

As an adult, Klah dressed as a man. The anthropologist Gladys Reichard observed that "there was nothing feminine about him unless an indescribable gentleness be so called. The reasons the Navajo called him 'one-who-has-been-changed' were chiefly that he wove blankets and was not interested in women."[80] He mastered the skills of weaving smooth, finely patterned rugs, and in 1893 he was invited to demonstrate his craft at New Mexico's exhibit at the World's Columbian Exposition in Chicago.[81]

When Arthur and Francis (known to friends as Franc) Newcomb took over a remote trading post near Klah's home in 1914, he was a prominent figure in the area. Whereas most medicine men learned one or two ceremonies in a lifetime, Klah mastered eight.[82] At his first Ye-ibichai dance in 1917, Newcomb estimated that nearly two thousand Indians from several tribes attended. Klah distributed goods and sheep representing one-third of his worldly wealth and declared his intention to devote his life to spiritual concerns. Wheelwright's friendship with Klah began soon after, when she purchased one of his weavings in 1921.

In 1919, Franc Newcomb proposed that Klah incorporate sandpainting designs into his weavings. "I assured him that a blanket of this type would never be used on the floor but would be hung on the wall of some museum. He said he would think about it."[83] Klah's first sandpainting tapestry created a stir. Because of its religious content, some Navajos demanded that it be destroyed. Klah believed that his powers as a medicine man could protect him. Among Americans, his tapestries were an immediate success. In the midst of the Depression, they sold for as much as five thousand dollars.[84] Most are now in museums. Klah's bold innovation helped transform what had been a craft into a fine art.

When Klah's assistant unexpectedly died in 1931 it was a bitter disappointment. In his sixties, he no longer had time to train another student. Wheelwright asked him if he would be willing to place his ceremonial equipment and weavings in a place where they would be preserved and could be studied. Klah agreed and plans were begun for the museum in Santa Fe.

In 1934, Klah returned to Chicago to demonstrate sandpainting and display his tapestries at the Century of Progress International Exhibition.[85] En route, a newspaper reporter asked him for his impression of Americans. Klah replied,

> The Americans hurry too much. All the time you hurry and worry how you are going to hurry and worry more. You go thru life so fast you can't see beauty. I live the way I did when I came here first in 1893. I

am happy. That is why I come. I want to show the white people that I am happier than they are because I don't have all those things to worry about.[86]

Hastíín Klah died at the age of seventy in February 1937, a few months before the dedication of the museum he helped envision.

Qánqon-kámek-klaúlha, Ohchiish, We'wha, and Hastíín Klah are a few of the Native American two spirits who made important contributions to their communities and to American history. They alert us to the diversity of individuals and gender roles in native societies. Their tribes were distinct from each other in fundamental ways; their careers shaped by distinct historical contexts. They expressed their gender and sexuality in distinct ways as well. Qánqon appeared at different times as a man and a woman; We'wha and Ohchiish dressed as women from childhood; Klah, as a man. If there is a common thread, it is the spiritual powers and attributes they possessed, which were an integral part of their two-spirit status.

Conclusion: History Matters

Knowledge of the sexual and gender diversity of American Indians, Alaskan Natives, and native Hawaiians has real implications for Americans of all backgrounds. The 2010 film *Two Spirits* relates the story of a young Navajo named Fred Martinez Jr.[87] As a teenager in Cortez, Colorado, Fred expressed many of the mix-gender traits and temperament typical of a traditional *nádhleeh*. In the film, his mother recalls, "He's the kind of person so willing to give what he has. If he seen somebody, a boy that has a shoe that's not good . . . 'I got lots of shoes, I got lots of shirts. Let me give this to them.' He would give it to them." Fred wore makeup and often used female names. His mother supported him, but living off the reservation he had no access to traditional extended family support systems or mentoring. Nor did school officials intervene when he was subjected to bullying. Tragically, in 2001, as the film relates, a young Anglo man murdered Fred in a brutal hate crime.

The incident shocked the community, and in its aftermath the local high school changed its dress code and instituted anti-bullying programs to protect gay and transgender children, while local law enforcement officials gained awareness of the seriousness of crimes motivated by homophobia and transphobia. But another lesson is to be learned, as well.

Two-spirit/LGBTQ history not only challenges stereotypes and bias, it provides the path to self-esteem, empowerment, and community for two-spirit/LGBTQ native people, while teaching all Americans about sexual and gender diversity and the cultural contributions they offer.

Dr. Will Roscoe is an independent scholar and author.

Notes

1. Timucuan Ecological and Historic Preserve, Florida (National Preserve established and listed on the NRHP on 16 February 1988); Fort Caroline National Memorial, Florida (established 16 January 1953; listed on the NRHP on 15 October 1966).
2. René Goulaine de Laudonnière, in Richard Hakluyt, ed., *The Principal Navigations, Voyages, Traffiques, and Discoveries of the English Nation*, vol. 9 (Glasgow: James MacLehose and Sons, 1904), 16, 56, 69.
3. Jacques Le Moyne de Morgues, *Brevis Narratio Eorum quae in Florida Americae Provicina Gallis Acciderunt, Secunda in illam Navigatione, duce Renato de Laudoníere Classis Praefaecto Anno MDLXIIII; quae est Secunda pars Americae*, ed. Theodore de Bry (Frankfurt, Germany: Theodore de Bry, 1591), pl. 17, 23.
4. Fernando Alarcón, "Report of Alarcon's Expedition," in *Narratives of the Coronado Expedition 1540–1542*, ed. George P. Hammond and Agapito Rey, 124–155 (Albuquerque: University of New Mexico Press, 1940), 130, 148; Robert J. Morris, "*Aikāne*: Accounts of Hawaiian Same-Sex Relationships in the Journals of Captain Cook's Third Voyage (1776–80)," *Journal of Homosexuality* 19, no. 4 (1990): 21–54; and Stephen O. Murray, "The Traditional Kodiak and Aleutian Islanders' Non-Sacralized Trans-generational, Trans-gender Role," in *Oceanic Homosexualities*, ed. Stephen O. Murray (New York: Garland, 1992), 341–352.
5. Peter Martyr, "De Orbe Novo Petri Martyris ab Angleria, Mediolanensis Protonotarii Caesaris Senatoris Decades," *Opera*, facs. ed. (Graz, Austria: Akademische Druck and Verlagsanstalt, [1516] 1966), 106.
6. Pedro Font, *Font's Complete Diary: A Chronicle of the Founding of San Francisco*, trans. Herbert E. Bolton (Berkeley: University of California Press, 1931), 105.
7. The earliest documentation for its use in North America occurs in Pierre Deliette, "The Memoir of Pierre Liette," in *The Western Country in the 17th Century: The Memoirs of Lamothe Cadillac and Pierre Liette*, ed. Milo Milton Quaife, 87–174 (Chicago: Lakeside Press, 1947), 112–113, 124. Deliette served at a trading post in the region of the Illinois Indians between 1688 and 1698.

8. John F. McDermott, *A Glossary of Mississippi Valley French, 1673–1850,* Washington University Studies New Series, Language and Literature no. 12 (St. Louis: Washington University, 1941), 22–23.

9. See Will Roscoe, *Changing Ones: Third and Fourth Genders in Native North America* (New York: St. Martin's Press, 1998), 173–78; George Gibbs, *A Dictionary of the Chinook Jargon or Trade Language of Oregon,* Smithsonian Miscellaneous Collections 161 (Washington: Smithsonian Institution, 1863), 2.

10. The renowned Ojibwe two-spirit Ozaawindib (Yellow Head) from northern Minnesota, active in the 1790s and early 1800s, was referred to by traders as "La Berdash." See Elliott Coues, ed., *New Light on the Early History of the Greater Northwest: The Manuscript Journals of Alexandeo Henry and of David Thompson, 1799–1814,* vol. 2 (New York: Francis P. Harper, 1897), 53; Jean Baptiste Perrault, "Narrative of the Travels and Adventures of a Merchant Voyageur in the Savage Territories of Northern America Leaving Montreal the 28th of May 1783 (to 1820)," ed. John Sharpless Fox, *Historical Collections and Researches Made by the Michigan Pioneer and Historical Society* 37 (1909–1910): 560–61. Similarly, a Cayuse known to traders as "the Berdash" was a prominent member of the tribe in the 1830s; see Theodore Stern, *Chiefs and Chief Traders: Indian Relations at Fort Nez Percés, 1818–1855* (Corvallis: Oregon State University Press, 1993), 81, 162. See also the account of Qánqon below, who was called Bundosh and Bowdash.

11. See Roscoe, *Changing,* 7, 249; Randy P. Conner, *Blossom of Bone* (San Francisco: HarperSanFrancisco, 1993), 186–87.

12. First Nations is the term used to designate most of the indigenous peoples of Canada. Legislatively, the Canadian Inuit and Metis are not encompassed by the term First Nations, just as Native Alaskans and Native Hawaiians and Pacific Islanders are also recognized as distinct from Native Americans.

13. Roscoe, *Changing Ones,* chap. 5; Sue-Ellen Jacobs, Wesley Thomas, and Sabine Lang, eds., *Two-Spirit People: Native American Gender Identity, Sexuality, and Spirituality* (Urbana: University of Illinois Press, 1997); and "Revisiting the 'North American Berdache' Empirically and Theoretically: A Wenner-Gren Conference," 17–21 November 1993, Quality Inn, 1900 Connecticut Avenue, Washington, DC.

14. "Two spirit" has been widely embraced but some commentators have pointed to its limitations. In many native belief systems *all* individuals are understood to combine male and female modes of being, whether intellectually, psychologically, socially, or ceremonially. In these contexts, identifying specific tribal members as "two spirits" implies that they achieve this balance while others do not, which can lead to confusion and division. In other cases, when "two spirit" is translated back into native languages, it acquires unintended meanings (see Bea Medicine and Sue-Ellen Jacobs, eds., *Learning to Be an Anthropologist and Remaining "Native": Selected Writings* [Urbana: University of Illinois Press, 2001], 147–48). Yet others have

noted the way in which its use fosters blanket statements about the universal presence and social acceptance of "two-spirit people." The case for presence and status needs to be established for each tribe through careful research grounded in written and oral sources. As the dialogue among scholars and in native communities evolves, the most encompassing way to identify the subject of this chapter is "two-spirit/LGBTQ" native people. For additional discussion, see Wesley Thomas and Sue-Ellen Jacobs, ". . . And We Are Still Here": From *Berdache* to Two-Spirit People," *American Indian Culture and Research Journal* 23 no. 2 (1993): 91–107; Joseph Gilley, *Becoming Two-Spirited: Gay Identity and Social Acceptance in Indian Country* (Lincoln: University of Nebraska Press, 2006); and the various contributors to Jacobs, Thomas, and Lang, *Two-Spirit People*. For a discussion of the interrelationships of white colonialism, modern queer identity, and two-spirit activism, see Scott L. Morgensen, *Spaces Between Us: Queer Settler Colonialism and Indigenous Decolonization* (Minneapolis: University of Minnesota Press, 2011).

15. For an index of anthropological and historical sources by tribe see Roscoe, *Changing Ones*, 223–47. The evidence is heavily weighted toward tribes west of the Mississippi River. Various factors account for this. Unlike the Spaniards, who sought to missionize intact native communities and often recorded details of their cultures, English settlers were singularly uninterested in the cultures of the people whose lands they were determined to occupy and recorded little about them. Indeed, Puritans such as John Winthrop conflated the entire native population with the Biblical Sodomites (Charles M. Segal and David C. Stineback, *Puritans, Indians, and Manifest Destiny* [New York: G. P. Putnam's Sons, 1977], 50). By the time anthropologists began documenting native cultures in the late nineteenth century, few descendants of Eastern tribes remained with knowledge of traditional practices and beliefs. Limited, but questionable, evidence has been cited for the presence of two spirits among the Iroquois, and a single reference from 1825 suggests that male two spirits had at one time been present in Cherokee society. See Roscoe, *Changing Ones*, 250–51 and Gregory D. Smithers, "Cherokee 'Two Spirits': Gender, Ritual, and Spirituality in the Native South," *Early American Studies* 3 (2014): 626–51 (Smithers discusses the challenges and opportunities for recovering two-spirit traditions in the face of limited documentation using the methodology of ethnohistory). Stronger evidence for male and female two spirits exists for the Algonkian-speaking tribes of the Mississippi Valley, including the Sauk and Fox, Illinois, Miami, and Potawatomi. Marquette observed Illinois males called *ikoueta*, who engaged in women's work, assisted men on war parties, sang at ceremonies, and gave advice at tribal councils. See Jacques Marquette, "Of the First Voyage Made by Father Marquette toward New Mexico, and How the Idea Thereof Was Conceived," in *The Jesuit Relations and Allied Documents: Travels and Explorations of the Jesuit Missionaries in New France 1610–1791,*

Vol. 59: *Lower Canada, Illinois, Ottawas 1667–1669*, ed. Reuben G. Thwaites, 86–163 (Cleveland, OH: Burrows Brothers, 1900), 128–129; Louis Armand de Lahontan, *Memoires de l'Amérique Septentrionale, ou la suite des voyages de Mr. Le Baron La Hontan*, vol. 2 (Amsterdam: Jonas L'Honoré, 1705), 144.

16. The term *nádleehí* refers to an individual who is a member of the gender class *nádleeh*; see Jacobs, Thomas, and Lang, eds., *Two-Spirit People*, 15.

17. For a listing of native language terms for alternative gender roles see Roscoe, *Changing Ones*, 213–22.

18. See Roscoe, *Changing Ones*; Jacobs, Thomas, and Lang, *Two-Spirit People*; Sabine Lang, *Men as Women, Women as Men: Changing Gender in Native American Cultures* (Austin: University of Texas Press, 1998); Sandra E. Hollimon, "The Archaeology of Nonbinary Genders in Native North American Societies," in *Handbook of Gender in Archaeology*, ed. Sarah M. Nelson (Lanham, MD: Altamira Press, 2006), 435–50.

19. Ruth Benedict, *Patterns of Culture* (Boston: Houghton Mifflin, 1959), 264.

20. See Roscoe, *Changing Ones*, chap. 4. Weetamo was present at the Great Swamp Fight in 1675 (Great Swamp State Management Area, West Kingston, Rhode Island). After drowning while attempting to escape the English in 1675, her head was displayed on a pole in Taunton, Massachusetts (Taunton Green Historic District; listed on the NRHP on 1 March 1985). Key sites associated with Lozen include the Fort Apache Historic District, located on the Fort Apache Indian Reservation, Arizona (listed on the NRHP on 14 October 1976), Castillo de San Marcos National Monument, St. Augustine, Florida (designated a National Monument on 15 October 1924; listed on the NRHP on 15 October 1966), and Mount Vernon Arsenal-Searcy Hospital Complex, Mount Vernon, Alabama (listed on the NRHP on 26 May 1988), where she died as a prisoner of war in 1889.

21. Willard W. Hill. "The Status of the Hermaphrodite and Transvestite in Navaho Culture," *American Anthropologist* 37, no. 2 (1935): 276.

22. Terms for a similar status in other Polynesian languages include *fa'fafine* in Samoan and *wakawawine* in Pukapukan. See Raleigh Watts, "The Polynesian Mahu," in *Oceanic Homosexualities*, 171–84.

23. Andrew Matzner, *'O Au No Keia: Voice from Hawai'i's Mahu and Transgender Communities* (n.p.: Xlibris, 2001); Carol E. Robertson, "The Māhū of Hawai'i," *Feminist Studies* 15, no. 2 (1989): 312–26; Watts, "The Polynesian Mahu"; Mario Vargas Llosa, "The Men-Women of the Pacific," *Tate Etc.* 2 (Autumn 2010), accessed 4 April 2015, www.tate.org.uk/context-comment/articles/men-women-pacific. See also the documentary by Dean Hamer and Joe Wilson, *Kumu Hina: A Place in the Middle*, QWaves, 2014.

24. Morris, "*Aikāne*," 32; Robert J. Morris, "Same-Sex Friendships in Hawaiian Lore: Constructing the Canon," in *Oceanic Homosexualities*, 71–102.

25. Matzner, "*'O Au No Keia*," 222; Robert J. Morris, "*Hulihia Ke Au*: Implications of Hawai'i Same-Sex Marriage for Policy, Practice, & Culture," *Asian Pacific American Law Journal* 20, no. 1 (2015): 1–23.

26. Abraham Fornander, *Fornander Collection of Hawaiian Antiquities and Folklore,* Memoirs of the Bernice Pauahi Bishop Museum (Honolulu: Bishop Museum, 1918–1919), 4: 384–405, 5: 498–517.

27. Kealakekua Bay Historic District, Hawai'i (listed on the NRHP on 12 December 1973).

28. Morris, "*Aikāne*," 33–34.

29. Roscoe, *Changing Ones,* 101. Alcatraz, San Francisco Bay, California (became a National Recreation Area in 1972; listed on the NRHP on 23 June 1976; designated an NHL District on 17 January 1986).

30. Maurice Kenny, "Tinselled Bucks: An Historical Study in Indian Homosexuality," *Gay Sunshine* 26–27 (Winter 1975–76): 17–48; Paula Gunn Allen, "Lesbians in American Indian Cultures" *Conditions* 7 (1981): 65–87.

31. Burns, Cameron, and other founding members met while participating in the American Indian Art Workshop at the American Indian Center, 225 Valencia Street, San Francisco, California.

32. See the bibliography of Native American LGBTQ writers in Roscoe, *Changing Ones,* 279–80.

33. "The Basket and the Bow: A Gathering of Lesbian and Gay Native Americans," 18–19 June 1988, American Indian Center, 1530 East Franklin Avenue and Gay 90's Bar, 408 Hennepin Avenue, Minneapolis, Minnesota. See Megan L. McDonald, "Two-Spirits Organizing: Indigenous Two-Spirit Identity in the Twin Cities Region," in *Queer Twin Cities,* ed. Twin Cities GLBT Oral History Project (Minneapolis: University of Minnesota Press, 2010), 150–70; See also Qwo-Li Driskill, Daniel Heath Justice, Deborah Miranda, and Lisa Tatonetti, eds., *Sovereign Erotics: A Collection of Two-Spirit Literature* (Tucson: University of Arizona Press, 2011).

34. Bay Area American Indian Two-Spirits Fourth Annual Two-Spirit Powwow, 7 February 2015, Cow Palace, 2600 Geneva Avenue, Daly City, California.

35. Jorge Rivas, "Native Americans Talk Gender Identity at 'Two-Spirit' Powwow," *Fusion,* 9 February 2015, accessed 22 March 2015, www.fusion.net/story/46014/native-americans-talk-gender-identity-at-a-two-spirit-powwow.

36. According to Robertson, "The *māhū* population today embraces an astounding variety of individuals. It can designate women who dress and work as men, men who dress and work as women, women or men who dress and act so as to obscure their biological classification, women who will only associate with other women, men who dress 'festively,' men who undergo hormone treatments and/or eventually change their sex surgically, true hermaphrodites, and women and men who might, in English, call themselves 'gay.' Any of these people may choose to procreate or to raise children through the traditional adoption arrangement known as *hanai.* In fact, parents sometimes put their children in the care of *māhū,* for mixed gender individuals are recognized as special, compassionate, and creative" ("The Māhū of Hawai'i," 314–15).

37. Matzner, *'O Au No Keia,* 221.

38. "Legal Recognition of Non-binary Gender," Wikipedia, accessed 19 July 2019, https://en.wikipedia.org/wiki/Legal_recognition_of_non-binary_gender. The interpretation of traditional two-spirit roles as a third (and sometimes fourth) gender was initially advanced by Roscoe, *The Zuni Man-Woman* (published in 1991) and further developed in *Changing Ones*.

39. The Stones of Kapaemāhū, Kuhio Beach, adjacent to Waikiki City Police Station, 2425 Kalakaua Avenue, Honolulu, Hawaii.

40. Mary K. Pukui, E. W. Haertig, and Catherine A. Lee, *Nana I Ke Kumu (Look to the Source)* (Honolulu: Queen Lili'uokalani Children's Center, 1972), 2: 108, 110; June Gutmanis, *Pohaku: Hawai'ian Stones* (Laie, HI: Institute for Polynesian Studies, Brigham Young University, Hawaii, 1986), 33–36. Andrea Feeser speculates that they may have settled in O'ahu during the second wave of Polynesian immigration to Hawaii, which introduced Tahitian religious and sociopolitical practices to the islands (*Waikīkī: A History of Forgetting and Remembering* [Honolulu: University of Hawaii Press, 2006], 79).

41. Matzner, *'O Au No Keia,* 279; Feeser, *Waikīkī,* 78–82.

42. Feeser, *Waikīkī,* 78–82; Gutmanis, *Pohaku,* 35.

43. Luan Fauteck Makes Marks, *A Typology of Native North American Sacred Lands and Places* (Little Canada, MN: Indian Land Tenure Foundation, 2008), 45, http://sacrednaturalsites.org/wp-content/uploads/2013/07/Natures oftheSacredTypology.pdf.

44. Ibid.

45. See Will Roscoe, "Native American Two Spirits at National Historic Sites," 2014, http://willsworld.org/Roscoe-2SpiritAtNationalHistoricSites.pdf. In the case of sites with spiritual significance to tribal communities, however, formal recognition—which would expose them to intrusion—would be inappropriate.

46. Claude E. Schaeffer, "The Kutenai Female Berdache: Courier, Guide, Prophetess, and Warrior," *Ethnohistory* 12, no. 3 (1965): 193–236.

47. David Thompson, *David Thompson's Narrative of His Explorations in Western America,* ed. J. B. Tyrrell (Toronto, Canada: Champlain Society, 1916), 512–13.

48. Schaeffer, "The Kutenai Female Berdache," 196–97.

49. Ibid., 224.

50. Fort Astoria, Astoria, Oregon (contributing property to the Astoria Downtown Historic District; listed individually on the NRHP on 15 October 1966; designated an NHL on 5 November 1961).

51. Schaeffer, "The Kutenai Female Berdache," 202.

52. Ibid., 212.

53. Ibid., 206.

54. Fort Okanogan, Okanogan County, Washington (listed on the NRHP on 4 June 1973. The fort site was flooded in 1967 by the Lake Pateros reservoir, following the construction of the Wells Dam).

55. John Franklin, *Narrative of a Second Expedition to the Shores of the Polar Seas in the Years 1825, 1826, and 1827* (Philadelphia: Carey, Lea, and Carey, 1828), 251–52.

56. Schaeffer, "The Kutenai Female Berdache," 214.

57. Leslie Spier, *The Prophet Dance of the Northwest and Its Derivatives: The Source of the Ghost Dance, General Series in Anthropology* 1 (Menasha, WI: George Banta, 1935).

58. Located several miles upstream from Saleesh House, established by David Thompson in 1809. The latter was located on the Clark Fork River near Highway 200, one mile east of Thompson Falls, Montana, and is identified by a Montana State Historical Marker.

59. The Whitman Mission was added to the NRHP on 15 October 1966. The site was designated in 1936 as the Whitman National Monument, and designated the Whitman Mission National Historic Site (an NPS unit) on 1 January 1963.

60. Schaeffer, "The Kutenai Female Berdache," 214–15.

61. Ibid., 217.

62. See Roscoe, *Changing Ones,* chap. 4.

63. Watson Smith, Richard B. Woodbury, and Nathalie F. S. Woodbury, *The Excavation of Hawikuh by Frederick Webb Hodge: Report of the Hendricks-Hodge Expedition 1917–1923,* Contributions from the Museum of the American Indian, Heye Foundation, vol. 20 (New York: Museum of the American Indian, Heye Foundation, 1966). Hawikuh, Cibola County, New Mexico was added to the NRHP on 15 October 1966 and designated an NHL on 9 October 1960. It is part of the Zuni-Cibola Complex NHL designated on 2 December 1974.

64. Matilda Coxe Stevenson, "The Zuñi Indians: Their Mythology, Esoteric Fraternities, and Ceremonies," *Twenty-Third Annual Report of the Bureau of American Ethnology, 1901–1902* (Washington, DC: Government Printing Office, 1904), 20, 37, 310–11. Stevenson uses both male and female pronouns in referring to We'wha. We'wha's life is the subject of Will Roscoe, *The Zuni-Man Woman* (Albuquerque: University of New Mexico Press, 1991).

65. Home of James and Matilda Coxe Stevenson, 1913 N Street NW, Washington, D.C. (no longer extant).

66. Smithsonian Building, Jefferson Drive at Tenth Street SW, Washington, D.C. (added to the NRHP on 15 October 1966; designated an NHL on 12 January 1965), National Mall (added to the NRHP on 15 October 1966).

67. See Dwight P. Lanmon and Francis H. Harlow, *The Pottery of Zuni Pueblo* (Santa Fe: Museum of New Mexico Press, 2008).

68. Fort Wingate Historic District, near Gallup, New Mexico (added to the NRHP on 26 May 1978).

69. Stevenson, "The Zuñi Indians," 311–12.

70. Ibid., 310.

71. For a full account of the episode and its aftermath see Roscoe, *The Zuni Man-Woman,* chap. 4.

72. Rosebud Battlefield–Where the Girl Saved Her Brother, near Kirby, Montana (added to the NRHP on 21 August 1972; designated an NHL on 19 August 2008). "Where the Girl Saved her Brother" is the Cheyenne name for the site, based on an incident that occurred during the battle when a Cheyenne woman, Buffalo Calf Road Woman, charged into the fray to rescue her brother. She was not a *hetaneman,* or two-spirited female, however, as indicated by her appearance in a ledger drawing depicting the event (National Anthropological Archives, MS 166,032, 08704700). She is dressed in the typical manner of a Cheyenne woman. In contrast, the Cheyenne female depicted in figure 1 is fighting *as a man,* bare-chested, and wearing a man's breechclout.

73. See Roscoe, *Changing Ones,* chap. 2. I follow the transcription of the name in Lillian Bullshows Hogan, *The Woman Who Loved Mankind: The Life of a Twentieth-Century Crow Elder* (Lincoln: University of Nebraska Press, 2012). Hogan, a Crow elder, uses both male and female pronouns in referring to Ohchiish and notes, "They don't call him 'him' or 'her.' They just say 'a person'" (124).

74. Frank B. Linderman, *Red Mother* (New York: John Day Company, 1932), 227–31.

75. Walter L. Williams, *The Spirit and the Flesh: Sexual Diversity in American Indian Culture* (Boston: Beacon Press, 1986), 179. Chief Plenty Coups (Alek-Chea-Ahoosh) Home, Pryor, Montana (added to the NRHP on 6 October 1970; designated an NHL on 20 January 1999).

76. Martin F. Schmitt, ed., *General George Crook: His Autobiography* (Norman: University of Oklahoma Press, 1946), 197.

77. Wheelwright Museum of the American Indian, 704 Camino Lejo, Santa Fe, New Mexico (added to the NRHP on 18 December 1990).

78. The following account of Klah's life is based on Roscoe, *Changing Ones,* chap. 3, and Franc Johnson Newcomb, *Hosteen Klah: Navaho Medicine Man and Sand Painter* (Norman: University of Oklahoma Press, 1964).

79. Newcomb, *Hosteen Klah,* 97.

80. Gladys A. Reichard, "Individualism and Mythological Style," *Journal of American Folklore* 57 (1944): 23.

81. Burnham Park, Lakefront and Northerly Island, 5491 South Shore Drive, Chicago, Illinois.

82. James C. Faris, *The Nightway: A History and a History of Documentation of a Navajo Ceremonial* (Albuquerque: University of New Mexico Press, 1990), 87.

83. Newcomb, *Hosteen Klah,* 157.

84. $5,000 in 1935 (roughly the middle of the Great Depression) equates to approximately $93,400 in 2019 dollars. Samuel H. Williamson, "Seven Ways

to Compute the Relative Value of a U.S. Dollar Amount, 1774 to Present," *MeasuringWorth*, 2017. http://www.measuringworth.com/uscompare/.

85. Jackson Park, 6401 South Stony Island Avenue, Chicago, Illinois.
86. Roscoe, *Changing Ones*, 57.
87. Lydia Nibley and Russell Martin, *Two Spirits*, DVD (Los Angeles: Independent Lens/Riding the Tiger Productions, LLC, 2010).

Bibliography

Alarcon, Fernando. "Report of Alarcon's Expedition." In *Narratives of the Coronado Expedition 1540–1542*, edited by George P. Hammond and Agapito Rey, 124–55. Albuquerque: University of New Mexico Press, 1940.

Allen, Paula Gunn. "Lesbians in American Indian Cultures." *Conditions* 7 (1981): 65–87.

Benedict, Ruth. *Patterns of Culture*. Boston: Houghton Mifflin, 1959.

Conner, Randy P. *Blossom of Bone*. San Francisco: HarperSanFrancisco, 1993.

Coues, Elliott, ed. *New Light on the Early History of the Greater Northwest: The Manuscript Journals of Alexander Henry and of David Thompson, 1799–1814*, vol. 2. New York: Francis P. Harper, 1897.

de Lahontan, Louis Armand. *Memoires de l'Amerique Septenrionale, ou la suite des voyage de Mr. Le Baron La Hontan*, vol. 2. Amsterdam: Jonas L'Honore, 1705.

Deliette, Pierre. "The Memoir of Pierre Liette." In *The Western Country in the 17th Century: The Memoirs of Lamothe Cadillac and Pierre Liette*, edited by Milo Milton Quaife, 87–174. Chicago: Lakeside Press, 1947.

Driskill, Quo-Li, Daniel Heath Justice, Deborah Miranda, and Lisa Tatonetti, eds. *Sovereign Erotics: A Collection of Two-Spirit Literature*. Tucson: University of Arizona Press, 2011.

Faris, James C. *The Nightway: A History and a History of Documentation of a Navajo Ceremonial*. Albuquerque: University of New Mexico Press, 1990.

Feeser, Andrea. *Waikiki: A History of Forgetting and Remembering*. Honolulu: University of Hawaii Press, 2006.

Font, Pedro. *Font's Complete Diary: A Chronicle of the Founding of San Francisco*. Translated by Herbert E. Bolton. Berkeley: University of California Press, 1931.

Fornander, Abraham. *Fornander Collection of Hawaiian Antiquities and Folklore*. Memoirs of the Bernice Pauahi Bishop Museum. Honolulu: Bishop Museum, 1918–19.

Franklin, John. *Narrative of a Second Expedition to the Shores of the Polar Seas in the Years 1825, 1826, and 1827*. Philadelphia: Carey, Lea, and Carey, 1828.

Gibbs, George Gibbs. *A Dictionary of the Chinook Jargon or Trade Language of Oregon*. Smithsonian Miscellaneous Collections 161. Washington: Smithsonian Institution, 1863.

Gilley, Joseph. *Becoming Two-Spirited: Gay Identity and Social Acceptance in Indian Country*. Lincoln: University of Nebraska Press, 2006.

Gutmanis, June. *Pohaku: Hawaiian Stones*. Laie, HI: Institute for Polynesian Studies, Brigham Young University, Hawaii, 1986.

Hakluyt, Richard, ed. *The Principal Navigations, Voyages, Traffiques, and Discoveries of the English Nation*. Vol. 9, 1–100. Glasgow: James MacLehose and Sons, 1904.

Hill, Willard W. "The Status of the Hermaphrodite and Transvestite in Navaho Culture." *American Anthropologist* 37, no. 2 (1935): 273–79.

Hogan, Lillian Bullshows. *The Woman Who Loved Mankind: The Life of a Twentieth-Century Crow Elder*. Lincoln: University of Nebraska Press, 2012.

Hamer, Dean, and Joe Wilson, dirs. *Kumu Hina: A Place in the Middle*. Film. QWaves, 2014.

Hollimon, Sandra E. "The Archaeology of Nonbinary Genders in Native North American Societies." In *Handbook of Gender in Archaeology*, edited by Sarah M. Nelson, 435–50. Lanham, MD: AltaMira, 2006.

Jacobs, Sue-Ellen, Wesley Thomas, and Sabine Lang, eds. *Two-Spirit People: Native American Gender Identity, Sexuality, and Spirituality*. Urbana: University of Illinois Press, 1997.

Kenny, Maurice. "Tinselled Bucks: An Historical Study in Indian Homosexuality." *Gay Sunshine* 26–27 (Winter 1975–76): 17–48.

Lang, Sabine. *Men as Women, Women as Men: Changing Gender in Native American Cultures*. Austin: University of Texas Press, 1998.

Lanmon, Dwight P., and Francis H. Harlow. *The Pottery of Zuni Pueblo*. Santa Fe: Museum of New Mexico Press, 2008.

Le Moyne de Morgues, Jacques. *Brevis Narratio Eorum quae in Florida Americae Provincina Gallis Acciderunt, Secunda in illam, Navigatione, duce Renato de Laudoniere Classis Praefaecto Anno MDLCIII; quae est Secunda pars Americae*. Edited by Theodore de Bry. Frankfurt, Germany: Theodore de Bry, 1591.

Linderman, Frank B. *Red Mother*. New York: John Day, 1932.

Llosa, Mario Vargas. "The Men-Women of the Pacific." *Tate Etc.* 2 (Autumn 2010). http://www.tate.org.uk/context-comment/articles/men-women-pacific.

Makes Marks, Luan Fauteck. *A Typology of Native North American Sacred Lands and Places*. Little Canada, MN: Indian Land Tenure Foundation, 2008. http://sacrednaturalsites.org/wp-content/uploads/2013/07/NaturesoftheSacred Typology.pdf.

Marquette, Jacques. "Of the First Voyage Made by Father Marquette toward New Mexico, and How the Idea Thereof Was Conceived." In *Travels and Explorations of the Jesuit Missionaries in New France, 1610–1791*, Vol. 59: *Lower Canada, Illinois, Ottawas: 1667–1669*, edited by Reuben G. Thwaites, 86–163. Cleveland, OH: Burrows Brothers, 1900.

Martyr, Peter. "De Orbe Novo Petri Martyris ab Angleria, Mediolanensis Protonotarii Caesaris Decades." *Opera*, facs. ed. Graz, Austria: Akademische Druck and Verlagsanstalt, [1516] 1966.

Matzner, Andrew. *'O Au No Keia: Voice from Hawai'i's Mahu and Transgender Communities*. N.p.: Xlibris, 2001.

McDermott, John F. *A Glossary of Mississippi Valley French, 1673–1850*. Washington University Studies New Series, Language and Literature no. 12. St. Louis: Washington University, 1941.

McDonald, Megan L. "Two-Spirits Organizing: Indigenous Two-Spirit Identity in the Twin Cities Region." In *Queer Twin Cities*, edited by Twin Cities GLBT Oral History Project, 150–70. Minneapolis: University of Minnesota Press, 2010.

Medicine, Bea, and Sue-Ellen Jacobs, eds. *Learning to be an Anthropologist and Remaining "Native": Selected Writings*. Urbana: University of Illinois Press, 2001.

Morgensen, Scott L. *Spaces between Us: Queer Settler Colonialism and Indigenous Decolonization*. Minneapolis: University of Minnesota Press, 2011.

Morris, Robert J. "*Aikane*: Accounts of Hawaiian Same-Sex Relationships in the Journals of Captain Cook's Third Voyage (1776–80)." *Journal of Homosexuality* 19, no. 4 (1990): 21–54.

———. "*Hulihia Ke Au*: Implications of Hawai'i Same-Sex Marriage for Policy, Practice, & Culture," *Asian Pacific American Law Journal* 20, no. 1 (2015): 1–23.

———. "Same-Sex Friendships in Hawaiian Lore: Constructing the Canon." In *Oceanic Homosexualities*, edited by Stephen O. Murray, 71–102. New York: Garland, 1992.

Murray, Stephen O. "'The Traditional Kodiak and Aleutian Islanders' Non-Sacralized Trans-generational, Trans-gender Role." In *Oceanic Homosexualities*, edited by Stephen O. Murray, 341–52. New York: Garland, 1992.

Newcomb, Franc Johnson. *Hasteen Klah: Navaho Medicine Man and Sand Painter*. Norman: University of Oklahoma Press, 1964.

Nibley, Lydia, and Russell Martin, dirs. *Two Spirits*. DVD. Los Angeles: Independent Lens/Riding the Tiger Productions, 2010.

Perrault, Jean Baptiste. "Narrative of the Travels and Adventures of a Merchant Voyageur in the Savage Territories of Northern America Leaving Montreal the 28th of May 1783 (to 1820)." Edited by John Sharpless Fox. *Historical Collections and Researches Made by the Michigan Pioneer and Historical Society* 37 (1909–10): 508–619.

Pukui, Mary K., E. W. Haertig, and Catherine A. Lee. *Nana I Ke Kumu (Look to the Source)*. Honolulu: Queen Lili'uokalani Children's Center, 1972.

Reichard, Gladys A. "Individualism and Mythological Style." *Journal of American Folklore* 57 (1944): 16–25.

Rivas, Jorge. "Native Americans Talk Gender Identity at 'Two-Spirit' Powwow." *Fusion*, 9 February 2015. http://www.fusion.net/story/46014/native-americans-talk-gender-identity-at-a-two-spirit-powwow.

Robertson, Carol E. "The Mahu of Hawai'i." *Feminist Studies* 15, no. 2 (1989): 312–26.

Roscoe, Will. *Changing Ones: Third and Fourth Genders in Native North America.* New York: St. Martin's Press, 1998.

———. *The Zuni Man-Woman.* Albuquerque: University of New Mexico Press, 1991.

Schaeffer, Claude E. "The Kutenai Female Berdache: Courier, Guide, Prophetess, and Warrior." *Ethnohistory* 12, no. 3 (1965): 193–236.

Schmitt, Martin F., ed. *General George Crook: His Autobiography.* Norman: University of Oklahoma Press, 1946.

Segal, Charles M., and David C. Stineback. *Puritans, Indians, and Manifest Destiny.* New York: G. P. Putnam's Sons, 1977.

Smith, Watson, Richard B. Woodbury, and Nathalie F. S. Woodbury. *The Excavation of Hawikuh by Frederick Webb Hodge: Report of the Hendricks-Hodge Expedition, 1917–1923.* Contributions from the Museum of the American Indian, Heye Foundation, vol. 20. New York: Museum of the American Indian, Heye Foundation, 1966.

Smithers, Gregory D. "Cherokee 'Two Spirits': Gender, Ritual, and Spirituality in the Native South." *Early American Studies* 3(2014): 626–51.

Spier, Leslie. *The Prophet Dance of the Northwest and Its Derivatives: The Source of the Ghost Dance.* General Series in Anthropology 1. Menasha, WI: George Banta, 1935.

Stern, Theodore, *Chiefs and Chief Traders: Indian Relations at Fort Nez Percés, 1818–1855* (Corvallis: Oregon State University Press, 1993).

Stevenson, Matilda Coxe. "The Zuni Indians: Their Mythology, Esoteric Fraternities, and Ceremonies." *Twenty-Third Annual Report of the Bureau of American Ethnology, 1901–1902.* Washington, DC: Government Printing Office, 1904.

Thomas, Wesley, and Sue-Ellen Jacobs. ". . . And We Are Still Here": From *Berdache* to Two-Spirit People." *American Indian Culture and Research Journal* 23, no. 2 (1993): 91–107.

Thompson, David. *David Thompson's Narrative of His Explorations in Western America.* Edited by J. B. Tyrrell. Toronto, Canada: Champlain Society, 1916.

Thwaites, Reuben Gold, ed. *The Jesuit Relations and Allied Documents: Travels and Explorations of the Jesuit Missionaries in New France 1610–1791,* Vol. 59: *Lower Canada, Illinois, Ottawas: 1667–1669.* Cleveland, OH: Burrows Brothers, 1900.

Watts, Raleigh. "The Polynesian Mahu." In *Oceanic Homosexualities,* edited by Stephen O. Murray, 171–84. New York: Garland, 1992.

Williamson, Samuel H. "Seven Ways to Compute the Relative Value of a U.S. Dollar Amount, 1774 to Present." MeasuringWorth.com, 2017. http://www.measuringworth.com/uscompare/.

Williams, Walter L. *The Spirit and the Flesh: Sexual Diversity in American Indian Culture.* Boston: Beacon Press, 1986.

Transgender History in the United States and the Places That Matter

Susan Stryker

The word "transgender" first appeared in print in American English in 1965, and entered widespread use only in the 1990s.[1] Thus, it might seem to name a relatively recent phenomenon without much of a history—one that has had scant time to leave many traces in the built environment or inhabited landscape. In most respects, "transgender" is just today's term for referring to the ways people can live lives that depart from the conventional patterns according to which all bodies are assigned a sex at birth (male or female) and enrolled in a social gender (girl or boy), form gendered personalities (subjective feelings of being a man or a woman or something else), and come to occupy the social and kinship roles considered normal for people assigned to their particular birth-sex (for example, becoming a wife or father). In departing from these conventional patterns, such people cross over (*trans-*) the gender categories that organize the historically specific ways we all imagine ourselves to be the particular kind of persons that we are. Such "gender variance" is a common feature in human cultures. It seems that however a given culture constructs its typical ways of being a person, some members of that culture do it differently, for whatever reason.[2]

Different cultures deal with gender variance differently.[3] Over the past few hundred years, gender variance in societies of Western European origin, including dominant U.S. culture, has most often been understood as something antisocial, sinful, criminal, or psychopathological—and thus in need of correction. People with what we might now call transgender feelings about themselves have often resisted the moral, legal, and medical characterizations of their lives that have resulted in their social oppression. At the same time, they often have sought to be recognized legally and socially as the kind of gendered person they consider themselves to be, and may also have sought medical treatment or psychotherapeutic support for expressing their gender. Since the nineteenth century, the struggles of such people have formed one thread in the larger historical tapestry of identity-based social movements that have sought to better the conditions of life for people in marginalized minority communities in the United States. Transgender social history has definitely left its mark on America, and these stories are increasingly coming to the public's attention. As the title of a 2016 web-based series of trans-history mini-documentaries puts it, "We've Been Around."[4] Place-based history can satisfy a need felt by contemporary transgender people hungry to see themselves reflected back from their social and physical environments, while at the same time performing an important pedagogical function for others to the degree that it un-erases the actual, persistent, and longstanding presence of gender-variant people in the world.

Prior to European colonization, and continuing until the present day, many cultures indigenous to North America have organized gender, sexuality, and social roles quite differently than settler societies of modern European origin.[5] Transgender histories in the United States, like the broader national histories of which they form a part, originate in colonial contact zones where members of the arriving culture encountered kinds of people it struggled to comprehend. This is *not* to say that such indigenous persons can or should be slotted into a contemporary "transgender" category, but to note that Eurocentric notions of transgender are inextricably caught up in colonial practices for the management of cultural difference. Important sites for transgender history thus include places where soldiers, missionaries, and settlers encountered indigenous practices that did not align with their own sense of proper expressions of gender and sexuality.

In the first published narrative of European exploration in what is now the United States, Álvar Núñez Cabeza de Vaca, writing of his overland journey from what is now southeastern Texas to Mexico City between 1527 and 1536, described encounters with apparent males who lived and worked as women, whom he called *hombres amarionados impotente* (impotent effeminate men). Jacques Marquette, the first European known to have visited the Upper Mississippi, observed "men who do everything women do" in his travels in what is now Illinois, between 1673 and 1677.[6] Relatedly, indigenous scholar Deborah Miranda (Esselen and Chumash) characterizes as "gendercide" the compulsory regendering, or outright extermination, of indigenous persons at Spanish missions in California and the Southwest who did not conform to Eurocentric ideas of proper gendered personhood.[7]

While such encounters left no physical landmarks, interpretive signage and other explanatory text on websites and in visitor centers devoted to historic trails and early colonial sites could describe European perceptions of gender variance, and note that the perception of gender variance in indigenous cultures typically functioned as a justification for colonization: i.e., that gender-variant people and the societies that tolerated them were worthy of death, in need of salvation, or unfit to occupy the land.[8] Similarly, interpretive materials could also incorporate indigenous worldviews local to that place that demonstrate how "gender" was—and still can be—conceptualized differently than it currently is in the dominant settler society.

Looking at the lives of transgender, transsexual, cross-dressing, and gender-variant individuals and groups reveals the geographical dimension of American transgender history, documenting how they transpired within the main currents of Euro-American society. Cases involving gender-variant people are present in some of the earliest legal records of the Anglo-American colonies. In 1629, the Virginia Court in Jamestown heard testimony to decide the fate of one Thomas or Thomasine Hall, apparently an individual born with physically ambiguous genitalia who lived as both a man and a woman at different periods of life. Raised in England as a girl, Hall presented as a man to become a sailor, presented again as a woman to work as a lacemaker, and eventually became an indentured servant in Virginia as a man. Hall ran afoul of community norms there when they started dressing again in feminine attire. Accused of performing an illicit sexual act with a female servant, the question before the Virginia Court was to determine whether Hall was male, and therefore guilty of fornication, or female, and therefore guilty of no crime, given that sexual activity between women was considered physically impossible. Remarkably, the court accepted Hall's claim to be both a man and a woman, and ordered them to wear a mix of men's and women's clothing.[9] It is unknown whether Hall, who seems to have died a few years later, complied, but their case highlights the degree to which law—which varied from place to place—played a central role in shaping the contours of gender-variant lives from the earliest days of North America's colonization.

In 1652, Joseph Davis of Haverhill, Massachusetts, was presented to the Court of Strawberry Banke (Portsmouth, New Hampshire) and charged with "putting on women's apparel and going from house to house in the night time with a female."[10] In 1677, Dorothie Hoyt of Essex

County, Massachusetts, was summoned to the Salem Court "for putting on man's apparel;" Hoyt failed to appear, having "gone out of the county." These and other such cases, such as Mary Henly's appearance in the Middlesex County Court in 1692 to face a charge of wearing men's clothing, undoubtedly contributed to Massachusetts Bay Colony's passage of an anti-cross-dressing law in 1696.[11] Of significance here is the *kind* of spaces and institutions within which gender-variant people become visible in the colonial period: primarily in courts, attesting to the perception of gender-variant practices as problems of social order. Such lives leave traces on the physical and social landscape, shaping the laws and spaces designed to regulate gender and sexuality.

It is often not possible to determine what motivated the behavior of people who entered the historical record centuries ago for wearing clothing not typically worn by people of their apparent sex. Sometimes the reasons have nothing to do with how we now typically understand transgender identity. In 1776, a person formerly known as Jemima Wilkinson, from a prominent Rhode Island Quaker merchant family, became seriously ill during a typhoid epidemic. To the astonishment of friends and family who had gathered around Wilkinson's deathbed, the comatose body suddenly became conscious, announced that Wilkinson had died and gone to heaven, and that it was now the corporeal vessel of an ungendered celestial entity known as the Comforter, or Publick Universal Friend. The Friend, who never wavered in their supernatural identity claims, thereafter asked to be addressed by the universal masculine pronoun *he* rather than the specifically feminine *she,* adopted a uniquely androgynous manner of dress, refused typically female kinship roles, rejected marriage, and set out on a decades-long ministry to proclaim the coming Kingdom of God on Earth, where gender and racial distinctions would be abolished, just as they were in heaven. In the 1790s, on the shores of Keuka Lake in Upstate New York, the Friend's followers eventually built a separatist religious community they named Jerusalem. The community's buildings, whose architecture reflected the celibate and communal lifestyle of its adherents (and thus their atypical ideas about gender and sexuality), are still extant, and many are registered historic sites in Yates County, New York. The "Jemima Wilkinson House" listing on the National Register of Historic Places uses feminine pronouns for the Friend, erasing the actual, historically existing manner in which he understood himself and was accepted by his community of believers.[12]

It would be remiss to interpret the perception of cross-dressing by others as an expression of transgender identification by the person thus dressed. Deborah Sampson, for example, born 17 December 1760 in Plympton, Plymouth County, Massachusetts, assumed the identity of Robert Shurtleff to enlist in the Continental Army, Fourth Massachusetts Regiment. She participated in combat and was wounded in battle, but treated her wound herself to keep her anatomy a secret, resulting in life-long disability. After the war, she resumed life as a woman, married, mothered children, lectured publicly on her years passing as a man, and eventually received a government pension as a veteran of the Revolutionary War. While she certainly engaged in transgender *practices* during one period of her life in order to participate in activities denied to women, there is little evidence she expressed a transgender *identity*. That she cross-dressed only temporarily, and did not ultimately challenge the stability of gender categorization, goes a long way toward explaining how Sampson could be celebrated as a heroine in her own day and remembered positively in the present.[13] At the same time, the need to maintain her temporary presentation as a man in order to work as a soldier cost her the full use of one leg, while the discovery of her female anatomy jeopardized her eligibility for a pension because women were excluded from military service. In other words, Sampson paid a price for crossing the gender binary, whether or not she identified as transgender.

Sampson's story contrasts that of Albert Cashier, an Irish immigrant given the name Jennie Hodgers at birth, who saw combat in the Civil War as a member of the 95th Illinois Infantry. Cashier had been sent out by his impoverished parents to work as a boy from an early age. Masculinity seems to have suited him. He changed his name and continued living as a man upon arrival in the United States in 1862. After being honorably discharged at the end of the war, Cashier went on living as a man without incident in the small town of Saunemin, Illinois, where he worked as a farmhand and jack-of-all-trades. In 1910, Cashier's employer accidently hit him with a car, badly breaking his leg, whereupon the employer arranged for Cashier's admission to the Soldiers' and Sailors' Home in Quincy, Illinois. By now an old man, Cashier developed dementia and needed to be moved to the Watertown State Hospital, where his biological sex was discovered.[14] No longer able to assert his sense of being a man, the staff dressed Cashier in women's clothes and housed him in the women's ward. The federal government attempted to revoke his military pension, claiming fraud, until Cashier's former infantry comrades rallied on his behalf and testified about his commendable service. When he died in 1915, Cashier was buried back in Saunemin, under his male name and military rank. Although Cashier has been characterized as a woman who went to war—and the name on his gravestone subsequently changed by well-intentioned but misguided feminist historians—his persistent presentation as a man both before and after his military service suggests that it would be more accurate to characterize Cashier as a transgender man. The persistence of his masculine presentation, his quiet insistence on it as a daily reality, is precisely what enabled the government to accuse him of fraud, of being someone other than he claimed to be.[15] At a time when transgender people were only briefly allowed to serve openly in the U.S. military, after their ability to serve was revoked by the Trump administration's 2019 ban, stories of long-gone transgender veterans like Cashier attest to the long historical persistence of seemingly quite contemporary transgender social issues.[16]

Cashier's story illustrates as well the ongoing importance for transgender history of such built environments as cemeteries, care facilities, mental hospitals, and prisons, which are often sex-segregated, or sex-specific. These physical institutions where practices of nonconsensual gender ascription play themselves out can survive for decades or even centuries, compelling people with historically different forms of identity and embodiment in the present to navigate spatially anachronistic institutional forms. At the same time, it must be noted that sex-segregated institutions always faced challenges regarding people with discordant expressions of sex/gender. As early as 1799, for example, a person named Samuel (a.k.a. Sarah) Johnson "who had accustomed herself to wear men's cloaths for several years" was discovered to be female after being arrested for housebreaking in Allegheny County, Pennsylvania, and sentenced to three years in Philadelphia's Walnut Street Prison—the first modern penitentiary. Johnson was incarcerated with women, but was allowed to continue dressing as a man.[17]

With the exception of the 1692 anti-cross-dressing law in Massachusetts Bay Colony, the law took little note of people who crossed the gender binary until the middle of the nineteenth century. Starting in the 1840s, a string of cities passed ordinances that forbade anyone from appearing in public "in a dress not belonging to his or her sex."[18] These cities included St. Louis (1843); Columbus, Ohio (1848); Chicago (1851); Wilmington, Delaware (1856); Springfield, Illinois (1856); Newark, New Jersey (1858); and Kansas City, Missouri (1860).[19] These cities were all undergoing rapid economic and social transformation due to industrialization and the construction of new high-speed transportation infrastructure such as railroads, canals, and the new national highway, and were experiencing a great influx of heterogeneous new residents with few if any ties to the places they now found themselves living. Their anti-cross-dressing laws need to be understood as part of a broader context characterized by a preoccupation with immigration, class formation, racial and ethnic identity, and voting rights—they were part of a more extensive project to sort, classify, and rank masses of people in an effort to grant or deny privilege or citizenship based on bodily characteristics and ancestry. They played a particularly important role in determining patterns of urban spatialization—designating some parts of the city appropriate for some people and activities, and other parts of the city off limits. Through criminalization, they functioned to confine public gender variance to "red light" or "tenderloin" districts that ghettoized and criminalized certain sexual behaviors or forms of gender expression, while constructing the rest of public space as compulsorily gender-normative. Transgender history is thus intimately related to the historical development of urban geography. The rise of North American cities introduced new means of spatial regulation of gender-diverse lives, as did the proliferation of institutions organized according to the principle of sex segregation.

The life of Joseph Lobdell, christened Lucy Ann at birth, ended in 1912, at age eighty-three, in the Willard Asylum for the Chronic Insane in Ovid, New York.[20] Born in 1829 on the outskirts of Albany, New York, and raised around Long Eddy in the Delaware River Valley, Lobdell rebelled against feminine expectations from an early age. Lobdell won fame as an excellent hunter and marksman, and published an autobiography that doubled as an impassioned feminist denunciation of inequality between the sexes. He changed name and gender presentation in his mid-twenties, lived in various locations on the western fringes of white settlement in Minnesota and western New York, and entered into a marriage—a decades-long romantic, cohabiting relationship whose union was presided over by a justice of the peace—with Marie Louise Perry, who called Joseph her husband and herself his wife. Prone to episodes of mania by middle age, Lobdell's siblings had him declared legally insane, told Perry that he had died, and locked him away for the rest of his long life under his former name and gender.[21] A psychiatrist's report on Lobdell's case, which emphasizes his physical sex rather than his gender identity—he told his doctor "I am a man in all that the name implies"—is among the earliest uses in the U.S. medical literature of the term *lesbian,* and exemplifies a growing forensic interest in gender variance.[22]

Lobdell's story represents two important trends in nineteenth-century U.S. transgender history: the development of new medical and scientific ideas that increasingly reframed transgender behavior as illness (discussed immediately below), and a relationship between gender nonnormativity and westward migration (discussed further below). During the late nineteenth century, the fledgling life sciences vastly expanded knowledge about basic biological processes, and medicine began to gain unprecedented social power. Some transgender people found ways of working within this emerging biomedical nexus, such as the early radiologist Alan Lucille Hart, a Stanford-educated doctor who began life with the name Alberta Lucille Hart. Hart used the eugenic argument that "inverts" such as himself should not be allowed to reproduce, and thereby was given a hysterectomy, making him the first known person in the United States to request a surgical procedure for the purpose of expressing his gender identity differently (figure 4.1).[23]

Typically, this new medicolegal configuration of power and knowledge was harnessed to the task of shoring up legal distinctions between people in order to maintain hierarchies between races and sexes. It enabled arguments that blacks were biologically inferior to whites, and women inferior to men.[24] People with transgender feelings increasingly became targets of medical intervention precisely because they represented problems of biopsychosocial classification, as well as opportunities for demonstrating the power of medicolegal and social-scientific knowledge. Johns Hopkins University in Baltimore played a central role in the development of these new conceptual frameworks starting in the nineteenth century. By the early twentieth century, its Brady Urological Clinic, under the direction of Hugh Hampton Young, became closely linked to the development of genital reconstructive surgeries, and it played a pioneering role in the development of endocrinology.[25] Working there in the 1950s, Lawson Wilkins and his student John Money developed the modern treatment protocols for medically managing intersex conditions. In later decades, as an extension of Money's earlier work on intersex, Johns Hopkins became home to the first clinical surgical sex-reassignment program in the United States, in 1966.[26]

As discussed above, transgender expression significantly predates its medicalization, and as Lobdell's case makes clear, people who expressed their gender differently sometimes wound up on the margins of settler culture, both socially and geographically. Peter Boag has noted, in his history of gender variance in areas opened to settlement in North America from the 1850s forward, that "cross-dressers were not simply ubiquitous, but were very much part of daily life on the frontier and in the West."[27] The relative anonymity and transience that characterized mining camps, lumber towns, and new "instant cities" such as Denver and San Francisco proved fertile ground for people whose gender iden-

Figure 4.1. The Selling Building, Portland, Oregon, ca. 1907–18. The medical office of Dr. J. Allen Gilbert was in this building. Dr. Gilbert was Dr. Alan Hart's physician during his transition to male. Postcard courtesy of Megan E. Springate.

tity or expression made geographical movement seem necessary or desirable (and, not surprisingly, both Denver and San Francisco were places that instituted anti-cross-dressing laws in the mid-nineteenth century). Gender ambiguity was so prevalent during the California Gold Rush that one of the most popular souvenirs was a daguerreotype purporting to be of a "girl miner" dressed in male attire; that the androgynous figure later turned out be a long-haired young man named John Colton only highlights the extent to which gender ambiguity was a common feature in the settlement of the West.[28]

Moreover, the post–Civil War years witnessed a marked upsurge in cross-dressing within many forms of popular entertainment, with historians of the theater noting that cross-dressing stage performances were first popularized by the so-called wench roles in blackface minstrelsy. Cross-dressing, particularly female-to-male cross-dressing, was also quite common in early cinema. Until the 1920s, theatrical and cinematic cross-dressing was typically considered "respectable" entertainment, and was not associated with social perceptions of "deviance." Consequently, the spectacle of cross-dressed bodies was a familiar sight on stage and screen, in theaters, vaudeville houses, and cinemas throughout the late nineteenth and early twentieth centuries. While most of the entertainers working in this field did not identify as some version of transgender, these forms of entertainment nevertheless provided relatively safe havens and pockets of greater freedom for individuals who did.[29]

Gender variance played a different role in the movements of communities of color into the United States than it did for whites. Asian immigrants to the West Coast faced social conditions that cast them all as gender variant vis-à-vis white gender norms.[30] The skewed sex ratios among Chinese immigrants—the female percentage of the total Chinese population in the United States ranged between 3 and 7 percent in the second half of the nineteenth century—skewed white perceptions of Chinese gender roles and sexuality.[31] White settlers in the West repeatedly commented on their inability to distinguish Chinese men and women, and disparagingly feminized Chinese men for wearing their hair in long queues and for performing labor, such as laundering, that was considered "women's work" when done by whites.[32] The celebrated Western writer Ambrose Bierce drew on these sociological conditions in his short story, "The Haunted Valley," which appeared in *Overland* magazine in 1871. Bierce described an interracial love triangle transpiring in the Sierra Nevada mother-lode country between two white men and a Chinese person named Ah Wee, who is initially understood to be a man (thus imparting homoerotic overtones to the story), but is later revealed to be a woman who works as a man.[33]

Scholars of African-American slavery have noted that their enslavement involved a stripping away of many elements of gender—not just of the cultural dimensions of what it meant to be a man or a woman in particular African societies, but a brute reduction of enslaved people to unsexed laboring bodies.[34] Those escaping slavery sometimes used cross-gender disguise to evade capture, as was the case with Ann Maria Weems, who posed as a male carriage driver on her flight north from Maryland to Canada in 1855.[35] Blacks often had to assert their belonging in gender categories in ways that whites took for granted, as Sojourner Truth's famous "Ain't I a Woman?" speech to her white abolitionist sisters makes clear.[36]

The life of Johanna or John O., which is known only through the account in Magnus Hirschfeld's 1913 casebook *The Transvestites*, exemplifies the relationship between gender variance and white settler migration. Assigned male at birth in the Tyrolean Alps in 1862, Johanna had grown up feeling girl-identified. When it became evident that her family would not support her plans to live as a woman, she did so anyway—running away as a teenager to Switzerland, and later France, before immigrating to the United States in 1882. Often it was the discovery of her biological sex, or on-the-job sexual harassment that compelled Johanna to move and to change jobs. She worked as an embroiderer in a Jersey City clothing factory, as a milkmaid on a dairy farm in upstate New York, and as a camp cook on a cattle trail in Montana. In 1885, she settled in San Francisco, where she supported herself as an itinerant bookseller and kept house for a group of sex-workers in the city's red-light district. Increasingly, her life became confined to those social spaces reserved for activities deemed deviant and illicit that are so often erased from history, memory, and from the physical fabric of our living places. As she aged, Johanna felt it became more difficult to be seen as a woman by others than when she was young and considered herself pretty. Fearing arrest, she reverted to dressing as a man in public, while continuing to dress as she pleased at home, without ever changing her persistent feelings of being a woman.[37]

Johanna's fear of arrest as a transgender person was not unfounded, given the manner in which Tenderloin districts functioned.[38] Because of the high degree of employment and housing discrimination faced by people who expressed their gender in nonnormative ways, these urban districts, which functioned for most people as destinations for late-night vice tourism, functioned for many transgender people as residential ghettos; confined to such districts, transgender people faced higher levels of surveillance and potential exposure to extrajudicial violence or exploitation from the corrupt police officers, who typically ran Tenderloin vice economies for their own profit, than did the population at large. Most late nineteenth- and early to mid-twentieth-century U.S. cities harbored such districts, with some of the more well-known being the Tenderloin neighborhoods of New York City and San Francisco, New Orleans' Storyville and French Quarter, Seattle's Pioneer Square, Philadelphia's Northern Liberties, Boston's Combat Zone, and the neighborhoods in Los Angeles's historic downtown core around Pershing Square, Bunker Hill, and the old Main Street Theater District.[39]

A number of building types in such red-light and nightlife districts are historically associated with transgender and gender-variant people, including bars, brothels, theaters, dance halls, nightclubs, and single-room-occupancy (SRO) hotels. Many SRO hotels in red-light districts catered primarily to transgender clientele, such as the El Rosa and Hyland Hotels in San Francisco.[40] Lucy Hicks Anderson, an African American transgender woman from Oxnard, California, was a Prohibition-era bootlegger who ran a boarding house and brothel on the city's waterfront.[41] Many clubs—such as the Garden of Allah in the basement of the Arlington Hotel in Seattle's Pioneer Square, the Club My-O-My in New Orleans, or Finocchio's in San Francisco's North Beach neighborhood—developed long-standing reputations for hosting "drag" entertainment.[42] Drag, distinct from the forms of gender impersonation that enjoyed mainstream acceptance, connoted cross-dressing with a campy or ironic homosexual aesthetic. Urban homosexual *demimonde* clubs featuring risqué forms of drag certainly existed in New York City by the late nineteenth century, and historian George Chauncey suggests that "threads of continuity" might, with care, be traced between such venues and the "molly houses" of seventeenth-, eighteenth- and nineteenth-century London. This gay subculture, in which cross-dressing slyly signified homosexual desire through the transposition of gender signifiers, first came to greater public attention in the United States during the so-called Pansy Craze of the 1920s, through the scandalous publicity given to lesbian masculinity in Mae West's notorious play *The Captive*, and through the popularization of psychological and sexological theories of sexual inversion.[43] In subsequent decades, theatrical cross-gender dressing would become associated primarily with homosexual and transgender subcultures and subcultural venues, and would lose the sense of being a mainstream form of entertainment that it had long enjoyed.

In *Autobiography of an Androgyne* (1919), Ralph Werther, who also used the names Jenny June and Earl Lind, described one such "resort for sex perverts," colloquially known as Paresis Hall, on Fourth Avenue a few blocks south of 14th Street in New York City, which exemplifies an entire genre of such establishments.[44] According to Werther, "In front was a modest bar-room; behind, a small beer-garden. The two floors above were divided into small rooms for rent," and drag performances were frequently staged in the evenings. In 1895, Werther was invited by other patrons of the Hall to join "a little club" called the Cercle Hermaphroditos, which rented one of the upstairs rooms. It admitted "only extreme types, such as like to doll themselves up in feminine finery," and its purpose was "to unite for defense against the world's bitter persecution."[45] The Cercle Hermaphroditos is the first known quasi-formal association of people we might now well consider to be transgender. Its rationale for existing seems to have drawn not just on a desire for sociability, but also on nascent notions of social justice for gender-variant people. The formation of the club at Paresis Hall attests to the importance of such subcultural spaces for members of marginalized communities, where the cultivation of social bonds can plant seeds that may ripen into political activism and social movements.

The second known quasi-political association of transgender people was the short-lived American Society for Equality in Dress, which began publishing the journal *Transvestia* in 1952.[46] It took root across the continent and a world away from the seedy urban environs of Werther's Paresis Hall, amid the decentralized, semisuburban sprawl of Los Angeles. Both the society and journal were spearheaded by Virginia Prince, née Arnold Lowman, one of the most influential and divisive figures in mid-twentieth-century transgender history. Prince, a secret cross-dresser since childhood who gradually started coming out to others in her late thirties, eventually took feminizing hormones and lived full time as a woman, but remained adamantly opposed to genital surgery; her views helped draw still-current distinctions between transsexuals, heterosexual transvestites, and homosexuals. She went on to found the first long-lasting organization for cross-dressers, notably the Foundation for Full Personality Expression (1962), which later became the Society for the Second Self (Tri-Ess).[47]

Prince was born in Los Angeles in 1912 and raised on the 100 block of South Hobart Avenue, in a fashionable upper-middle-class neighborhood near Beverly and Western Avenues, until age eight, at which time the family relocated to the 800 block of Victoria Avenue in the even more fashionable Hancock Park neighborhood. Her father was a prominent orthopedic surgeon, and her mother a successful businesswoman with a talent in real estate. Prince herself went on to earn a Ph.D. in pharmacology from the University of California, San Francisco (UCSF) by 1939, specializing in the development of new medicines. She later worked for several different pharmaceutical companies, which helped support her unpaid transgender activism in later decades.[48]

The UCSF campus on Parnassus Heights, particularly the Langley Porter Psychiatric Clinic located there, is an important site in the history of transgender medicalization and community formation.[49] It was there, on a postdoctoral fellowship in the early 1940s, that Prince met Louise Lawrence, a San Francisco resident who, like her, was a life-long cross-dresser born in 1912. Lawrence had started corresponding with other transvestites whom she had contacted through personal ads in various magazines as early as 1937, and her contact list of more than fifty individuals became the first subscription list for Prince's *Transvestia* magazine. Unlike the still-closeted Prince, however, Lawrence had started living full time as a woman by 1942, and spoke regularly at Langley Porter to help educate medical professionals about people like herself.[50] Her longtime residence would become an informal way station for transsexual women seeking medical services for gender-transition in the 1950s and 1960s.[51] The clinic was directed by Dr. Karl Bowman, a former president of the American Medical Association, who had written extensively on homosexuals as well as individuals we would now call transgender or transsexual. Through UCSF, people like Prince and Lawrence came in contact with sexuality researchers such as Alfred Kinsey (who ran the famous Institute that bore his name at the University of Indiana in Bloomington) and Harry Benjamin (a German American doctor with private practices in New York and San Francisco), who in turn began to study, treat, and write about people in Prince's and Lawrence's networks.[52]

Transgender topics burst into spectacular mass media visibility in 1952 through the unprecedented coverage given to Christine Jorgensen, the first truly global transgender celebrity. Jorgensen, of Danish-American heritage, had been born in 1926 to working-class parents in the Bronx.[53] She had had transgender feelings since early childhood, and by the late 1940s had educated herself about the possibilities for using hormones and surgery to change her body. The body-shaping effects of the so-called sex hormones had been discovered only in the 1910s, synthesized only in the 1920s, and became widely commercially available only in the 1930s and 1940s.[54] Genital plastic surgeries had actually been practiced in the United States since the 1840s, but these procedures were carried out on people born with anomalous genitals, and were not available to people with apparently normal genitals who wished them to resemble the genitals usually associated with another social gender. The concept of "transsexualism" (though not the term itself) began to take shape in Europe as early as 1906—that is, that by medically treating individuals to transform their bodies through surgery, and later hormones, such individuals could be granted a new legal and social identity that matched their innate sense of self. Such practices were well established at Magnus Hirschfeld's Institute for Sexual Science by the early 1930s, but these ideas did not take root in the United States until after World War II—largely in response to the Jorgensen story.[55] Although Christine Jorgensen was by no means the first transsexual, she became the person who popularized the concept for mass audiences after she set sail for her ancestral Scandinavia, and news of her surgical and hormonal transformation there leaked to the press.

Jorgensen did not imagine that media coverage of her genital conversion surgeries in Copenhagen would make headlines around the world, but it did. Through her, the idea of medical "sex-change" became part of common knowledge for anyone old enough to read a newspaper in the 1950s. Jorgensen, who had aspired to be a photographer and filmmaker before becoming a celebrity, capitalized on her newfound fame by developing a successful night club act and traveling the globe, staying in the media spotlight for more than a decade and earning a comfortable living. She bought a retirement home for her parents, with whom she continued to live until their deaths, in Massapequa, Long Island, New York; she later lived at various locations in Southern California, including the Chateau Marmont Hotel in Los Angeles, the home of friends in Riverside, and various apartments in Hollywood; for many years, she owned a home in Laguna Niguel.[56]

The world in which Jorgensen achieved her fame was changing rapidly with regard to transgender issues. For many white people, the 1950s scene was still characterized by places like Casa Susanna, a secretive resort in New York's Catskill Mountains for closeted heterosexual cross-dressers in the mold of Virginia Prince.[57] Other transsexual women, many of them women of color, began to live much more publicly in (and as) what Africana and gender studies scholar C. Riley Snorton has punningly called "Jorgensen's shadows."[58] These women made tabloid headlines of their own, including Delisa Newton, an African American Chicago cabaret singer, and belly dancer Bessie Mukaw, who billed herself as "the first Eskimo sex-change."[59] Of all those who followed in Jorgensen's wake, only Charlotte McLeod, another white transsexual woman who came to public attention within months of Jorgensen's sudden celebrity, initially came close to matching her level of fame, but McLeod's star faded quickly.[60]

Jorgensen' success also brought attention to a longstanding transgender presence in vernacular entertainment venues such as carnival sideshows, circuses, and strip clubs, as well as in traveling song-and-dance revues.[61] Comic entertainer Rae (or Ray) Bourbon moved for decades in such milieus. A person of apparently mixed Anglo-Latino heritage from south Texas, sometimes claiming Rámon Ícarez as a birth name, Bourbon had a fascinating career in cross-dressed silent film acting, vaudeville, and nightclub performance that spanned the Pansy Craze of the 1920s, as well as the post-Jorgensen fascination with transgender representation in the 1950s. Bourbon claimed (probably spuriously) to have had genital conversion surgery, and humorously recounted these supposed experiences on comedy albums such as *Let Me Tell You about My Operation*.[62]

Urban inner-city neighborhoods that had long provided homes for more marginalized, racially and ethnically mixed transgender communities began showing signs of social unrest by the later 1950s. In 1959, patrons at Cooper Do-Nut, a late-night hangout in downtown Los Angeles popular with street queens, gays, and hustlers, resisted arrest en masse when police made a "street sweep" to round up people accused of loitering, vagrancy, or public lewdness.[63] In Philadelphia in 1964, patrons of Dewey's lunch counter conducted a successful informational picket and sit-in protest, resulting in three arrests that challenged the management's discrimination against "youth in unconventional attire."[64] And, in 1966, patrons at Compton's Cafeteria, in San Francisco's Tenderloin, rioted against a police raid aimed at arresting the transgender women and street queens who frequented that establishment (figure 4.2). They smashed windows, demolished a police car, set the corner newsstand on fire, and fought with police up and down the surrounding streets.[65] The disturbance there preceded by three years the much larger and better-known resistance to police oppression of gay and transgender people that took place at New York's Stonewall Inn in 1969.[66]

In the aftermath of the Compton's riot, San Francisco's Tenderloin became a national hub for early transgender activism and social services—the result of a "perfect storm" of anti-trans, anti-gay, and racist policing practices that galvanized resistance, coupled with a generally permissive social environment, along with long traditions of cultural bohemianism and radical politics, that created opportunities for structural change based on social mobilization. The city's many SRO

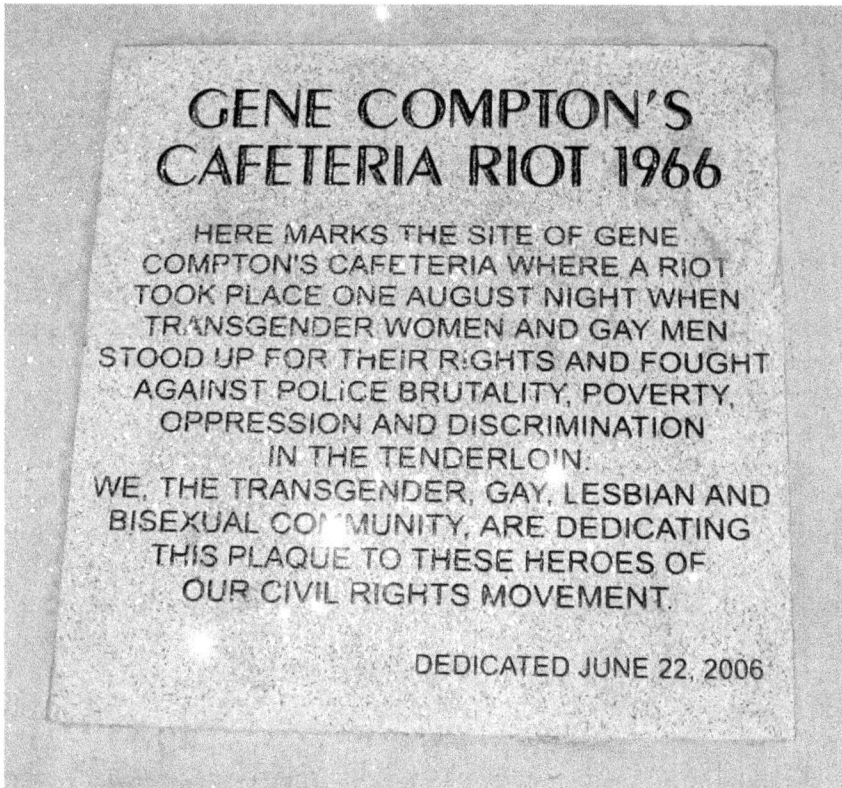

GENE COMPTON'S
CAFETERIA RIOT 1966

HERE MARKS THE SITE OF GENE
COMPTON'S CAFETERIA WHERE A RIOT
TOOK PLACE ONE AUGUST NIGHT WHEN
TRANSGENDER WOMEN AND GAY MEN
STOOD UP FOR THEIR RIGHTS AND FOUGHT
AGAINST POLICE BRUTALITY, POVERTY,
OPPRESSION AND DISCRIMINATION
IN THE TENDERLOIN.
WE, THE TRANSGENDER, GAY, LESBIAN AND
BISEXUAL COMMUNITY, ARE DEDICATING
THIS PLAQUE TO THESE HEROES OF
OUR CIVIL RIGHTS MOVEMENT.

DEDICATED JUNE 22, 2006

Figure 4.2. Historical marker commemorating the fortieth anniversary of the Compton's Cafeteria Riot, San Francisco, California. Photo by Gaylesf (public domain; https://commons.wikimedia.org/wiki/File:Plaque_commemorating_Comptonpercent27s_Cafeteria_riot.jpg).

hotels were home to hundreds of transgender people. Glide Memorial Methodist Church, a neighborhood institution, hosted the first gay and transgender street youth organization, Vanguard, starting in 1965, as well as the first transsexual support group, Conversion Our Goal, starting in 1967.[67] The Tenderloin is adjacent to the Polk Street neighborhood, where a unit of the San Francisco Department of Public Health, called the Center for Special Problems, offered some of the nation's first social services for transgender people, as well as to fashionable Union Square, where Harry Benjamin sometimes saw transsexual patients in the suite of rooms at the Sir Francis Drake Hotel where he lived during his annual summer visits. The Tenderloin was also home to the National Transsexual Counseling Unit (NTCU), one of many efforts funded by the wealthy female-to-male transsexual Reed Erickson.[68] The Erickson

Educational Foundation (EEF), based in Baton Rouge, Louisiana, provided crucial support not only for the NTCU, but also for publication of *The Transsexual Phenomenon,* Harry Benjamin's paradigm-defining book on medical treatment protocols for transgender people. The EEF also supported the first wave of clinical "sex-change" programs at Johns Hopkins, Stanford, UCLA, University of Minnesota, and elsewhere.[69]

The pace of transgender social-change activism quickened in the later 1960s. In Los Angeles, Sir Lady Java, an African American trans-feminine performer at the Redd Foxx nightclub, helped overturn police rules that criminalized cross-dressing, and Angela Douglas founded TAO, the Transsexual Activist Organization.[70] In New York City, the support groups Transsexuals and Transvestites (TAT) and Labyrinth, the first group dedicated to transsexual men, formed along with STAR, the Street Transvestite Action Revolutionaries. STAR House, founded by Sylvia Rivera and Marsha P. Johnson, provided free shelter, food, and peer support for marginalized transgender street youth of color.[71] Another New York group, the Queens Liberation Front, published *Drag* magazine, which reported on political happenings all across the country.[72] In Philadelphia, the Radical Queens collective worked to integrate transgender concerns into multi-issue social-change activism, often in collaboration with the radical lesbian collective DYKETACTICS. Fantasia Fair, an annual gathering on Cape Cod that catered to the sort of people who once would have attended Casa Susanna, began in 1975, and is now the longest-running transgender event in the world.[73] It was organized by Ari Kane and Betty Lind, both of Boston's Cherrystone Club, a transgender social club.

By the end of the 1970s, however, many of the advances of recent years had been undone. Setbacks included federal cutbacks to social-service funding as well as new ideas in gay and feminist communities that began to characterize transgender people as less liberated than themselves, or even as dangerous or mentally ill people trying to infiltrate progressive movements. The 1980s were an especially difficult decade for transgender people, who were largely excluded from other social justice activism, even as they faced new levels of pathologization. In 1980, "Gender Identity Disorder" appeared for the first time in the DSM-IV, the fourth revised version of the *Diagnostic and Statistical Manual of Mental Disorders,* published by the American Psychiatric Association. That same year a new organization was formed for medical and psychotherapeutic service providers who worked with transgender populations, the Harry Benjamin International Gender Dysphoria Association (later renamed the World Professional Association for Transgender Health). Perversely, this official pathologization did not make medical treatment more accessible for transgender people who needed it. Health insurance providers classified sex-reassignment procedures as "experimental" or "cosmetic" and thus ineligible for coverage. Most counseling for transgender people seeking medical services was provided from within the community itself, notably the organization J2PC, named for its founders Jude Patton and Joanna Clark (now Sister Mary Elizabeth), in San Juan Capistrano, California.

One of the most significant developments of the 1980s was the formation of a national network of female-to-male transsexuals, primarily through the efforts of Louis G. Sullivan. Born and raised in the Milwaukee suburb of Wauwatosa, Wisconsin, Sullivan had transgender feelings from a very early age, which confused him because he was also attracted to men. Sullivan eventually realized that he was a gay transsexual man—that is, attracted to men as a man, in spite of starting life with a female anatomy. He not only helped medical professionals understand that people like him existed, but also worked to educate and bring together all sorts of masculine-identified people assigned female at birth through publications such as *Information for the Female-to-Male Cross-Dresser and Transsexual* and the *FTM Newsletter*. Sullivan, who moved to San Francisco in the later 1970s, was sexually active there in the gay men's community at a time when HIV was already circulating but before the AIDS epidemic had become visible. Like many other gay men of his generation, Sullivan became infected, and eventually died of AIDS-related illnesses in 1991.[74]

The AIDS epidemic transformed transgender politics in the 1990s. Transgender women of color who shared needles for hormones and engaged in survival sex-work were among the most vulnerable to, and at risk for, infection.[75] Transgender people became involved in AIDS-activist organizations such as ACT UP (AIDS Coalition to Unleash Power) in New York and Queer Nation in San Francisco, and with other militant protest groups such as the Lesbian Avengers.[76] The word "transgender" itself (rather than some other term for gender variance) was popularized around this time through the publication of Leslie Feinberg's 1992 pamphlet *Transgender Liberation: A Movement Whose Time Has Come*.[77] Groups such as Transgender Nation in San Francisco and Transexual Menace in New York brought a new style of confrontational, in-your-face activism to transgender politics that drew on queer militancy's punk sensibility. The Women's Building in San Francisco hosted many transgender-related events in the 1990s, including, ironically, the first-ever International FTM (Female-to-Male) Conference in 1995.[78] It was also during this time that the Tom Waddell Health Center, a branch of the San Francisco Department of Public Health, began offering "Tranny Tuesday," the first low-cost health clinic run specifically for transgender clients. It adopted a harm-reduction rather than trans-pathologization model of healthcare provision, providing services that transgender people needed to live self-directed lives rather than diagnosing them with gender identity disorder and medically managing their transitions.[79]

Two flashpoints brought heightened awareness of transgender activism during these years. In 1991, organizers of the Michigan Womyn's Music Festival expelled transsexual attendee Nancy Burkholder from the lesbian-run women-only event because they did not consider transsexuals to be women. Burkholder's expulsion inspired the creation of Camp Trans, which gathered each year across the road from the music festival to engage in dialog with attendees and help change transphobic attitudes in some quarters of the lesbian and feminist communities.[80] In 1993, the murder of Brandon Teena, a transgender youth who lived and died in rural Nebraska, inspired vigils outside the courthouse where his killers were eventually convicted.[81] In Houston, the country's first openly transgender judge, Phyllis Randolph Frye, hosted the International Conference on Transgender Law and Employment Policy for several years beginning in 1992, which laid the foundation for a new generation of legal activism in the decades ahead.[82] Houston's Transgender Foundation of America, founded in 1998, hosted the Transgender Archive, the only publicly oriented walk-in research collection in the United States dedicated to transgender history, until losing its lease in the rapidly gentrifying Montrose neighborhood in 2015.[83]

By the later 1990s, several U.S. cities had passed ordinances protecting transgender people from discrimination, which—in a more positive manner than the anti-cross-dressing laws dating from the 1840s—influenced where transgender people might choose to live and work. Fledgling transgender lobbying groups such as GenderPAC were finally beginning to draw funding from major philanthropic foundations. In the wake of the 9/11 attacks in 2001, issues that had long concerned transgender people took on a new sense of urgency, particularly those that involved obtaining state-issued identification documents that accurately reflected a person's current gender. Heightened levels of security and surveillance, tightened border controls, and fears of terrorism deepened existing difficulties for transgender people who could have difficulty proving to others that they really were who they said they were. Civil liberty concerns about the expansion of the national security apparatus after 9/11 led military intelligence analyst Chelsea (née Bradley) Manning to divulge classified documents detailing U.S. spying—the so-called Wiki-Leaks case—resulting in the most high-profile legal proceedings against a transgender person in U.S. history, and in Manning's eventual conviction and incarceration at Fort Leavenworth, Kansas.[84] The first professionally staffed transgender advocacy organizations took shape during these tense early years of the War on Terror and the wars in Afghanistan and Iraq, including the Transgender Law Center in San Francisco and the Sylvia Rivera Law Project in New York (both founded in 2002), the National Center for Transgender Equality in Washington, D.C. (founded in 2003), the TGI (Transgender, Gender-Variant, and Intersex) Justice Project in San Francisco (founded in 2004), and, Global Action for Trans* Equality (GATE) in New York in 2009.[85]

In 2007, openly gay Democratic congressman Barney Frank landed on the wrong side of history when he cut transgender protections from the proposed federal Employment Non-Discrimination Act in an ultimately futile attempt to enact that landmark piece of legislation. That was the last time, as of this writing, that transgender issues were sacrificed to a larger gay and lesbian liberal agenda. Under the Obama administration, the transgender movement became thoroughly mainstreamed, making advances unthinkable only a few short years before. Particularly after the Supreme Court ruled conclusively on the constitutionality of same-sex marriage in 2015, transgender issues came to be considered a cutting edge of the civil rights agenda, and as such have been a hot button topic in the culture wars of the Trump presidency. The political backlash against transgender people has been particularly obvious in the wave of "bathroom bills" that have swept the country since the revocation of the Houston Equal Rights Ordinance in 2015, and the passage of HB2 in North Carolina in 2016. Public toilets, locker rooms, and other sex-segregated built environments, particularly when they are located in public schools that receive federal funds, have become the latest architectural sites of importance in the transgender history of the United States.

In spite of heightened levels of anti-transgender sentiment and policy since 2016, transgender people and topics remain ubiquitous in the mass media. The appearance of transgender actress Laverne Cox on the cover of *Time* magazine in 2014 and the wall-to-wall tabloid and reality-television coverage of Caitlyn Jenner in 2015 were breakthrough moments comparable in scale to Christine Jorgensen's celebrity in the 1950s. The critically acclaimed show *Orange Is the New Black* features positive representation of transgender people, while *Transparent* employed numerous transgender people as writers, directors, producers, crew members, and on-camera talent. *Sense8,* directed by the transgender sisters Lana and Lilly Wachowski, achieved an unprecedented level of creative control for a big-budget project that expresses transgender sensibilities, but it is only one of many recent media productions that allow for greater transgender self-representation; other notable works include *Tangerine,* about two trans women in Los Angeles, and *Drunktown's Finest,* the debut feature of Sydney Freeland, the first Native American transgender film director to gain a mainstream movie distribution deal.

Perhaps even more significant than transgender representation in commercial media is the explosion of transgender content in user-generated social media. The Internet, which has reconfigured the relationship between presence, identity, embodiment, community, and sociality relative to the offline world, is now one of the most significant places where transgender history happens. Much of the transgender content available online is produced and circulated by transgender youth such as Leelah Alcorn, a transgender teen who committed suicide in 2014 after posting her suicide note on Tumblr. Such nonprofessional media production can play an important role in providing emotional support and creative outlets, as well as "how to" information for individuals seeking gender transition.

Although the most conservative estimates of transgender adults in the United States place their numbers around one and a half million people, the same research methodologies for arriving at those numbers place the number of transgender-identified youth somewhere between four and ten million.[86] Clearly, we are in the midst of a sea change in how our culture understands gender and accepts gender variance. That this history is unfolding all across the country, in structures as banal as a public toilet and in spaces as visible as antifascist street fighting, attests to the truly fundamental level of change our society is undergoing. It is not just that the long-standing presence of transgender people in our national life is finally becoming more visible; it is that gender itself is changing radically in ways we can now scarcely comprehend. Any contemporary representation, analysis, or memorialization of the past that seeks to be relevant to the present or near future will fail to the extent that it does not take this profound shift in the social understanding of gender into account.

Dr. Susan Stryker is a professor of gender and women's studies at the University of Arizona in Tucson.

Notes

1. Cristan Williams, "Transgender," *TSQ: Transgender Studies Quarterly* 1, no. 1–2 (2014): 232–34.
2. Susan Stryker, *Transgender History* (Emeryville, CA: Seal Press, 2008), 1.
3. There is an extensive literature on cross-cultural gender variance; some helpful starting places are Trystan Cotten, ed., *Transgender Migrations: The Bodies, Borders, and Politics of Transition* (New York: Routledge, 2011); Gilbert Herdt, ed., *Third Sex, Third Gender: Beyond Sexual Dimorphism in History and Culture* (Cambridge, MA: Zone Books, 1996); Toni Lester, ed., *Gender Nonconformity, Race, and Sexuality: Charting the Connections* (Madison: University of Wisconsin Press, 2002); DeWight R. Middleton, *Exotics and Erotics: Human Cultural and Sexual Diversity* (Long Grove, IL: Waveland Press, 2001); Serena Nanda, *Gender Diversity: Crosscultural Variations,* 2nd ed. (Long Grove, IL: Waveland Press, 2014); Evan B. Towle and Lynn M. Morgan, "Romancing the Transgender Native: Rethinking the Use of the 'Third Gender' Concept," *GLQ: A Journal of Lesbian and Gay Studies* 8, no. 4 (2002): 469–97; David Valentine, *Imagining Transgender: An Ethnography of a Category* (Durham, NC: Duke University Press, 2007).
4. *We've Been Around,* directed by Rhys Ernst (Los Angeles: Nonetheless Productions, 2016); available online at www.wevebeenaround.com.
5. See Will Roscoe, "Sexual and Gender Diversity in Native America and the Pacific Islands," this volume.
6. Primary documents in English translation are included in Jonathan Katz, *Gay American History: Lesbians and Gay Men in the U.S.A.* (New York: Thomas Y. Crowell, 1976), see 281–84 for Cabeza de Vaca, and 287 for Marquette.
7. Deborah A. Miranda, "Extermination of the *Joyas:* Gendercide in Spanish California," *GLQ: A Journal of Lesbian and Gay Studies* 16, no. 1–2 (2010): 253–84. Many missions in California and elsewhere are listed on the NRHP and/or designated NHLs. Specifically mentioned in the article are the Mission San Carlos Borromeo del Rio Carmelo (Carmel Mission), Mission San Antonio de Padua (Mission San Antonio), Mission Basilica San Diego de Alcala (Mission San Diego), Mission Santa Barbara, Mission San Jose, Mission San Francisco de Asis (Mission Dolores), Mission Santa Clara de Asis (Mission Santa Clara), and Mission Santa Ynez (Mission Santa Ines). The Carmel Mission, 3080 Rio Road, Carmel-by-the-Sea, California, was listed on the NRHP on 15 October 1966 and designated an NHL on 9 October 1960. Mission San Antonio de Padua, near Jolon, Monterey County, California, was listed on the NRHP on 26 April 1976 and is located along the Juan Bautista de Anza National Historic Trail (a unit of the NPS) established in 1990. Mission San Diego, 10818 San Diego Mission Road, San Diego, California, was listed on the NRHP and designated an NHL as the San Diego Mission Church on 15 April 1970. Mission Santa Barbara, 2201 Laguna Street, Santa Barbara, Cali-

fornia, was added to the NRHP on 15 October 1966 and designated an NHL on 9 October 1960. Mission San Jose, 43300 Mission Boulevard, Fremont, California, was listed on the NRHP on 14 July 1971. Mission San Francisco de Asis, 320 Dolores Street, San Francisco, California, was listed on the NRHP on 16 March 1972. Mission Santa Clara, 500 El Camino Real, Santa Clara, California, not listed; Mission Santa Ynez, 1760 Mission Drive, Solvang, California, was listed on the NRHP on 8 March 1999 and designated an NHL on 20 January 1999.

8. Drawing on this article, the following are examples of places that could include the recognition of native variance from European norms, and European responses to it, in interpretive materials: for Cabeza de Vaca, see Donald E. Sheppard, "Cabeza de Vaca: Journeys across North America 1528–36," http://www.floridahistory.com/cabeza.html; for Marquette, see Melinda Roberts, "Jacques Marquette and Louis Joliet," *Wisconsin Historical Markers* (blog), http://wisconsinhistoricalmarkers.blogspot.com/2013/04/jacques-marquette-and-louis-joliet.html; for California Missions, see Mission Tour, "El Camino Real," http://missiontour.org/wp/related/el-camino-real.html. Other indigenous and colonial locations include the area around Yuma, Arizona, along the Juan Bautista de Anza National Historic Trail, where on 7 December 1775 a member of the group described "effeminate men" among the Yuma; the Stones of Kapaemahu on Kuhio Beach, Waikiki, Hawai'i, which commemorate the arrival of the gender-variant mahu; Fort Caroline National Memorial, which commemorates the founding of Fort Caroline in 1564, an event that brought Europeans into contact with gender-variant Timucua Indians; and the Chief Plenty Coups (Alek-Chea-Ahoosh) Home, residence of Chief Plenty Coups who, in the late 1880s, told federal Indian Agents to leave the reservation after they tried to make the two-spirit *bote* dress in male clothing. The Juan Bautista de Anza National Historic Trail (a unit of the NPS) was created in 1990; Fort Caroline National Memorial was listed on the NRHP on 15 October 1966 and designated a National Memorial on 16 January 1953; the Chief Plenty Coups (Alek-Chea-Ahoosh) Home at 1 Pryor Road, Pryor, Montana, was added to the NRHP on 6 October 1970 and designated an NHL on 20 January 1999.

9. H. R. McIlwaine, ed., *Minutes of the Council and General Court of Colonial Virginia, 1622–1632, 1670–76* (Richmond, VA: Colonial Press/Everett Waddey, 1924), 194–95; the court convened twice yearly. For an insightful discussion of the Hall case, see Mary Beth Norton, *Founding Mothers and Fathers: Gendered Power and the Forming of American Society* (New York: Vintage, 1997), 183–202. Founded in 1609, Jamestown was the first permanent English settlement in what is now the United States. The Jamestown National Historic Site (an NPS unit) was listed on the NRHP on 15 October 1966.

10. Strawberry Banke was added to the NRHP on 20 June 1975.

11. All examples of seventeenth-century cross-dressing are taken from Elizabeth Reis, *Bodies in Doubt: An American History of Intersex* (Baltimore, MD: Johns Hopkins Press, 2009), 15.

12. Herbert Wisbey Jr., *Pioneer Prophetess: Jemima Wilkinson, the Publick Universal Friend* (Ithaca, NY: Cornell University Press, 2009); Paul B. Moyer, *The Public Universal Friend: Jemima Wilkinson and Religious Enthusiasm in Revolutionary America* (Ithaca, NY: Cornell University Press, 2015). The Jemima Wilkinson House in Jerusalem, New York, was added to the NRHP on 24 August 1994.

13. Alfred Fabian Young, *Masquerade: The Life and Times of Deborah Sampson, Continental Soldier* (New York: Alfred A. Knopf, 2004); Sheila Solomon Klass, *Soldier's Secret: The Story of Deborah Sampson* (New York: Henry Holt, 2009). The town of Sharon, Massachusetts, is home to the Deborah Sampson Gannett House on East Street, a Deborah Sampson Park, and a commemorative Deborah Sampson statue in front of the public library. The Plympton city flag incorporates Sampson as the Official Heroine of the Commonwealth of Massachusetts.

14. The Soldiers' and Sailors' Home (now the Illinois Veterans' Home) is at 1707 North Twelfth Street, Quincy, Illinois. Watertown State Hospital, now operating as the East Moline Correctional Center, is located at 100 Hillcrest Road, East Moline, Illinois.

15. In May 1863, Private Cashier was captured at the Siege of Vicksburg before escaping; see "Jennie Hodgers, aka Private Albert Cashier," National Park Service website, https://www.nps.gov/resources/story.htm?id=187. Vicksburg National Military Park (an NPS unit), located in Vicksburg, Mississippi, and Delta, Louisiana, was established 21 February 1899; it was added to the NRHP on 15 October 1966. Cashier's post–Civil War residence and grave are designated historical sites in Saunemin, Illinois. On the broader history of female-bodied people serving in the Civil War, see Elizabeth D. Leonard, *All the Daring of the Soldier: Women of the Civil War Armies* (New York: W. W. Norton & Co, 1999); and Larry G. Eggleston, *Women in the Civil War: Extraordinary Stories of Soldiers, Spies, Nurses, Doctors, Crusaders, and Others* (Jefferson, NC: McFarland, 2003). On how Cashier's gender and identity should be conceptualized, see Amy Benck, "Albert D. J. Cashier: Woman Warrior, Insane Civil War Veteran, or Transman?" *OutHistory.org*, http://outhistory.org/exhibits/show/tgi-bios/albert-cashier.

16. National Center for Transgender Equality, "Trump Administration Announces Beginning of Transgender Military Ban on April 12," https://transequality.org/press/releases/trump-administration-announces-beginning-of-transgender-military-ban-on-april-12.

17. Jen Manion, *Liberty's Prisoners: Carceral Culture in Early America* (Philadelphia: University of Pennsylvania Press, 2016), 164; Johnson's case is noted in the Walnut Street Prison Sentence Docket Book on 4 December 1799. The Walnut Street Prison was located on a lot on Walnut Street, bounded by

Locust and Sixth Streets, Philadelphia, Pennsylvania. The prison was razed following its closure in 1835.

18. William N. Eskridge, *Gaylaw: Challenging the Apartheid of the Closet* (Cambridge, MA: Harvard University Press, 2009), see 326–55 for lists of anti-cross-dressing laws.

19. See also Marc Stein, "Historical Landmarks and Landscapes of LGBTQ Law," in *Communities and Place: A Thematic Approach to the Histories of LGBTQ Communities in the United States,* edited by Katherine Crawford-Lackey and Megan E. Springate (New York: Berghahn Books, 2020).

20. The Willard Asylum for the Chronic Insane, Ovid, New York, was added to the NRHP on 7 June 1975.

21. Bambi Lobdell, *A Strange Sort of Being: The Transgender Life of Lucy Ann/ Joseph Israel Lobdell, 1829–1912* (Jefferson, NC: McFarland, 2011).

22. P. M. Wise, "A Case of Sexual Perversion," *Alienist and Neurologist: A Quarterly Journal of Scientific, Clinical and Forensic Psychiatry and Neurology* 4, no. 1 (1883): 87–91.

23. Hart's medical treatment is discussed in J. Allen Gilbert, "Homo-Sexuality and Its Treatment," *Journal of Nervous and Mental Disease* 2, no. 4 (October 1920): 297–332; Gilbert's office was located in the Selling Building at 610 SW Alder Street, Seventh Floor, Portland, Oregon. It was added to the NRHP on 17 October 1991. On Hart's life, see Emile Devereaux, "Doctor Alan Hart: X-Ray Vision in the Archive," *Australian Feminist Studies* 25, no. 64 (2010): 175–87; Brian Booth, *The Life and Career of Alberta Lucille / Dr. Alan L. Hart with Collected Early Writings* (Portland, OR: Friends of the Aubrey Watzek Library, Lewis & Clark College, 2003); and Colin Patrick Close, "Manifesting Manhood: Dr. Alan Hart's Transformation and the Embodiment of Sex in Early Twentieth-Century Sexology," master's thesis, Sonoma State University, 2014, available online at https://www.researchgate.net/publica tion/272831386_Manifesting_Manhood_Dr_Alan_Hart's_Transformation_ and_the_Embodiment_of_Sex_in_Early_Twentieth-Century_Sexology.

24. On the relationship between race and sex classification in scientific sexology, see Siobhan B. Somerville, *Queering the Color Line: Race and the Invention of Homosexuality in American Culture* (Durham, NC: Duke University Press, 2000); on the long history of Johns Hopkins University in the biomedicalization of race and sex, see Rebecca Skloot, *The Immortal Life of Henrietta Lacks* (New York: Random House, 2010).

25. On the development of genital surgeries at Hopkins, see Hugh Hampton Young, *Genital Abnormalities, Hermaphroditism, and Related Adrenal Diseases* (Baltimore: Williams and Wilkins, 1937); on the development of endocrinology as a field, see Chandak Sengoopta, *The Most Secret Quintessence of Life: Sex, Glands, and Hormones, 1850–1950* (Chicago: University of Chicago Press, 2006). The Johns Hopkins Hospital Complex, 601 North Broadway, Baltimore, Maryland, was added to the NRHP on 24 February 1975.

26. On Money's role in bridging intersex and transsexual medicine, see John Money and Anke A. Ehrhardt, *Man and Woman, Boy and Girl* (Baltimore: Johns Hopkins University Press, 1972).

27. Peter Boag, *Re-Dressing America's Frontier Past* (Berkeley: University of California Press, 2011), is an invaluable source for directing researchers to Western U.S. newspaper accounts, 1850s–1920s, documenting the lives of scores of individuals who were publicly discovered to be presenting as one gender while having the anatomy usually associated with the other.

28. Clare Sears, *Arresting Dress: Cross-Dressing, Law, and Fascination in Nineteenth-Century San Francisco* (Durham, NC: Duke University Press, 2014), 36–37. See also John Jeffrey Auer IV, "Queerest Little City in the World: LGBTQ Reno," in *Communities and Place: A Thematic Approach to the Histories of LGBTQ Communities in the United States*, edited by Katherine Crawford-Lackey and Megan E. Springate (New York: Berghahn Books, 2020) and Donna J. Graves and Shayne E. Watson, "San Francisco: Placing LGBTQ Histories in the City by the Bay," in *Preservation and Place: Historic Preservation by and of LGBTQ Communities in the United States*, edited by Katherine Crawford-Lackey and Megan E. Springate (NY: Berghahn Books, 2019).

29. Leslie Ferris, ed., *Crossing the Stage: Controversies on Cross-Dressing* (London: Routledge, 1993); Laurence Senelick, *The Changing Room: Sex, Drag, and Theater* (New York: Routledge, 2000); Laura Horak, *Girls Will Be Boys: Crossed-Dressed Women, Lesbians, and American Cinema, 1908–1920* (New Brunswick, NJ: Rutgers University Press, 2015).

30. See Amy Sueyoshi, "Remembering Asian Pacific American Activism in Queer History," this volume.

31. Sucheng Chan, *This Bittersweet Soil: The Chinese in California Agriculture, 1860–1910* (Berkeley: University of California Press, 1989).

32. Sears, *Arresting Dress*, 34–35, 83–84, 113–14, and *passim*.

33. See Helen Lee-Keller, "Civilizing Violence: 'The Haunted Valley,'" *The Ambrose Bierce Project: The ABP Journal* 2, no. 1 (Fall 2006), http://www.ambrosebierce.org/journal2lee-keller.html.

34. Hortense Spillers, "Mama's Baby, Papa's Maybe: An American Grammar Book," *Diacritics* 17, no. 2 (Summer 1987): 64–81.

35. See "Ann Maria Weems," National Park Service website. https://www.nps.gov/subjects/ugrr/discover_history/vignette_details.htm?ID=4073143.

36. See "Sojourner Truth," National Park Service website, https://www.nps.gov/wori/learn/historyculture/sojourner-truth.htm. Sojourner Truth gave her "Ain't I a Woman" speech at the 1851 Women's Rights Convention held at the Old Stone Church, corner of North High and Perkins Streets, Akron, Ohio (demolished). See also Jeffrey Harris, "'Where We Could Be Ourselves': African American LGBTQ Historic Places and Why They Matter," this volume.

37. Magnus Hirschfeld, *The Transvestites: The Erotic Urge to Cross-Dress*, trans. Michael Lombardi-Nash (Buffalo, NY: Prometheus Books, 1991), 83–94.

38. Clare Sears, "Electric Brilliancy: Cross-Dressing Laws and Freak Show Displays in Nineteenth-Century San Francisco," *WSQ: Women's Studies Quarterly* 36, no. 3–4 (Fall/Winter 2008): 170–87.

39. For treatments of two paradigmatic "tenderloins," see Randy Shaw, *The Tenderloin: Sex, Crime and Resistance in the Heart of San Francisco* (San Francisco: Urban Reality Press, 2015); and Marilynn S. Johnson, *Street Justice: A History of Police Violence in New York City* (Boston: Beacon Press, 2004). San Francisco's Uptown Tenderloin Historic District was added to the NRHP on 5 February 2009. New Orleans' French Quarter was listed on the NRHP as the Vieux Carre Historic District on 15 October 1966 and designated an NHL on 21 December 1965. Seattle's Pioneer Square-Skid Road Historic District was added to the NRHP on 22 June 1970, with boundary increases on 7 July 1978 and 16 June 1988. Philadelphia's Northern Liberties Historic District was added to the NRHP on 31 October 1985.

40. The El Rosa Hotel was located at 166 Turk Street, San Francisco, California, and the Hyland Hotel at 101 Taylor Street, above the Compton's Cafeteria site.

41. Frank P. Barajas, "Work and Leisure in La Colonia: Class, Generation, and Interethnic Alliances among Mexicanos in Oxnard, California, 1890–1945," Ph.D. diss., Claremont Graduate University, 2001.

42. The Arlington Hotel was on First Avenue between University and Seneca Streets, Seattle, Washington (now demolished). See Don Paulson, *An Evening at the Garden of Allah: A Gay Cabaret in Seattle* (New York: Columbia University Press, 1996). Finocchio's, established by Italian American impresario Joseph Finocchio, began as an illegal speakeasy in the basement of 406 Stockton Street, San Francisco, in 1929, and moved upstairs in the same building in 1933 with the repeal of Prohibition. After a police raid temporarily closed the club in 1936, it soon reopened (protected by police graft) at its larger and longtime location at 506 Broadway, where it remained until its closing on 27 November 1999. See Susan Stryker, "Finocchio's: A Short Retrospective," http://www.foundsf.org/index.php?title=Finocchio%27s,_a_ Short_Retrospective. Perhaps coincidentally, "finocchio," Italian for "fennel," is a derogatory slang term for homosexual. Club My-O-My began as the Wonder Bar just after the end of Prohibition. In 1936, the owner asked for an injunction against police raids on the club, which featured female impersonators. Refused an injunction on the grounds that the club was a menace to morals, the owner moved the bar (renamed the Wonder Club) to pilings extending into Lake Pontchartrain on the Jefferson-Orleans parish line. The goal was to get as far away from the police as possible. In the late 1940s, Club My-O-My took over the business. Rebuilt after a fire in 1948, the club was destroyed by fire in 1972. See John Kelly, "1972: Fire Destroys Club My-O-My on Lakefront," *Times-Picayune*, 5 September 2010, http://www.nola.com/living/index.ssf/2010/09/1972_fire_destroys_club_my-o-m.html; see also "Club My-O-My: New Orleans Vintage Drag," YouTube

video, posted by NewOrleansHistorical, 13 September 2012, https://www
.youtube.com/watch?v=2U_IvJLROdw.

43. George Chauncey, *Gay New York: Gender, Urban Culture, and the Making of the Gay Male World, 1890–1940* (New York: Basic Books, 1995), see 12 for quote, but *passim* for detailed discussion of gay cross-gender expression, underground venues for drag performance, "fairies," and the pansy craze. Esther Newton, *Mother Camp: Female Impersonators in America* (Chicago: University of Chicago Press, 1972), offers the classic anthropological account of the topic.

44. Paresis Hall, more formally known as Columbia Hall, was located at 32 Cooper Square (a continuation of Fourth Avenue), New York City, New York.

45. Ralph Werther, *Autobiography of an Androgyne,* ed. Scott Herring (New Brunswick, NJ: Rutgers University Press, 2008), originally published 1918.

46. *Transvestia* published only two issues in 1952, at which time the American Society for Equality in Dress seems to have folded; after a hiatus, publisher Virginia Prince's Chevalier Publications began issuing the journal again, 1960–1979, from a post office box in Tulare, California.

47. On Prince, see Richard F. Docter, *From Man to Woman: The Transgender Journey of Virginia Prince* (Northridge, CA: Docter Press, 2004); Richard Ekins and David King, eds., *Virginia Prince: Pioneer of Transgendering,* special issue of *International Journal of Transgenderism* 8, no. 4 (2005); and Darell G. Raynor, *A Year among the Girls* (London: Mayflower-Dell, 1968).

48. Docter, *From Man to Woman,* 19, 26.

49. Langley Porter Psychiatric Hospital and Clinics are located at 401 Parnassus Avenue, San Francisco, California.

50. "Journal," Louise Lawrence Collection, Series II D, Folder 2, Archives of the Kinsey Institute for Research in Sex, Gender, and Reproduction, Bloomington, Indiana.

51. Lawrence lived at 11 Buena Vista Terrace, San Francisco, California (now demolished).

52. Virginia "Charles" Prince, *The Transvestite and His Wife* (Tulare, CA: Chevalier Publications, 1967), 5; Joanne Meyerowitz, *How Sex Changed: A History of Transsexuality in the United States* (Cambridge, MA: Harvard University Press, 2002), 181–86. Harry Benjamin's New York Offices were located at 728 Park Avenue; his San Francisco offices were at the Medical-Dental Building, 450 Sutter Street, but he also sometimes saw patients at his suite at the Sir Francis Drake Hotel (450 Powell Street, San Francisco, California), where he made his residence during his annual summer practice. In New York City, Dr. Benjamin lived in the Flatiron District. The 450 Sutter Street building was listed on the NRHP on 22 December 2009.

53. Jorgensen's father, a carpenter and building contractor, built the family home on Dudley Avenue in the Throgs Neck section of the Bronx, where Jorgensen was born and lived her first twenty-six years. See Christine Jorgensen, *A Personal Autobiography* (San Francisco: Cleis Press, 2000), 4, orig-

inally published 1967. In addition to Jorgensen's own autobiography, see Richard Docter, *Becoming A Woman: A Biography of Christine Jorgensen* (New York: Haworth Press, 2008); and Emily Skidmore, "Constructing the 'Good Transsexual': Christine Jorgensen, Whiteness, and Heteronormativity in the Mid-Twentieth-Century Press," *Feminist Studies* 37, no. 2 (Summer 2011): 270–300.

54. On the history of genital surgeries, see Reis, *Bodies in Doubt*; on the history of endocrinology, see Sengoopta, *The Most Secret Quintessence of Life*; and Nelly Oudshoorn, *Beyond the Natural Body: An Archeology of the Sex Hormones* (New York: Routledge, 1994).

55. On the development of a "transsexual discourse," see Meyerowitz, *How Sex Changed,* 16–28; and Reis, *Bodies in Doubt,* 45–54. For the earliest known case of a person requesting medical transformation to support a change in legal and social gender, see the case of Karl (née Martha) Baer, director of the Berlin B'nai B'rith in Berlin until his emigration from Germany in 1938; Baer wrote a somewhat fictionalized autobiography under a pseudonym, which has recently become available in English translation with a scholarly preface: N. O. Body, with a preface by Sander L. Gilman, and afterward by Hermann Simon, *Memoirs of a Man's Maiden Years,* trans. Deborah Simon (Philadelphia: University of Pennsylvania Press, 2009).

56. Jorgensen's father also built the family's home in the 100 block of Pennsylvania Avenue, at the corner of Ocean Avenue, in Massapequa, New York. ndocrinologist Harry Benjamin referred many of his patients for surgery, were located ssexual women seeking medical services on The Chateau Marmont Hotel is located at 8221 Sunset Boulevard, Los Angeles, California.

57. Casa Susanna, described by the *New York Times* as a "slightly run-down bungalow camp in Hunter, N.Y.," was a retreat for cross-dressers that existed in the late 1950s and early 1960s; see Penelope Green, "A Safe House for the Girl Within," *New York Times,* 7 September 2006, http://www.nytimes .com/2006/09/07/garden/07trann.html?_r=1. A collection of photographs from the resort have been published: Michael Hurst and Robert Swope, eds., *Casa Susanna* (New York: Powerhouse Books, 2006). A play by Harvey Fierstein based on the history of the resort, *Casa Valentina,* premiered on Broadway in 2014. For a firsthand account of a consequential visit to Casa Susanna by noted sex researchers Alfred Kinsey and Wardell Pomeroy, see Katherine Cummings, *Katherine's Diary: The Story of a Transsexual* (Sydney: William Heinemann Australia, 1992).

58. Snorton has delivered many public lectures, circa 2014–16, under the title "Jorgensen's Shadows," related to his forthcoming book on black transgender history in the United States; for a synopsis of this larger project, see H. Roger Segelken, "Examining Black Transness through Contemporary Media," *Cornell Chronicle,* 8 June 2015, http://www.news.cornell.edu/stories/2015/06/ examining-black-transness-through-contemporary-media.

59. On Newton and Mukaw, see Meyerowitz, *How Sex Changed,* 86.

60. After her moment in the media spotlight, McLeod married, adopted her husband's two children, and retreated from public life. A native of Dyersburg, Tennessee, she returned home to care for her aging and infirm mother in the mid-1960s, and remained to run a convalescent home until her own retirement. She died in 2007. As the child of a prominent local family, a headstone bearing her given name, Charles, had been erected in the family plot in Fairview Cemetery, at the time of her birth. McLeod took great satisfaction, after all her older relatives had died, in purchasing a plot in the same cemetery under her chosen name, and leaving the grave set aside for "Charles" permanently empty. See oral history interview by the author with Aleshia Brevard Crenshaw, GLBT Historical Society, OHC Number 97-040, recorded 2 August 1997. The author visited McLeod in May 2002, and was shown both grave sites.

61. On transgender carnival, circus, sideshow, and strip club performers, see Minette (as told to Steve Watson), *Minette: Recollections of a Part-Time Lady* (Chicago: Novel Books, 1965); Hedy Jo Star, *I Changed My Sex!* (Chicago: Allied Books, 1955); Tamara Rees, *Reborn: A Factual Life Story of a Transition from Male to Female.* (Los Angeles: Irene Lipman, 1955); and the film *Forever's Gonna Start Tonight,* about the entertainer Vicki Marlane, directed by Michelle Lawler (Los Angeles: Aggressively Enthusiastic Films, 2009). Of the traveling revues, the best known was Doc Brenner and Danny Brown's Jewel Box Revue, founded in Miami in 1939, and touring until 1969; see Zagria, "The Jewel Box Revue," *A Gender Variance Who's Who* (blog), 15 August 2010, http://zagria.blogspot.it/2010/08/jewel-box-revue.html#.V2 shFWN1Hwx; see also Julio Capó Jr. "Locating Miami's Queer History," in *Communities and Place: A Thematic Approach to Histories of LGBTQ Communities in the United States,* ed. Katherine Crawford-Lackey and Megan E. Springate (New York: Berghahn Books, 2020). The troupe was notable for being racially integrated, featuring African American transmasculine emcee Stormé DeLarverie, as well as Miss Major Griffin-Gracy, who became a leading transgender prisoner's rights activist in the 1990s and subject of the documentary film *Major!,* directed by Annalise Ophelian (San Francisco: Floating Ophelia Productions, 2015).

62. Don Romesburg, "Longevity and Limits in Rae Bourbon's Life in Motion," in *The Transgender Studies Reader 2,* ed. Susan Stryker and Aren Z. Aizura (New York: Routledge, 2013), 479–91. An extensive and well-researched website constructed by Randy Riddle, containing many digital media versions of Bourbon's written and performed works, can be found at Randy Riddle, "Don't Call Me Madam: The Life and Work of Rae Bourbon," 2005, http://www.coolcatdaddy.com/bourbon.html. See also Auer, "Queerest Little City in the World."

63. Cooper Do-Nut, sometimes remembered as Cooper's Donuts, was located at either 553 or 557 W. Main in Los Angeles, between two of the city's oldest gay bars, the Waldorf and Harold's; see Lillian Faderman and Stuart Tim-

mons, *Gay L.A.: A History of Sexual Outlaws, Power Politics and Lipstick Lesbians* (New York: Basic Books, 2006), 1.

64. Marc Stein, *City of Sisterly and Brotherly Loves: Lesbian and Gay Philadelphia, 1945–1972* (Chicago: University of Chicago Press, 2000), 245–46. There was more than one Dewey's location; the sit-in and arrests took place at the location near Seventeenth Street and Locust.

65. There were several Compton's locations; the riot took place at the Compton's Cafeteria located at 101 Taylor Street, at the corner of Turk and Taylor. See Raymond Broshears, "History of Christopher Street West—San Francisco," *Gay Pride Quarterly* 1 (San Francisco, 1972), n.p., for the best firsthand account; for fuller contextualization see Susan Stryker, *Transgender History* (Emeryville, CA: Seal Press, 2008), 63–75; and *Screaming Queens: The Riot at Compton's Cafeteria,* directed by Victor Silverman and Susan Stryker (San Francisco: Frameline, 2005), a documentary film that includes first-person interviews.

66. Stonewall, the site of the Stonewall Riots at 51–53 Christopher Street and the surrounding streets and Christopher Park, New York City, New York, was listed on the NRHP on 28 June 1999, designated an NHL on 16 February 2000, and designated the Stonewall National Monument on 24 June 2016.

67. Glide Memorial Church, 330 Ellis Street, San Francisco, California, is a contributing element to the Uptown Tenderloin Historic District, and was added to the NRHP on 5 February 2009.

68. The Center for Special Problems was located at 1700 Jackson Street; the NTCU was in the 200 block of Turk Street; the Sir Francis Drake Hotel is at 450 Powell Street, all in San Francisco, California.

69. The Erickson Education Foundation office in Baton Rouge was located in what is now a private residence on Moreland Drive. Locations of early "sex change" programs include Johns Hopkins University, Hopkins Hospital, 1800 Orleans Street, Baltimore, Maryland (from 1965 to 1979); Stanford University, Stanford Medical Center Gender Identity Clinic, 300 Pasteur Drive, Stanford, California (from 1968 to 1980, when the clinic became a nonprofit foundation not associated with the university); Northwestern University, Feinberg School of Medicine, 303 East Chicago Avenue, Chicago, Illinois; University of Texas Galveston, UT Galveston Medical Branch, 301 University Boulevard, Galveston, Texas (1966–1980); University of Michigan, Transgender Services, 2025 Traverwood Drive, Ann Arbor, Michigan; University of Minnesota Hospital, 505 East Harvard Street, Minneapolis, Minnesota; Oregon Health and Science University Hospital, 3181 SW Sam Jackson Park Road, Portland, Oregon; Case Western Reserve University School of Medicine, 2109 Adelbert Road, Cleveland, Ohio; and Integris Baptist Medical Center, Gender Identity Foundation, 3300 NW Expressway, Oklahoma City, Oklahoma (1973 to 1977). Rachel Witkin, "Hopkins Hospital: A History of Sex Reassignment," *Johns Hopkins News-Letter,* 1 May 2014, http://www.jhunewsletter.com/2014/05/01/hopkins-hospital-a-history-of-sex-

reassignment-76004/; Dawn Levy, "Transsexuals Talk about Stanford's Role in their Complex Lives," Stanford News Service website, 2 May 2000, http://news.stanford.edu/pr/00/sexchange53.html; Brandon Wolf, "Galveston's Invisible LGBT History," *Out Smart Magazine,* 1 July 2016, http://www.outsmartmagazine.com/2016/07/galvestons-invisible-lgbt-history/; Vern L. Bullough and Bonnie Bullough, *Cross Dressing, Sex, and Gender* (Philadelphia: University of Pennsylvania Press, 1993), 259; Meyerowitz, *How Sex Changed.* Johns Hopkins Hospital Complex was added to the NRHP on 24 February 1975. The Ashbel Smith Building, part of the UT Galveston Medical Branch, was added to the NRHP on 28 October 1969.

70. Redd Foxx's nightclub, often referred to simply as "Redd's," was located on La Cienega Boulevard, opening in 1959. Joe X. Price, *Redd Foxx, B.S. (Before Sanford)* (Chicago: Contemporary Books, 1979), 1. For numerous locations for the peripatetic Angela Douglas, who was living in a trailer in Sneads, Florida, at the time of her death, see her self-published 1982 autobiography, *Triple Jeopardy*; a copy is held at the GLBT Historical Society in San Francisco, California.

71. STAR House was located at 640 East Twelfth Street, Apartment C, New York City, New York (now demolished).

72. The Queens Liberation Front, founded in 1969, was closely associated with Lee Brewster; it, and *Drag Magazine*, were largely run out of Lee's Mardi Gras Boutique, a transgender emporium located in the Meatpacking District at 400 West Fourteenth Street, New York City, New York. The Meatpacking District, as the Gansevoort Market Historic District, was added to the NRHP on 30 May 2007.

73. Fantasia Fair is held in multiple locations in Provincetown, Massachusetts, usually during the third week in October. The Provincetown Historic District was listed on the NRHP on 30 August 1989.

74. Brice Smith, "'Yours in Liberation': Lou Sullivan and the Construction of FTM Identity," Ph.D. diss., History Department, University of Wisconsin-Milwaukee, 2010.

75. David Valentine, *Imagining Transgender: An Ethnography of a Category* (Durham, NC: Duke University Press, 2007), describes, in part, how the introduction of the term "transgender" itself in HIV/AIDS prevention activism remapped the relationship between particular kinds of gender-variant people, new forms of public health surveillance and service provision, and the geographical territory in which gender-nonconforming sex-work and black and Latino/a street socializing took place in lower Manhattan in the first half of the 1990s.

76. ACT UP and Queer Nation were both founded at the Lesbian, Gay, Bisexual and Transgender Community Center, 208 West Thirteenth Street, New York City, New York. Lesbian Avengers also met at the center, following their founding meeting held at the home of Ana Maria Simo in New York City's East Village neighborhood. ACT UP and Queer Nation groups were founded

across the country. In San Francisco, both groups met at the Women's Building at 3543 Eighteenth Street. In New York, transgender activist Riki Wilchins was an active member of Lesbian Avengers; in San Francisco, the first activist organization to use the term "transgender" in its name, Transgender Nation, began as a special-interest focus group of Queer Nation in 1992.

77. At the time of Feinberg's death in 2014, Feinberg, who used gender-neutral pronouns, was living with long-term partner and spouse, Minnie Bruce Pratt, in Syracuse, New York.

78. FTM Conference of the Americas, San Francisco, California, 18–20 August 1995.

79. The Tom Waddell Health Center, opened in 1993, was at 50 Lech Walesa (Ivy) Street, San Francisco, California. On the clinic, see Mark Freeman and Nathaniel Walters-Koh, dirs., *Transgender Tuesdays: A Clinic in the Tender-loin* (San Francisco: Healing Tales Productions, 2012). Freeman, a medical service provider, was instrumental in establishing the Tranny Tuesday clinic; note that the original name of the clinic used a slang term then considered to evoke a familiar, welcoming, insider, community-oriented sensibility, which has since fallen into disfavor by a younger generation of transgender people; the title of Freeman's film bows to these newer sensibilities.

80. Hart Township, Oceana County, Michigan, adjacent to privately held festival property known as "the Land."

81. Brandon Teena's murder inspired the Academy Award–winning film *Boys Don't Cry*, directed by Kimberly Peirce (Beverly Hills, CA: Twentieth Century Fox Home Entertainment, 2000), for which Hilary Swank won best actress for playing Brandon; the house in which Brandon and others were murdered is located on the outskirts of Humboldt, Nebraska. Transexual Menace organized vigils outside the Richardson County Courthouse in nearby Falls City, Nebraska, 1700 Stone Street, during the murder trial. The Richardson County Courthouse was listed on the NRHP on 5 July 1990. For an account of this activism, see Riki Wilchins, *Read My Lips: Sexual Subversion and the End of Gender* (New York: Riverdale, 2013). For more information on Brandon's life, see J. Jack Halberstam, *In a Queer Time and Place: Transgender Bodies, Subcultural Lives* (New York: NYU Press, 2005).

82. The first conference was held at the Hilton Hotel, 6780 Southwest Freeway, Houston, Texas, on 28 August 1992. For more information, see Phyllis Randolph Frye, "History of the International Conference on Transgender Law and Employment Policy, Inc.," Transgender Legal website, 2001, http://www.transgenderlegal.com/ictlephis1.htm.

83. The Transgender Foundation of America, including the Transgender Archive, has occupied several locations in Houston's Montrose and Heights neighborhoods; most recently it was located at 604 Pacific Street, until its 2015 closure. Though not legally incorporated until 1998, the TFA is an

outgrowth of Gulf Coast Transgender Community (GCTC), which traces its roots to 1965.

84. Manning was incarcerated at the United States Disciplinary Barracks, Fort Leavenworth, Kansas, until President Obama commuted her sentence on 17 January 2017. This did not erase Manning's conviction, but mitigated her sentence from the original thirty-five years to time served. Transgender populations in the United State experience incarceration rates more than twice that of the cisgender population. Most of those incarcerated are trans women of color who are incarcerated in men's facilities; see Eric A. Stanley and Nat Smith, eds., *Captive Genders: Trans Embodiment and the Prison Industrial Complex* (Oakland, CA: AK Press, 2011).

85. Long located in the historic Flood Building, 870 Market Street, San Francisco, the Transgender Law Center was, like many nonprofits, priced out of the city's real estate market by the high-tech boom. It is currently located at 1629 Telegraph Avenue, Oakland, California. The Sylvia Rivera Law Project is located at 147 West Twenty-Fourth Street, New York City, New York, in the Miss Major-Jay Toole Building for Social Justice, which also houses four other LGBTQ social justice organizations; the National Center for Transgender Equality is located at 1400 Sixteenth Street NW, Washington, D.C.; TGI Justice is located at 1372 Mission Street, San Francisco; GATE, a virtual international organization, operates online, with no physical office space.

86. Andrew Flores, Jody Herman, Gary Gates, and Taylor Brown, "How Many Adults Identify as Transgender in the United States," Williams Institute, UCLA Law School, June 2016, http://williamsinstitute.law.ucla.edu/wp-content/uploads/How-Many-Adults-Identify-as-Transgender-in-the-United-States.pdf. On transgender youth population estimates, see Jody Herman, Christy Mallory, and Bianca Wilson, "Estimates of Transgender Populations in States with Legislation Impacting Transgender People," Williams Institute, UCLA Law School, June 2016, http://williamsinstitute.law.ucla.edu/wp-content/uploads/Estimates-of-Transgender-Populations.pdf. In this report, the authors cite other scholars who, based on a review of multiple local probability samples and national convenience samples, found that between 1.3 and 3.2 percent of all youth are transgender; in other words between four and ten million youth.

Bibliography

Auer, John Jeffrey, IV. "Queerest Little City in the World: LGBTQ Reno." In *Communities and Place: A Thematic Approach to the Histories of LGBTQ Communities in the United States*, edited by Katherine Crawford-Lackey and Megan E. Springate. New York: Berghahn Books, 2020.

Barajas, Frank P. "Work and Leisure in La Colonia: Class, Generation, and Inter-ethnic Alliances among Mexicanos in Oxnard, California 1890–1945." Ph.D. diss., Claremont Graduate University, 2001.

Benck, Amy. "Albert D. J. Cashier: Woman Warrior, Insane Civil War Veteran, or Transman?" *OutHistory.org.* http://outhistory.org/exhibits/show/tgi-bios/albert-cashier.

Boag, Peter. *Re-Dressing America's Frontier Past.* Berkeley: University of California Press, 2011.

Body, N. O. *Memoirs of a Man's Maiden Years.* Translated by Deborah Simon. Philadelphia: University of Pennsylvania Press, 2009.

Booth, Brian. *The Life and Career of Alberta Lucille / Dr. Alan L. Hart with Collected Early Writings.* Portland, OR: Friends of the Aubrey Watzek Library, Lewis & Clark College, 2003.

Broshears, Raymond. "History of Christopher Street West—San Francisco." *Gay Pride Quarterly* 1 (San Francisco, 1972).

Bullough, Vern L., and Bonnie Bullough. *Cross Dressing, Sex, and Gender.* Philadelphia: University of Pennsylvania Press, 1993.

Capo, Julio, Jr. "Locating Miami's Queer History." In *Communities and Place: A Thematic Approach to the Histories of LGBTQ Communities in the United States,* edited by Katherine Crawford-Lackey and Megan E. Springate. New York: Berghahn Books, 2020.

Chan, Sucheng. *This Bittersweet Soil: The Chinese in California Agriculture, 1860–1910.* Berkeley: University of California Press, 1989.

Chauncey, George. *Gay New York: Gender, Urban Culture, and the Making of the Gay Male World, 1890–1940.* New York: Basic Books, 1995.

Close, Colin Patrick. "Manifesting Manhood: Dr. Alan Hart's Transformation and the Embodiment of Sex in Early Twentieth-Century Sexology." Master's thesis, Sonoma State University, 2014. https://www.researchgate.net/publication/272831386_Manifesting_Manhood_Dr_Alan_Hart's_Transformation_and_the_Embodiment_of_Sex_in_Early_Twentieth-Century_Sexology.

Cotten, Trystan, ed. *Transgender Migrations: The Bodies, Borders, and Politics of Transition.* New York: Routledge, 2011.

Cummings, Katherine. *Katherine's Diary: The Story of a Transsexual.* Sydney: William Heinemann Australia, 1992.

Devereaux, Emile. "Doctor Alan Hart: X-Ray Vision in the Archive." *Australian Feminist Studies* 25, no. 64 (2010): 175–87.

Docter, Richard F. *Becoming A Woman: A Biography of Christine Jorgensen.* New York: Haworth Press, 2008.

———. *From Man to Woman: The Transgender Journey of Virginia Prince.* Northridge, CA: Docter Press, 2004.

Douglas, Angela. *Triple Jeopardy.* Self-published, 1982.

Eggleston, Larry G. *Women in the Civil War: Extraordinary Stories of Soldiers, Spies, Nurses, Doctors, Crusaders, and Others.* Jefferson, NC: McFarland, 2003.

Ekins, Richard, and David King, eds. *Virginia Prince: Pioneer of Transgendering,* special issue of *International Journal of Transgenderism* 8, no. 4 (2005).

Ernst, Rhys, dir. *We've Been Around.* Los Angeles: Nonetheless Productions, 2016.

Eskridge, William N. *Gaylaw: Challenging the Apartheid of the Closet.* Cambridge, MA: Harvard University Press, 2009.

Faderman, Lillian, and Stuart Timmons. *Gay L.A.: A History of Sexual Outlaws, Power Politics and Lipstick Lesbians.* New York: Basic Books, 2006.

Ferris, Leslie, ed. *Crossing the Stage: Controversies on Cross-Dressing.* London: Routledge, 1993.

Flores, Andrew, Jody Herman, Gary Gates, and Taylor Brown. "How Many Adults Identify as Transgender in the United States." Williams Institute, UCLA Law School, June 2016. http://williamsinstitute.law.ucla.edu/wp-content/uploads/How-Many-Adults-Identify-as-Transgender-in-the-United-States.pdf.

Freeman, Mark, and Nathaniel Walters-Koh, dirs. *Transgender Tuesdays: A Clinic in the Tenderloin.* San Francisco: Healing Tales Productions, 2012.

Frye, Phyllis Randolph. "History of the International Conference on Transgender Law and Employment Policy, Inc." Transgender Legal, 2001. http://www.transgenderlegal.com/ictlephis1.htm.

Gilbert, J. Allen. "Homo-Sexuality and Its Treatment." *Journal of Nervous and Mental Disease* 2, no. 4 (October 1920): 297–332.

Graves, Donna J., and Shayne E. Watson. "San Francisco: Placing LGBTQ Histories in the City by the Bay." In *Preservation and Place: Historic Preservation by and of LGBTQ Communities in the United States,* edited by Katherine Crawford-Lackey and Megan E. Springate. New York: Berghahn Books, 2019.

Green, Penelope. "A Safe House for the Girl Within." *New York Times,* 7 September 2006. http://www.nytimes.com/2006/09/07/garden/07trann.html?_r=1.

Halberstam, J. Jack. *In A Queer Time and Place: Transgender Bodies, Subcultural Lives.* New York: NYU Press, 2005.

Harris, Jeffrey. "'Where We Could Be Ourselves': African American LGBTQ Historic Places and Why They Matter." In *Identities and Place: Changing Labels and Intersectional Communities of LGBTQ and Two-Spirit People in the United States,* edited by Katherine Crawford-Lackey and Megan E. Springate. New York: Berghahn Books, 2020.

Herdt, Gilbert, ed. *Third Sex, Third Gender: Beyond Sexual Dimorphism in History and Culture.* Cambridge, MA: Zone Books, 1996.

Herman, Jody, Christy Mallory, and Bianca Wilson. "Estimates of Transgender Populations in States with Legislation Impacting Transgender People." Williams Institute, UCLA Law School, June 2016. http://williamsinstitute.law.ucla.edu/wp-content/uploads/Estimates-of-Transgender-Populations.pdf.

Hirschfeld, Magnus. *The Transvestites: The Erotic Urge to Cross-Dress.* Translated by Michael Lombardi-Nash. Buffalo: Prometheus Books, 1991.

Horak, Laura. *Girls Will Be Boys: Cross-Dressed Women, Lesbians, and American Cinema, 1908–1920.* New Brunswick, NJ: Rutgers University Press, 2015.

Hurst, Michael, and Robert Swope, eds. *Casa Susanna*. New York: Powerhouse Books, 2006.

Johnson, Marilynn S. *Street Justice: A History of Police Violence in New York City*. Boston: Beacon Press, 2004.

Jorgensen, Christine. *A Personal Autobiography*. San Francisco: Cleis Press, 2000.

Katz, Jonathan. *Gay American History: Lesbians and Gay Men in the U.S.A.* New York: Thomas Y. Crowell, 1976.

Kelly, John. "1972: Fire Destroys Club My-O-My on Lakefront." *Times-Picayune*, 5 September 2010. http://www.nola.com/living/index.ssf/2010/09/1972_fire_destroys_club_my-o-m.html.

Klass, Sheila Solomon. *Soldier's Secret: The Story of Deborah Sampson*. New York: Henry Holt, 2009.

Lamothe, Dan. "The Pentagon's Ban on Transgender Service Just Fell—But the Details are Complicated." *Washington Post*, 30 June 2016. https://www.washingtonpost.com/news/checkpoint/wp/2016/06/30/the-pentagons-ban-on-transgender-service-just-fell-but-the-details-are-complicated/.

Lawler, Michelle, dir. *Forever's Gonna Start Tonight*. Los Angeles: Aggressively Enthusiastic Films, 2009.

Lee-Keller, Hellen. "Civilizing Violence: 'The Haunted Valley.'" *The Ambrose Bierce Project: The ABP Journal* 2, no. 1 (Fall 2006). http://www.ambrosebierce.org/journal2lee-keller.html.

Leonard, Elizabeth D. *All the Daring of the Soldier: Women of the Civil War Armies*. New York: W. W. Norton & Co., 1999.

Lester, Toni, ed. *Gender Nonconformity, Race, and Sexuality: Charting the Connections*. Madison: University of Wisconsin Press, 2002.

Levy, Dawn. "Transsexuals Talk about Stanford's Role in their Complex Lives." *Stanford News Service*, 2 May 2000. http://news.stanford.edu/pr/00/sexchange53.html.

Lobdell, Bambi. *A Strange Sort of Being: The Transgender Life of Lucy Ann/Joseph Israel Lobdell, 1829–1912*. Jefferson, NC: McFarland, 2011.

Manion, Jen. *Liberty's Prisoners: Carceral Culture in Early America*. Philadelphia: University of Pennsylvania Press, 2016.

McIlwaine, H. R., ed. *Minutes of the Council and General Court of Colonial Virginia, 1622–1632, 1670–76*. Richmond, VA: Colonial Press/Everett Waddey, 1924.

Meyerowitz, Joanne. *How Sex Changed: A History of Transsexuality in the United States*. Cambridge, MA: Harvard University Press, 2002.

Middleton, DeWight R. *Exotics and Erotics: Human Cultural and Sexual Diversity*. Long Grove, IL: Waveland Press, 2001.

Minette (as told to Steve Watson). *Minette: Recollections of a Part-Time Lady*. Chicago: Novel Books, 1965.

Miranda, Deborah A. "Extermination of the *Joyas*: Gendercide in Spanish California." *GLQ: A Journal of Lesbian and Gay Studies* 16, no. 1–2 (2010): 253–84.

Mission Tour. "El Camino Real." http://missiontour.org/wp/related/el-camino-real.html.

Money, John, and Anke A. Ehrhardt. *Man and Woman, Boy and Girl.* Baltimore, MD: Johns Hopkins University Press, 1972.

Moyer, Paul B. *The Public Universal Friend: Jemina Wilkinson and Religious Enthusiasm in Revolutionary America.* Ithaca, NY: Cornell University Press, 2015.

Nanda, Serena. *Gender Diversity: Crosscultural Variations.* 2nd ed. Long Grove, IL: Waveland Press, 2014.

National Park Service. "Jennie Hodgers, aka Private Albert Cashier." https://www.nps.gov/resources/story.htm?id=187.

———. "Sojourner Truth." https://www.nps.gov/wori/learn/historyculture/sojourner-truth.htm

NewOrleansHistorical. "Club My-O-My: New Orleans Vintage Drag." YouTube, 13 September 2012. https://www.youtube.com/watch?v=2U_IvJLROdw.

Newton, Esther. *Mother Camp: Female Impersonators in America.* Chicago: University of Chicago Press, 1972.

Norton, Mary Beth. *Founding Mothers and Fathers: Gendered Power and the Forming of American Society.* New York: Vintage, 1997.

Ophelian, Annalise, dir. *Major!* San Francisco: Floating Ophelia Productions, 2015.

Oudshoorn, Nelly. *Beyond the Natural Body: An Archeology of the Sex Hormones.* New York: Routledge, 1994.

Paulson, Don. *An Evening at the Garden of Allah: A Gay Cabaret in Seattle.* New York: Columbia University Press, 1996.

Peirce, Kimberly, dir. *Boys Don't Cry.* Beverly Hills, CA: Twentieth Century Fox Home Entertainment, 2000.

Price, Joe X. *Redd Foxx, B.S. (Before Sanford).* Chicago: Contemporary Books, 1979.

Prince, Virginia "Charles." *The Transvestite and His Wife.* Tulare, CA: Chevalier Publications, 1967.

Raynor, Darell G. *A Year among the Girls.* London: Mayflower-Dell, 1968.

Rees, Tamara. *Reborn: A Factual Life Story of a Transition from Male to Female.* Los Angeles: Irene Lipman, 1955.

Reis, Elizabeth. *Bodies in Doubt: An American History of Intersex.* Baltimore, MD: Johns Hopkins Press, 2009.

Riddle, Randy. "Don't Call Me Madam: The Life and Work of Rae Bourbon." 2005. http://www.coolcatdaddy.com/bourbon.html.

Roberts, Melinda. "Jacques Marquette and Louis Joliet." *Wisconsin Historical Markers* (blog), http://wisconsinhistoricalmarkers.blogspot.com/2013/04/jacques-marquette-and-louis-joliet.html.

Romesburg, Don. "Longevity and Limits in Rae Bourbon's Life in Motion." In *The Transgender Studies Reader 2,* edited by Susan Stryker and Aren Z. Aizura, 479–91. New York: Routledge, 2013.

Roscoe, Will. "Sexual and Gender Diversity in Native America and the Pacific Islands." In *Identities and Place: Changing Labels and Intersectional Com-*

munities of LGBTQ and Two-Spirit People in the United States, edited by Katherine Crawford-Lackey and Megan E. Springate. New York: Berghahn Books, 2020.

Sears, Clare. *Arresting Dress: Cross-Dressing, Law, and Fascination in Nineteenth-Century San Francisco.* Durham, NC: Duke University Press, 2014.

———. "Electric Brilliancy: Cross-Dressing Laws and Freak Show Displays in Nineteenth-Century San Francisco." *WSQ: Women's Studies Quarterly* 36, no. 3–4 (Fall/Winter 2008): 170–87.

Segelken, H. Roger. "Examining Black Transness through Contemporary Media." *Cornell Chronicle,* 8 June 2015. http://www.news.cornell.edu/stories/2015/06/examining-black-transness-through-contemporary-media.

Senelick, Laurence. *The Changing Room: Sex, Drag, and Theater.* New York: Routledge, 2000.

Sengoopta, Chandak. *The Most Secret Quintessence of Life: Sex, Glands, and Hormones, 1850–1950.* Chicago: University of Chicago Press, 2006.

Shaw, Randy. *The Tenderloin: Sex, Crime and Resistance in the Heart of San Francisco.* San Francisco: Urban Reality Press, 2015.

Sheppard, Donald E. "Cabeza de Vaca: Journeys across North America 1528–36." Florida History. http://www.floridahistory.com/cabeza.html.

Silverman, Victor, and Susan Stryker, dirs. *Screaming Queens: The Riot at Compton's Cafeteria.* San Francisco: Frameline, 2005.

Skidmore, Emily. "Constructing the 'Good Transsexual': Christine Jorgensen, Whiteness, and Heteronormativity in the Mid-Twentieth-Century Press." *Feminist Studies* 37, no. 2 (Summer 2011): 270–300.

Skloot, Rebecca. *The Immortal Life of Henrietta Lacks.* New York: Random House, 2010.

Smith, Brice. "'Yours in Liberation': Lou Sullivan and the Construction of FTM Identity." Ph.D. diss., History Department, University of Wisconsin-Milwaukee, 2010.

Somerville, Siobhan B. *Queering the Color Line: Race and the Invention of Homosexuality in American Culture.* Durham, NC: Duke University Press, 2000.

Spillers, Hortense. "Mama's Baby, Papa's Maybe: An American Grammar Book." *Diacritics* 17, no. 2 (Summer 1987): 64–81.

Stanley, Eric A., and Nat Smith, eds. *Captive Genders: Trans Embodiment and the Prison Industrial Complex.* Oakland, CA: AK Press, 2011.

Star, Hedy Jo. *I Changed My Sex!* Chicago: Allied Books, 1955.

Stein, Marc. *City of Sisterly and Brotherly Loves: Lesbian and Gay Philadelphia, 1945–1972.* Chicago: University of Chicago Press, 2000.

———. "Historical Landmarks and Landscapes of LGBTQ Law." In *Communities and Place: A Thematic Approach to the Histories of LGBTQ Communities in the United States,* edited by Katherine Crawford-Lackey and Megan E. Springate. New York: Berghahn Books, 2020.

Stryker, Susan. "Finocchio's: A Short Retrospective." *Found SF.* http://www.foundsf.org/index.php?title=Finocchio%27s,_a_Short_Retrospective.

———. *Transgender History*. Emeryville, CA: Seal Press, 2008.

Sueyoshi, Amy. "Remembering Asian Pacific American Activism in Queer History." In *Identities and Place: Changing Labels and Intersectional Communities of LGBTQ and Two-Spirit People in the United States,* edited by Katherine Crawford-Lackey and Megan E. Springate. New York: Berghahn Books, 2020.

Towle, Evan B., and Lynn M. Morgan. "Romancing the Transgender Native: Rethinking the Use of the 'Third Gender' Concept." *GLQ: A Journal of Lesbian and Gay Studies* 8, no. 4 (2002): 469–97.

Valentine, David. *Imagining Transgender: An Ethnography of a Category.* Durham, NC: Duke University Press, 2007.

Werther, Ralph. *Autobiography of an Androgyne.* Edited by Scott Herring. New Brunswick, NJ: Rutgers University Press, 2008.

Wilchins, Riki. *Read My Lips: Sexual Subversion and the End of Gender.* New York: Riverdale, 2013.

Williams, Cristan. "Transgender." *TSQ: Transgender Studies Quarterly* 1, no. 1–2 (2014): 232–34.

Wisbey, Herbert, Jr. *Pioneer Prophetess: Jemina Wilkinson, the Publick Universal Friend.* Ithaca, NY: Cornell University Press, 2009.

Wise, P. M. "A Case of Sexual Perversion." *Alienist and Neurologist: A Quarterly Journal of Scientific, Clinical and Forensic Psychiatry and Neurology* 4, no. 1 (1993): 87–91.

Witkin, Rachel. "Hopkins Hospital: A History of Sex Reassignment." *Johns Hopkins News-Letter,* 1 May 2014. http://www.jhunewsletter.com/2014/05/01/hopkins-hospital-a-history-of-sex-reassignment-76004/.

Wolf, Brandon. "Galveston's Invisible LGBT History." *OutSmart Magazine,* 1 July 2016. http://www.outsmartmagazine.com/2016/07/galvestons-invisible-lgbt-history/.

Young, Alfred Fabian. *Masquerade: The Life and Times of Deborah Sampson, Continental Soldier.* New York: Alfred A. Knopf, 2004.

Young, Hugh Hampton. *Genital Abnormalities, Hermaphroditism, and Related Adrenal Diseases.* Baltimore, MD: Williams and Wilkins, 1937.

Zagria. "The Jewel Box Revue." *A Gender Variance Who's Who* (blog), 15 August 2010. http://zagria.blogspot.it/2010/08/jewel-box-revue.html.

CHAPTER 5

Remembering Asian Pacific American Activism in Queer History

Amy Sueyoshi

On 1 July 2015, the Respect After Death Act (California Assembly Bill 1577) took effect in California enabling transgender people to record their chosen gender on their death certificates. At least three Asian queers stood at the center of the passage of this bill. When Chinese and Polish American Christopher Lee, who identified as a transgender man, killed himself in 2012, the coroner listed him as female on his death certificate. Troubled by their friend's misgendering, Chinese Mexican Chino Scott-Chung, also a transgender man, brought the death certificate to the attention of the Transgender Law Center, which initiated and lobbied for the passage of AB 1577. Three years later, Japanese American Kris Hayashi stood at the helm of the Transgender Law Center as its executive director when the organization celebrated the passage of the bill.[1] When CBS reported on the victory, however, they lauded the organization's previous executive director, Masen Davis, and a statement from Davis, rather than Hayashi, evocatively defined the historic moment, "It brings us one significant step closer to making sure that all transgender people are able to live—and die—authentically in accordance with who they really are."[2]

Notably, Asian Pacific Americans have also played central roles in what many political scientists mark as the two most important issues in gay politics of the twenty-first century—the repeal of "Don't Ask Don't Tell" and the fight for marriage equality.[3] Korean American and Lieutenant Dan Choi became a symbol of the fight against the military's policy of disallowing gays and lesbians from serving openly in the military when he came out on the Rachel Maddow Show in 2009 and a year later handcuffed himself to the White House fence in protest (figure 5.1).[4]

Figure 5.1. Lt. Dan Choi, 2014. Photo courtesy of Dan Choi.

Stuart Gaffney, whose mother is Chinese American, was one of several plaintiffs in the 2008 lawsuit that held that California's ban on same-sex marriage was unconstitutional. Gaffney advocated for marriage equality by invoking the legal prohibition against interracial marriage and how it affected his own parents' white and Asian union in advocating for marriage equality.[5] Despite these and many more instances of queer Asian Pacific American (APA) activism and engagement, their existence remains largely invisible.[6]

Structural operations of homophobia and racism have diminished if not erased the significance of queer APA genders and sexualities. Foundational writings in Asian American studies explicitly derided same-sex sexuality in the 1970s, establishing a less-than-queer-friendly beginning to the movement and the field.[7] Whiteness in queer studies, too, has stunted the growth of publications on the queer APA experience.[8] In fact, the professional field of history for nearly a century perceived sexuality broadly as a private matter and not worthy of intellectual inquiry.[9] In the midst of forces that deny the existence of LGBTQ Asians and Pacific Islanders in history, however, queer intimacies most certainly existed in even the earliest APA communities in the United States. And, since the 1980s, queer Asian Pacific Americans have become increasingly "out and proud," engaging in activism at the intersection of race, gender, and sexuality. APA queers have often occupied the leading wave of social transformation within the Asian Pacific American community.

Early Queer APA History

Likely, countless queers came to America during the first wave of Asian migration in the nineteenth century. Historians, however, have rendered their stories invisible through a heteronormative recounting of history. Chinese men languished painfully in "bachelor societies" in cities such as San Francisco and New York. The miniscule number of women immigrants appeared exclusively as prostitutes to serve these men deprived of "normal" heterosexual contact.[10] In nearly all of the existing literature, "queer" Chinese in America existed only as a discursive device in public health records and leisure culture that painted them as morally deviant in the 1860s and 1870s.[11] Same-sex intimacies and sex acts themselves seemed completely absent. Yet, queer acts, if not identity, existed in early Asian Pacific American history. As immigrants and indigenous Pacific Islanders sought out same-sex intimacies, they too contributed to the changing dynamic of America. A number of them more specifically shaped American modernism, the U.S. military, and Hollywood. Nearly all interacted with whites in unexpectedly intimate ways.

White missionaries and imperial zealots wrote often of the prevalence of same-sex intimacies in the Pacific, as they sought refuge from the stigma of their own sexual proclivities at home. In a letter to Walt Whitman, writer Charles Warren Stoddard, who had become famous for his travel logs from the 1870s, described the Pacific Islands as a sexual utopia that not even "California where men are tolerably bold" could provide.[12] Stoddard became disappointed when one of his young lovers from Hawai`i named Kahele came to San Francisco for a visit and immediately began to "sow his heterosexual oats." Days after his arrival, Kahele deserted Stoddard to move to Los Angeles with his new Mexican wife.[13] Pacific Islander men rendered faceless by authors who merely penned them as "savages" crucially influenced how white men came to understand their sexuality through widely popular travel publications about the "South Seas." According to literary critic Lee Wallace, Pacific Islander same-sex sexualities so powerfully informed nineteenth-century western imaginings of masculinity that "male homosexuality as we have come to understood it . . . was constituted in no small part through the collision with Polynesian culture."[14]

For the unlucky ones, the criminal court system etched their illicit activities into historical record. In the 1890s, authorities in San Francisco arrested a number of Chinese men who were impersonating women in order to attract fellow countrymen for sex work.[15] Across the bay in Oakland, Chin Ling in 1908 dressed as a "handsome Chinese maiden of the better class" in hopes of obtaining a husband.[16] Ten years later in downtown Sacramento, California, two South Asian men, Jamil Singh and Tara Singh, separately sought out male intimacy from two men in their late teens, one white and the other Native American.[17] So prevalent did incidents of South Asian men anally penetrating young white men appear in police records that, according to Nayan Shah, criminal courts in the 1910s and 1920s began to blame "Oriental depravity" for promoting degeneracy among America's transient youth, a population understood to be particularly susceptible to sodomy.[18] Alaskan canneries at which Japanese and Chinese immigrants labored also became productive sites of business for male sex workers, most often Chinese, African American, or Portuguese in the 1920s and 1930s. Sex workers divided their earnings equally with cannery foremen who occasionally pimped for them.[19] These early immigrant men and their pursuit of frequently interracial same-sex affairs sheds a different light upon existing historical narratives that presume compulsory heterosexuality and little racial mixing among Asian immigrant men.

Chinese immigrants accustomed to homosocial spaces in their homeland may have actively enjoyed all-male spaces and forged meaningful same-sex relationships as they gathered for mahjong or benevolent association events as "bachelors" in America. Without the imposition of a Western lens that assumes heterosociality as the ideal, historian Madeline Hsu detailed how men from China, steeped in a tradition of same-sex social interaction, may not have been as deprived as more insistently heteronormative histories have declared.[20] In fact, Susan Johnson traces how male gold seekers during the 1850s in the Southern Mines of California—including Chinese—created multiracial families of cooperation and consent as they forged new forms of cross-ethnic male intimacy. The influx of white women in the 1860s and its accompanying valorization of "civilized" families—code for white het-erosexuality—would later fuel the formation of rigid racial hierarchies.[21]

In some cases, individuals did identify themselves as explicitly queer. In 1899, Kosen Takahashi, an illustrator for *Shin Sekai*,[22] one of San Fran-cisco's earliest Japanese American newspapers, declared himself an "ut-most queer Nipponese" to journalist Blanche Partington.[23] Takahashi, who had earlier shared kisses with fellow *issei* Yone Noguchi, missed him sorely when Noguchi went tramping from San Francisco to Los Angeles.[24] Noguchi, a poet in his own right who would later become better known as the father of acclaimed Asian American artist Isamu Noguchi, had struck up an affair with the aforementioned writer and one-time lover of Kahele, Charles Warren Stoddard.[25] At the turn of the century, Noguchi would collect bouquets of wild flowers in California's Oakland Hills and blow kisses to Stoddard's "bungalow" on M Street in Washington, D.C.[26] When Noguchi heard that Stoddard took walks atop Telegraph Hill in San Francisco, he raced there to look for his footprints. Charles Warren Stoddard, touted as San Francisco's first gay writer, was a cofounder of the Bohemian Club, an elite fraternal order that former President Richard Nixon later declared in 1971 "the most faggy god-damned thing you could imagine with that San Francisco crowd."[27] At the same time that Noguchi was writing letters of love to Stoddard, he impregnated editor Léonie Gilmour and became engaged to journal-ist Ethel Armes, who herself preferred relationships with women rather than men.[28]

Noguchi would not be the only Asian in America hobnobbing with well-known whites in queer circles long before the 1970s. Western writer Joaquin Miller particularly favored hosting Japanese "boys," whom he referred to as "brownies," as live-in domestics in his home in California's Oakland Hills.[29] Miller attracted such a following that, shortly after his death in 1913, Yone Noguchi—who had since returned to Japan—sailed back to the United States and organized a group of Japanese men to pay their respects at his home. Miller, also an active member of the San Francisco Bohemian Club, frequently declared his love of men as he remained married to a woman.[30]

In 1899, the same year Kosen Takahashi pined away over Yone Noguchi's absence as he tramped to Los Angeles, Ah Yane gave birth to her first child, Margaret Chung, in Santa Barbara, California. By the 1920s, Chung would become a successful physician, the first American surgeon of Chinese descent (figure 5.2).[31] Chung, known for wearing mannish attire, drove a sleek blue sports car around San Francisco and led many of her contemporaries, including lesbian poet Elsa Gidlow, to

Dr. Margaret Chung. San Francisco's Chinese woman physician

Figure 5.2. Portrait of Dr. Margaret Chung. Courtesy of the Gay, Lesbian, Bisexual, Transgender Historical Society (Lisa Gidlow Collection 91-16).

speculate that she might be a lesbian.[32] Gidlow actively courted Chung, drinking bootleg liquor at a local speakeasy of Chung's choosing in San Francisco's North Beach, an Italian community neighboring Chinatown. Later, in the 1940s, Chung may have had an intimate relationship with actor Sophie Tucker. Chung hosted grand parties in her home for soldiers traveling through San Francisco during World War II and served as "Mom Chung" to American soldiers by inviting them into her home while they were on leave in San Francisco.[33] She also raised funds for the war and supported the formation of the Women's Army Corps (WAC). In order to join the U.S. Navy herself, Chung initiated and lobbied congressional legislation to establish the Women Accepted for Volunteer Emergency Services (WAVES). Ironically, after the establishment of WAVES, government officials would never accept Chung's application to join due to rumors about her lesbianism unearthed by the Naval Intelligence Service. In 1943, the Professional Women's Club of San Francisco also asked Chung to resign from their membership over suspicions around her sexuality.[34]

Meanwhile, more than seven hundred miles away in the Utah desert, the United States government had incarcerated *issei* Jiro Onuma in the Topaz War Relocation Center—not for the crime of being a homosexual, but for being an "enemy alien."[35] Authorities forcibly removed Onuma and 120 thousand other Japanese Americans who had made homes along the Pacific coast to desolate camps in the nation's interior during the 1940s. Government officials claimed that Japanese living along the West Coast posed a threat to national security as the nation embarked on a war with Japan.[36] Throughout his life, Onuma had collected homoerotic kitsch, such as a postcard of a matador with a bronze penis pinned on. The penis could be detached and used as necktie pin. And, as Japanese Americans could only bring what they could carry into the incarceration camps, Onuma made it a point to pack the patriotic 1942 "Victory Issue" of male physique magazine *Strength and Health* and a medal of completion awarded by Earle Liederman, a professional muscle man who ran a popular twelve-week mail-order bodybuilding school throughout the 1920s and 1930s.[37] While historian John Howard suggests that camp provided unusual freedoms for women and gay men, visual studies scholar Tina Takemoto argues that incarceration ultimately squashed the aspirations of men such as Jiro and his lover, Ronald. Officials separated the two men due to their differing answers on the infamous "loyalty questionnaire," and surveillance implicit in any prison camp aggressively policed inappropriate activity from taking place.[38]

Literary critic Andrew Leong has proposed an "epistemology of the pocket" as opposed to queer theorist Eve Sedgwick's "epistemology of the closet" for those in America unable to afford their own room with a closet. Leong describes the pocket as a smaller space that "due to its proximity to the body, ought to be more 'private,' but because of its placement on the body, is subject to public view." It accommodates only partial concealment, since "you can hide a body in a closet but not in a pocket." Leong added, "For propertied, Anglo-American men with rooms of their own, the closet might be an appropriate figure for the possession of a hidden identity. The pocket might be more fitting for the countless others with more precarious relationships to individual property and identity: colonized peoples who have had their property taken from them; people who have been treated *as* property; aliens ineligible for citizenship; migrant workers."[39] For queer Asians who sought to keep their desires private particularly before the rise of a nationally visible LGBTQ movement, Leong's pocket serves as a useful metaphor for their all-too-small shelter, which more likely exposed rather than concealed their indiscretions from their contemporaries.

Being "out" would always be complicated for Asian Pacific Americans as for other queers of color. Political scientist Cathy Cohen has detailed how, in the late twentieth century, gay African Americans have also been out in less public ways to not risk losing their ethnic communities in racist America.[40] Asian Pacific Americans, too, would not have felt at liberty to be out in a society that already villainized and marginalized them for their race. Ironically, even when obviously queer Asians such as Yone Noguchi and Margaret Chung initiated significant action alongside history-making whites, their activities still remain barely visible. Clearly same-sex affairs did exist among Asians and Pacific Islanders in America or in territories later to be become part of the United States, even as those engaged in these intimacies may not have had a gay, lesbian, or bisexual identity. While many may perceive Asians in America as "closeted" in this earlier part of APA history, historians who privilege heterosexuality and whiteness more likely rendered them irrelevant and therefore invisible in America's past.

Radicalism on the Rise

The post–World War II period marked a shift for queer Asian Pacific American life as it did for the larger LGBT community. APA queers activated not only movements for gay and lesbian rights but also for racial and economic justice. In the mid-1950s when Daughters of Bilitis (DOB), the first lesbian civil and political rights group in the United States formed, Filipina Rose Bamberger played a crucial role in gathering a handful of women, including Del Martin and Phyllis Lyon, who would later become known as the founders. Bamberger invited a group of six women, including Martin and Lyon, to join her and her partner Rosemary Sliepen for drinks and dinner at their home in San Francisco on Friday, 21 September 1955. A second planning meeting took place on 5 October, again at Bamberger's home, at which time the group decided that she, along with her partner Sliepen, would bring fried chicken to the first official DOB meeting to be held two weeks later.[41] Yet, the purpose of DOB— a secret group of women gathered for private events versus a public organization pushing for political reform—divided the group. Historian Marcia Gallo noted how Bamberger left DOB in early 1956, refusing to be a part of an organization that hoped to welcome men and heterosexual women working publicly toward legislative changes. No doubt an outward facing DOB would increase the possibility that her own lesbianism would become more public.[42]

Bamberger had reason to protect herself from the instability that public knowledge of her sexuality might bring. During the 1950s, she had a different job nearly every year as a machine operator, brush maker, or factory worker, and additionally changed residences at least five times. Without job security and little residential stability, the consequences of coming out for Bamberger would have likely been unfathomable to bear.[43] Ironically, as DOB grew during the 1950s, a number of the officers—including Phyllis Lyon, one of the original founders who pushed for the group to be more public—in fact used pseudonyms in their newsletter, the *Ladder*, to protect their identities.[44]

Ten years after Bamberger left the group, Chinese American Crystal Jang attended a few San Francisco DOB meetings in search of other lesbians and still found the group, as well as the lesbian bars she frequented, to be "all white." When she turned to leftist groups working for Third World liberation, the broader Asian American movement seemed "very male."[45] Jang would not be alone in her sense of alienation. Activist Gil Mangaoang described himself as being in state of "schizophrenia" during the 1970s, trapped between his involvement in a homophobic Asian American political community and his intimate life in a racist LGBTQ community.[46] He matriculated into the City College of San Francisco in 1970 after being discharged from the U.S. Air Force. On campus, Mangaoang joined the Filipino Club, became an officer on the student council, and worked with other student groups of color to establish an ethnic studies program. He and other student activists negotiated with the administration to ensure that courses in Filipino history and Tagalog be included in the curricula.[47] Mangaoang, impatient for change within the college, soon after began doing volunteer work at the International

Hotel (I-Hotel), a low-income residence hotel at the corner of Jackson and Kearny Streets in San Francisco, which housed many *manong*, or elderly Filipino men.[48] It stood as the last bastion of the San Francisco's Manilatown before the city tore it down in 1979 as part of urban renewal.[49]

Countless other Asian gay and lesbian activists and writers, such as Daniel Tseng, Kitty Tsui, and Helen Zia, have reported on how people of color and queer progressive spaces remained unable to accommodate queer people of color in the 1970s.[50] Tseng vividly remembers a group comprised largely of African Americans at the Third World People's Solidarity Conference in Ann Arbor in 1974 growing angry over antigay sentiments expressed at the podium by "otherwise radical leaders." The most incendiary comments ironically came from Angela Davis, who mocked founding father George Washington for his "sissy shoes" long before her own queerness would become public knowledge.[51] The rise of the Asian American movement, as well, owed much of its ideological origins to Marxist-Leninist-Maoist beliefs that devalued same-sex sexuality as a product of bourgeois decadence and believed homosexuality would be eliminated with the eventual demise of capitalism.[52]

Still, APA queers remained committed to social justice and forged their own paths for community engagement. In the 1960s, Crystal Jang and her women friends began a petition at the City College of San Francisco calling for women students on campus to be allowed to wear pants, and successfully changed the dress code. On their way to and from City College and their homes in Chinatown, they also defiantly rode cable cars hanging off the side when the law still mandated women to sit safely inside.[53] In 1978, Jang publicly spoke against the Briggs Initiative to a news reporter who interviewed her at her workplace, the schoolyard of Benjamin Franklin Middle School.[54] The Briggs Initiative would have legalized the firing of all LGBTQ teachers and those who supported them.[55] When she appeared in the local newspapers as a result, she became one the faces of the anti–Briggs Initiative movement, participating in a rally with the United Educators of San Francisco even as the threat of losing her job loomed large.[56] For Jang, self-acceptance of her same-sex desires came through her investigations in the stacks at the public library. In 1960 at the North Beach branch, Jang, still an eighth grader, read about the Kinsey Scale just seven years after sexologist Alfred Kinsey published *Sexual Behavior in the Human Female*.[57]

Gil Mangaoang, too, forged a space where he could be both queer and Asian in his activism for social change. Through his work at the I-Hotel, Mangaoang became a member of the Kalayaan Collective, and would become one of the early members of Katipunan ng mga Demokratikong Pilipino (KDP), the first revolutionary Filipino nationalist group in the United States. Headquartered in Oakland, California, KDP appeared to be the only organization within the Asian American movement that accepted queer members. At least ten lesbians and two gay men comprised the membership and leadership of the organization.[58]

On the East Coast, bar patrons at New York City's Stonewall Inn in 1969 fought back against police harassment, marking what many historians cite as the beginning of the gay rights movement. Yet, three years earlier, in 1966 in San Francisco's Tenderloin District, sex worker and activist Tamara Ching, of Native Hawaiian, Chinese, and German descent, fought back against police harassment with other street queens at Compton's Cafeteria. The twenty-four-hour restaurant on the corner of Turk and Taylor streets had attracted a regular late-night crowd of drag queens, hustlers, and runaway teens. One weekend night in August, the management called the police to expel a particularly noisy crowd of queens lingering too long at one table while spending little money. When a police officer grabbed the arm of one of the queens to drag her away, an insurrection ensued. Dishware and silverware flew through the air, tables and chairs were upended, and patrons pushed the police out into the street. The Compton's Cafeteria revolt, in which Ching and other queens participated, initiated new transgender advocacy programs within the San Francisco Police Department and the city's Department of Public Health.[59] In the wake of Stonewall, too, queers in New York—and, soon after, across the nation—organized to form the Gay Liberation Front (GLF) to demand sexual liberation for all people. As GLF branches popped up across the country, Japanese American Kiyoshi Kuromiya cofounded the Gay Liberation Front–Philadelphia on 29 May 1970, when a group of approximately fifty people met at Gazoo, a gay collective at 230 South Street.[60]

In the arts as well, Asian lesbians took to the stage in 1979 in the form of a feminist Asian women's performance group called Unbound Feet. Kitty Tsui, Merle Woo, and Canyon Sam were three of the six women. Their very presence as performers proved radical due to the fact that few, if any, Asian American women appeared on stage at the time.[61] Tsui and Sam had previously met at Asian American Feminists, an Asian women's rap group initiated two years earlier by Doreena Wong and Canyon Sam.[62]

Unbound Feet's first show took place at the James Moore Oakland Museum Theater and proved to be immediately successful. As the group continued to perform over the next two years, audiences of up to six hundred flocked to their shows. While the performances of Tsui, Sam, and Woo did not address lesbianism, the program explicitly stated their sexuality. Unbound Feet thus exposed prominently and without shame the real existence of lesbians within the Asian American community and drew a significant Asian lesbian following.[63]

After performances, women crowded into the home of Zee Wong, which became a popular gathering place for lesbians of color generally. Wong, a master of party planning with a wide network, later initiated a series of Asian lesbian potlucks in which large groups of women would gather to share food and build community for the first time. Wong simultaneously began organizing multiracial BBQs. While the potlucks took place in Wong's home, the BBQs ironically convened at Joaquin Miller Park, a public space upon which Joaquin Miller, the lover of "brownies," had hosted countless young Japanese men in his home. By 1982, Wong had over seventy women on her list of people to invite. A year later, Lisa Chun, who had earlier in 1978 cofounded Asian Women, an Oakland-based nonpolitical support group for Asian lesbians, combined her list of contacts with Wong's and the number of APAs grew to 112.[64]

In 1981, Unbound Feet disbanded over member Merle Woo's grievance against University of California, Berkeley's refusal to renew her contract as a lecturer in Asian American Studies. Woo hoped Unbound Feet would publicly support her position when she charged that the university had discriminated against her as a lesbian and for her radical political ideology.[65] The group, unable to come to an agreement on whether they should make a public statement, splintered. Half of the members stood opposed to using Unbound Feet as a platform for workplace grievances that would put them in direct conflict with the Asian American community. Four years later, in 1985, when three of the original members regrouped as Unbound Feet Three, they more actively brought lesbian content to the stage.[66]

In the same year that Unbound Feet, in its original grouping, drew audiences to their radical performances, queer Asians from across the nation gathered in Washington, D.C., at the first National Third World Lesbian and Gay Conference. The conference, organized by the National Coalition of Black Gays, took place at Howard University in October 1979.[67] According to poet Michiyo Cornell, the meeting was "the first time in the history of the American hemisphere that Asian American gay men and lesbians joined to form a network of support."[68] Cornell, who would later change her last name to Fukaya, would go on to organize Vermont's first queer pride celebration, called "Lesbian and Gay Pride," in 1983.[69]

Four years later, in 1987, Asian lesbian and bisexual women organized the first West Coast Asian Pacific Lesbian Retreat in Sonoma, California, drawing eighty people, mostly from the San Francisco Bay Area. Then, in October, fifty Asian lesbian and gay men from across the nation gathered to form the first Asian contingent at the 1987 March on Washington for Gay Rights on the National Mall. As a national network of Asian lesbians solidified, the Asian/Pacific Lesbian Network (APLN) sponsored their first national retreat, titled "Coming Together, Moving Forward," in Santa Cruz, California, 1–4 September 1989. The event drew over 140 APA lesbians from the United States, Canada, and the United Kingdom.[70] For Asian lesbians, the 1980s marked a time of momentous community building. A burgeoning network of individuals created newsletters, held potlucks, and formed softball teams, coalescing into what sociologist Karin Aguilar-San Juan characterized as a "movement."[71]

What might be the first Asian American lesbian newsletter, *Phoenix Rising*, began in the mid-1980s, its title referring to these women's resilience and beauty, rising out of the ashes that racism, sexism, and homophobia might otherwise leave behind.[72] Their mailing list at one point counted eighty-seven women.[73] For Helen Zia, who as a community organizer in New Jersey hid her lesbianism, *Phoenix Rising* served as a lifeline, a vibrant symbol of how all her identities as a woman, Asian, and lesbian could coexist.[74]

Unbound Feet also laid the groundwork for Kitty Tsui to publish her poetry four years later in 1983.[75] Her book, *The Words of a Woman Who Breathes Fire*, inspired countless queer Asian women across two decades.[76] Tsui's work offered, in the words of Aguilar-San Juan, "an image of a 'proud, defiant, no bullshit woman, the dyke we all wanted to be.'"[77] While Kitty Tsui was the first Chinese American lesbian to come out with a book, Korean American Willyce Kim broke significant ground as the first published Asian American lesbian with *Eating Artichokes*, printed by the Woman's Press Collective nine years earlier in 1972.[78] In the 1980s, however, more than a handful of poets and writers, including Merle Woo and Chea Villanueva, began publishing their own single-authored books—a trend that continued into the 1990s.[79] In addition to publishing with established feminist publishers, such as Firebrand Books, the Women's Press Collective, and Spinsters Ink, queer writers of color also initiated their own printing houses, including Kitchen Table: Women of Color Press, founded in 1980 by Black lesbians Barbara Smith and Audre Lorde.[80]

Tsui, known not just for her poetry, additionally took up bodybuilding and won a bronze medal in 1986 and gold in 1990 at Gay Games I and II, held respectively in San Francisco and Vancouver. Her muscled body prominently appeared in the renegade lesbian erotica magazine *On Our Backs* in 1988 and 1990, as well as in New York City's *Village Voice*.[81] Tsui may have been the first Asian lesbian to appear on the cover of both publications. In 1995, she published *Breathless,* a book of SM erotica in which sex mingled with fermented bean curd, beef tendons, and bitter melon. Tsui created intense scenes of pleasure, pain, and Chinese food, and won the Firecracker Alternative Book (FAB) Award for *Breathless* in 1996.[82] Tsui wrote explicitly about desiring Asian lesbians, which became noteworthy to a white lesbian community who did not necessarily see Asian women as attractive.[83]

During the 1980s, many queer Asians defiantly sought to find each other. In New York City, two mixed-heritage Asians, Katherine Hall and Chea Villanueva, formed Asian Lesbians of the East Coast in 1983.[84] In Los Angeles, queer Asian American activists formed Asian Pacific Lesbians and Gays (A/PLG) in 1980, the first organization of its kind in Southern California.[85] The group would later become overrun with "rice queens"—a term used to describe white men interested in relationships with Asians based largely on their ethnicity.[86] Four years later in 1984, Steve Lew and Prescott Chow formed the Gay Asian Rap Group (GARP) in Long Beach, California. Though GARP did not initially form in direct response to A/PLGs internal divisions—debates around whether it should be a space that nurtures gay Asian leadership or serve primarily as a social network for white men to meet Asian men—early members of GARP organized the group to avoid what they perceived as mistakes in A/PLG. As more gay APA men within A/PLG defected to GARP, the two organizations became distinctly different. GARP would later become the Gay Asian Pacific Support Network (GAPSN) in 1989 to create a space specifically for APA men.[87] David Hong hosted many of the meetings in his West Hollywood home. Monthly rap sessions took place at the Chinatown Service Center Annex in Los Angeles.[88]

Queer South Asians contributed significantly to the explosion of queer APA community groups in the 1980s. In 1985 and 1986, queer South Asians—first in Brooklyn, New York; and then in the San Francisco Bay Area—formed two different groups, Anamika and Trikone respectively, to address the specific needs of LGBTQ people of South Asian descent from countries such as Afghanistan, Bangladesh, India, Sri Lanka, Pakistan, Bhutan, Nepal, Myanmar (Burma), and Tibet. The two organizations would be part of a half dozen groups that emerged in the following years across North America, the United Kingdom, and India.[89]

Other queer Asian Pacific Americans played key roles in community organizations that were not specifically queer, as well as in queer groups that were not exclusively APA. Mini Liu, who worked extensively in the New York–based Organization of Asian Women (OAW) and the Committee Against Anti-Asian Violence (CAAAV), pushed hard to include sexuality in the organizations' missions and priorities. She sought to bring a more intersectional approach to existing racial justice activism.[90] In San Francisco, Donna Keiko Ozawa cofounded the first and still largest queer youth organization, called the Lavender Youth Recreation & Information Center (LYRIC). A dance at the Women's Building celebrated their formation in 1988.[91] In 1991, the group transitioned from an autonomous collective to a service provider with financial support from the San Francisco Mayor's Office, and two years later purchased their permanent home at 127 Collingwood Street in the Castro District of San Francisco.[92] Lia Shigemura of Okinawan and Japanese heritage played a foundational role in establishing the Asian Women's Shelter (AWS) in 1988 to provide services for limited-English- and non-English-speaking refugee and immigrant survivors of domestic violence in the San Francisco Bay Area. Two years later, in 1990, AWS implemented its Lesbian Services Program to increase accessibility.[93] From 1989 to 1992, South Asian American LGBTQ activist and attorney Urvashi Vaid served as the executive director of the National Gay and Lesbian Task Force (NGLTF), now known as the LGBTQ Task Force. Filipina American activist Melinda Paras, former founder and national leader of the KDP, also served as the organization's executive director from 1994 to 1996.[94]

The 1980s simultaneously marked mass devastation for the gay male community due to the U.S. government's non-response to the AIDS epidemic.[95] People of color found themselves in a particular public health crisis due to disparate funding for services and education, as well as presumptions within their own communities that HIV/AIDS was only a "white disease."[96] Queer activists of color across the nation quickly organized to provide support. On the West Coast, Asian American Recovery Services (AARS) in San Francisco established the Asian AIDS Project (AAP) in 1987, the first organization to target APAs for HIV/AIDS prevention.[97] In the same year, AARS would call Asian American city leaders to initiate the Asian AIDS Taskforce (AAT), a group committed to mobilizing community-wide resources in the fight against AIDS. The Japanese American Cultural and Community Center of Northern California hosted these early meetings in Japan Town.[98] The following year, the Gay Asian Pacific Alliance (GAPA) implemented an informal support group for HIV-positive gay Asians, later called GAPA Community HIV Project (GCHP).[99] Chinese American Steve Lew served a critical role in these early efforts as a key organizer, educator, and role model for other HIV-positive men.[100] In 1990, when Vince Crisostomo left New York and traveled across the country with his Jewish boyfriend to live in San Francisco, he found community and family with GAPA, the Asian AIDS Project, and particularly Steve Lew. Crisostomo's boyfriend, who had AIDS, could also access the organization's services, and AAP offered Crisostomo a job in their theater program after he had applied for seven other jobs without success.[101]

Asian Pacific Americans also took formative roles in AIDS activism in other parts of the United States and the world. In 1989, just two years after the formation of the Asian AIDS Project in San Francisco, Kiyoshi Kuromiya, who earlier formed the Philadelphia branch of Gay Liberation Front, founded Critical Path, one of the earliest and most comprehensive resources available to the public for treating HIV.[102] Crisostomo, who was Chamorro, became the first publicly out HIV-positive Pacific Islander at World AIDS Day in 1991, and became directly involved in bringing increased HIV/AIDS awareness and education to Guam. In 2000, Crisostomo returned to Guam to become the executive director for the first funded, community-based organization to do AIDS work in the Pacific.[103] GAPA board member George Choy collaborated with OCCUR, Japan's first gay rights group, which successfully brought a discrimination suit against the Tokyo city government in 1990.[104] Also in 2000, Chinese American Choy had persuaded the San Francisco Board of Supervisors to pass Project 10, a teen youth counseling program within the San Francisco Unified School District.[105]

AIDS organizing in the 1980s and 1990s both gathered and nurtured countless community-minded APA activists committed to promoting Asian Pacific American health and wellbeing in the queer and transgender communities, as well as eradicating broad-based fear based on gender, sexuality, or HIV status. Tamara Ching from the Compton's Cafeteria revolt worked as an AIDS education outreach worker for the AAP and oversaw a support group for the APA transgender community for GCHP as the "God Mother of Polk [Street]".[106] Transwoman Nikki Calma, better known as "Tita Aida,"[107] who also worked at the Asian AIDS Project in 1990s, became a community icon through her advocacy work. She hosted countless fundraisers, and was one of three women to be featured in the first APA transgender public service announcement in 2008.[108] Transman Willy Wilkinson, who was active in HIV work with

Inner City Community Health Outreach and served as a founding board member of GCHP, would go on to become a leading transgender public health advocate in San Francisco.[109]

Historian Marc Stein has characterized the outpouring of community engagement in response to the conservatism of the 1980s as a "renaissance." Queer cultural productions and community activism flourished in the fight against AIDS and moral condemnation of LGBTQ people. The 1980s, however, was also a time of mounting anti-Asian sentiment and violence as the U.S. automobile industry crumbled in the face of Japanese car manufacturers. The Vincent Chin case became a flashpoint for organizing against Asian American violence, regardless of gender and sexual identities. On 19 June 1982 in Highland Park, Michigan, two white autoworkers with a baseball bat bludgeoned to death twenty-seven-year-old engineer Vincent Chin after hurling racial epithets at him and accusing him of taking away their jobs.[110] Chinese American lesbian Helen Zia, who was a community organizer at the time and would later become an award-winning journalist and editor of *Ms. Magazine*, cofounded and served as the president of American Citizens for Justice (ACJ), the first explicitly Asian American grassroots community advocacy effort with a national scope, and led the fight for justice for Vincent Chin.[111] Indeed, an explosion of the Asian literary and arts culture as well as community groups in the 1980s becomes particularly notable as queer Asian Pacific Americans came together during a time of extreme socioeconomic repression, moral conservatism, and anti-Asian sentiment.

On 6 April 1991 on Broadway in New York City, queers of color, leftist Asian Americans regardless of sexual orientation or gender diversity, antiracist white gays, bisexuals, and lesbians, and the Actors' Equity Association joined hands with Asian Lesbians of the East Coast (ALOEC) and Gay Asian and Pacific Islander Men of New York (GAPIMNY) to protest two prominent LGBTQ institutions' use of Cameron Mackintosh's musical *Miss Saigon* as their annual fundraiser extravaganza. ALOEC and GAPIMNY had long been in conversation with the two hosts— Lambda Legal Defense and Education Fund and New York City's Lesbian and Gay Community Services Center—to cancel their fundraiser at this musical, which promoted damaging images of submissive "Orientals" and used yellow face in the casting of one of the actors.[112] While the fundraiser took place as scheduled, the protest marked the formation of an incredible coalition of various communities publicly denouncing racism, misogyny, and Orientalism. Organizer Yoko Yoshikawa recalled, "James Lee taped a neon pink triangle to his leather jacket, emblazoned with the words: 'San Francisco-born Gay Man of Korean Descent.' On any other night, he could have been bashed for that. But that night, his back was covered. Gray-haired Japanese American wives and mothers and brash young white men from Queer Nation marched side by side. Dykes in dreads, campy queens, leftists of all persuasions: we owned Broadway."[113]

Queer APA publications too flourished through the 1990s. Asian Pacific Islander lesbians and bisexual women produced *The Very Inside,* an anthology of over one hundred pieces edited by Sharon Lim-Hing in 1994.[114] Lim-Hing began thinking about producing the book in the summer of 1990 as she walked home in Somerville, Massachusetts, in anticipation of the local teenagers calling her "Chink."[115] At the time, except for *Between the Lines,* a short anthology of Asian American lesbian writing that was out of print and hard to obtain, Asian women's writings had appeared only in small numbers as part of women of color anthologies or as tokens toward diversity in white anthologies.[116] Lim-Hing sought to create something as large as Gloria Anzaldúa's and Cherríe Moraga's *This Bridge Called My Back* to speak to Asian Pacific bisexual and lesbian women's strength, beauty, creativity, and rage so that these women would not be just "a blip on the graph at the intersection of 'race' and sexual preference, nor . . . the hub of triple oppressions."[117]

Six years later, Quang Bao and Hanya Yanagihara published *Take Out,* an anthology produced with the support of the Asian American Writer's Workshop in New York. The anthology brought gay Asian male authors into a literary community that had theretofore fostered a growing number of queer women writers.[118] Motivated more by artistry and less by activism, the editors nevertheless hoped their publication would force readers "to reevaluate [their] conceptions of gay Asian America." The collection was comprised mostly of works by men since the editors decided to not "worry too much about gender equity" since it was "far better to sacrifice quantity for quality."[119] Unfortunately, *Take Out* with its less-than-feminist impulse, might have served as the cap to a literary movement started by radical Asian lesbians thirty years earlier.

The most widely read queer APA writing of the 1990s, however, was Olympic medalist Greg Louganis's autobiography, titled *Breaking the Surface,* in which he publicly came out as HIV positive after nearly a decade of rumors in professional sports that he was gay. Louganis, an adoptee of mixed Samoan and white ancestry, endured a childhood of persecution being called "nigger" as well as "sissy." He went on to win four gold medals in diving—the three-meter springboard and the ten-meter platform in 1984 and 1988. *Breaking the Surface* became a

New York Times #1 Best Seller in 1995, initiating his public persona as a gay rights activist. As the first prominent athlete to come out as gay, Louganis faced tremendous challenges in professional sports that impacted him emotionally and lost him millions of dollars in endorsements.[120]

Other activists published landmark texts on not exclusively queer APAs. In 1991, Native Hawaiian Lani Ka`ahumanu coedited *Bi Any Other Name* with Loraine Hutchins, and the anthology has become recognized as the "Bi-ble" of the bisexual movement.[121] When Ka`ahumanu and Hutchins could only submit their book in the "lesbian anthology" category of the Lambda Literary Awards, BiNet, an umbrella organization for a network of bisexual communities, protested and initiated the creation of a "bisexual" category in the book awards.[122] Ka`ahumanu had long been recognized as the mother of the bisexual movement with her role in the founding of BiPOL in 1983, the first and oldest bisexual political organization.

The 1990s further marked an expansion of queer Asian American activism with the development of the Internet. A swell of South Asian queer groups formed outside of California—SALGA in New York City, Khush in Washington, D.C., Trikone in Atlanta, MASALA in Boston—as well as internationally. Online forums such as KhushList, SAGrrls, DesiDykes, GayBombay, and Khushnet.com multiplied as the web become more accessible.[123] A queer Vietnamese American support group in Southern California called Ô-Môi also took advantage of the Internet to grow significantly from its initial six members in 1995 to fifty-four members by 2000, according to sociologist Gina Masequesmay.[124]

Organizations within the ethnic mainstream also increasingly recognized LGBTQ members within their communities. In 1990, when much of the nation feared to even breathe the same air as gay men because of the AIDS epidemic, the San Fernando, California, chapter of the Japanese American Citizens' League (JACL) elected Takenori "Tak" Yamamoto as president. Yamamoto became the first openly gay president in any chapter of the JACL and played a critical role in the organization's endorsement of gay marriages at their national convention four years later in Salt Lake City.[125] In 1994, as AIDS became the leading cause of death for Americans between the ages of twenty-five and forty-four, Pine United Methodist Church in San Francisco, one of America's earliest Japanese American churches, became the first reconciling or queer-friendly Asian American church in America.[126] In the same year, Cherry Blossom Festival organizers in San Francisco invited more than one hundred LGBTQ women and men to march in the April parade, after hearing that a similar contingent had just marched in San

Francisco's Chinese New Year's parade in February after much struggle. Vice president at Union Bank and community leader June Sugihara
led the Cherry Blossom contingent, declaring, "It is so very important
to recognize and support the lesbian and gay people in our Japanese
American community."[127]

The 1990s also marked a period when more APA parents publicly vo-
calized support of their gay, lesbian, and bisexual children. In 1990, two
years after their daughter came out to them as gay, Okinawan American Harold and Ellen Kameya became actively involved in Parents and
Friends of Lesbians and Gays (PFLAG) as the first known Asian parents
in America to publicly advocate for their gay children. They first began
attending PFLAG meetings at the Westwood United Methodist Church,
and the two informally functioned as an API (Asian and Pacific Islander)
PFLAG for more than a decade as the only Asian parents they knew in
PFLAG. In 2012, the Kameyas along with other API parents would more
formally cofound the first API PFLAG chapter in the San Gabriel Valley.[128]
In Northern California, the API-PFLAG Family Project, later known as
API Family Pride, formed in 1996. Filipina lesbian Trinity Ordona played
a central role in collaboration with the API-PFLAG Family Project to produce the first documentary film of Asian parents discussing their queer
children, titled *Coming Out, Coming Home*.[129] In 1997, Al and Jane Nakatani, in collaboration with writer Molly Fumia, published *Honor Thy
Children*, a memoir of the loss of their three sons, two of whom were
gay. The oldest and youngest of the Nakatani sons died from AIDS-
related illnesses, and the middle son died from a gunshot wound in an
altercation. The father, Al Nakatani, later attributed his middle son's inability to walk away from the fight to his own mandate to maintain an
inflexible prideful masculinity. The father had already pushed his oldest
son out of their house at the age of fifteen when he found out he was
gay. However, after the death of his second son, he and his wife came to
actively support their youngest son in his final struggle against AIDS.[130]
These early works laid the groundwork for a flurry of publications and
memoirs by queer APAs or their parents in the decades that followed.[131]

Queer Asian America continues to grow tremendously in the twenty-
first century. Countless blogs from queer Asians expound on the importance of community engagement and queer empowerment. Artists and
community organizations have initiated the recognition of queer and
transgender APAs for their historic activism, further shedding light on
their previously hidden presence. Christopher Lee, the Asian American
transgender man whose death certificate motivated the Respect After
Death Act, was also cofounder of the San Francisco Transgender Film

Festival in 1997 and was the first openly transgender man to be elected as Grand Marshal in the 2002 San Francisco Pride Parade.[132] The afore-mentioned Tamara Ching, who revolted against police at Compton's Cafeteria in 1966, won a number of honors, including the Community Service Award from the Harvey Milk LGBT Democratic Club in 2006.[133] In 2012, artist Tanya Wischerath recognized her and other transwomen activists of color in a mural along Clarion Alley in San Francisco.[134] In 2013, San Francisco Pride honored retired schoolteacher Crystal Jang as Grand Marshal in recognition of her contributions to the LGBTQ com-munity as the first openly gay Asian lesbian teacher within the San Fran-cisco Unified School District. Not only had Jang first spoken out publicly against the Briggs Initiative, but, decades later in the early 1990s, offi-cials appointed her the middle school coordinator for the Office of Sup-port Services for Sexual Minority Youth and Families, the first office of its kind in the nation. For the following ten years, she assisted in creating K-12 curriculum for district-wide staff trainings to address issues of bul-lying, antigay discrimination, safe schools, and sensitivity to alternative families.[135] More recently in 2014, San Francisco AIDS activist George Choy was honored with a sidewalk plaque in the Castro District's Rain-bow Honor Walk, memorializing twenty "heroes and heroines of LGBT history."[136] Countless other activists, such as Native Hawaiian Kumu Hi-naleimoana Wong-Kalu, have, without formal recognition, been trans-forming people's lives daily by teaching love, honor, and respect for indigeneity and gender diversity in classrooms, workshops, and public spaces.[137]

In universities across the nation, queer and Asian student groups are cropping up. In the San Francisco Bay Area alone, four institutions of higher education—University of California, Berkeley; San Francisco State University; San Jose State University; and Stanford—all have student-run organizations by and for LGBTQ Asian Pacific Americans.[138] More recently, in 2014, the University of Pennsylvania formed its first queer and Asian student group, called Penn Q&A.[139] While much of queer APA activism historically has taken place at coastal metropoles, where both Asians and queers have congregated in larger numbers, the rise of suburbs of color since the 1990s will no doubt fuel queer APA community engagement and cultural production in other regions in the twenty-first century.[140] Most notably, a younger generation of queer APAs are taking interest in the histories of their LGBTQ predecessors. In the past three years, chapters of the queer advocacy organization API Equality in both Northern and Southern California have initiated oral history projects (the Pioneers Project in Los Angeles and Dragon Fruit

Project in San Francisco) and have sponsored educational workshops on APA queer history as well as Wikipedia Hackathons.[141] At the GLBT History Museum in San Francisco, the first of its kind in the nation, curators have mounted four exclusively queer APA exhibits since its opening in 2011.[142] Queer APA organizing and community engagement has consistently occurred at the intersection of race and sexuality even as much of the mainstream LGBTQ movement attempts to erase the significance of their race and ethnicity in what many Americans believe to be a postracial America.[143] For these APA activists, sexual freedom, economic justice, and gender and racial equity are inextricably intertwined in their fight for a more compassionate and inclusive world.

Dr. Amy Sueyoshi is Dean of the College of Ethnic Studies at San Francisco State University, with a joint faculty appointment in Sexuality Studies and Race and Resistance Studies.

Notes

1. Transgender Law Center, "Remembering Christopher Lee as Respect After Death Act Takes Effect," Transgender Law Center website, 7 July 2015, http://transgenderlawcenter.org/archives/11746. The Transgender Law Center is located at 1629 Telegraph Avenue, Oakland, California.
2. Jan Mabry, "'Respect After Death' Act Takes Effect Giving Transgenders Right to Have Chosen Gender on Death Certificates," CBS San Francisco, 1 July 2015, http://sanfrancisco.cbslocal.com/2015/07/01/respect-after-death-act-takes-effect-giving-transgenders-right-to-have-chosen-gender-on-death-certificates.
3. Stephen M. Engel, "Development Perspectives on Lesbian and Gay Politics: Fragmented Citizenship in a Fragmented State," Perspectives on Politics 13, no. 2 (2015): 287–311. "Don't Ask, Don't Tell" is formally known as Department of Defense Directive 1304.26. It was issued on 21 December 1993 and was in effect from 28 February 1994 through 20 September 2011.
4. A West Point graduate, an Arabic linguist, and an Iraq war veteran, Choi remains dishonorably discharged from the military even though "Don't Ask, Don't Tell" has been repealed. He handcuffed himself to the White House fence on 20 April 2010. The White House is located at 1600 Pennsylvania Avenue NW, Washington, DC. It was designated an NHL on 19 December 1960. Maria Streshinsky, "Dan Choi," Atlantic Monthly 306, no. 4 (2010): 88; Gabriel Arana, "The Passion of Dan Choi," American Prospect: Longform, 9 February 2014, http://prospect.org/article/passion-dan-choi.

5. "Stuart Gaffney," *Huffington Post,* http://www.huffingtonpost.com/stuart-gaffney.
6. I use the term Asian Pacific Americans to signal people who are in the United States who come from or have ancestors from Asia or the Pacific Islands. Because of the history of APA migration, the queer people documented here before 1965 are largely Chinese and Japanese. I include in a more abbreviated form Korean, Filipino, Indonesian, Vietnamese, Native Hawaiian, Okinawan, Samoan, and Indian activism mostly after 1965.
7. Frank Chin and Jeffery Paul Chan, "Racist Love," in *Seeing through Shuck,* ed. Richard Kostelanetz (New York: Ballantine Books, 1972), 65–79; Amy Sueyoshi, "Queer Asian American Historiography," in *The Oxford Handbook of Asian American History,* ed. David K. Yoo and Eiichiro Azuma (New York: Oxford University Press, 2016), 267–78.
8. David Eng speaks to the dearth of scholarship on queer people of color generally in queer studies, which includes APAs. David Eng, Judith Halberstam, and José Esteban Muñoz, "Introduction: What's Queer about Queer Studies Now," *Social Text* 23, no. 3–4 (2005): 2.
9. Susan Lee Johnson, "'My Own Private Life': Toward a History of Desire in Gold Rush California," *California History* 79, no. 2 (2000): 316–46.
10. Mary Roberts Coolidge, *Chinese Immigration* (New York: Henry Holt and Company, 1909); Yong Chen, *Chinese San Francisco, 1850–1943: A Trans-Pacific Community* (Stanford, CA: Stanford University Press, 2000); Yuji Ichioka, *Issei: The World of the First Generation Japanese Immigrants, 1885–1924* (New York: Free Press, 1988); Yuji Ichioka, "Ameyuki-san: Japanese Prostitutes in Nineteenth-Century America," *Amerasia Journal* 4, no. 1 (1977): 1–22; Lucie Cheng Hirata, "Free, Indentured, Enslaved: Chinese Prostitutes in Nineteenth-Century America," *Signs* 5, no. 1 (1979): 3–29; George Anthony Peffer, *If They Don't Bring Their Women Here: Chinese Female Immigration before Exclusion* (Urbana: University of Illinois Press, 1999).
11. Robert G. Lee, *Orientals: Asian Americans in Popular Culture* (Philadelphia: Temple University Press, 1999); Nayan Shah, *Contagious Divides: Epidemics and Race in San Francisco's Chinatown* (Berkeley: University of California Press, 2001).
12. Amy Sueyoshi, *Queer Compulsions: Race, Nation, and Sexuality in the Affairs of Yone Noguchi* (Honolulu: University of Hawaii Press, 2012), 16. See also Gregory Tomso, "The Queer History of Leprosy and Same-Sex Love," *American Literary History* 14, no. 2 (2002): 747–75. For more on Stoddard, see Roger Austen, *Genteel Pagan: The Double Life of Charles Warren Stoddard,* ed. John W. Crowley (Amherst: University of Massachusetts Press, 1991).
13. Austen, *Genteel Pagan,* 92.
14. Lee Wallace, *Sexual Encounters: Pacific Texts, Modern Sexualities* (Ithaca, NY: Cornell University Press, 2003).
15. See "*Emporia Daily Gazette,* 25 July 1893, 1," in Peter Boag, *Re-dressing America's Frontier Past* (Berkeley: University of California Press, 2011), 149.

16. See *"Oakland Tribune,* 22 July 1908, 3" in Boag, *Re-dressing America's Frontier Past,* 148.

17. Nayan Shah, *Stranger Intimacy: Contesting Race, Sexuality, and the Law in the North American West* (Berkeley: University of California Press, 2011), 75–76.

18. Nayan Shah, "Between 'Oriental Depravity' and 'Natural Degenerates': Spatial Borderlands and the Making of Ordinary Americans," *American Quarterly* 57, no. 3 (2005): 703–25.

19. Jack Mason and Donald Guimary, "Asian Labor Contractors in Alaska Canned Salmon Industry, 1880–1937," *Labor History* 22, no. 3 (1981): 391; Lauren Casady, "Labor Unrest and the Labor Movement in the Salmon Industry of the Pacific Coast," Ph.D. diss., University of California, Berkeley, 1938, 79, 201, 240. Chris Friday summarized the content of the above two citations and added his own analysis of "homosexuality" in the canneries in his book *Organizing Asian American Labor: The Pacific Coast Canned-Salmon Industry, 1870–1942* (Philadelphia: Temple University Press, 1994), 45–55, 114.

20. Madeline Y. Hsu, "Unwrapping Orientalist Constraints: Restoring Homosocial Normativity to Chinese American History," *Amerasia Journal* 29, no. 2 (2003): 230–53.

21. Susan Johnson, *Roaring Camp: The Social World of the California Gold Rush* (New York: W. W. Norton and Company, 2000).

22. The *Shin Sekai,* founded in 1894, functioned as the house organ for the San Francisco Japanese YMCA until 1897. The San Francisco YMCA was located at 121 Haight Street. See Brian Niiya, "Shin Sekai (newspaper)," *Densho En cyclopedia,* http://encyclopedia.densho.org/Shin_Sekai_%28newspaper%29; *Langley's San Francisco Directory, 1895* (San Francisco: J. B. Painter Co., 1895). In 1906, at the height of the newspaper's circulation, *Shin Sekai's* San Francisco office was located at 948 Geary Street. Japanese American History Archive, Japanese American Cultural and Community Center of Northern California, San Francisco, California.

23. Sueyoshi, *Queer Compulsions,* 83.

24. Ibid. "Issei," which means first generation in Japanese, refers to the first wave of immigrants from Japan who arrived in the United States before the 1924 passage of the Johnson-Reed Immigration Act. See "Issei," *Densho Encyclopedia,* accessed 7 May 2016, http://encyclopedia.densho.org/Issei.

25. Yone Noguchi was the father of Asian American artist Isamu Noguchi. He carved his name in Japanese into the wall of the Carmel Mission during his tramp to Los Angeles. Sueyoshi, *Queer Compulsions,* 54. The Carmel Mission, also known as Mission San Carlos Borromeo de Carmelo, is located at 3080 Rio Road, Carmel-by-the-Sea, California. It was listed on the NRHP on 15 October 1966 and designated an NHL on 9 October 1960.

26. Stoddard lived at 300 M Street NW at the corner of Third and M Streets in a two-story red brick house with six rooms and one bath. Ethel Armes, "Aloha,

Wela, Wela!" *National Magazine* 21, no. 3 (1904): 308; Austen, *Genteel Pagan,* 134.

27. Austen, *Genteel Pagan.* The Bohemian Club Clubhouse was located at the northeast corner of Post Street and Grant Avenue. Bohemian Club, *Certificate of Incorporation, Constitution, By-Laws and Rules, Officers, Committees, and Members* (San Francisco: H. S. Crocker Company, 1904). For Richard Nixon's quotation, see Sueyoshi, *Queer Compulsions,* 149.

28. Yone Noguchi's more famous son Isamu Noguchi was born in Pasadena, California, on 17 November 1904. Ethel Armes would become famous as Alabama's first historian. Amy Sueyoshi, *Queer Compulsions.* For more on Isamu Noguchi, see Masayo Duus, *The Life of Isamu Noguchi: Journey without Borders* (Princeton, NJ: Princeton University Press, 2007).

29. Miller's residence address is listed as "Upper Fruitvale" in the 1899 Oakland Directory. His home is located within Joaquin Miller Park at 3590 Sanborn Drive, Oakland, California. It was listed on the NRHP on 15 October 1966 and designated an NHL on 29 December 1962.

30. When Miller first met Noguchi, he called him a "beautiful Japanese flower"; see Sueyoshi, *Queer Compulsions.*

31. Judy Tzu-Chun Wu, *Doctor Mom Chung of the Fair-Haired Bastards: The Life of a Wartime Celebrity* (Berkeley: University of California Press, 2005). The 1929 San Francisco city directory lists Chung as living at 340 Stockton Place (now demolished). See *Crocker-Langley San Francisco City Directory, 1929* (San Francisco: R. L. Polk and Co., 1928).

32. Wu, *Doctor Mom Chung of the Fair-Haired Bastards.*

33. In 1942, Chung's home was in the Telegraph Hill neighborhood of San Francisco; from 1943 to 1945, she is listed as living in what is now the Lone Mountain neighborhood, according to the city directory. Her medical practice was located at 752 Sacramento Street, in San Francisco's Chinatown. See *Polk's Crocker-Langley San Francisco City Directory, 1942, 1943, 1944, 1945* (San Francisco: R. L. Polk and Co.).

34. Wu, *Doctor Mom Chung of the Fair-Haired Bastards.*

35. The Topaz War Relocation Center, also known as the Central Utah Relocation Center (Topaz), was built in 1942 in Millard County, Utah. It was listed on the NRHP on 2 January 1974 and designated an NHL on 29 March 2007.

36. Roger Daniels, *Concentration Camps USA: Japanese Americans and World War II* (Hinsdale, IL: Dryden Press, 1971); Greg Robinson, *A Tragedy of Democracy: Japanese Confinement in North America* (New York: Columbia University Press, 2009); Greg Robinson, *By Order of the President: FDR and the Internment of Japanese Americans* (Cambridge, MA: Harvard University Press, 2001).

37. Tina Takemoto, "Looking for Jiro Onuma: A Queer Meditation on the Incarceration of Japanese Americans during WWII," *GLQ: A Journal of Lesbian and Gay Studies* 20, no. 3 (2013): 241–75.

38. John Howard, *Concentration Camps on the Homefront: Japanese Americans in the House of Jim Crow* (Chicago: University of Chicago Press, 2008); Takemoto, "Looking for Jiro Onuma."

39. Andrew Leong, "The Pocket and the Watch: A Collective Individualist Reading of Japanese American Literature," *Verge: Studies in Global Asias* 1, no. 2 (2015): 76–114.

40. Cathy Cohen, *Boundaries of Blackness: AIDS and the Breakdown of Black Politics* (Chicago: University of Chicago, 1999).

41. In 1955, Rose Bamberger, or "Rosalie Bamberger," appears in the city directory as living in San Francisco's Silver Terrace neighborhood. See Marcia M. Gallo, *Different Daughters: A History of the Daughters of Bilitis and the Rise of the Lesbian Rights Movement* (Emeryville, CA: Seal Press, 2007), 4, 5.

42. Gallo, *Different Daughters,* 8.

43. *Polk's San Francisco City Directories, 1950–1959* (San Francisco: R. L. Polk and Co.)

44. Gallo, *Different Daughters,* 31.

45. Interview with Crystal Jang, conducted by author, 31 January 2012, San Francisco, California. For more on the Asian American movement see Daryl J. Maeda, *Rethinking the Asian American Movement* (New York: Routledge, 2012).

46. Eric C. Wat, *The Making of a Gay Asian Community: An Oral History of Pre-AIDS Los Angeles* (New York: Rowman and Littlefield, 2002), 102.

47. Gil Mangaoang, "From the 1970s to the 1990s: Perspective of a Gay Filipino American Activist," in *Asian American Sexualities: Dimensions of the Gay and Lesbian Experience,* ed. Russell Leong (New York: Routledge, 1996), 102–3.

48. The International Hotel was home to thousands of seasonal Asian laborers in the 1920s and 1930s, particularly Filipinos. It was added to the NRHP on 15 June 1977.

49. The demolition took place despite a fight that began in 1968 and continued for more than a decade between the residents of the hotel and the city. See Estella Habal, *San Francisco's International Hotel: Mobilizing the Filipino American Community in the Anti-Eviction Movement* (Philadelphia: Temple University Press, 2007).

50. Daniel Tseng, "Slicing Silence: Asian Progressives Come Out," in *Asian Americans: The Movement and the Moment,* ed. Steve Louie and Glenn Omatsu (Los Angeles: UCLA Asian American Studies Center Press, 2001), 200–39; Kitty Tsui, *The Words of a Woman Who Breathes Fire* (San Francisco: Spinsters Ink, 1983); Helen Zia, *Asian American Dreams: The Emergence of an American People* (New York: Farrar, Straus and Giroux, 2000).

51. Tseng, "Slicing Silence," 228.

52. Wat, *The Making of a Gay Asian Community,* 93.

53. Interview with Crystal Jang, conducted by author, 31 January 2012, San Francisco, California. Ocean Campus, the main campus of the City College

of San Francisco, is located at 50 Phelan Avenue, San Francisco, California. In May 1965, Mona Hutchin, a student at the University of California, Berkeley, more formally challenged the unofficial ban against women standing on the "outside step" of cable cars. Associated Press, "Women Start Riding 'Outside Step' of Frisco's Old Dinky Cable Cars," *Ocala Star Banner,* 13 May 1965, 8.

54. Benjamin Franklin Middle School is located at 1430 Scott Street, San Francisco, California.

55. Karen Graves, "Political Pawns in an Educational Endgame: Reflections on Bryant, Briggs, and Some Twentieth-Century School Questions," *History of Education Quarterly* 53, no. 1 (2013): 1–20.

56. Interview with Crystal Jang, conducted by author, 31 January 2012, San Francisco, California; Crystal Jang, email message to author, 17 October 2015.

57. Alfred C. Kinsey and the Institute for Sex Research, *Sexual Behavior in the Human Female* (Philadelphia: Saunders, 1953). The North Beach branch of the San Francisco Public Library recently reopened at 850 Columbus Avenue, San Francisco, California. This new construction replaces the previous building, constructed in 1959 on an adjacent lot.

58. Gil Mangaoang, "From the 1970s to the 1990s,"103–9; Trinity Ann Ordona, "Coming Out Together: An Ethnohistory of the Asian and Pacific Islander Queer Women's and Transgendered People's Movement of San Francisco," Ph.D. diss., University of California, Santa Cruz, 2000. The KDP National Headquarters was located at 4704 Shattuck Avenue in Oakland in the 1970s and moved to 526 Thirty-Second Street in Oakland in the late 1970s. In the 1980s, the office moved to 3600 Lincoln Way in Oakland. Trinity Ordona, email message to author, 16 December 2015.

59. Susan Stryker, *Transgender History* (Berkeley, CA: Seal Press, 2008), 63–66, 74, 75. The uprising at Compton's Cafeteria, 101 Taylor Street, San Francisco, was the first known militant action by LGBTQ people against police harassment. The building is a contributing resource to the Uptown Tenderloin Historic District, added to the NRHP on 5 February 2009.

60. Interview with Kiyoshi Kuromiya, conducted by Marc Stein. See Marc Stein, "Kiyoshi Kuromiya, 17 June 1997," Outhistory.org, 2009, http://outhistory .org/exhibits/show/philadelphia-lgbt-interviews/interviews/kiyoshi-kuromiya. Marc Stein, *City of Sisterly and Brotherly Loves: Lesbian and Gay Philadelphia, 1945–1972* (Philadelphia: Temple University Press, 2004).

61. Trinity Ordona, "Asian Lesbians in San Francisco: Struggles to Create a Safe Space, 1970s–1980s," in *Asian/Pacific Islander Women: A Historical Anthology,* ed. Shirley Hune and Gail Nomura (New York: New York University Press, 2003), 327. Merle Woo is of both Chinese and Korean ancestry.

62. Members of Asian American Feminists would share food and talk about racism and sexism in a group of nearly all queer Asian women. The first session of Asian American Feminists took place in Sam's Castro neighborhood San

Francisco apartment; see Ordona, "Coming Out Together," 128–32; Canyon Sam, email message to author, 24 November 2015.

63. Ordona, "Coming Out Together," 134–35.
64. Ordona, "Coming Out Together," 142; Stephen Stewart, *Positive Image: A Portrait of Gay America* (New York: William Morrow and Co., 1985), 181.
65. After a two-year legal battle, in 1984, the University of California, Berkeley reached a settlement with Woo of $73,584 and two years' reinstatement. See Stewart, *Positive Image,* 115.
66. Ordona, "Coming Out Together," 136–37. Unbound Feet Three, comprised of Kitty Tsui, Nellie Wong, and Merle Woo performed on Friday, October 16 at La Peña Cultural Center. Margaret Krouskoff, "Unbound Feet Three," *Off Our Backs* 11, no. 11 (December 31, 1985): 25. La Peña Cultural Center is located at 3105 Shattuck Avenue, Berkeley, California.
67. Tseng, "Slicing Silence," 231. Howard University is located at 2400 Sixth Street NW, Washington, D.C.
68. Michiyo Cornell, "Living in Asian America: An Asian American Lesbian's Address before the Washington Monument (1979)," in Leong, *Asian American Sexualities,* 83. See also Gwendolyn Shervington, ed., *A Fire is Burning, It Is in Me: The Life and Writings of Michiyo Fukaya* (Norwich, VT: New Victoria Publishers, 1996).
69. Shervington, *A Fire is Burning, It is in Me,* 145; Chuck Stewart, ed., *Proud Heritage: People, Issues, and Documents of the LGBT Experience* (Santa Barbara, CA: ABC-CLIO, LLC, 2015), 1208.
70. Christy Chung, Aly Kim, Zoon Nguyen, and Trinity Ordona, with Arlene Stein, "In Our Own Way: A Roundtable Discussion," in Leong, *Asian American Sexualities,* 91; Alice Hom, "Asian Americans and Pacific Islanders," in *Encyclopedia of Lesbian and Gay Histories and Cultures,* ed., George Haggerty and Bonnie Zimmerman (New York: Taylor and Francis, 2000), 72–75. Likely bisexual and transgender people also participated, though firsthand accounts only mention gays and lesbians.
71. Karin Aguilar-San Juan, "Landmarks in Literature by Asian American Lesbians," *Signs* 18, no. 4 (1993): 937.
72. For additional details on community discussions on the naming of the newsletter, see Ordona, "Coming Out Together," 151–53. *Phoenix Rising* maintained a post office box in Oakland for correspondence and met in people's homes.
73. *Phoenix Rising* mailing list, private collection of Crystal Jang.
74. Helen Zia, *Asian American Dreams*; Interview with Helen Zia, conducted by the author, 16 November 2013, San Francisco, California. In New Jersey, Helen Zia lived in an apartment in downtown Jersey City. Helen Zia, email message to author, 7 December 2015. Zia currently resides in Oakland, California.
75. Interview with Kitty Tsui, conducted by author, 21 December 2014, Long Beach, California; Ordona, "Coming Out Together," 134–35.

76. Kitty Tsui, *The Words of a Woman Who Breathes Fire* (San Francisco: Spinsters Ink, 1983). In 1981, Sherry Thomas, editor of Spinsters Ink, worked out of her San Francisco apartment. The press moved to a warehouse location in 1985 until it moved to Duluth, Minnesota, in 1993. From 1985 to 1986, Spinsters Ink was located at 803 DeHaro Street. From 1986 to 1992 the publishing company was located at 223 Mississippi. Spinsters Ink, Fall Catalogue 1993, GLC 105, Box 13, San Francisco Public Library, San Francisco, California; *San Francisco Telephone Directory,* 1981–1992.

77. Aguilar-San Juan, "Landmarks in Literature by Asian American Lesbians," 936.

78. Willyce Kim, *Eating Artichokes* (Oakland: Women's Press Collective, 1972). The Women's Press Collective was located at 5251 Broadway, Oakland, California. Kim additionally published *Dancer Dawkins and the California Kid* (Boston: Alyson Publications, 1985); Tseng, "Slicing Silence," 236; Interview with Kitty Tsui, conducted by author, 22 December 2014, Long Beach, California. Kim self-published an earlier book of poetry in 1970 titled *Curtains of Light.* See Alice Hom, "Kim, Willyce," *Encyclopedia of Lesbian, Gay, Bisexual and Transgendered History in America,* Gale Group, 2004, http://www.encyclopedia.com/social-sciences/encyclopedias-almanacs-transcripts-and-maps/kim-willyce.

79. Tsui, *Words of a Woman Who Breathes Fire*; Kitty Tsui, *Breathless: Erotica* (Ithaca, NY: Firebrand Books, 1996); Merle Woo, *Yellow Woman Speaks: Selected Poems* (Seattle: Radical Women Publications, 1986); Chea Villanueva, *Jessie's Song and Other Stories* (New York: Masquerade Books, 1995); Chea Villanueva, *Bulletproof Butches* (New York: Hard Candy Books, 1997). Queer Asian women writers also contributed individual essays, poetry, and prose to anthologies dedicated to women of color in hopes of changing the heteronormative discourse around race, inequality, and gender. See Cherrie Moraga and Gloria Anzaldúa, eds., *This Bridge Called My Back: Writings by Radical Women of Color* (Watertown, MA: Persephone Press, 1981); Asian Women United of California, eds., *Making Waves: An Anthology of Writings by and about Asian American Women* (Boston: Beacon Press, 1989).

80. Barbara Smith, "A Press of Our Own Kitchen Table: Women of Color Press," *Frontiers: A Journal of Women Studies* 10, no. 3 (1989): 11–13.

81. *On Our Backs* was located at 526 Castro Street in San Francisco. See *On Our Backs* 5, no. 1 (1988); *On Our Backs* 7, no. 2 (1990).

82. Interview with Kitty Tsui, conducted by author, 22 December 2014, Long Beach, California. Kitty Tsui, *Breathless* (Ithaca, NY: Firebrand Books, 1996). Firebrand Books was located in offices at 141 The Commons, Ithaca, New York.

83. Writer Judith Stelboum, who reviewed Tsui's book for the *Lesbian Review of Books,* commented with surprise, "The narrator is especially attracted to Asian lesbians." See Judith Stelboum, "Catching Your Breath," *Lesbian Review of Books* 3, no. 1 (1996): 24.

84. Ordona, "Coming Out Together," 219; Emi Minemura, "Asian Pacific Islander Lesbian and Bisexual Women in North America: Activism and Politics," master's thesis, Michigan State University, 1996, 10.

85. A/PLG was established in the home of Morris Kight in Los Angeles. An early gay rights activist, Kight cofounded the Los Angeles branch of the Gay Liberation Front, the Stonewall Democratic Club, and the Gay and Lesbian Community Service Center of L.A., now known as the Los Angeles LGBT Center. Well known for his "love" of Asians, Kight initiated the formation of A/PLG due to concern that his Asian partner Roy Z. would not have Asian friends and would not have community after the older Kight passed. Karen Ocamb, "Morris Kight, 1919–2003," *Advocate* 884 (2003): 16; Wat, *The Making of a Gay Asian Community*, 110, 115. Morris Kight lived in the Westlake neighborhood of Los Angeles, California. See "Morris Kight Residence," Los Angeles Conservancy website, https://www.laconservancy.org/locations/morris-kight-residence.

86. Wat, *The Making of a Gay Asian Community*.

87. Wat, *The Making of a Gay Asian Community*, 166–67. Chow and Lew later moved back to the San Francisco Bay area, where they helped to form important Asian Pacific Islander groups for gay men, including Gay Asian Pacific Islanders (GAPA) and the GAPA Community HIV Project (GCHP).

88. David Hong's home was located just off Santa Monica Boulevard in West Hollywood, California. The Chinatown Service Center Annex was located at 300 West Cesar E. Chavez Boulevard, Los Angeles, California. Alex Fukui, email message to author, 7 January 2016.

89. Trikone's current address is 60 Twenty-Ninth Street, #614, San Francisco, California; see "Contact Us," Trikone website, http://www.trikone.org/index.php/about-us/contact-us. The other four organizations that formed in the 1980s are Khush Kayal in Canada, Shakti Khabar in the United Kingdom, Freedom in India, and Bombay Dost in India as well. Nayan Shah, "Sexuality, Identity, and the Uses of History," in *Q&A: Queer in Asian America*, ed. David L. Eng and Alice Y. Hom (Philadelphia: Temple University Press, 1998), 141.

90. Liu was a member of both organizations from 1984 to 1997. Alice Y. Hom, "Unifying Differences: Lesbian of Color Community Building in Los Angeles and New York, 1970s–1980s," Ph.D. diss., Claremont Graduate University, 2011, 114–15. CAAAV is located at 55 Hester Street, New York City, New York.

91. The Women's Building is located at 3543 Eighteenth Street, San Francisco, California. The Women's Building was the first women-owned community center established in 1979 in the Mission District of San Francisco that advocates self-determination, gender equality, and social justice. See "History & Mission," The Women's Building website, accessed 31 October 2015, http://womensbuilding.org/about/mission-history; Sushawn Robb, *Mothering the Movement: The Story of the San Francisco Women's Building* (Denver: Outskirts Press, 2011).

92. Ozawa cofounded LYRIC with Beth Kivel; see "History," LYRIC website, accessed 1 August 2015, http://lyric.org/history.

93. Interview with Lia Shigemura, conducted by author, 31 July 2015, Oakland, California. "Timeline—Achievements and Milestones," Asian Women's Shelter website, http://www.sfaws.org/about-us/history/timeline-%E2%80%93-achievements-and-milestones.aspx.

94. Website of Urvashi Vaid, http://urvashivaid.net/wp/?page_id=578; "NGLTF's Paras to Leave; Lobel Appointed ED," National Gay and Lesbian Task Force press release, 30 September 1996, http://www.qrd.org/qrd/orgs/NGLTF/1996/paras.to.leave-09.30.96.

95. Deborah Gould, *Moving Politics: Emotion and ACT UP's Fight against AIDS* (Chicago: University of Chicago Press, 2009).

96. Nancy E. Stoller, *Lessons from the Damned: Queers, Whores, and Junkies Respond to AIDS* (New York: Routledge, 1998), 63–79.

97. The Asian American Recovery Services housed the Asian AIDS Project when it first began in 1987. AARS' office was at 2041 Hayes Street, San Francisco, California.

98. The Japanese American Cultural and Community Center of Northern California was located at 1840 Sutter Street in San Francisco. Letter from Davis Y. Ja, 14 July 1987, Folder Meeting Minutes: General, 1987, Carton 1, Asian/ Pacific AIDS Coalition 96–14, GLBT Historical Society, San Francisco, California.

99. The support group often met at the Metropolitan Community Church located at the time at 150 Eureka Street in San Francisco, or in people's private homes. M. J. Talbot, email message to author, 23 November 2015. The group would later include women and youth, and grow into what is today the Asian & Pacific Islander Wellness Center (A&PI Wellness Center). The center is located at 730 Polk Street, San Francisco, California. "History," A&PI Wellness Center website, http://apiwellness.org/site/history.

100. Stoller, *Lessons from the Damned,* 64.

101. Crisostomo had already been volunteering for AAP as a peer counselor before he was hired. Interview with Vince Crisostomo conducted by Toby Wu, 13 November 2013, San Francisco, California.

102. The current address for Critical Path is 1233 Locust Street, Fifth Floor, Philadelphia, Pennsylvania. At its founding Critical Path was located in Kuromiya's home in Philadelphia's Fitler Square neighborhood. See Interview with Kiyoshi Kuromiya, conducted by Marc Stein, http://outhistory.org/exhibits/show/philadelphia-lgbt-interviews/interviews/kiyoshi-kuromiya; "History," Critical Path Project website, http://www.critpath.org/about-us/history; Alyssa Richman, email message to author, 7 October 2015.

103. Interview with Vince Crisostomo, conducted by Toby Wu, 13 November 2013, San Francisco, California.

104. George Choy Papers, GLBT Historical Society, San Francisco, California. For more on the discrimination suit in Tokyo, see Wim Lunsing, "LGBT Rights in Japan," *Peace Review* 17, no. 2 (2005): 143–48.

105. Choy was also a member of ACT UP and organizer for GCHP. Just two years later, in 1993, Choy died of AIDS. George Choy Papers, GLBT Historical Society, San Francisco, California. The three most important prevention and service organizations for APAs at the time in Northern California were the GAPA Community HIV Project, Asian AIDS Project, and Filipino Task Force on AIDS, all run by gay or bisexual men. See Stoller, *Lessons from the Damned,* 66.

106. Tamara Ching, "Piece of Mind: Stranger in Paradise," *A. Magazine* 3, no. 1 (1994): 85.

107. "Tita Aida," translated as Auntie AIDS in Tagalog, is a fantastical transmogrification of AIDS from a deadly disease into a familiar feminine figure. For more on the sociopolitical use of "Tita Aida," see Martin Manalansan, *Global Divas: Filipino Gay Men in the Diaspora* (Durham, NC: Duke University Press, 2003).

108. *AsianWeek,* "PSA Targeting API Transgender Communities for World AIDS Day," *AsianWeek,* 5 December 2008, 17; Celeste Chan, "Tita Aida—A Community Icon," *Hyphen Magazine,* 26 July 2014, http://hyphenmagazine .com/blog/2014/7/26/tita-aida-community-icon.

109. Steve Lew, email message to author, 5 June 2016; Willy Wilkinson, *Born on the Edge of Race and Gender: A Voice of Cultural Competency* (Oakland, CA: Hapa Papa Press, 2015).

110. While prosecutors charged suspects Ronald Ebens and Michael Nitz with second-degree murder, the father and stepson pair pleaded to manslaughter. The judge, Charles Kauffman, in March 1983 sentenced the two men to three years of probation and a fine of $3,780. A federal trial the following year determined that the murder had been a hate crime, convicting only Ebens of violating Chin's civil rights. However, a retrial in 1987 acquitted Ebens, and both men would never spend a day in jail for their crime. Robert S. Chang, *Disoriented: Asian Americans, Law, and the Nation State* (New York: New York University Press, 1999). See also Henry Yu and Mai Ngai, eds., "The Politics of Remembering," special issue, *Amerasia Journal* 28, no. 3 (2002).

111. The first community meeting that would later formally become American Citizens for Justice (ACJ) took place on 20 March 1983 at Golden Star Restaurant at 22828 Woodward Avenue in Ferndale, Michigan. The founding ACJ meeting took place on 31 March 1983 at the Detroit Chinese Welfare Council building at 3153 Cass Avenue in Detroit, Michigan. See Zia, *Asian American Dreams,* 64–66.

112. Yoko Yoshikawa, "The Heat is on Miss Saigon Coalition: Organizing across Race and Sexuality," in *Q&A: Queer in Asian America,* 41–56; Alex Witchel, "Actor's Equity Attacks Casting of 'Miss Saigon,'" *New York Times,* 26 July 1990, http://www.nytimes.com/1990/07/26/theater/actors-equity-attacks-casting-of-miss-saigon.html.

113. Yoshikawa, "The Heat is on Miss Saigon Coalition," 55.

114. Sharon Lim-Hing, *The Very Inside: An Anthology of Writing by Asian and Pacific Islander Lesbian and Bisexual Women* (Toronto, ONT: Sister Vision Press, 1994).

115. After arriving home, in the heat of her apartment and with the neighbor's dog barking incessantly, Lim-Hing in her discomfort decided that Asian and Pacific Islander lesbians should have a book of their own.

116. C. Chung, A. Kim, and A. K. Lemeshewsky, *Between the Lines: An Anthology by Pacific/Asian Lesbians of Santa Cruz, California* (Santa Cruz, CA: Dancing Bird Press, 1987).

117. Lim-Hing, *The Very Inside,* Introduction.

118. The Asian American Writer's Workshop was located at 16 West Thirty-Second Street, Suite 10A, New York City, New York. See Quang Bao and Ha-nya Yanagihara, *Take Out: Queer Writing from Asian Pacific America* (New York: Asian American Writer's Workshop, 2000).

119. Bao and Yanagihara, *Take Out.*

120. Greg Louganis, *Breaking the Surface* (New York: Random House, 1994); Larry Reibstein and Gregory Beals, "Public Glory, Secret Agony," *Newsweek,* 5 March 1995, http://www.newsweek.com/public-glory-secret-agony-180724. See also Richard Sandomir, "Movement Builds to Honor Greg Louganis on a Wheaties Box," *New York Times,* 22 August 2015, http://www.nytimes.com/2015/08/23/sports/olympics/movement-builds-to-honor-greg-louganis-on-a-wheaties-box.html?_r=0; and Katherine Schweighofer, "LGBTQ Sport and Leisure," in *LGBTQ America: A Theme Study of Lesbian, Gay, Bisexual, Transgender, and Queer History,* ed. Megan E. Springate (Washington, DC: National Park Foundation and National Park Service, 2016), https://nps.gov/articles/lgbtqtheme-sport.htm.

121. Ka`ahumanu was born Lani Farrell and took the last name Ka`ahumanu in 1979 at the suggestion of her mother. Trinity Ordona details Ka`ahumanu's heritage as the following: "[Her] maternal grandmother was part Native Hawaiian, her maternal grandfather was Eurasian. Her mother Minerva Helani, was born in Japan and raised in Japan and later Hawaii. Her father, a man of Irish and Polish ancestry, married her mother in Hawaii where they met." Ordona, "Coming Out Together," 292. See also Loraine Hutchins, "Making Bisexuals Visible" (this volume).

122. Claude J. Summers, "BiNet USA," GLBTQ Encyclopedia Project website, http://www.glbtqarchive.com/ssh/binet_usa_S.pdf.

123. Mala Nagarajan, "Queer South Asian Organizing in the United States," *Trikone Magazine* 28, no. 1 (2014): 4–7.

124. Gina Masequesmay, "Becoming Queer and Vietnamese American: Negotiating Multiple Identities in an Ethnic Support Group of Lesbians, Bisexual Women, and Female-to-Male Transgenders," Ph.D. diss., University of California, Los Angeles, 2001.

125. Harold Kameya, "Asian American LGBT Pioneers Recognized," San Fernando Valley JACL website, 27 July 2012, http://sfvjacl.weebly.com/1/

post/2012/07/apa-lgbt-pioneers-recognized.html; "Tak Yamamoto, Pioneer Nikkei Gay Activist, Dies at 74," *Rafu Shimpo,* 19 November 2012, http://www .rafu.com/2012/11/tak-yamamoto-pioneer-nikkei-gay-activist-dies-at-74.

126. "A Timeline of HIV/AIDS," AIDS.gov website, http://www.aids.gov/hiv-aids-basics/hiv-aids-101/aids-timeline; "Pine is Proud to be a Reconciling Church," Pine United Methodist Church website, http://www.pineumc .org/reconciling.htm. Pine United Methodist Church is located at 426 Thirty-Third Avenue, San Francisco, California.

127. Linh H. Pham, "Another First: Lesbian and Gay Asian Americans to March in Cherry Blossom Parade," Gay Asian Pacific Alliance, Asian/Pacific Sisters, and Older Asian Sisters in Solidarity press release, Google Groups website, 13 April 1994, https://groups.google.com/forum/#!topic/bit.listserv .gaynet/0n2kPOFp7_s; Elisa Lee, "Lavender Godzilla," *Third Force* 2, no. 2 (1994): 7.

128. The Kameyas live in the Granada Hills neighborhood of Los Angeles. The Westwood Methodist Church is located at 10947 Wilshire Boulevard, Los Angeles, California. The San Gabriel Valley API PFLAG meets at Sage Granada Methodist Church in Alhambra at 1850 West Hellman Avenue. Harold Kameya, email message to author, 2 October 2015. Harold Kameya, "A Sansei Family's Unexpected Journey," *Pacific Citizen,* December 2001.

129. "First Person: Trinity Ordona Recently Helped Make a Video Aimed at Opening Discussion between Asian Parents and Their Gay Children," *San Francisco Examiner,* 26 June 1996, A-8.

130. Molly Fumia, *Honor Thy Children: One Family's Journey to Wholeness* (Berkeley, CA: Conari Press, 1997); Harold Kameya, "Our Journey," Network on Religion and Justice website, archived at https://web.archive .org/web/20150530060824/http://www.netrj.org/?p=library&id=2; Lina Hoshino, dir., *In God's House: Asian American Lesbian and Gay Families in the Church,* (Berkeley, CA: PANA Institute, 2007).

131. For examples of memoirs by Asian Americans, see Kenji Yoshino, *Covering: The Hidden Assault on our Civil Rights* (New York: Random House, 2006); Thomas Beatie, *Labor of Love: The Story of One Man's Extraordinary Pregnancy* (Berkeley, CA: Seal Press, 2008); and Marsha Aizumi, *Two Spirits, One Heart: A Mother, Her Transgender Son and Their Journey to Love and Acceptance* (Bronx, NY: Magnus Books, 2012).

132. Transgender Law Center, "Remembering Christopher Lee as Respect After Death Act Takes Effect."

133. The Harvey Milk Democratic Club honored Ching at their annual dinner on 25 May 2006 at the Ramada Plaza Hotel on 1231 Market Street at Eighth Street in San Francisco, California. See Cynthia Laird, "News in Brief: Milk Club dinner tonight," *Bay Area Reporter,* 25 May 2006, http://www.ebar .com/news/article.php?article=868&sec=news.

134. Caitlin Donohue, "Trans Activists Honored in Clarion Alley Mural," *San Francisco Bay Guardian Online,* 24 October 2012, archived at https://web.archive

.org/web/20150911001552/http://www.sfbg.com/pixel_vision/2012/10/24/
trans-activists-honored-clarion-alley-mural.

135. Interview with Crystal Jang, conducted by author, 31 January 2012, San Francisco, California; Crystal Jang, email message to author, 17 October 2015.

136. The plaque is located in front of 468 Castro Street. Bill Lipsky, "Rainbow Honor Walk: Passionate Activist George Choy," *San Francisco Bay Times*, 2015, http://sfbaytimes.com/rainbow-honor-walk-passionate-activist-george-choy; Rainbow Honor Walk website, http://rainbowhonorwalk.org; *Queerty*, "San Francisco's New 'Rainbow Honor Walk' Littered with Offensive Typos and Misinformation," *Queerty*, 3 September 2014, 2015, http://www.queerty.com/san-franciscos-new-rainbow-honor-walk-littered-with-offensive-typos-and-misinformation-20140903.

137. Dean Hamer and Joe Wilson, eds., *Kumu Hina: The True Meaning of Aloha* (Qwaves, 2014).

138. Cal Q&A at UC Berkeley, originally called CAL B GAY, and Q&A at Stanford formed in the 1990s. AQUA at San Francisco State University and Q&A at San Jose State University began later, in the 2000s. See Cal Q&A web page, http://calqanda.tumblr.com; Q&A at San Jose State Tumblr page, http://qnasjsu.tumblr.com; Queer and Asian at Stanford web page, http://web.stanford.edu/group/queerasians/index.html; Asians and Queers United for Awareness Twitter page, https://twitter.com/AQUASFSU; Tiffany Chen, email message to author, 2 October 2015; Joseph Lee, email message to author, 2 October 2015.

139. Victoria, "Queer, Asian, and Proud," *South Asian Americans Leading Together* (blog), 6 October 2014, http://saalt.org/queer-asian-and-proud.

140. For history of Asian Americans settling dominantly in the Western United States, see Chan, *Asian Americans*. For the West and specifically San Francisco as a place of sexual freedom, see Kath Weston, "Get Thee to a Big City: Sexual Imaginary and the Great Gay Migration," *GLQ: A Journal of Lesbian and Gay Studies* 2, no. 3 (1995): 253–77; Nan Alamilla Boyd, *Wide Open Town: A History of Queer San Francisco to 1965* (Berkeley: University of California Press, 2003). For more on cultural production by suburban queers of color, see Karen Tongson, *Relocations: Queer Suburban Imaginaries* (New York: New York University Press, 2011).

141. API Equality-LA website, http://apiequalityla.org; API Equality-Northern California website, http://www.apiequalitync.org. API Equality-LA is located at 1137 Wilshire Boulevard, Los Angeles, California. API Equality-Northern California is located at 17 Walter U. Lum Place, San Francisco, California.

142. Jessica Kwong, "SF Gay History Museum Finds Home, Identity," *SFGate*, 12 January 2011, http://www.sfgate.com/news/article/SF-gay-history-museum-finds-home-identity-2478991.php; Win Mixter, "All about the Castro's

GLBT Historical Society and Museum," *Hoodline,* 9 February 2015, http://hoodline.com/2015/02/all-about-the-castro-s-glbt-historical-soci ety-and-museum.
143. For more on postracial America, see David Eng, *The Feeling of Kinship: Queer Liberalism and the Racialization of Intimacy* (Durham, NC: Duke University Press, 2010); and Michelle Alexander, *The New Jim Crow: Mass Incarceration in the Age of Colorblindness* (New York: New Press, 2010), 1–57.

Bibliography

Aguilar-San Juan, Karin. "Landmarks in Literature by Asian American Lesbians." *Signs* 18, no. 4 (1993): 936–43.

AIDS.gov. "A Timeline of HIV/AIDS." AIDS.gov. http://www.aids.gov/hiv-aids-basics/ hiv-aids-101/aids-timeline.

Aizumi, Marsha. *Two Spirits, One Heart: A Mother, Her Transgender Son and Their Journey to Love and Acceptance.* Bronx, NY: Magnus Books, 2012.

Alexander, Michelle. *The New Jim Crow: Mass Incarceration in the Age of Color-blindness.* New York: New Press, 2010.

Arana, Gabriel. "The Passion of Dan Choi." *American Prospect: Longform,* 9 February 2014. http://prospect.org/article/passion-dan-choi.

Armes, Ethel. "Aloha, Wela, Wela!" *National Magazine* 21, no. 3 (1904): 308–18.

Asian & Pacific Islander Wellness Center. "History." Asian & Pacific Islander Wellness Center. http://apiwellness.org/site/history.

AsianWeek. "PSA Targeting API Transgender Communities for World AIDS Day." *AsianWeek,* 5 December 2008.

Asian Women's Shelter. "Timeline—Achievements and Milestones." Asian Women's Shelter. http://www.sfaws.org/about-us/history/timeline-%E2%80%93- achievements-and-milestones.aspx.

Asian Women United of California, eds. *Making Waves: An Anthology of Writings by and about Asian American Women.* Boston: Beacon Press, 1989.

Associated Press. "Women Start Riding 'Outside Step' of Frisco's Old Dinky Cable Cars." *Ocala Star Banner,* 13 May 1965.

Austen, Roger. *Genteel Pagan: The Double Life of Charles Warren Stoddard.* Edited by John W. Crowley. Amherst: University of Massachusetts Press, 1991.

Bao, Quang, and Hanya Yanagihara. *Take Out: Queer Writing from Asian Pacific America.* New York: Asian American Writer's Workshop, 2000.

Beatie, Thomas. *Labor of Love: The Story of One Man's Extraordinary Pregnancy.* Berkeley, CA: Seal Press, 2008.

Boag, Peter. *Re-dressing America's Frontier Past.* Berkeley: University of California Press, 2011.

Bohemian Club. *Certificate of Incorporation, Constitution, By-Laws and Rules, Officers, Committees, and Members.* San Francisco: H. S. Crocker Company, 1904.

Boyd, Nan Alamilla. *Wide Open Town: A History of Queer San Francisco to 1965.* Berkeley: University of California Press, 2003.

Casady, Lauren. "Labor Unrest and the Labor Movement in the Salmon Industry of the Pacific Coast." Ph.D. diss., University of California, Berkeley, 1938.

Chan, Celeste. "Tita Aida—A Community Icon." *Hyphen Magazine,* 26 July 2014. http://hyphenmagazine.com/blog/2014/7/26/tita-aida-community-icon.

Chang, Robert S. *Disoriented: Asian Americans, Law, and the Nation State.* New York: New York University Press, 1999.

Chen, Yong. *Chinese San Francisco, 1850–1943: A Tran-Pacific Community.* Stanford, CA: Stanford University Press, 2000.

Chin, Frank, and Jeffery Paul Chen. "Racist Love." In *Seeing through Shuck,* edited by Richard Kostelanetz, 65–79. New York: Ballantine Books, 1972.

Ching, Tamara. "Piece of Mind: Stranger in Paradise." *A. Magazine* 3, no. 1 (1994): 85.

Chung, C., A. Kim, and A. K. Lemeshewsky. *Between the Lines: An Anthology by Pacific/Asian Lesbians of Santa Cruz, California.* Santa Cruz: Dancing Bird Press, 1987.

Chung, Christy, Aly Kim, Zoon Nguyen, and Trinity Ordona, with Arlene Stein. "In Our Own Way: A Roundtable Discussion." In *Asian American Sexualities: Dimensions of the Gay and Lesbian Experience,* edited by Russell Leong, 91–100. New York: Routledge, 1996.

Cohen, Cathy. *Boundaries of Blackness: AIDS and the Breakdown of Black Politics.* Chicago: University of Chicago, 1999.

Coolidge, Mary Roberts. *Chinese Immigration.* New York: Henry Holt and Company, 1909.

Cornell, Michiyo. "Living in Asian America: An Asian American Lesbian's Address before the Washington Monument (1979)." In *Asian American Sexualities: Dimensions of the Gay and Lesbian Experience,* edited by Russell Leong, 83–84. New York: Routledge, 1996.

Critical Path Project. "History." Critical Path Project. http://www.critpath.org/about-us/history.

Daniels, Roger. *Concentration Camps USA: Japanese Americans and World War II.* Hinsdale, IL: Dryden Press, 1971.

Densho Encyclopedia. "Issei." *Densho Encyclopedia.* http://encyclopedia.densho.org/Issei.

Donohue, Caitlin. "Trans Activists Honored in Clarion Alley Mural." *San Francisco Bay Guardian Online,* 24 October 2012. Archived at https://web.archive.org/web/20150911001552/http://www.sfbg.com/pixel_vision/2012/10/24/trans-activists-honored-clarion-alley-mural.

Duus, Masayo. *The Life of Isamu Noguchi: Journey without Borders.* Princeton, NJ: Princeton University Press, 2007.

Eng, David. *The Feeling of Kinship: Queer Liberalism and the Racialization of Intimacy.* Durham, NC: Duke University Press, 2010.

Eng, David, Judith Halberstam, and Jose Esteban Munoz. "Introduction: What's Queer about Queer Studies Now." *Social Text* 23, no. 3–4 (2005): 1–17.

Engel, Stephen M. "Development Perspectives on Lesbian and Gay Politics: Fragmented Citizenship in a Fragmented State." *Perspectives on Politics* 13, no. 2 (2015): 287–311.

Friday, Chris. *Organizing Asian American Labor: The Pacific Coast Canned-Salmon Industry, 1870–1942.* Philadelphia: Temple University Press, 1994.

Fumia, Molly. *Honor Thy Children: One Family's Journey to Wholeness.* Berkeley, CA: Conari Press, 1997.

Gallo, Marcia M. *Different Daughters: A History of the Daughters of Bilitis and the Rise of the Lesbian Rights Movement.* Emeryville, CA: Seal Press, 2007.

Gould, Debora. *Moving Politics: Emotion and ACT UP's Fight against AIDS.* Chicago: University of Chicago Press, 2009.

Graves, Karen. "Political Pawns in an Educational Endgame: Reflections on Bryant, Briggs, and Some Twentieth-Century School Questions." *History of Education Quarterly* 53, no. 1 (2013): 1–20.

Habal, Estella. *San Francisco's International Hotel: Mobilizing the Filipino American Community in the Anti-Eviction Movement.* Philadelphia: Temple University Press, 2007.

Hamer, Dean, and Joe Wilson, dirs. *Kumu Hina: The True Meaning of Aloha.* Qwaves, 2014.

Hirata, Lucie Cheng. "Free, Indentured, Enslaved: Chinese Prostitutes in Nineteenth-Century America." *Signs* 5, no. 1 (1979): 3–29.

Hom, Alice. "Asian Americans and Pacific Islanders." In *Encyclopedia of Lesbian and Gay Histories and Cultures,* edited by George Haggerty and Bonnie Zimmerman, 72–75. New York: Taylor and Francis, 2000.

———. "Kim, Willyce." *Encyclopedia of Lesbian, Gay, Bisexual and Transgendered History in America.* The Gale Group, 2004. http://www.encyclopedia.com/social-sciences/encyclopedias-almanacs-transcripts-and-maps/kim-willyce.

———. "Unifying Differences: Lesbian of Color Community Building in Los Angeles and New York, 1970s–1980s." Ph.D. diss., Claremont Graduate University, 2011.

Hoshino, Lina, dir. *In God's House: Asian American Lesbian and Gay Families in the Church.* Berkeley, CA: PANA Institute, 2007.

Howard, John. *Concentration Camps on the Homefront: Japanese Americans in the House of Jim Crow.* Chicago: Chicago University Press, 2008.

Hsu, Madeline Y. "Unwrapping Orientalist Constraints: Restoring Homosocial Normativity to Chinese American History." *Amerasia Journal* 29, no. 2 (2003): 230–53.

Huffington Post. "Stuart Gaffney." *Huffington Post.* http://www.huffingtonpost.com/stuart-gaffney.

Hutchins, Loraine. "Making Bisexuals Visible." In *Identities and Place: Changing Labels and Intersectional Communities of LGBTQ and Two-Spirit People in the United States,* edited by Katherine Crawford-Lackey and Megan E. Springate. New York: Berghahn Books, 2020.

Ichioka, Yuji. "Ameyuki-san: Japanese Prostitutes in Nineteenth-Century America." *Amerasia Journal* 4, no. 1 (1977): 1–22.

———. *Issei: The World of the First Generation Japanese Immigrants, 1885–1924.* New York: Free Press, 1988.

Johnson, Susan Lee. "My Own Private Life: Toward a History of Desire in Gold Rush California." *California History* 79, no. 2 (2000): 316–46.

———. *Roaring Camp: The Social World of the California Gold Rush.* New York: W. W. Norton and Company, 2000.

Kameya, Harold. "Asian American LGBT Pioneers Recognized." San Fernando Valley Japanese American Citizens League, 27 July 2012. http://sfvjacl .weebly.com/1/post/2012/07/apa-lgbt-pioneers-recognized.html.

———. "Our Journey." Network on Religion and Justice. Webpage archived at https:// web.archive.org/web/20150530060824/http:/www.netrj.org/?p=library &id=2.

———. "A Sansei Family's Unexpected Journey." *Pacific Citizen,* December 2001.

Kim, Willyce. *Curtains of Light.* Self-published, 1971.

———. *Dancer Dawkins and the California Kid.* Boston: Alyson Publications, 1985.

———. *Eating Artichokes.* Oakland, CA: Women's Press Collective, 1972.

Kinsey, Alfred C., and the Institute for Sex Research. *Sexual Behavior in the Human Female.* Philadelphia: Saunders, 1953.

Krouskoff, Margaret. "Unbound Feet Three." *Off Our Backs* 11, no. 11 (1985): 25.

Kwong, Jessica. "SF Gay History Museum Finds Home, Identity." *SFGate,* 12 January 2011. http://www.sfgate.com/news/article/SF-gay-history-museum-finds-home-identity-2478991.php.

Laird, Cynthia. "News in Brief: Milk Club Dinner Tonight." *Bay Area Reporter,* 25 May 2006. http://www.ebar.com/news/article.php?article=868&sec=news.

Langley, Henry G. *Langley's San Francisco Directory, 1895.* San Francisco: J. B. Painter, 1895.

Lee, Elisa. "Lavender Godzilla." *Third Force* 2, no. 2 (1994): 2, 7.

Lee, Robert G. *Orientals: Asian Americans in Popular Culture.* Philadelphia: Temple University Press, 1999.

Leong, Andrew. "The Pocket and the Watch: A Collective Individualist Reading of Japanese American Literature." *Verge: Studies in Global Asias* 1, no. 2 (2015): 76–114.

Lim-Hing, Sharon. *The Very Inside: An Anthology of Writing by Asian and Pacific Islander Lesbian and Bisexual Women.* Toronto, ONT: Sister Vision Press, 1994.

Lipsky, Bill. "Rainbow Honor Walk: Passionate Activist George Choy." *San Francisco Bay Times,* n.d. http://sfbaytimes.com/rainbow-honor-walk-passionate-activist-george-choy.

Los Angeles Conservancy. "Morris Kight Residence." Los Angeles Conservancy. https://www.laconservancy.org/locations/morris-kight-residence.

Louganis, Greg. *Breaking the Surface.* New York: Random House, 1994.

Lunsing, Wim. "LGBT Rights in Japan." *Peace Review* 17, no. 2 (2005): 143–48.

LYRIC. "History." LYRIC. http://lyric.org/history.

Mabry, Jan. "Respect After Death Act Takes Effect Giving Transgenders Right to Have Chosen Gender on Death Certificates." *CBS San Francisco,* 1 July 2015. http://sanfrancisco.cbslocal.com/2015/07/01/respect-after-death-act-takes-effect-giving-transgenders-right-to-have-chosen-gender-on-death-certificates.

Maeda, Daryl J. *Rethinking the Asian American Movement.* New York: Routledge, 2012.

Manalansan, Martin. *Global Divas: Filipino Gay Men in the Diaspora.* Durham, NC: Duke University Press, 2003.

Mangaoang, Gil. "From the 1970s to the 1990s: Perspective of a Gay Filipino American Activists." In *Asian American Sexualities: Dimensions of the Gay and Lesbian Experience,* edited by Russell Leong, 101–12. New York: Routledge, 1996.

Masequesmay, Gina. "Becoming Queer and Vietnamese American: Negotiating Multiple Identities in an Ethnic Support Group of Lesbians, Bisexual Women, and Female-to-Male Transgenders." Ph.D. diss., University of California, Los Angeles, 2001.

Mason, Jack, and Donald Guimary. "Asian Labor Contractors in the Alaska Canned Salmon Industry, 1880–1937." *Labor History* 22, no. 3 (1981): 377–97.

Minemura, Emi. "Asian Pacific Islander Lesbian and Bisexual Women in North America: Activism and Politics." Master's thesis, Michigan State University, 1996.

Mixter, Win. "All about the Castro's GLBT Historical Society and Museum." *Hoodline,* 9 February 2015. http://hoodline.com/2015/02/all-about-the-castro-s-glbt-historical-society-and-museum.

Moraga, Cherrie, and Gloria Anzaldua, eds. *This Bridge Called My Back: Writings by Radical Women of Color.* Watertown, MA: Persephone Press, 1981.

Nagarajan, Mala. "Queer South Asian Organizing in the United States." *Trikone Magazine* 28, no. 1 (2014): 4–7.

National Gay and Lesbian Task Force. "NGLTF's Paras to Leave; Lobel Appointed ED." National Gay and Lesbian Task Force press release, 30 September 1996. http://www.qrd.org/qrd/orgs/NGLTF/1996/paras.to.leave-09.30.96.

Niiya, Brian. "Shin Sekai (newspaper)." *Densho Encyclopedia.* http://encyclopedia.densho.org/Shin_Sekai_%28newspaper%29.

Ocamb, Karen. "Morris Kight, 1919–2003." *Advocate* 884 (2003): 16.

Ordona, Trinity Ann. "Coming Out Together: An Ethnohistory of the Asian and Pacific Islander Queer Women's and Transgendered People's Movement of San Francisco." Ph.D. diss., University of California, Santa Cruz, 2000.

———. "Asian Lesbians in San Francisco: Struggles to Create a Safe Space, 1970s–1980s." In *Asian/Pacific Islander Women: A Historical Anthology,* edited by Shirley Hune and Gail Nomura, 319–34. New York: New York University Press, 2003.

Peffer, George Anthony. *If They Don't Bring Their Women Here: Chinese Female Immigration before Exclusion.* Urbana: University of Illinois Press, 1999.

Pham, Linh H. "Another First: Lesbian and Gay Asian Americans to March in Cherry Blossom Parade." Gay Asian Pacific Alliance, Asian/Pacific Sisters, and Older Asian Sisters in Solidarity press release, Google Groups website, 13 April 1994. https://groups.google.com/forum/%23!topic/bit.listserv .gaynet/0n2kPOFp7_s.

Pine United Methodist Church. "Pine is Proud to be a Reconciling Church." Pine United Methodist Church, n.d. http://www.pineumc.org/reconciling.htm.

Queerty. "San Francisco's New 'Rainbow Honor Walk' Littered with Offensive Typos and Misinformation." *Queerty,* 3 September 2014. http://www.queerty .com/san-franciscos-new-rainbow-honor-walk-littered-with-offensive-ty pos-and-misinformation-20140903.

Rafu Shimpo. "Tak Yamamoto, Pioneer Nikkei Gay Activist, Dies at 74." *The Rafu Shimpo,* 19 November 2012. http://www.rafu.com/2012/11/tak-yamamoto-pioneer-nikkei-gay-activist-dies-at-74/.

Reibstein, Larry, and Gregory Beals. "Public Glory, Secret Agony." *Newsweek,* 5 March 1995. http://www.newsweek.com/public-glory-secret-agony-180724.

R. L. Polk & Co. *Crocker-Langley San Francisco City Directory.* San Francisco: R. L. Polk and Co., 1928, 1942, 1943, 1944, 1945, 1950–1959.

Robb, Sushawn. *Mothering the Movement: The Story of the San Francisco Women's Building.* Denver: Outskirts Press, 2011.

Robinson, Greg. *By Order of the President: FDR and the Internment of Japanese Americans.* Cambridge, MA: Harvard University Press, 2001.

———. *A Tragedy of Democracy: Japanese Confinement in North America.* New York: Columbia University Press, 2009.

Sandomir, Richard. "Movement Builds to Honor Greg Louganis on a Wheaties Box." *New York Times,* 22 August 2015. http://www.nytimes.com/2015/08/23/ sports/olympics/movement-builds-to-honor-greg-louganis-on-a-wheat ies-box.html.

San Francisco Examiner. "First Person: Trinity Ordona Recently Helped Make A Video Aimed at Opening Discussion between Asian Parents and Their Gay Children." *San Francisco Examiner,* 26 June 1996.

Schweighofer, Katherine. "LGBTQ Sport and Leisure." In *LGBTQ America: A Theme Study of Lesbian, Gay, Bisexual, Transgender, and Queer History,* edited by Megan E. Springate. Washington, DC: National Park Foundation and National Park Service, 2016. https://nps.gov/articles/lgbtqtheme-sport.htm.

Shah, Nayan. "Between 'Oriental Depravity' and 'Natural Degenerates': Spatial Borderlands and the Making of Ordinary Americans." *American Quarterly* 57, no. 3 (2005): 703–25.

———. *Contagious Divides: Epidemics and Race in San Francisco's Chinatown.* Berkeley: University of California Press, 2001.

——. "Sexuality, Identity, and the Uses of History." In *Q&A: Queer in Asian America*, edited by David L. Eng and Alice Y. Hom, 141–56. Philadelphia: Temple University Press, 1998.

——. *Stranger Intimacy: Contesting Race, Sexuality, and the Law in the North American West.* Berkeley: University of California Press, 2011.

Shervington, Gwendolyn, ed. *A Fire is Burning, It Is in Me: The Life and Writings of Michiyo Fukaya.* Norwich, VT: New Victoria Publishers, 1996.

Smith, Barbara. "A Press of Our Own: Kitchen Table: Women of Color Press." *Frontiers: A Journal of Women Studies* 10, no. 3 (1989): 11–13.

Stein, Marc. *City of Sisterly and Brotherly Loves: Lesbian and Gay Philadelphia, 1945–1972.* Philadelphia: Temple University Press, 2004.

——. "Kiyoshi Kuromiya, June 17, 1997." OutHistory.org, 2009. http://outhistory.org/exhibits/show/philadelphia-lgbt-interviews/interviews/kiyoshi-kuromiya.

Stelboum, Judith. "Catching Your Breath." *Lesbian Review of Books* 3, no. 1 (1996): 24.

Stewart, Chuck, ed. *Proud Heritage: People, Issues, and Documents of the LGBT Experience.* Santa Barbara, CA: ABC-CLIO 2015.

Stewart, Stephen. *Positive Image: A Portrait of Gay America.* New York: William Morrow and Company, 1985.

Stoller, Nancy E. *Lessons from the Damned: Queers, Whores, and Junkies Respond to AIDS.* New York: Routledge, 1998.

Streshinsky, Maria. "Dan Choi." *Atlantic Monthly* 306, no. 4 (2010): 88.

Stryker, Susan. *Transgender History.* Berkeley, CA: Seal Press, 2008.

Sueyoshi, Amy. *Queer Compulsions: Race, Nation, and Sexuality in the Affairs of Yone Noguchi.* Honolulu: University of Hawaii Press, 2012.

——. "Queer Asian American Historiography." In *The Oxford Handbook of Asian American History,* edited by David K. Yoo and Eiichiro Azuma, 267–78. New York: Oxford University Press, 2016.

Summers, Claude J. "BiNet USA." GLBTQ Encyclopedia Project. http://www.glbtqarchive.com/ssh/binet_usa_S.pdf.

Takemoto, Tina. "Looking for Jiro Onuma: A Queer Meditation on the Incarceration of Japanese Americans during WWII." *GLQ Journal: A Journal of Lesbian and Gay Studies* 20, no. 3 (2013): 241–75.

The Women's Building. "History & Mission." The Women's Building. http://womensbuilding.org/about/mission-history.

Tomso, Gregory. "The Queer History of Leprosy and Same-Sex Love." *American Literary History* 14, no. 2 (2002): 747–75.

Transgender Law Center. "Remembering Christopher Lee as Respect After Death Act Takes Effect." Transgender Law Center, 7 July 2015. http://transgenderlawcenter.org/archives/11746.

Trikone. "Contact Us." Trikone. http://www.trikone.org/index.php/about-us/contact-us.

Tseng, Daniel. "Slicing Silence: Asian Progressives Come Out." In *Asian Amer-*

icans: The Movement and the Moment, edited by Steve Louie and Glenn Omatsu. Los Angeles, 200–39. Los Angeles: UCLA Asian American Studies Center Press, 2001.

Tsui, Kitty. *Breathless: Erotica.* Ithaca, NY: Firebrand Books, 1996.

———. *The Words of a Woman Who Breathes Fire.* San Francisco: Spinsters Ink, 1983.

Vaid, Urvashi. "More Information—Urvashi Vaid." Urvashi Vaid personal website. http://urvashivaid.net/wp/?page_id=578.

Victoria. "Queer, Asian, and Proud." *South Asian Americans Leading Together,* 6 October 2014. http://saalt.org/queer-asian-and-proud.

Villanueva, Chea. *Bulletproof Butches.* New York: Hard Candy Books, 1997.

———. *Jessie's Song and Other Stories.* New York: Masquerade Books, 1995.

Wallace, Lee. *Sexual Encounters: Pacific Texts, Modern Sexualities.* Ithaca, NY: Cornell University Press, 2003.

Wat, Eric C. *The Making of a Gay Asian Community: An Oral History of Pre-AIDS Los Angeles.* New York: Rowman and Littlefield, 2002.

Weston, Kath. "Get Thee to a Big City: Sexual Imaginary and the Great Gay Migration." *GLQ: A Journal of Lesbian and Gay Studies* 2, no. 3 (1995): 253–77.

Willyce, Kim. *Curtains of Light.* Self-published, 1970.

———. *Dancer Dawkins and the California Kid.* Boston: Alyson Publications, 1985.

———. *Eating Artichokes.* Oakland: Women's Press Collective, 1972.

Wilkinson, Willy. *Born on the Edge of Race and Gender: A Voice of Cultural Competency.* Oakland, CA: Hapa Papa Press, 2015.

Witchel, Alex. "Actor's Equity Attacks Casting of 'Miss Saigon.'" *New York Times,* 26 July 1990. http://www.nytimes.com/1990/07/26/theater/actors-equity-attacks-casting-of-miss-saigon.html.

Woo, Merle. *Yellow Woman Speaks: Selected Poems.* Seattle: Radical Women Publications, 1986.

Wu, Judy Tzu-Chun. *Doctor Mom Chung of the Fair-Haired Bastards: The Life of a Wartime Celebrity.* Berkeley: University of California Press, 2005.

Yoshikawa, Yoko. "The Heat is on Miss Saigon Coalition: Organizing across Race and Sexuality." In *Q&A: Queer in Asian America,* edited by David L. Eng and Alice Y. Hom, 41–56. Philadelphia: Temple University Press, 1998.

Yoshino, Kenji. *Covering: The Hidden Assault on our Civil Rights.* New York: Random House, 2006.

Yu, Henry, and Mai Ngai, eds. "The Politics of Remembering." Special Issue, *Amerasia Journal* 28, no. 3 (2002).

Zia, Helen. *Asian American Dreams: The Emergence of an American People.* New York: Farrar, Straus and Giroux, 2000.

CHAPTER 6

Latina/o Gender and Sexuality

Deena J. González and Ellie D. Hernández

Introduction

Gender and sexuality among U.S. Latina/o populations encompass a continuum of experiences—historical, cultural, religious, and lived. Gender and sexuality varied by culture or ethnicity and by era across the many different Latino populations descended from Latin Americans. Latino national histories, born inside the thirty-three different Latin American countries in existence today, are united in one irrefutable link to the conquest by Spain and the Iberian peninsula. The Spanish and Portuguese warred against many indigenous empires, towns, and communities encountered in 1519, and the wars continued subsequently into the 1800s, during the colonization of the Americas by other countries, including the United States.

In 1519, when the Spaniards landed on the Veracruz shore and made their way into Tenochtitlan, the most populated city in the Americas, and in the two years it took for them to lay claim to what would become Mexico City and its environs, gender and sexuality played a key role among people who survived the conquest and those who as conquerors remained in Mexico as well as in Central and South America to create nations across three centuries (from 1521 to 1898). A primary example is Malintzin Tenepal (Malinche or Doña Marina as the Spanish called her), the mistress and lover of the conqueror, Hernán Cortés, who had two children with him (figure 6.1). From the outset, this racial and ethnic mixing of people, known as *mestizaje,* shaped gender and sexuality because it imbued the outcomes of these unions, many of them violent, with legal, economic, and sexual consequences. Gender and sexuality were foundational in the story of Malinche and Cortés because the woman was memorialized as the mother of the first mes-

Figure 6.1. La Malinche, detail from the Monumento al Mestizaje by Julian Martinez and M. Maldonado (1982). The monument is of Hernan Cortes, La Malinche, and their son, Martin Cortes. The monument was originally located in the Center of Coyoacan, Mexico City, but was moved to Jardin Xicotencatl (a lesser known park), Barrio de San Diego Churubusco, Mexico City, due to public protests. Photo by Javier Delgado Rosas, 2009 (public domain; https://commons.wikimedia.org/wiki/File:La_Malinche_statue.jpg).

tizo children of the Americas, which was not the case, but also as the supreme betrayer of the Mexicans. Malinche's sexuality in the form of her relationship to the Spanish conqueror subsequently became a metaphor for loss, by women, against the more powerful Europeans, or men. Many contemporary theorists argue that the relationship was also a metaphor for rape, immortalized in Mexican lexicons by use of the term *la chingada* for someone who suffers rape.[1] These constant and persistent references in Mexican essays, movies, and folklore indeed suggest the considerable strength a metaphor based on someone as prominent as Malinche carries across time; few hail her interpretive abilities, her diplomatic status, or her multilingual facility. Instead, she—a woman—became equated with treachery and a loss of trust. In this reflection of a less-than-glorious Mexican past, men are never blamed for the loss to the Spaniards: Cuauhtémoc, the underprepared nephew of the deceased ruler, Moctezuma, actually surrendered the city, but is rarely assigned blame or shame. Malinche escapes no such special treatment.

Race and ethnicity, like gender and sexuality, complicated the story of women's centrality in the conquest, much of it similarly assigned for the wrong reasons. That is, women generally were not considered central as powerful agents in the conquest, but rather as its by-product, or their mixed-race children were. In some regions of Latin America, over seventeen different terms classified race or ethnic status, from "mestizo" to "mulatto" to "lobo" and "coyote."[2] These were not simple obsessions of a race-conscious state, but derived from Catholic and European legal codes seeking control over labor and most certainly over women and children.

The institutional apparatuses of the empire, including the Catholic Church, and later, the nation-state, conspired to sustain a hierarchy driven by fear and terror. Women could not venture far from home, or out on their own, even in urban areas. In the rural areas where the majority lived, working for bare subsistence dictated dependencies on men, children, and if possible, on fathers and families of origin. The powerful Catholic and hierarchical traditions imposed God, disciples, and the Pope or priests over parishioners, men, and households, with women and children at the bottom, and far below only African descent peoples and Native peoples; and the controlling effects of such persistent views and legal codes provided the basis upon which an empire was created. Church and state helped craft laws that ordered life in relationship to economies of production, work, and an occasional celebration around the sacraments of baptism, confirmation, or marriage. There were few opportunities for women's autonomy in a social or legal sense, and only activities hidden from public scrutiny or juridical sight allowed women to act in their own defense or protection. Native people similarly endured harsh treatment, subject to their employer's whims, forced to work on ranches, in mines, and, later, in factories simply because they were thought not to possess the talent, skills, or values to do more. Labor's link to gender and sexuality existed in the interplay between those with economic power (European men), and those without it (women, children, Native peoples, mixed-race people, and Latinos of African descent).

Against this past, gender and sexuality today have achieved a different status in a lived Latino/a reality, that is, they pose new and exciting challenges for historic and cultural traditions, but are based on modern ideas about the utter necessity of women's equality to men and access to opportunity for all. They also require new conceptualizations of what we mean by gender and what we mean when we define sexuality, including a rereading of the past.

While many imagine that the world is divided into male and female, masculine and feminine, or men and women, research in the past half century undermines the supposition that there are only two genders, only two sexes, or that what is normal in one community is normal across all others. In the nineteenth-century United States, pink was considered a masculine color, and boys as well as girls wore dresses and kept their hair long until they reached age seven.[3] The historical record provides an exceptional vantage point for looking at the dynamics of a multiplicity of experiences among Latina/o people. Many Native traditions across the Americas recognized (and continue to recognize) multiple combinations of gender and sexuality that intersected in different ways with social roles and responsibilities. Each of these groups had different categories and roles, as well as words to name them: from 1990, many Natives have adopted the umbrella term "two-spirit."[4] Spanish chroniclers described two-spirit people using their own ideas of sexuality and gender—for example, as men "feminized" into women's roles. Women were known to have passed their lives as men and/or soldiers in the conquest era and late into the twentieth century during the Mexican Revolution.[5] These examples are not necessarily given to prove that homosexuality or bisexuality have existed in the Americas for many centuries, which evidently they did, but rather to illustrate that what we think of as modern concepts of sexuality might have a longer history than is accorded traditionally.

As varied and diverse as the histories of the Latino people, so are their expressions of gender and sexuality. Most obvious is the understanding that gender and sexuality share some similarities with the larger experience of being human: in other words, we all have and express our gender and our sexuality, but at the same time, not all genders are the same, and not all expressions of sexuality and sexual identity share the same qualities. Gender and sexuality are also influenced largely by the specific parameters established by religion, culture, ethnicity, nationality, and race or class distinctions. This chapter discusses Latina/o gender and sexual experiences within a broad historical context to focus as well on a contemporary Latina/o context, for present understandings, like historical ones, enrich our analysis of how men and women defined one another and lived their lives as the gender codes organizing their behaviors changed over time.[6]

Conquest and Colonialism

From the nascent beginnings of the Americas, the period known as the Conquest, followed by the colonial period, is normally considered the origin that led to the formation of Latina/o people. The blending of races through *mestizaje* and miscegenation created regional and national distinctions. Within that landscape, the indigenous and Spanish advanced new bi- and multiracial configurations. In the areas we identify as the U.S. Southwest and the Caribbean, various indigenous and native groups blended racially with European conquistadors. Concomitant to the era of conquest and colonization (1492–1800), the period was distinguished by the force and domination of a new European cultural system, distinct from the indigenous, with eventual Spanish and Catholic dominance in the three continents—North American, Central American, and South American—known as Latin America today. In this vast geographic terrain, a dynamic people and dynamic societies developed.

Given the large territories, countries, and continents that comprise Latin America, it is impossible to trace a true chronological sequence or periodization of Chicana or Latina history, or of a singular role gender and sexuality played in that past or geography. This is because chronology and periods are the purview of tidily organized, written historiographical studies, of which Latina/o history remains defiant. Much resistance, for example, to domination or conquest was erased because few written or recorded documents detailed successful efforts to overcome the conquerors. Although court records and church records attest to many efforts against Spanish control, the truth is that those who collected the written record had a vested interest in securing one side of the story, despite the findings in recent decades of historians who are working to cast the wars and political picture in ways that account for both sides of the story. Archeologists have worked for centuries to assist the written record and are making progress in detailing how native communities and Spanish-Catholic ones shaped their pasts.

The best way to illustrate an important element related to where our story should begin is to ask when Latina/o or Chicano/a history began. There is no agreeable answer. Does it begin in 1519 when the Spaniards arrived on the coast of Mexico? Was there even a geographic identification that could be called Mexico? We know that the country named Spain existed because the Pope and a king and queen authorized it to set off to new lands. Mexico, on the other hand, was a constellation of over two hundred different indigenous communities, federations, and cities or towns that did not identify as a country, nation, or nation-state.

Mexico City (Tenochtitlan) was the oldest city in the Americas and the largest city up until the middle of the seventeenth century, and boasted a multiethnic, multi-caste, and multi-class society. Out of this varied history or past, it is impossible to trace effectively the meaning of gender and sexuality across time for any one group, and less so for as multiethnic and multiracial a group as Mexicans, Latino/as, or Chicano/as of today. Some general understanding of the events and cultural artifacts, however, provide clues about the significance or meaning of gender and sexuality across time.

One characteristic of the Spanish Empire's domination of the regions of the United States and the Caribbean is that the experiences of sexuality were less determined by the pleasures we normally ascribe to sexuality today; rather, sexuality was determined by need and survival, as this was foreign terrain for the Spanish and a new experience for the indigenous people native to the land. For the indigenous groups who endured the wrath of conquest and occupation, sexuality became a means of domination over their various indigenous traditions, especially the women and children. Many of the early inhabitants of the "New World" lived in tribal cultures that relied on nature and their surroundings for survival, and this organized their understandings of sexuality and of sexual expressiveness. The Spanish thought differently and codified as heretical or criminal many native understandings of the human body. Some native groups were bare breasted, or exposed chests and legs as the climate allowed. The Spanish were draped in cloth from neck to their feet, if not in armor or leather, and considered native dress codes promiscuous or offensive.

Native sophistication and what today would be labeled a modern way of life (nudity or frequent sexual partners, for example), were considered anti-Catholic and illegal. The anxiety of the Spaniards extended beyond the body. Many cities in Native America had developed sophisticated agricultural techniques, relied on scientific knowledge to feed and organize their cosmopolitan way of life (Mexico City especially), and organized their life according to an understanding of the cosmos, including mathematics and theology. The early conquistadores were mostly military men removed from the homeland and came to the New World to conquer the land and to force indigenous populations to submit to the twin goals of installing religious and state imperatives, Catholicism, and loyalty to the king.

The poststructuralist theoretician Tzvetan Todorov notes that the Mexican conquest is distinct from all other forms of empire building. He asks how a vast number of inhabitants could have fallen supposedly so easily. The singular direction of the Spanish to seek gold and valuables, along with their advanced weaponry, made it possible to win battles, but the truth also lies in the rapid spread of diseases that within twenty-five years of the arrival of the Spanish caused the demise of more than 90 percent of the native populations. Smallpox, measles, influenzas, and infections assisted the Spanish more than brilliant maneuvers on the battlefield. An ill population could not resist an onslaught. On the day Cortés finally laid claim to the ancient city of Tenochtitlan, those suffering from diseases, or dead in their beds because they could not reach their water supply, created a visible reminder of weakness and surrender. Had the Aztecs or Mexicanos not been so badly infected, their struggle to fortify and evacuate the city would have resulted in a different outcome.[7]

Some of these aspects of Mexican history, and of the histories of other regions in Central and South America that repeated the pattern after 1521, resulted in the creation of obtuse rules and the assertion of laws about gender and sexuality, some of which are still in existence today. Laws easily dictated the cultural practices of the early Latina/os. Of this, the most recognized figure of the conquest of Mexico has also become synonymous with the modern nation-state. The public and widely mythologized history of Doña Marina or Malinztin Tenépal, or La Malinche, mentioned above, situates one of the main elements of historiographical attitudes about the role of women in the New World and as its emblem of domination.[8] The early conquistadores used force in the early encounters with the Native Indians. Within a short amount of time, a matter of 150 years, the Spanish church and state institutionalized their rules of governance through the issuances of law and religious codes. Masculinity and femininity were institutionalized as oppositional rather complimentary aspects of gender and sexuality as the Spanish Crown created a division of labor according to gender, and this was seen clearly in the adjudication of specific sets of laws. *Las Leyes de Burgos* (Laws of Burgos) of 1512, for example, established a set of laws (and in actual practice, guidelines) on the treatment of the Native people in the first island conquered, Hispaniola.[9]

The laws constituted the first attempt to specifically outline conduct in matters of marriage and raising children; however, the law code made some attempt to regulate the treatment and conduct of the Spanish settlers and their encounters with the native Indians. The laws specifically created a family (tribal) structure and instructed priests to instill Catholic teachings and convert the Natives to Christianity. The creation of *Las Leyes de Burgos* was an attempt by the Spanish Crown to attend to the many abuses of the Native peoples in the decades after the conquest, but failed on many levels because the Native peoples were disempowered with the conversion of the society into a system of labor, which was the primary goal of the law, and to Catholicism, which was its second goal. Another attempt to create laws for the treatment of the natives came in 1542 with the *Leyes Nuevas* (New Laws) under Charles V. Once again, these laws sought to provide for the mistreatment of Native people but only reinforced the encomienda system of labor—an assignment, often in perpetuity, of a person's labor or work—and offered little protection for the Indians in the end.

The seventeenth century added to the major legal apparatus with the *Recopilacíon de las Leyes de los Reinos de Indias,* a copious and pedantic sequence of laws enacted in 1681 to supplant the previous two codifications, which were deemed ineffectual on a local level and excluded the many regions overtaken by Spanish rule over the next century. One of the main accomplishments of the *Recopilacíon* was to standardize the Spanish Law over the vast and enormous territories under Spanish occupation, also encompassing the areas of the Southwest, including Tucson, Los Angeles, Santa Fe, Laredo, and Albuquerque, and extending as far as the Philippines, Cuba, and Puerto Rico.[10]

The laws' geographic reach established a wide sweep for the legal and religious codes whose influences can be found in today's attitudes and economic trade relationships. The most distinctive of these codes was girded by a supreme understanding of the division of labor. Men and women became separated in their lived and working experiences and were bound by the separate spheres that divide men and women into private and public.

But the order and regulation of sexuality fell under the purview of the dreaded and somewhat fickle Spanish Inquisition. Few think or believe that the Spanish Inquisition pertained to Mexico or the New World, but recent historical excavation shows that the Inquisition did in fact regulate sexual behaviors and served more as a regulatory system in the New World than in Europe. Inquisitional repression also included many offenses that pertained to sexuality, such as bestiality, rape, and sodomy (male and female), as well as other forms of stated heresy against the church. Phillip II established the Inquisition officially in Mexico in 1569.[11] By 1662, accounts of homosexual behavior led the Duke of Albuquerque to indict over a hundred people and execute a substantial number of them.[12] Within the colonial period and heritage, the laws and codes of conduct began to shape the codification of proper sexuality, situating it within the domain of heterosexuality, with the church and state as purveyors of the law guiding it.

Naturally, people began to perceive heterosexuality not only as the "natural" order of things, but as the only order of things. It would become clear through the actions of the church and state that they became more interested in regulating behaviors and in associating morality with the regulation of sexual behaviors and were far less interested in heresy. The Inquisition in Spain did not actively pursue the persecution of sodomy as it would in the Americas and the New World.[13] Most of the active persecution of sodomy by the Inquisition belonged to the New World.[14] According to historian Richard C. Trexler, the arena of conquest placed sexuality and gender clearly within the paradigm of the victor or vanquished, where rape became an "insult" of war for both men and women.[15] Sexual and gender identity were not based on individual rights, pleasure, or desires, or even on group rights. The role and function of gender and sexual identity pertained to the natural order or biological basis of reproduction and conquest.

Anthropologist June Nash observes the distinctive roles men and women played in the transition under Spanish Colonialism.[16] Nash observes that "while women continued to have important roles in the domestic economy, they were [ultimately] excluded from the predatory economy."[17] In another location, historian Antonia Castañeda associates the "*entrada*" or "incursion" of the Spanish soldiers and priests with sexual violence of women and girls in Alta California.[18] Castañeda recognizes that limited information on the subject of gender and sexuality exists, but nevertheless found similar findings as many others have noted previously that the subordination of women did in fact lead toward sexual violence and many other abuses that are well documented in the former Spanish Borderlands.

In the centuries where the origin of the multi-continental Americas lies, and especially for the United States, the predicament of the Spanish Conquest left behind an arcane system of laws and religious codes without the benefit of a cultural Renaissance or a Protestant Reformation as had been experienced in Europe, and thus continued as facets of canonical and state law that would carry over into the United States' expansion through the eighteenth and nineteenth centuries. Just as the Spanish language that is spoken today in many regions of the Americas is an arcane vestige of the Old World, so, too, is the legal apparatus and cultural view of gender and sexuality residing within the remnants of a culture of conquest.

Our effort in this essay has always been to re-center Latina/o/x people outside the glare of U.S. imperialism. Our worldview and our history did not begin in 1848—our effort is by design intended to feature a gender and sexuality before U.S. hegemonic frontier dominance.

The nineteenth century brought about expansion and new frontier attitudes through changes precipitated by the United States' expansion. These culminated in an ever denser context for gender and sexuality among Latina/o people as they came under U.S. domination, physically in the former Mexican northern territories, and economically toward the end of the nineteenth century as the United States extended its reach toward the natural resources that Latin America provided, including its labor force.

While it is common to view the impact of the U.S.-Mexican War of 1846–1848 as a training ground for U.S. soldiers later engaged in the Civil War, and common to overlook the U.S. invasion of Mexico beyond the border formed by the Rio Grande, there is more to see: gender and sexuality proved powerful agents in the hands of the U.S. takeover as Mexican lands were acquired and as gender and sexual politics shaped the dynamics of acquisition. Historian Deena González concludes that the centrality of such figures as Doña Gertrudis Barceló, who operated businesses in Santa Fe, was its wealthiest citizen for over three decades, and was maligned by the invading Euro-Americans as a common whore or a madam, is the best example of the centrality of gender in the U.S. colonization of the Mexican north. When Euro-Americans crossed illegally first into Texas, and later into New Mexico, they argued that the people were "as barren as the land," "lazy," and "ugly."[19] These undocumented merchants, soldiers, and vagabonds used such rhetoric to denounce the local population, making it easier to occupy their land and achieve domination over the work force.

After the Treaty of Guadalupe Hidalgo of 1848 resolved the armed conflict between the two countries, if not the bitter feelings between locals and imposers, women who had owned property as allowed under Spanish law were at a loss in a court system that did not allow women to adjudicate differences. Because women outlived men and tended to own property, land, houses, and livestock, they lost more than men when the Euro-Americans went to court to establish ownership under pretext. The Widow Chaves of Santa Fe best exemplified how even wealthy women were duped by agents of the state, in this case a lawyer and claims surveyor who managed to conspire to produce a will in English that was not a translation of her wishes rendered in the original Spanish.[20] Such occurrences were far from rare, and the colonizers, who cast women as gullible or dependent, managed to exert legal influence to such an extent that many resident Spanish-Mexican people of the Southwest endured land and property losses without recourse.

Because the northern Mexican territories figured so critically in U.S. history, particularly after the California gold rush and the need for a transcontinental railroad, and because Latino/as played such an important role in the growth of the territories west of the Mississippi, it is clear why Spanish Borderlands history—and writers, historians, and artists—consistently reference the roles of women. Especially prominent are the stereotypes of women as virgins or martyrs, as saloon keepers or as pious maternal figures, then and later in the twenty-first century, concluding that a pattern of loss, intimidation, and violence characterized memory and life through to the present. While it is the case that abuses of power and imposition of gender codes occurred and continue, the most recent focus on response and resistance, on defiance of assigned roles—whether racialized, sexualized, gendered, or classed—underscores new directions in our views of sexuality and male/female roles or patterns across time and geography. For that reason, we examine next the contemporary application of some previously mentioned gender codes and roles where sexuality and sexual expressiveness most endure as agents of political action as well as of derision. In understanding these dynamics, and through them, we find a great deal of hope for a future less determined by limitation and misunderstanding.

Twentieth Century: Codes of Transformation

Throughout the twentieth century, moral codes about gender and sexuality underwent a tumultuous period characterized by inconsistencies and scattered progressions. For Latina/os, the triumph of the United States over the Southwest transferred the focus from a Spanish system to an Anglo-European and Protestant perspective, or at least the uneasy coexistence of both. One of the main areas that has transformed perspectives on gender and sexuality has been the gender codes. With modernization came a new industrialized labor force that brought women out of the confines of the home. This carried over to other American sensibilities that gave new possibilities for identity and self-expression.

One of the enduring influences shaping Latino/a gender and sexuality since the era of the Spanish conquest is the Catholic Church, which has taken a strong and influential stance on sexual conduct and gender attributes. In the sacrament of marriage, also called matrimony, for example, the covenant describes a partnership to be exclusively between a man and woman, and, until just recently, women were asked to assent to a life as "man and wife."[21] A man thus retained his gender, but a woman's was filtered through her marital identity as the wife of someone. The covenant of marriage in Catholicism requires that the two partners be a man and a woman, and the Catholic religion holds that marriage is the only acceptable place for sex and procreation.[22]

Until very recently, the laws of a nation, both municipal and state, followed religion's canonical law and recognized the partnership of marriage in accordance with those of religious practices. In June 2015, the United States Supreme Court decision Obergefell v. Hodges guaranteed same-sex couples across the country the fundamental right to marry.[23] The movements for same-sex marriage initiatives and for civil unions that preceded the decision were met with a backlash that views them as part of a "liberal agenda" or a conspiracy against heterosexuality.[24] Heterosexual marriage still enjoys a privileged position in the majority of Latina/o communities. Heterosexual privilege signifies a public recognition and support for an intimate relationship between a man and woman, and is recognized and supported by different social networks, such as the workplace, governmental bodies, educational institutions, housing, health care, and, of course, acceptance and recognition by many religious organizations. It is a privilege often enjoying the status of a "right," and only in the past half century has it been challenged as inaccurately reflecting people's lives, romantic interests, or the real lived experiences of gays and lesbians as well as bisexual and transgender people. A later section of this chapter gives examples of specific Latino- and Latina-based challenges to heteronormativity, or the belief that everyone is and must be heterosexual.

The expression of a male or female identity thus becomes embedded in institutions that support a masculine identity for men and a feminine one for women. Another way of making this point is that masculinity and femininity express what it means to be a heterosexual male or female in a court of law, and in hospitals, schools, or churches—that is, in institutions that sanctify those privileges. The more obvious Latino expression of heterosexual masculinity is located in the term "macho," which is defined as a strong, often exaggerated, sense of masculine pride. To be macho has mixed meanings in the U.S. context. Its meaning can have both positive and negative connotations. Male athletes are considered a proper role model of masculinity.[25] The more negative aspect is that of the stereotype of a macho man as someone who is aggressive and demonstrates excessive dominance over women through male chauvinism. Most gay men, in traditional Latino/a thinking, would be considered less masculine and not sufficiently macho.[26]

The counterpart to the macho or male figure is to be found in the concept of *Marianismo*. *Marianismo* derives from the worship or following of the Virgin Mary (Maria) and her central role in active Catholicism. It is an ideal of true femininity that women are supposed to embody— that is, to be modest, virtuous, and sexually abstinent until marriage, and then faithful and subordinate to their husbands. *Marianismo* serves as the female companion to "machismo," or hypermasculinity, and originated as its counterpoint during the time of the Spanish conquest. It began as a direct response to the overused *machismo* and was intended to explain a female phenomenon in Latin America in which women were either depicted as saints or as whores. Female superiority was at the heart of *Marianismo*, but its opposite also accounts for how easily, in this dichotomous construction, women could also be seen as overly and overtly sexual—that is, as super-sexed. Beginning in 1973, scholars have located the concept across many Latino/a cultures, meaning that it is a gender construction shared across national borders. Since the 1980s, however, other scholars introduced into the lexicon of femininity and womanhood more feminist-based ideas, including *mujerismo*, or woman-centeredness, which locates women's power and struggles within a Catholic context, but engages religious equality and social liberation for all. A *mujerista* theology was also a response to male-constructed notions of how women should behave in social and religious contexts; in this case, the message was directed toward the traditional Catholic hierarchy.[27]

Other characteristics of machismo that are often hidden include an ostensibly valorous and chivalrous code of protection that extends into the Spanish and Latin-derived romantic virtues of sexual potency and prowess. Less obvious is the *mujer passiva* (or, *la mujer abnegada*) who negates herself for the love of her husband and children and sacrifices her individualism for the benefit of the family. This traditional role orients women toward home life and religious dedication. Gender and sexuality have their own unique expressions within Latina/o communities.

In the most basic sense, gender refers to the biological identity assigned at birth, usually boy or girl; some newborns on rare occasions have genitalia that might be male and female at once.[20] In Western culture, male and female predominate as the primary assigned or prescribed gender categories.[29] As a cultural facet of every Spanish-speaking nation across the Americas—shaped by unique traditions, religious influences, and laws—most gender codes of conduct in the vast Latina/o experience emphasize femininity for women and masculinity for men. Ideally, these gender codes of masculinity and femininity have served as the basis of heterosexuality and, with them, support the formation of the family social structure as a central basis for constructing gender and sexual identities.[30]

Latinas experience negative stereotyping as frequently as their male counterparts. The virgin/whore complex refers to the way Latinas are situated between two completely opposite views: the virgin and the whore, or the martyr and the witch, are ideals embedded in cultural practices, religious or spiritual values, and in social life, and they require women to behave and position themselves as either celibate (virginal) or as sacrificing themselves for the good of the family, the community, or the collective (martyr). Like the terms suggest, the virgin is the idealized woman in Latina/o culture, while the term "witch" refers to the maligned aspects of a woman who shows too much independence. Sexual promiscuity is central to the virgin/whore or martyr/witch dichotomies.[31] To be "virginal" suggests an attitude of moral refinement and right action, and to be labeled a whore or prostitute suggests sexual autonomy and freedom, including the possibility of prostitution. Mainstream culture exploits this notion in advertising and the media, underscoring Latinas' hypersexuality, or availability for sex. Popular culture focuses on Latinas' bodies and eroticizes them on the basis of a traditional idea that Latinas had more children (meaning they had more sex) than white women. While attitudes about sexuality have changed during the last five decades, some of these attitudes about Latina/o men and women remain despite efforts to move away from cultural prescriptions and established preconceptions.[32]

Now regarded as a socially constructed set of rules and behaviors, orthodox assumptions about heterosexuality and the view that men were superior and women inferior are being challenged. The belief that heterosexuality was the only option for sexual behavior no longer dominates Latina/o perspectives. Heteronormativity, the belief that heterosexuality is the only acceptable way of expressing and enjoying sexuality in the human experience, is further challenged by science, psychology, and religious and cultural mores. The belief that heterosexuality is "normal" and all other forms of sexuality outside of heterosexuality are abnormal, deviant, and disordered has given way to an understanding of the complexity of human gender and sexual expression, including homosexuality, bisexuality, asexuality, and gender variation, from those who are genderqueer to those who are transgender.[33] Due to the work of many academics and activist political organizations, sexuality is increasingly seen as complex; there are more persuasive arguments, including scientific information, that support variety in human expression and behaviors and, to a great extent, among mammals and other animals. These only reinforce the idea that sex and sexuality are not simple concepts to be understood as uniformly or divinely ordained.[34] Many Native American cultures recognized sexual and gender variations that go beyond the male/female understandings of Western European cultures.[35] In the Americas for example, the Zapotec of Mexico recognize a third gender category, the *Muxe* (pronounced Mu-SHAY), who are identified as male when they are born, but who dress and live as women. *Muxe* are generally accepted by the Zapotec Indian culture and are not viewed negatively, as they might be in Western industrialized cultures. *Muxe* are not necessarily homosexual and do not fit neatly into identity categories one may find in U.S. LGBTQ communities.

Gender identity and sexual orientation are related but distinct cultural identities. There are many people in the United States who do not identify with the gender assigned to them at birth. Some people find that they identify opposite to the gender they were identified as; others may feel that they exist somewhere on the continuum between the two binaries, or as some gender not represented by male or female, or as no gender at all (agender). In sexuality and sexually fluid identities, the terms used are expressly significant. The same is the case in ethnic identity, where a recent trend is to use "Latinx" to be inclusive of Latino/a, or of all self-identified people of Latin American origins. Most broadly, the term "transgender" encompasses all those who do not identify with the gender they were identified with at birth; the terms "gender fluid" and "gender queer" are also used by people to describe themselves.[36] Sexuality is defined as the expression of one's sexual desire and may or may not include a certain partner. It is no longer widely seen as being limited to conventional terms of marriage and heterosexuality.[37]

There are many different ways that people in the LGBTQ community and beyond it identify, depending on how they perceive their sexual and gender identities and how they express them. The terms used to describe these various attractions and identities have varied over time.[38] After the 1950s, when, for example, "lesbian" referred to women's attraction for other women, and "gay" referred to men who expressed desire for and partnership with each other, the sexual revolution following these understandings changed the way we describe contemporary sexual identity. The Latina/o LGBTQ communities emerged to claim spaces in the larger queer movements of the past decades from experiences

in the sexual and feminist political debates, including those addressing civil rights and the rights of minorities, including sexual minorities.
In sum, they drew from contemporary legacies, including civil rights,
federal and state debates, and student movements that changed how
minorities viewed their position in society.[39]

History and Activism of Latina/o Sexual Politics

Latinas/os had been situated at the margins in queer political movements, often overlooked in major historical moments—their political,
cultural, social, and sexual activisms intertwined with radical economic
and demographic changes to underscore gay rights issues. The general influence of queer Latinas/os became more prominent during the
1980s and 1990s, and visibility and representation posed less of a challenge. During these decades, the marginalized role queer Latinos played
within some of the larger LGBTQ political movements continued to per-
meate issues and organizations. Several pivotal and historical factors
contributed to the emergence and visibility of Latinas/o queers. In these
early decades, the plight of AIDS and Latina feminism transformed the
issue of visibility as Latinos sought to transform their cultural "outsider"
status—being ethnic and political minorities—often sidelined as contributing leaders and players in the larger spheres of LGBTQ politics.
Since the 1950s and even in today's politics of self-representation, the
terms "Latino," "Latina," and "queer" have moved away from their pejorative meanings into a positive reflection of "Latinidad," a label of consciousness about Latin American roots and, in the case of embracing
a queer Latinidad, a politicized and political identity.[40] The same thing
occurred in the 1960s in the Chicano movement: as women claimed
their stake and interests in struggles for equality, access to education,
and farmworkers' and other laborers' rights, the word "Chicano" (derived
perhaps from *Mexicano* pronounced in the original Nahuatl language
as Me-SHEE-cano) lost its pejorative flavor and slipped into popular acceptance. Today, three established Ph.D. programs in Chicana/o Studies indicate the widespread acceptance of the concept of selfhood—of
naming oneself and embracing an identity for varied political, cultural,
or socially acceptable reasons.

Until the most recent census, as the invisibility of Latino/as persisted
among the majority population as a whole, admitting one's homosexuality was difficult; racial disenfranchisement made it even more difficult
to be proud of any identity at all. In the Latina experience, misogyny and

homophobia created complications because lesbian women were often single parents, unpartnered, or disowned by their families of origin. The popular term used until the 1960s was "homosexual." "Gay" only began to gain legitimacy in later decades as gays and lesbians openly declared and reclaimed their sexual identities. "Gay" was often used to refer to gay men's experience, and women began to use "lesbian" alongside "gay" to contrast the gender distinctions. Only in the 1990s was the term "queer" used to encompass all groups from a wide range of gender identities and sexualities. AIDS activism radicalized lesbian and gay men's movements in the early 1990s, and their leaders continued a quest to elect local sympathetic officials, found or run businesses, and create families within this expanding display of sexual desires and sexuality. Some resisted the idea of "flamboyance," while others were proudly flamboyant. Most gay and lesbian politicians and social activists argued strenuously for the inclusion of all sexual expression, no matter how disdainful some would find them, citing First and Second Constitutional Amendments as rights given to any American citizen without regard to their sexuality. Others also used "queer" to formulate artistic, political, and social initiatives, particularly in the urban centers of the country.[41]

The pre-Stonewall period, before 1969, is often cited as an era marked by closeted life for many gays and lesbians, though there were those who worked publicly for LGBTQ civil rights.[42] It was incredibly difficult to be open about homosexuality, and this proved to be a fearful time, with little to no societal acceptance of any gay/lesbian lifestyle. Senator Joseph McCarthy's witch hunts included searching for homosexuals in the early 1950s, blacklisting actors who might have had even an affiliation with known or suspected gay actors and actresses; the FBI under J. Edgar Hoover was discovered to have been obsessed about locating the secret lives of many left-leaning, supposedly communist-sympathizing Americans.[43] Adding to that experience of marginalization, racial politics and especially anti-Latino sentiment across the United States hardly encouraged honesty or open declarations. Despite such marginalization and erasure from the larger historical picture, Latinas/os played a role in the nascent gay liberation movements.[44] The summer of 1969 ushered in a new perspective on sexuality for gays and lesbians. On 28 June 1969, a group of gay and lesbian people, many of them Latina/o and of color, rebelled against police harassment at the Stonewall Inn in Greenwich Village in New York City.[45] During the Stonewall riots and in its aftermath, several Latina/o activists were critical players in forming the vocabulary and understanding of what was to become known as the "gay liberation" movement.[46] Before the Stonewall riots, many of the queer political movements were limited to organizations such as the Mattachine Society and Daughters of Bilitis, and were focused primarily on fighting discrimination.[47] These organizations believed in assimilation over marginalization and difference, but the agenda of these groups emphasized Anglo-American values, middle-class interests, and the desire to blend in with mainstream society, despite the fact that each group contained gays and lesbians of color.[48]

Despite the Anglo, middle-class values of the earliest LGBTQ or queer movements, some Latino activists clearly and cleverly resisted the assimilationist models that predominated a pre–civil rights era. In San Francisco, for example, José Sarria rejected the secrecy of the Mattachine Society and founded instead the League for Civil Education in 1960, which sought to educate queer and straight communities about homophobia and especially police abuse.[49] The group worked to find a solution to the police raids of gay bars and the harassment that was pervasive at the time. Sarria subsequently founded the Royal Court System in 1965, which now serves as the collective body for over sixty-five local chapters worldwide, each of which organizes drag-related fundraisers for queer charities.

Latina Sylvia Rivera was born Ray Rivera in New York City to Puerto Rican and Venezuelan parents, and took the name Sylvia while still a child. Rivera was present at Stonewall during the 1969 Stonewall Riots. Told through testimony, Rivera purportedly threw one of the first bricks at the police during the riot.[50] She also played an important role in the organization of other queer organizations, among them the Gay Liberation Front (GLF) and another offshoot of the GLF called the Gay Activists Alliance (GAA). These organizations were active primarily from 1970 to 1974 and included Latino/as. Rivera would also move on to cofound, with Marsha P. Johnson, the Street Transvestite Action Revolutionaries (STAR), which focused on providing social services to those we would now identify as transgender and queer youth, and to offer a safe space for transgender political voices to speak.

In response to many instances of erasure and lack of consideration, many Latina/o queers began setting up their own representational organizations, such as the Third World Gay Revolution in New York, the Gay Liberated Chicanos of Los Angeles, or the Gay Latino Alliance (GALA) of San Francisco. In yet another example of representational political efforts, a New York–based Latino gay men's group, described as a coalitional group from several countries in Latin America, published a

Figure 6.2. The Edificio Comunidad de Orgullo Gay de Puerto Rico (Casa Orgullo), in San Juan, Puerto Rico, was the home of the Comunidad de Orgullo Gay de Puerto Rico. Inspired by the Stonewall Riots in New York City, the group was founded in 1974 and was Puerto Rico's first gay liberation organization. They occupied this building from 1975 to 1976. Casa Orgullo was listed on the NRHP on 1 May 2016. Photo by Santiago Gala, 2015, courtesy of the Puerto Rico State Historic Preservation Office.

pamphlet in Spanish, *AFUERA* (Out).[51] Focused on the politics of "coming out," the booklet examined leftist ideas—drawing from Third World–liberation, Marxist thought—and challenged patriarchy, as Darren Rosenblum, a scholar of Latino gay rights, notes.[52] In 1974 in Puerto Rico, inspired by the 1969 Stonewall Riots, LGBTQ Puerto Ricans founded the Comunidad de Orgullo Gay de Puerto Rico (figure 6.2). They published *Pa'fueral* and offered educational and community services out of the second-floor space in a residential neighborhood.[53] Of major significance to the coming out process were the public events and social celebrations, such as parades, pageants, and political activism. Understanding that "coming out" and public visibility were important to LGBTQ rights, organizations such as Comité Homosexual Latinoamericano, or the Latin American Homosexual Committee, attempted to march in New York's annual Puerto Rican Day Parade. Denied participation, activists were successful in drawing attention to gay realities in Puerto Rican communities, a move that scholar David Gibson believes presaged later battles over St. Patrick's Day Parades, which ended in the United States Supreme Court.[54]

Sexuality, Gender, and Representation

LGBTQ communities have routinely been impacted by issues of access and adequate care and representation. One of the most difficult aspects of being "out" is working through the homophobic attitudes against LGBTQ people, who have often faced discrimination in legal matters and life-threatening decisions in areas of health care and immigration. These concerns over homophobia in the legal system became the basis of many legal disputes over cases related to child custody, immigration, and survivor benefits. Mariana Romo-Carmona underwent such a legal battle over the custody of her son. She notes, "Sometimes our own families act in collusion with the state to deprive us of the right to raise our own children."[55]

Issues with immigration also surfaced as lesbian or bisexual and transsexual women seeking asylum in to the United States have been denied entry. Ironically, many LGBTQ people were among the thousands of Cubans allowed to come to the United States as part of the Marielito boatlift, sent out of Cuba as the nation drained the undesirables.[56] Until recently, immigration laws have generally excluded LGBTQ people from entering the United States and other nations also do not offer considerations for LGBTQ refugees. It has only been since the 2015 Supreme Court decision regarding same-sex marriage that spouses of LGBTQ people have been eligible for immigration privileges and death benefits. Elba Cedeno's life partner was killed in the World Trade Center attacks on 11 September 2001.[57] Her efforts to access survivor benefits from the Federal Victim's Compensation Fund were denied. After denial of her claims, she sought representation from the Lambda Legal Defense Fund.[58]

Homophobia in health care, one of the largest industries in the United States, discourages gays, lesbians, and bisexual and transgender people from accessing adequate medical care. This is exacerbated by cultural and financial barriers that discourage Latino/as in general from seeking health care.[59] While some changes in the health care industry have developed, like increasingly noting sexual preference and preferred name and gender pronouns in a chart so that accurate information can be conveyed, health care in the United States continues to practice heteronormativity. Suzanne Newman, producer of the film *Nuestra Salud,* discusses lesbian health issues. Newman notes, "Many Latinas believe that you only go to the OB-GYN when you're sick or dying . . . . And that when you do go, you always get bad news."[60]

Conclusion: Contemporary Sites of Political Organizing

Latina lesbian organizations that emerged during the 1990s and later included Latina Lesbians United Never Apart (LLUNA, Boston); Ellas en Acción (San Francisco); Las Buenas Amigas (New York City); Entre Ellas (Austin); and Amigas Latinas (Chicago). Chicago LGBTQ activists are often overlooked by LGBTQ historians, but a number of notables can be found in the Chicago Gay and Lesbian Hall of Fame, including Latinas Mona Noriega and Evette Cardona.[61] Latino/a LGBTQ organizations are increasingly found across the country, including the Association of Latinos/as Motivating Action (ALMA) in Chicago; Latino LinQ in Atlanta; the Austin Latina/Latino Lesbian and Gay Organization (ALLGO) in Austin; the Latino Pride Center in New York City; AGUILAS in San Francisco; the Unity Coalition in Florida; and from 1987 to 2004, the National Latino/a Lesbian and Gay Organization (LLEGÓ).[62] The Latino GLBT History Project works to preserve LGBTQ Latina/o history.[63]

Lesbians have made significant inroads in local community politics and serve social justice causes in critical ways. In San Antonio, Texas, Graciela Sánchez and a group of young feminists with visions of ending discrimination founded the Esperanza Peace and Justice Center. When homophobic interests sought to cut the center's funding, Esperanza sued and won.[64] In Los Angeles, attorney and housing advocate Elena Popp helped elect Antonio Villaraigosa to a seat on the Los Angeles City Council. She was expected to, but did not, run for the seat lesbian Jackie Goldberg won in the California State Senate. In Washington, D.C., attorney Mercedes Marquez served as deputy general counsel for fair housing at the U.S. Department of Housing and Urban Development. In 1993, with the help of Ellas in Acción, Susan Leal was appointed to the San Francisco Board of Supervisors. Olga Vives, a Cubana, served as vice president of action for the National Organization for Women (NOW) until her death in 2012. She said that in NOW she could focus on a mix of issues that affected her life as a "Latina, immigrant, mother, and lesbian from the Midwest."[65] Ingrid Durán works in the national political arena through the Congressional Hispanic Caucus Institute. She has served as a social justice broker and change agent, mitigating homophobia in

Latina/Latino political organizations and countering racism in LGBTQ organizations.[66]

Other rich forms of activism manifest in lesbian and feminist cultural representations. During the 1990s, Tatiana de la Tierra, a Colombian writer, activist, and librarian (now deceased), published three Latina lesbian magazines: *Conmoción, Esto No Tiene Nombre,* and *Telaraña.*[67] In Los Angeles, Tongues is a Latina lesbian group and publication that grew out of VIVA, a 1980s LGBTQ Latina/Latino arts group. Members included artist Alma López, whose controversial reimagination of Our Lady caused a furor in New Mexico in 2001.[68] MACHA Theatre (Mujeres Advancing Culture, History, and Art), led by Cuban American Odalys Nanin, produces plays with lesbian content.[69] Laura Aguilar is a Los Angeles–based Chicana photographer whose images examine body image and cultural identity.[70] A long list of Latina and Latino LGBTQ writers, activists, and other notables can be found on the Lesbian History Project website, which suggests not only how enduring this legacy of both activism and presence or visibility has been, but also what a leading role in gender and sexuality studies such writers and researchers, artists, and others have played in contemporary feminist circles including among gay Latino men as well as heterosexual allies.

Many theories today argue that the hegemonic narratives of identity politics (said to be grounded in nationalist or religious identities) are an essentialist error, but some Latina lesbians argue that identity politics have been their survival strategy. In other words, possessing an identity politics founded on gender and sexuality allows a person to sustain a strong politics of identity. Emma Pérez has written that "strategic essentialism is practiced resistance against dominant ideologies that silence and/or model marginalized groups."[71] Regardless of theoretical and political disruptions, straight, lesbian, and bisexual Latina feminists who began exploring gender and sexuality as important elements of their human condition maintained a standpoint of resistant consciousness and created important movements of interaction with *familia, cultura,* and the larger society. For a unique moment, historically speaking, such consciousness existed apart from patriarchal reach or male visions of women's proper roles. In this way, the new Latina feminisms of the contemporary era also shed light on men's gender roles and encourage their re-examination as well. Such an accomplishment attests to the significance of understanding the varied, central roles that gender and sexuality have played in Latino/a life.[72]

Dr. Deena J. González is Provost and Senior Vice President at Gonzaga University in Spokane, Washington, where she is also a professor in the History Department.

Dr. Ellie D. Hernández is an associate professor in the Department of Chicana/o Studies at the University of California, Santa Barbara.

Notes

1. For the most cited example, see Octavio Paz, "Labyrinth of Solitude" (New York: Grove Press, 1961).
2. See, for example, Barbara L. Voss, *The Archaeology of Ethnogenesis: Race and Sexuality in Colonial San Francisco* (Berkeley: University of California Press, 2008).
3. See Ruth Padawer, "BoyGirl," *New York Times Magazine,* 12 August 2012, 19–36.
4. For a detailed treatment, see Will Roscoe, "Sexual and Gender Diversity in Native America and the Pacific Islands," this volume.
5. On the *soldaderas* of the Mexican Revolution, see Elizabeth Salas, *Soldaderas in the Mexican Military: Myth and History* (Austin: University of Texas Press, 1990).
6. For an overview, see Luz Calvo and Catriona Esquibel, "Latina Lesbians, BiMujeres, and Trans Identities: Charting Courses in the Social Sciences," in *Latino/a Sexualities: Probing Powers, Passions, Practices, and Policies,* ed. Marysol Asencio (New Brunswick, NJ: Rutgers University Press, 2010), 217–29.
7. Tzvetan Todorov, "The Reasons for Victory," in *The Conquest of America: The Question of the Other* (New York: Harper and Row, 1984).
8. See Adelaida del Castillo, "Malintzin Tenépal: A Preliminary Look into a New Perspective," in *Essays on la Mujer,* ed. Rosaura Sánchez and Rosa Martinez Cruz (Los Angeles: UCLA Chicano Studies Research Center, 1977), 124–49.
9. See Leyes de Burgos in John A. Crow, *The Epic of Latin America* (Oakland: University of California Press, 1992).
10. For the full list of laws, see Spain/Council of the Indies, *Recopilación de leyes de los reynos de las Indias, 1681,* 5 vols. (Mexico: M. A. Porrúa, 1987).
11. Louis Crompton, *Homosexuality and Civilization* (Cambridge, MA: Harvard University Press, 2003).
12. Ibid., 319.
13. Cristian Berco, *Sexual Hierarchies, Public Status: Men, Sodomy, and Society in Spain's Golden Age* (Toronto: University of Toronto Press, 2007).

14. Ibid.

15. Richard C. Trexler, *Sex and Conquest: Gendered Violence, Political Order, and the European Conquest of the Americas* (Ithaca, NY: Cornell University Press, 1995).

16. June Nash, "Aztec Women: The Transition from Status to Class in Empire and Colony," in *Women and Colonization: Anthropological Perspectives,* ed. Mona Etienne and Eleanor Leacock (New York: Praeger, 1980), 134–48.

17. Ibid., 67.

18. Antonia I. Castañeda, "Engendering the History of Alta California, 1769–1848: Gender, Sexuality, and the Family," *California History* 76, no. 2–3 (1997): 230–59.

19. See Deena J. González, *Refusing the Favor: The Spanish-Mexican Women of Santa Fe, 1820–1880* (New York: Oxford University Press, 1999), chapter ii.

20. Ibid., 86.

21. Castañeda, "Engendering," 150.

22. See Catholic News Service, "U.S. Bishops to Urge Constitutional Amendment to Protect Marriage," *AmericanCatholic.org,* 2003, http://www.ameri cancatholic.org/News/Homosexuality/default.asp.

23. The text of the decision is available online: United States Supreme Court, Obergefell v. Hodges, 576 U.S. ___ (2015), http://www.supremecourt.gov/opinions/14pdf/14-556_3204.pdf.

24. See the resources at the Williams Institute website, http://williamsinstitute .law.ucla.edu.

25. See Katherine Schweighofer, "LGBTQ Sport and Leisure," in *LGBTQ America: A Theme Study of Lesbian, Gay, Bisexual, Transgender, and Queer History,* ed. Megan E. Springate (Washington, DC: National Park Foundation and National Park Service, 2016), https://nps.gov/articles/lgbtqtheme-sport.htm, for a discussion of masculinity in sport.

26. See Tomás Almaguer, "Chicano Men: Cartography of Homosexual Identity and Behavior," in *The Lesbian and Gay Studies Reader,* ed. Henry Abelove, Michèle Aina Barale, and David M. Halperin (New York: Routledge, 1993), 255–73.

27. See R. M. Hill and C. I. Vasquez, *The Maria Paradox: How Latinas Can Merge Old World Traditions with New World Self-Esteem* (New York: G. P. Putnam & Sons, 1996).

28. Judith Halberstam, *In a Queer Time and Place: Transgender Bodies, Subcultural Lives* (New York: New York University Press, 2005).

29. See Roscoe, "Sexual and Gender Diversity," for a discussion of multiple genders recognized by Native American societies.

30. See Olivia Espín, "Cultural and Historical Influences on Sexuality in Hispanic/Latin Women: Implications for Psychotherapy," in *Pleasure and Danger: Exploring Female Sexuality,* ed. Carole S. Vance (London: Pandora Press, 1989), 164–94.

31. For a review of the Spanish Mediterranean origins of these concepts, see Mary Elizabeth Perry, *Gender and Disorder in Early Modern Seville* (Princeton, NJ: Princeton University Press, 1990).

32. Elena R. Gutiérrez, *Fertile Matters: The Politics of Mexican-Origin Women's Reproduction* (Austin: University of Texas Press, 2008); on cultural tradition, a young woman's fifteenth birthday "coming of age" ritual, see Karen Mary Davalos, "La Quinceañera: Making Gender and Ethnic Identities," in *Velvet Barrios: Popular Culture and Chicana/o Sexualities*, ed. Alicia Gaspar de Alba (New York: Palgrave Macmillan, 2003), 141–62.

33. See Leisa Meyer and Helis Sikk, "Introduction to Lesbian, Gay, Bisexual, Transgender, and Queer (LGBTQ) History in the United States," in *LGBTQ America: A Theme Study of Lesbian, Gay, Bisexual, Transgender, and Queer History*, ed. Megan E. Springate (Washington, DC: National Park Foundation and National Park Service, 2016), chapter 3, https://nps.gov/articles/lgbtqtheme-history.htm; Susan Stryker, "Transgender History in the U.S. and the Places that Matter," this volume; and Loraine Hutchins, "Making Bisexuals Visible," this volume.

34. See Bruce Bagemihl, *Biological Exuberance: Animal Homosexuality and Natural Diversity* (New York: Macmillan, 2000).

35. For details about cultures within what is now the United States, see Roscoe, "Sexual and Gender Diversity."

36. For more on transgender identities, see Stryker, "Transgender History in the U.S."

37. The breadth of examples and of influence about the entire topic of Latina literary narratives can be traced in Katherine Sugg, "The Ultimate Rebellion: Chicana Narratives of Sexuality and Community," *Meridians: Feminism, Race, and Transnationalism* 3, no. 2 (2003): 139–70.

38. For a list of popular definitions and terms, see Fedwa Malti-Douglas, ed., *Encyclopedia of Sex and Gender* (Detroit, MI: Macmillan Reference, 2007).

39. See Elizabeth M. Iglesias and Francisco Valdes, "Religion, Gender, Sexuality, Race, and Class in Coalitional Theory: A Critical and Self-Critical Analysis of LatCrit Social Justice Agendas, 19," in *LATCRIT Primer*, vol. 1 (Boston: Harvard Latino Law Review, 1997), 395–463, http://latcrit.org/media/media library/2014/01/lcprimeri.pdf.

40. See Susan Oboler, ed., *Latino Studies Journal* 1, no. 1 (March 2003).

41. For sensationalizing media coverage of early gay rights marches, see as examples, Sex and Love Editor, "Will the Gay Rights Movement Make for Fabulous History?," *Creative Loafing*, 25 July 2011, http://cltampa.com/dailyloaf/archives/2011/07/25/will-the-gay-rights-movement-make-for-fabulous-history; or for primary sources designed to develop lesson plans for gay and lesbian studies, see "Media Construction of Social Justice, Teacher's Guide, Unit 7: Gay Liberation" at http://www.projectlooksharp.org/?action=justice.

42. See Megan E. Springate, "LGBTQ Civil Rights in America," in *LGBTQ America: A Theme Study of Lesbian, Gay, Bisexual, Transgender, and Queer History* (Washington, DC: National Park Foundation and National Park Service, 2016), https://nps.gov/articles/lgbtqtheme-civilrights.htm.

43. Anthony Summers, *Official and Confidential: The Secret Life of J. Edgar Hoover* (New York: Putnam, 1993).

44. Tim Retzloff, "Eliding Trans Latino/a Queer Experience in U.S. LGBT History: José Sarria and Sylvia Rivera Reexamined," *CENTRO: Journal of the Center for Puerto Rican Studies* 19, no. 1 (2007): 140–61.

45. Stonewall, including the Stonewall Inn (51–53 Christopher Street, New York City, New York) and the area in the street and Christopher Park where the riots took place, was added to the NRHP on 28 June 1999, designated an NHL on 16 February 2000, and declared the Stonewall National Monument on 24 June 2016.

46. See Martin Duberman's account of the Stonewall riots in his book, *Stonewall* (New York: Dutton, 1993).

47. Harry Hay, *Radically Gay: Gay Liberation in the Words of Its Founder,* ed. Will Roscoe (Boston: Beacon Press, 1996); Kristen Esterberg, "From Accommodation to Liberation: A Social Movement Analysis of Lesbians in the Homophile Movement," *Gender and Society* 8, no. 3 (1994): 424–43.

48. See also Amy Sueyoshi, "Remembering Asian Pacific American Activism in Queer History," this volume; and Jeffrey A. Harris, "'Where We Could Be Ourselves': African American LGBTQ Historic Places and Why They Matter," this volume.

49. Sarria performed drag at the Black Cat Club, 710 Montgomery Street, San Francisco, California. It was from the Black Cat that he launched his 1961 campaign for a seat on the San Francisco Board of Supervisors—the first time an openly gay person ran for elected office. The Black Cat Club location is a contributing resource to the Jackson Square Historic District, added to the NRHP on 18 November 1971.

50. Sylvia Rivera, "Sylvia Rivera's Talk at LGMNY, June 2001, Lesbian and Gay Community Services Center, New York City," *CENTRO: Journal of the Center for Puerto Rican Studies* 19, no. 1 (2007): 116–23.

51. Darren Rosenblum, "Queer Political Movements," in the *Oxford Encyclopedia of Latinos and Latinas in Contemporary Politics, Law, and Social Movements,* ed. Suzanne Oboler and Deena J. González. (New York: Oxford University Press, 2015).

52. Darren Rosenblum, "Queer Intersectionality and the Failure of Recent Lesbian and Gay 'Victories,'" *Law and Sexuality* 83 (1994), online at http://digital commons.pace.edu/lawfaculty/210/.

53. The Comunidad de Orgullo Gay de Puerto Rico was founded on 4 August 1974 at a meeting held at the San Juan Unitarian Fellowship, 53 Sevilla Street, San Juan, Puerto Rico. In 1975, they rented their own space, the Edificio Comunidad de Orgullo Gay de Puerto Rico (Casa Orgullo) at 3 Calle

Saldaña, San Juan, Puerto Rico. The group lasted until 1976. Casa Orgullo was added to the NRHP on 1 May 2016.

54. United States Supreme Court, Hurley v. Irish-American Gay, Lesbian, and Bisexual Group of Boston, 515 U.S. 557 (1995), is a landmark decision regarding the right to assemble. Much to the dismay of gay rights groups, the court ruled that private organizations, even if they were planning on and had permits for a public demonstration, were permitted to exclude groups if those groups presented a message contrary to the one the organizing group wanted to convey. Organizers of the St. Patrick's Day event were under no obligation to include gays, lesbians, and transgender people in the annual parade. In 2015, LGBTQ people were allowed to march in St. Patrick's Day parades in Boston, Massachusetts, and New York City, New York, for the first time. See David Gibson, "Catholic Debate over Gays in St. Patrick's Parades Roils Irish on Big Day," *Huffington Post,* 17 March 2015, http://www.huffing tonpost.com/2015/03/17/st-patrick-day-parade-lgbt_n_6880892.html.

55. Juanita Ramos, *Compañeras: Latina Lesbians (An Anthology)* (New York: Latina Lesbian History Project, 1987), xxvii. See also Marc Stein, "Historical Landmarks and Landscapes of LGBTQ Law," in *Communities and Place: A Thematic Approach to the Histories of LGBTQ Communities in the United States,* ed. Katherine Crawford-Lackey and Megan E. Springate (New York: Berghahn Books, 2020).

56. See Julio Capó Jr., "Locating Miami's Queer History," in Crawford-Lackey and Springate, *Communities and Place* (New York: Berghahn Books, 2020).

57. The seven buildings of the World Trade Center were located in Lower Manhattan, New York City. They were destroyed by terrorist attacks on 11 September 2001.

58. See Barbara Raab, "Same-Sex Partners Face Discrimination," *NBC News,* 20 December 2011, http://tampabaycoalition.homestead.com/files/1220 SameSexPartnersFaceDiscrimination911.htm (web page no longer online; see archived link at https://web.archive.org/web/20051227141702/http:// tampabaycoalition.homestead.com/files/1220SameSexPartnersFaceDis crimination911.htm).

59. See, for example, Jennifer Kates, Usha Ranji, Adara Beamesderfer, Alina Salganicoff, and Lindsey Dawson, "Health and Access to Care and Coverage for Lesbian, Gay, Bisexual, and Transgender Individuals in the U.S.," Kaiser Family Foundation website, last updated 6 June 2016, http://kff .org/disparities-policy/issue-brief/health-and-access-to-care-and-cov erage-for-lesbian-gay-bisexual-and-transgender-individuals-in-the-u-s; and Amanda Machado, "Why Many Latinos Dread Going to the Doctor," *Atlantic,* 7 May 2014, http://www.theatlantic.com/health/archive/2014/05/ why-many-latinos-dread-going-to-the-doctor/361547.

60. *Nuestra Salud: Lesbianas Latinas Rompiendo Barreras (Our Health: Latina Lesbians Breaking Barriers),* directed by Teresa Cuadra and Suzanne Newman (Brooklyn, NY: Fan Light Productions, 2002).

61. See the Chicago Gay and Lesbian Hall of Fame website at http://www.gl halloffame.org.

62. ALMA is located at 3656 North Halsted Street, Chicago, Illinois. ALLGO was founded in 1985 and is currently located at 701 Tillery Street, Austin, Texas. The Latino Pride Center, founded in 2013, is an evolution of the Hispanic AIDS Forum, the first Latino organization in the United States established to fight HIV/AIDS, itself founded in 1983; it is currently located in East Harlem, New York City, New York. AGUILAS was founded in 1991, and met in people's homes until early 1992, when they began regular meetings at St. Francis Lutheran Church, 152 Church Street, San Francisco, California; they are currently located at the San Francisco LGBT Center, 1800 Market Street, San Francisco, California. The Unity Coalition/Coalicion Unida was founded in 2002. LLEGÓ was founded in 1987 during the National March for Lesbian and Gay Rights in Washington, D.C., and had their headquarters in D.C. See "National Latino/a Lesbian and Gay Organization (LLEGÓ) Records, 1987–2004," Texas Archival Resources Online, University of Texas Libraries website, http://www.lib.utexas.edu/taro/utlac/00273/lac-00273.html; and Patrick Saunders, "New Organization Tackles Latino LGBT Needs in Georgia," Georgia Voice, 21 August 2015, http://thegavoice.com/new-org anization-tackles-latino-lgbt-needs-in-georgia.

63. The Latino GLBT History Project was founded in Washington, D.C., by José Gutierrez in 2000. See the organization's website at http://www.latinoglbt history.org.

64. See National Coalition Against Censorship, Esperanza vs. the City of San Antonio, 2001, http://ncac.org/resource/esperanza-peace-and-justice-cen ter-v-city-of-san-antonio. The Esperanza Peace & Justice Center is located at 922 San Pedro Avenue, San Antonio, Texas.

65. Vives passed away in March 2012. See "In Memoriam: Olga Vives," National Organization for Women website, 19 March 2012, http://www.now.org/ history/vives-memoriam.html (web page no longer online, see archived web link at https://web.archive.org/web/20131011091857/http://www.now .org/history/vives-memoriam.html).

66. For examples of Ingrid Duran's work in Washington and with elected officials, see http://www.dpcreativestrategies.com/#!ingrid-duran/w83no.

67. See http://delatierra.net.

68. See Alicia Gaspar de Alba and Alma López, eds., Our Lady of Controversy: Alma López's "Irreverent Apparition" (Austin: University of Texas Press, 2011). On the earlier Chicana reconfigurations of the Virgen de Guadalupe, see the work of the artist, Yolanda López, in Karen Mary Davalos, Yolanda López (Minneapolis: University of Minnesota Press, 2009).

69. See the MACHA Theatre website at http://www.machatheatre.org.

70. Luz Calvo, "Embodied at the Shrine of Cultural Disjunction," in Beyond the Frame: Women of Color and Visual Representation, ed. Neferti X. M. Tadiar and Angela Y. Davis (New York: Palgrave MacMillan, 2005), 207–18. On the

Lesbian History Project, see the Latino LGBT History Project website at http://www.latinoglbthistory.org/about-the-archive.

71. Emma Pérez, *The Decolonial Imaginary: Writing Chicanas into History* (Indianapolis: Indiana University Press, 1999), 105.

72. Additional resources used in preparing this chapter: Gloria Anzaldúa, *Borderlands/La Frontera: The New Mestiza* (San Francisco: Spinsters/Aunt Lute, 1987); Anzaldúa, *The Gloria Anzaldúa Reader*, ed. Ana Louise Keating (Durham: Duke University Press, 2009); Luis Aponte-Parés and Jorge Merced, "Páginas Omitidas: The Gay and Lesbian Presence" in *The Puerto Rican Movement: Voices from the Diaspora*, ed. Andrés Torres and José E. Velázquez (Philadelphia: Temple University Press, 1998), 296–315; Emilio Bejel, *Gay Cuban Nation* (Chicago: University of Chicago Press, 2001); Combahee River Collective, "The Combahee River Collective Statement," in *Homegirls: A Black Feminist Anthology*, ed. Barbara Smith (New York: Kitchen Table: Women of Color Press, 1983), 264–74; Tatiana de la Tierra, *Para las Duras/For the Hard Ones: A Lesbian Phenomenology* (San Diego: Calaca, 2002); Terence Kissack, "Freaking Fag Revolutionaries: New York's Gay Liberation Front," *Radical History Review* 62 (1995): 105–34; Lawrence La Fountain-Stokes, *Queer Ricans: Cultures and Sexualities in the Diaspora* (Minneapolis: University of Minnesota, 2009); La Fountain-Stokes, "De un pájaro las dos alas: Travel Notes of a Queer Puerto Rican in Havana," *GLQ: A Journal of Lesbian and Gay Studies* 8, no. 1–2 (2002): 7–33; Yolanda Chávez Leyva, "Listening to the Silences in Latina/Chicana Lesbian History," in *Living Chicana Theory*, ed. Carla Trujillo (Berkeley, CA: Third Woman Press, 1998), 429–34; Jacqueline M. Martinez, *Phenomenology of Chicana Experience and Identity: Communication and Transformation in Practice* (Lanham, MD: Rowman & Littlefield, 2000); Cherríe Moraga and Gloria Anzaldúa, *This Bridge Called My Back: Writings by Radical Women of Color* (Watertown, MA: Persephone Press, 1981); José Esteban Muñoz, *Cruising Utopia: The Then and There of Queer Futurity* (New York: New York University Press, 2009); Muñoz, *Disidentifications: Queers of Color and the Performance of Politics* (Minneapolis: University of Minnesota, 1999); Emma Pérez, "Irigaray's Female Symbolic in the Making of Chicana Lesbian Sitios y Lenguas (Sites and Discourses)," in *The Lesbian Postmodern*, ed. Laura Doan (New York: Columbia University Press, 1994), 104–17; Yolanda Retter, "Identity Development of Lifelong vs. Catalyzed Latina Lesbians," master's thesis, School of Social Work, University of California, Los Angeles, 1987; Juana Maria Rodríguez, *Queer Latinidad: Identity Practices, Discursive Spaces* (New York: New York University Press, 2003); Richard T. Rodríguez, *Next of Kin: The Family in Chicano/a Cultural Politics* (Durham: Duke University Press, 2009); Horacio Roque Ramírez, "'That's My Place': Negotiating Racial, Sexual, and Gender Politics in San Francisco's Gay Latino Alliance (GALA), 1975–1983," *Journal of the History of Sexuality* 12, no. 3 (2003): 224–58; Yvette Saavedra with Deena J. González, "Latino/Latina Americans and LGBTQ Issues," in

LGBTQ America Today: An Encyclopedia, ed. John C. Hawley (Westport, CT: Greenwood Press, 2009); Eve Sedgwick, *Touching Feeling: Affect, Pedagogy, and Performativity* (Durham, NC: Duke University Press, 2003); Carla Trujillo, *Chicana Lesbians: The Girls Our Mothers Warned Us About* (Berkeley, CA: Third Woman Press, 1991); Antonia Villaseñor, "Latina Lesbians," in *The Reader's Companion to U.S. Women's History,* ed. Wilma Pearl Mankiller (Boston: Houghton Mifflin, 1998), 340; Antonio Viego, *Dead Subjects: Toward a Politics of Loss in Latino Studies* (Durham, NC: Duke University Press, 2007).

Bibliography

Almaguer, Tomas. "Chicano Men: Cartography of Homosexual Identity and Behavior." In *The Lesbian and Gay Studies Reader,* edited by Henry Abelove, Michele Aina Barale, and David M. Halperin, 255–73. New York: Routledge, 1993.

Anzaldúa, Gloria. *Borderlands/La Frontera: The New Mestiza.* San Francisco: Spinsters/Aunt Lute, 1987.

———. *The Gloria Anzaldúa Reader.* Edited by Ana Louise Keating. Durham, NC: Duke University Press, 2009.

Aponte-Parés, Luis, and Jorge Merced. "Páginas Omitidas: The Gay and Lesbian Presence." In *The Puerto Rican Movement: Voices from the Diaspora,* edited by Andrés Torres and José E. Velázquez, 296–315. Philadelphia: Temple University Press, 1998.

Bagemihl, Bruce. *Biological Exuberance: Animal Homosexuality and Natural Diversity.* New York: Macmillan, 2000.

Bejel, Emilio. *Gay Cuban Nation.* Chicago: University of Chicago Press, 2001.

Berco, Cristian. *Sexual Hierarchies, Public Status: Men, Sodomy, and Society in Spain's Golden Age.* Toronto: University of Toronto Press, 2007.

Calvo, Luz. "Embodied at the Shrine of Cultural Disjunction." In *Beyond the Frame: Women of Color and Visual Representation,* edited by Neferti X. M. Tadiar and Angela Y. Davis, 207–18. New York: Palgrave MacMillan, 2005.

Calvo, Luz, and Catriona Esquibel. "Latina Lesbians, BiMujeres, and Trans Identities: Changing Courses in the Social Sciences." In *Latino/a Sexualities: Probing Powers, Passions, Practices, and Policies,* edited by Marysol Asencio, 217–29. New Brunswick, NJ: Rutgers University Press, 2010.

Capó, Julio, Jr. "Locating Miami's Queer History." In *Communities and Place: A Thematic Approach to the Histories of LGBTQ Communities in the United States,* edited by Katherine Crawford-Lackey and Megan E. Springate. New York: Berghahn Books, 2020.

Castañeda, Antonia I. "Engendering the History of Alta California, 1769–1848: Gender, Sexuality, and the Family." *California History* 76, no. 2–3 (1977): 230–59.

Catholic News Service. "U.S. Bishops to Urge Constitutional Amendment to Protect Marriage." *AmericanCatholic.org,* 2003. http://www.americancatholic.org/News/Homosexuality/default.asp.

Chicago Gay and Lesbian Hall of Fame. Website. http://www.glhalloffame.org.

Combahee River Collective. "The Combahee River Collective Statement." In *Homegirls: A Black Feminist Anthology,* edited by Barbara Smith, 264–74. New York: Kitchen Table: Women of Color Press, 1983.

Crompton, Louis. *Homosexuality and Civilization.* Cambridge, MA: Harvard University Press, 2003.

Crow, John A. *The Epic of Latin America.* Oakland: University of California Press, 1992.

Cuadra, Teresa, and Suzanne Newman, dirs. *Nuestra Salud: Lesbianas Latinas Rompiendo Barrerras (Our Health: Latina Lesbians Breaking Barriers).* Brooklyn: Fan Light Productions, 2002.

Davalos, Karen Mary. "La Quinceanera: Making Gender and Ethnic Identities." In *Velvet Barrios: Popular Culture and Chicana/o Sexualities,* edited by Alicia Gaspar de Alba, 141–62. New York: Palgrave Macmillan, 2003.

———. *Yolanda Lopez.* Minneapolis: University of Minnesota Press, 2009.

de la Tierra, Tatiana. *Para las Duras/For the Hard Ones: A Lesbian Phenomenology.* San Diego: Calaca, 2002.

del Castillo, Adelaida. "Malintzin Tenepal: A Preliminary Look into a New Perspective." In *Essays on la Mujer,* edited by Rosaura Sanchez and Rosa Martinez Cruz, 124–49. Los Angeles: UCLA Chicano Studies Research Center, 1977.

Duberman, Martin. *Stonewall.* New York: Dutton, 1993.

Espín, Olivia. "Cultural and Historical Influences on Sexuality in Hispanic/Latin Women: Implications for Psychotherapy." In *Pleasure and Danger: Exploring Female Sexuality,* edited by Carole S. Vance, 194–64. London: Pandora Press, 1989.

Esterberg, Kristen. "From Accommodation to Liberation: A Social Movement Analysis of Lesbians in the Homophile Movement." *Gender and Society* 8, no. 3 (1994): 424–43.

Gaspar de Alva, Alicia, and Alma Lopez, eds. *Our Lady of Controversy: Alma Lopez's "Irreverent Apparition."* Austin: University of Texas Press, 2011.

Gibson, David. "Catholic Debate over Gays in St. Patrick's Parades Roils Irish on Big Day." *Huffington Post,* 17 March 2015. http://www.huffingtonpost.com/2015/03/17/st-patrick-day-parade-lgbt_n_6880892.html.

González, Deena J. *Refusing the Favor: The Spanish-Mexican Women of Santa Fe, 1820–1880.* New York: Oxford University Press, 1999.

Gutiérrez, Elena R. *Fertile Matters: The Politics of Mexican-Origin Women's Reproduction.* Austin: University of Texas Press, 2008.

Halberstam, Judith. *In a Queer Time and Place: Transgender Bodies, Subcultural Lives.* New York: New York University Press, 2005.

Harris, Jeffrey A. "'Where We Could Be Ourselves': African American LGBTQ Historic Places and Why They Matter." In *Identities and Place: Changing La-*

bels and Intersectional Communities of LGBTQ and Two-Spirit People in the United States, edited by Katherine Crawford-Lackey and Megan E. Springate. New York: Berghahn Books, 2020.

Hay, Harry. Radically Gay: Gay Liberation in the Words of Its Founder, edited by Will Roscoe. Boston: Beacon Press, 1996.

Hill, R. M., and C. I. Vasquez. The Maria Paradox: How Latinas Can Merge Old World Traditions with New World Self-Esteem. New York: G. P. Putnam & Sons, 1996.

Hutchins, Loraine. "Making Bisexuals Visible." In Identities and Place: Changing Labels and Intersectional Communities of LGBTQ and Two-Spirit People in the United States, edited by Katherine Crawford-Lackey and Megan E. Springate. New York: Berghahn Books, 2020.

Iglesias, Elizabeth M., and Francisco Valdes. "Religion, Gender, Sexuality, Race and Class in Coalitional Theory: A Critical and Self-Critical Analysis of LatCrit Social Justice Agendas." In LATCRIT Primer, vol. 1, 395–463. Boston: Harvard Latino Law Review 19, 1998. http://latcrit.org/media/media library/2014/01/lcprimeri.pdf.

Kates, Jennifer, Usha Ranji, Adara Beamesderfer, Alina Salganicoff, and Lindsey Dawson. "Health and Access to Care and Coverage for Lesbian, Gay, Bisexual, and Transgender Individuals in the U.S." Kaiser Family Foundation, 6 June 2016. http://kff.org/disparities-policy/issue-brief/health-and-access-to-care-and-coverage-for-lesbian-gay-bisexual-and-transgender-individuals-in-the-u-s.

Kissack, Terence. "Freaking Fag Revolutionaries: New York's Gay Liberation Front." Radical History Review 62 (1995): 105–34.

La Fountain-Stokes, Lawrence. "De un pájaro las dos alas: Travel Notes of a Queer Puerto Rican in Havana." GLQ: A Journal of Lesbian and Gay Studies 8, no. 1–2 (2002): 7–33.

———. Queer Ricans: Cultures and Sexualities in the Diaspora. Minneapolis: University of Minnesota, 2009.

Latino GLBT History Project. "About the Archive." http://www.latinoglbthistory .org/about-the-archive.

———. Website. http://www.latinoglbthistory.org.

Leyva, Yolanda Chávez. "Listening to the Silences in Latina/Chicana Lesbian History." In Living Chicana Theory, edited by Carla Trujillo, 429–34. Berkeley: Third Woman Press, 1998.

Machado, Amanda. "Why Many Latinos Dread Going to the Doctor." Atlantic, 7 May 2014. http://www.theatlantic.com/health/archive/2014/05/why-many-latinos-dread-going-to-the-doctor/361547.

MACHA Theatre. Website. http://www.machatheatre.org.

Malti-Douglas, Fedwa, ed. Encyclopedia of Sex and Gender. Detroit: Macmillan Reference, 2007.

Martínez, Jacqueline M. Phenomenology of Chicana Experience and Identity: Communication and Transformation in Practice. Lanham, MD: Rowman & Littlefield, 2000.

Media Construction of Social Justice. Teacher's Guide, Unit 7: Gay Liberation. http://www.projectlooksharp.org/?action=justice.

Meyer, Leisa, and Helis Sikk. "Introduction to Lesbian, Gay, Bisexual, Transgender, and Queer (LGBTQ) History in the United States." In *LGBTQ America: A Theme Study of Lesbian, Gay, Bisexual, Transgender, and Queer History,* edited by Megan E. Springate (Washington, DC: National Park Foundation and National Park Service, 2016), chapter 3. https://nps.gov/articles/lgbtqtheme-history.htm.

Moraga, Cherrie, and Gloria Anzaldúa. *This Bridge Called My Back: Writings By Radical Women of Color.* Watertown, MA: Persephone Press, 1981.

Muñoz, José Esteban. *Cruising Utopia: The Then and There of Queer Futurity.* New York: New York University Press, 2009.

———. *Disidentifications: Queers of Color and the Performance of Politics.* Minneapolis: University of Minnesota, 1999.

Nash, June. "Aztec Women: The Transition from Status to Class in Empire and Colony." In *Women and Colonization: Anthropological Perspectives,* edited by Mona Etienne and Eleanor Leacock, 134–48. New York: Praeger, 1980.

National Coalition Against Censorship. Esperanza Peace and Justice Center v. City of San Antonio, 2001. http://ncac.org/resource/esperanza-peace-and-justice-center-v-city-of-san-antonio.

National Organization for Women. "In Memoriam: Olga Vives." National Organization for Women. http://www.now.org/history/vives-memoriam.html (web page no longer online; see archived web link at https://web.archive.org/web/20131011091857/http://www.now.org/history/vives-memoriam.html).

Oboler, Susan, ed. *Latino Studies Journal* 1, no. 1 (March 2003).

Padawer, Ruth. "BoyGirl." *New York Times Magazine,* 12 August 2010, 16–19.

Paz, Octavio. *Labyrinth of Solitude.* New York: Grove Press, 1961.

Pérez, Emma. *The Decolonial Imaginary: Writing Chicanas into History.* Indianapolis, Indiana University Press, 1999.

———. "Irigaray's Female Symbolic in the Making of Chicana Lesbian Sitios y Lenguas (Sites and Discourses)." In *The Lesbian Postmodern,* edited by Laura Doan, 104–17. New York: Columbia University Press, 1994.

Perry, Mary Elizabeth. *Gender and Disorder in Early Modern Seville.* Princeton, NJ: Princeton University Press, 1990.

Raab, Barbara. "Same-Sex Partners Face Discrimination." *NBC News,* 20 December 2011. http://tampabaycoalition.homestead.com/files/1220SameSexPartnersFaceDiscrimination911.htm (web page no longer online; see archived linkathttps://web.archive.org/web/20051227141702/http://tampabaycoalition.homestead.com/files/1220SameSexPartnersFaceDiscrimination911.htm).

Ramirez, Horacio Roque. "That's My Place: Negotiating Racial, Sexual, and Gender Politics in San Francisco's Gay Latino Alliance (GALA), 1975–1983." *Journal of the History of Sexuality* 12, no. 3 (2003): 224–58.

Ramos, Juanita. *Companeras: Latina Lesbians (An Anthology).* New York: Latina Lesbian History Project, 1987.

Retter, Yolanda. "Identity Development of Lifelong vs. Catalyzed Latina Lesbians." Master's thesis, School of Social Work, University of California, Los Angeles, 1987.

Retzloff, Tim. "Eliding Trans Latino/a Queer Experience in U.S. LGBT History: Jose Sarria and Sylvia Rivera Reexamined." *CENTRO: Journal of the Center for Puerto Rican Studies* 19, no. 1 (2007): 140–61.

Rivera, Sylvia. "Sylvia Rivera's Talk at LGMNY, June 2001, Lesbian and Gay Community Services Center, New York City." *CENTRO: Journal of the Center for Puerto Rican Studies* 19, no. 1 (2007): 116–23.

Rodríguez, Juana Maria. *Queer Latinidad: Identity Practices, Discursive Spaces.* New York: New York University Press, 2003.

Rodrigues, Richard T. *Next of Kin: The Family in Chicano/a Cultural Politics.* Durham, NC: Duke University Press, 2009.

Roscoe, Will. "Sexual and Gender Diversity in Native America and the Pacific Islands." In *Identities and Place: Changing Labels and Intersectional Communities of LGBTQ and Two-Spirit People in the United States,* edited by Katherine Crawford-Lackey and Megan E. Springate. New York: Berghahn Books, 2020.

Rosenblum, Darren. "Queer Intersectionality and the Failure of Recent Lesbian and Gay 'Victories.'" *Law and Sexuality* 83 (1994). http://digitalcommons.pace.edu/lawfaculty/210/.

———. "Queer Political Movements." In *The Oxford Encyclopedia of Latinos and Latinas in Contemporary Politics, Law, and Social Movements,* edited by Suzanne Oboler and Deena J. Gonzalez. New York: Oxford University Press, 2015.

Saavedra, Yvette, with Deena J. González. "Latino/Latina Americans and LGBTQ Issues." In *LGBTQ America Today: An Encyclopedia,* edited by John C. Hawley. Westport, CT: Greenwood Press, 2009.

Salas, Elizabeth. *Soldaderas in the Mexican Military: Myth and History.* Austin: University of Texas Press, 1990.

Saunders, Patrick. "New Organization Tackles Latino LGBT Needs in Georgia." *Georgia Voice,* 21 August 2015. http://thegavoice.com/new-organization-tackles-latino-lgbt-needs-in-georgia.

Schweighofer, Katherine. "LGBTQ Sport and Leisure." In *LGBTQ America: A Theme Study of Lesbian, Gay, Bisexual, Transgender, and Queer History,* edited by Megan E. Springate (Washington, DC: National Park Foundation and National Park Service, 2016). https://nps.gov/articles/lgbtqtheme-sport.htm.

Sedgwick, Eve. *Touching Feeling: Affect, Pedagogy, and Performance.* Durham, NC: Duke University Press, 2003.

Sex and Love Editor. "Will the Gay Rights Movement Make for Fabulous History?" *Creative Loafing,* 25 July 2011. http://cltampa.com/dailyloaf/archives/2011/07/25/will-the-gay-rights-movement-make-for-fabulous-history.

Spain/Council of the Indes. *Recopilación de leyes de los reynos de las Indias, 1681.* 5 vols. Mexico: M. A. Porrúa, 1987.

Springate, Megan E. "LGBTQ Civil Rights in America." In *LGBTQ America: A Theme Study of Lesbian, Gay, Bisexual, Transgender, and Queer History* (Washington, DC: National Park Foundation and National Park Service, 2016). https://nps.gov/articles/lgbtqtheme-civilrights.htm.

Stein, Marc. "Historical Landmarks and Landscapes of LGBTQ Law." In *Communities and Place: A Thematic Approach to the Histories of LGBTQ Communities in the United States,* edited by Katherine Crawford-Lackey and Megan E. Springate. New York: Berghahn Books, 2020.

Stryker, Susan. "Transgender History in the U.S. and the Places That Matter." In *Identities and Place: Changing Labels and Intersectional Communities of LGBTQ and Two-Spirit People in the United States,* edited by Katherine Crawford-Lackey and Megan E. Springate. New York: Berghahn Books, 2020.

Sueyoshi, Amy. "Remembering Asian Pacific American Activism in Queer History." In *Identities and Place: Changing Labels and Intersectional Communities of LGBTQ and Two-Spirit People in the United States,* edited by Katherine Crawford-Lackey and Megan E. Springate. New York: Berghahn Books, 2020.

Sugg, Katherine. "The Ultimate Rebellion: Chicana Narratives of Sexuality and Community." *Meridians: Feminism, Race, and Transnationalism* 3, no. 2 (2003): 139–70.

Summers, Anthony. *Official and Confidential: The Secret Life of J. Edgar Hoover.* New York: Putnam, 1993.

Trexler, Richard C. *Sex and Conquest: Gendered Violence, Political Order, and the European Conquest of the Americas.* Ithaca, NY: Cornell University Press, 1995.

Trujillo, Carla. *Chicana Lesbians: The Girls Our Mothers Warned Us About.* Berkeley: Third Woman Press, 1991.

Tzvetan Todorov. "The Reasons for Victory." In *The Conquest of America: The Question of the Other.* New York: Harper and Row, 1984.

United States Supreme Court. Hurley v. Irish-American Gay, Lesbian, and Bisexual Group of Boston, 515 U.S. 557 (1995).

———. Obergefell v. Hodges, 576 U.S. (2015). http://www.supremecourt.gov/opinions/14pdf/14-556_3204.pdf.

University of Texas Libraries. "National Latino/a Lesbian and Gay Organization (LLEGÓ) Records, 1987–2004." Texas Archival Resources Online. http://www.lib.utexas.edu/taro/utlac/00273/lac-00273.html.

Viego, Antonio. *Dead Subjects: Toward a Politics of Loss in Latino Studies.* Durham, NC: Duke University Press, 2007.

Villaseñor, Antonia. "Latina Lesbians." In *The Reader's Companion to U.S. Women's History,* edited by Wilma Pearl Mankiller, 340–42. Boston: Houghton Mifflin, 1988.

Voss, Barbara L. *The Archaeology of Ethnogenesis: Race and Sexuality in Colonial San Francisco.* Berkeley: University of California Press, 2008.

Williams Institute. Website. http://williamsinstitute.law.ucla.edu.

CHAPTER 7

"Where We Could Be Ourselves"

African American LGBTQ Historic Places and Why They Matter

Jeffrey A. Harris

Introduction

My first forays into African American LGBTQ history were purely for self-edification. As an out African American man, I sought out whatever information I could find, from novels to anthologies, to biographies, to documentaries. In many ways, I was looking for a sense of community, and a sense of belonging. Yet it wasn't until I started working in historic preservation that I began asking different questions and seeking new information. Though I began my work in history by following the traditional academic path, historic preservation proved to be a revelation for me. I began to understand more fully the power and importance of visiting historic places. I took note of the impact on people that historic sites had. I also saw how academic history and historic preservation could work in tandem to broaden our overall understanding of the past.

I remember visiting Montpelier, the home of our fourth president, James Madison, and I had something of an epiphany.[1] As a docent conducted our tour of the grounds, she spoke of the praise the Madison family received regarding the beauty of their estate. As I looked toward the mountains in the distance and did a visual sweep of the manicured lawns, I turned around and looked at the home itself (it was in the midst of a major renovation at that time). Then it hit me, as though I were struck by lightning, that everything I was taking in had been the work of the enslaved Africans who were owned by the Madison family. I understood that the praise the docent mentioned earlier needed to be directed toward those who actually did the work to make Montpelier beautiful. I began to swell with pride at *their* work. I looked at my surroundings again, imagining what it would have looked like back when James and Dolley Madison were living, and I felt a sense of ownership of Montpelier on behalf of those who were forced to work there, as well as on behalf of the descendants of those who worked there. I realized, for myself, that there was no need to feel shame over slavery, something that many people do feel (along with anger and sadness). Instead, I offered congratulations, silently, to those spirits who did that work, and did it well. If no one in their lives offered genuine thanks for *their* work, I wanted to do it those many years later, and I did.

I share that anecdote, because I want to convey the impact that visiting a historic site can have on a person. I felt a similar sense of pride when I moved to the Logan Circle neighborhood of Washington, D.C., in the mid-2000s.[2] Occasionally, I would walk around the surrounding neighborhoods looking for the residences of noted African Americans, and I took special care to look for the homes of African American LGBTQ Washington residents. I hoped to build on the legacies that they had left behind, because I was following in their footsteps. That is why I accepted the opportunity to participate in this LGBTQ theme study. I recognized the deep need for the African American LGBTQ community not only to know where our predecessors made their history, but also to identify places that are still available for us to visit, even if that visit constitutes standing outside of a door, or driving by a building where something incredible happened. And it certainly is important for historic places associated with African American LGBTQ history to be recognized as places worthy of inclusion on the National Register of Historic Places (NRHP).

Though I will focus more attention on some of these historic sites within the body of this study, I wanted to share a partial list of the few African American LGBTQ-related historic sites that either are National Historic Landmarks (NHL) or are currently listed on the NRHP. Three NHL sites that have African American LGBTQ historic relevance are the residence of writer Claude McKay in Harlem, New York; the childhood home of civil rights and women's rights activist Pauli Murray; and Villa Lewaro, the estate of Madame C. J. Walker, the hair-straightening and beauty products magnate, and her daughter, A'Lelia, in Irvington-on-Hudson, New York.[3] Six sites on the NRHP that have African American LGBTQ historic relevance include the residence of writer Langston Hughes; the

Apollo Theater in Harlem; the apartment complex where Countee Cullen lived (the Dunbar Apartments), as well as the residence of civil and LGBTQ rights activist Bayard Rustin, all of which are in New York City; the residence of Gertrude "Ma" Rainey in Columbus, Georgia (figure 7.1); and Azurest South, the Ettrick, Virginia, home of architect Amaza Lee Meredith.[4] Of the sites listed, only the Bayard Rustin and Pauli Murray sites have express African American LGBTQ narratives highlighted. Of course, as scholars and researchers discover new information or revisit existing information and find missed LGBTQ context clues, the number of these sites will grow.

It was during my tenure as program coordinator of the African American Historic Places Initiative at the National Trust for Historic Preservation that I learned of Azurest South. Located on the campus of Virginia State University, a historically black university, Azurest South was the home of architect Amaza Lee Meredith. The home itself, completed in 1939, is an example of the International style in architecture, and Meredith was, at that time, one of the nation's few African American female architects.

Figure 7.1. "Ma" Rainey's home in Columbus, Georgia. Photo by Katyrw, 2017 (CC BY SA 4.0; https://commons.wikimedia.org/wiki/File:Columbus_ma_rainey_house.jpg).

Though trained as a teacher, Meredith explored her artistic expression through architecture, and she designed homes for family and friends. Meredith also dabbled in real estate development, with the creation of Azurest North, an African American resort community in Sag Harbor, New York. Azurest South was listed on the NRHP in 1993, particularly for its architectural distinction. However, as I read through the National Register nomination, I noticed that Dr. Edna Meade Colson, a former dean of the university's School of Education, was identified as Meredith's "companion." The nomination also provided a description of the second bedroom in the home, a room identified as Dr. Colson's. Meredith preceded Colson in death, and in the two years before Colson passed away, the university co-owned Azurest South with Colson.[5] It was clear to me that I'd stumbled upon an African American LGBTQ historic place that was listed on the NRHP, but wasn't identified expressly as such. Meredith and Colson likely did not live in an LGBTQ vacuum, meaning that there likely was an LGBTQ community at Virginia State, no matter how clandestine it may have been, to which they belonged. But at Azurest South, they were able to create a space where they could be themselves.

Purpose of the Chapter

This chapter is part of a longstanding effort to identify African American historic places that should be considered for listing on the NRHP. But it is more specifically an examination of African American historic places that are directly related to the African American LGBTQ experience. The historic places that will be highlighted are currently listed on the National Register but without specific mention of their LGBTQ historical ties, or unlisted historic places that are extant, or African American LGBTQ historic places that have been lost. As Gail Dubrow, author of "Deviant History, Defiant Heritage" notes, there are those who view sexual orientation as a private matter: "Corollary thinking suggests that we have no business 'outing' closeted gay people and that sexual orientation is largely irrelevant to the interpretation of the past."[6] In spite of that concern, it is of particular importance that the African American LGBTQ community be represented openly through its sites of historic significance. The African American community as a whole has experienced efforts at historical erasure. Through scholarship, however, historians and preservationists have enriched the American historical narrative and have identified historic places tied to African Americans, including historic places that many would not automatically consider

African American historic places. The White House and the U.S. Capitol Building are great examples.[7] Historical erasure has also been experienced by the African American LGBTQ community both in broader LGBTQ history and in African American history. This study will help to move us in the direction not only of combatting that erasure, but also of gaining national recognition for African American LGBTQ historic places.

The African American LGBTQ community, for the most part, and unlike the broader white LGBTQ community, was integrated into, and has remained within, broader African American historic communities. Even following the Stonewall rebellion, and with the growing acceptance and visibility of the LGBTQ community as a whole, there have not been significant movements to create African American LGBTQ enclaves or for LGBTQ African Americans to leave African American communities for LGBTQ-identified communities. Racism and economic disparities, both social and structural, have certainly contributed to this circumstance. As professor of rhetoric Charles Nero noted in his study tracing the development of the Faubourg Marigny neighborhood of New Orleans into a "gay ghetto," this racialized social and physical segregation was often by design: "Exploiting personal and friendship networks that had been established because of shared sexual—and racial and gender—identities was crucial ... in the Marigny."[8] African American LGBTQ people were excluded from home ownership in the neighborhood "because they were neither a part of their formal networks of middle class gay men nor were they employed in the low wage service sector of gay owned businesses."[9] As a result, the gay enclave of Faubourg Marigny is largely white. These circumstances are not unique to Faubourg Marigny. Alex W. Costley, in his note prefacing the late anthropologist William Hawkeswood's study of Harlem's African American gay male community, noted that "given the relative social and economic marginalization experienced by most residents of Harlem, [Hawkeswood] firmly believe[d] that apart from organized religion's traditional dogma against homosexuality, gayness does not in itself draw condemnation from others in the community."[10] Historian Timothy Stewart-Winter, in his study on gay politics in Chicago, notes that African American LGBTQ life was a visible component of the broader African American community in the city, which definitely was not the case for Chicago's white LGBTQ community.[11] It is not surprising that many African American LGBTQ people have historically remained within African American communities; therefore, the vast majority of African American LGBTQ historic places are located there.

There is no question that the vast majority of the earliest LGBTQ historical studies focused primarily on the experiences of white males, largely reflecting the experiences of their authors—themselves predominantly white men.[12] Historian Kevin J. Mumford notes that "many of the best and most important studies have avoided further investigation into the meanings of race for the gay past."[13] Despite the avoidance of race, almost every general LGBTQ history covering the early twentieth century features information about Harlem and/or the Harlem Renaissance. This, I believe, is a testament to the power and visibility of Harlem's African American LGBTQ community, and the willingness of Harlemites to provide spaces for interracial interactions rarely allowed elsewhere during this period.[14] In part, this was helped by the vice industry that had established itself in Harlem (keeping the vice out of places like the white LGBTQ enclave of Greenwich Village), so "Harlem clubs . . . continued to mix straight and gay, thereby providing homosexuals with a proportionally greater number of gathering spots than were available in the more uptight downtown white world."[15] Because white members of the LGBTQ community could make the trip uptown to "slum" among the Harlemites, they too could be themselves—even if for an evening.[16] As a result, early chroniclers of LGBTQ history found many references to Harlem in the archives and papers that they mined.

Harlem Renaissance Era

Harlem has a special place in African American LGBTQ history. Not only was there a concentration of African American LGBTQ folk there, but their presence was visible and documented—uncommonly so—in the early twentieth century. The participants of the Harlem Renaissance left a historical record, from Richard Bruce Nugent's "Smoke, Lilies and Jade," the first known African American literary work with an explicit gay theme, to the various drag balls that were attended (and chronicled) by interracial audiences. The Harlem African American LGBTQ community, which included people from across the country, left an indelible mark on African American, LGBTQ, and American history. But this was not without limits; as George Chauncey noted, though LGBTQ people "were casually accepted by many poor Harlemites and managed to earn a degree of begrudging respect from others, they were excoriated by the district's moral guardians."[17] Cultural studies scholar Shane Vogel notes that many of the more famous artists of this era, members of what he calls the "Cabaret School," "rejected the narratives and logics of normative racial uplift and sexual respectability that initially guided the Harlem Renaissance."[18] Scholars and preservationists of African American LGBTQ history owe much to the "Cabaret School" of the Harlem Renaissance.

Decades after the Harlem Renaissance ended, its LGBTQ history has survived in stories told across the generations: "Many stories abound about the legendary figures of the Harlem Renaissance. There is the 'Langston Hughes chair' in one gay bar, the apartment where Countee Cullen and Harold Jackman played out their long-term affair, the solicitation of young college students by the eminent Alain Locke, and tales of the restroom and park sex of Richard Bruce Nugent and Wallace Thurman."[19] These oral histories mention places that researchers may be able to find, like the specific apartment of the Cullen/Jackman affair, or the park Nugent and Thurman enjoyed. African American women certainly weren't excluded from these sorts of recollections. "Harlemites might ridicule stereotypic bulldaggers or drag queens, but in the twenties especially, bisexuality had a certain cachet in sophisticated circles, and in the world of show biz the rumored lesbianism of such favored entertainers as Bessie Smith, Ma Rainey, Alberta Hunter and Ethel Waters tended to be ignored as irrelevant."[20]

The historical scholarship focused on the era of the Harlem Renaissance, as well as on gay life in the 1920s and 1930s, has been particularly helpful in identifying African American LGBTQ historic places.[21] LGBTQ literary luminaries such as Langston Hughes and Claude McKay have residences that are currently listed on the NRHP; McKay's residence has also been designated a NHL.[22] The Dunbar Apartments were home to Countee Cullen, and the complex is listed on the National Register.[23] In addition to historical research, the literary canon of the Harlem Renaissance itself provides the names of LGBTQ writers and the places associated with them. Unfortunately, one of the most significant historic places tied to African American LGBTQ literature, the 267 House, was demolished in 2002, and a new building was built in its place.[24] The 267 House (also referred to as Niggerati Manor by its residents) was a rooming house where Zora Neale Hurston, Langston Hughes, Wallace Thurman, and Richard Bruce Nugent all used to live. It was here where Wallace Thurman sought contributions from other young artists for a publication made for them, as opposed to being targeted to an outside audience. The 1926 publication was *Fire!!*, and it included the aforementioned short story from Richard Bruce Nugent, "Smoke, Lilies and Jade."[25] Thurman would go on to use the 267 House as a primary locale in his novel, *Infants of the Spring* (1932). Despite its historical significance, the building was not landmarked before its demolition.

Figure 7.2. Villa Lewaro, Irvington, New York. Photo from the Historic American Buildings Survey, n.d. (HABS NY, 60-IRV, 5-1).

Another important site for African American LGBTQ history was the Dark Tower, named after Countee Cullen's poem "From the Dark Tower."[26] This was the home and salon of A'Lelia Walker, the daughter of Madame C. J. Walker. A'Lelia Walker was not only an ally of LGBTQ Harlemites, but her "romantic partiality to accomplished women was an open secret in Harlem."[27] The Dark Tower was demolished in 1941. Surviving is Walker's Irvington-on-Hudson estate, Villa Lewaro, which is an NHL (1976) (figure 7.2). The narrative for the National Landmark designation, in light of the evidence of Walker not only being a strong supporter of the LGBTQ community (publicly), but also being a member of the LGBTQ community herself (privately), could be updated to include that information.[28]

The losses of the Dark Tower and the 267 House were genuine blows to African American LGBTQ history, but were not the only such places in Harlem to have been lost. The Rockland Palace, which hosted some of the most legendary of drag balls during the Harlem Renaissance, is also gone.[29]

Other lost sites include places that were integrated (heterosexual/homosexual) gathering spaces, such as the Savoy Ballroom and Harry Hansberry's Clam House, where the drag king Gladys Bentley held court.[30] Despite these losses, there remain places from the Harlem Renaissance era that have been identified as historically significant, but efforts at designations either have stalled or have not begun. There are efforts to improve the pace of designations in Harlem generally, but they still proceed slowly.[31]

Harlem was not the only African American community where LGBTQ denizens felt a sense of freedom. Many urban communities "provided Black gays, lesbians, and bisexuals, who might have been closeted in small towns or other cities, an opportunity to meet one another in clubs, or street corners, and in storefront churches."[32] And there has been a marked increase in interest in the history of the African American LGBTQ folks in various communities across the nation. Historians, anthropologists, and local organizations have been scouring sources, conducting oral histories, and identifying historic sites in an effort to expand our knowledge and understanding of the lives of LGBTQ African Americans. For example, even though he wasn't a Harlemite, Howard University professor Dr. Alain Locke, the nation's first African American Rhodes Scholar, was central to the Harlem Renaissance.[33] Not only did Locke seek to identify writers and artists with potential for success during his travels, but he also encouraged those he met who weren't living in Harlem to move there to have more direct access to the various publications (such as the *Crisis* from the NAACP or *Opportunity* from the Urban League) and publishing houses. Langston Hughes was one who followed Locke's suggestion to move from Washington, D.C., to Harlem.[34] It is likely that the combination of Hughes's talent and good looks greatly influenced Locke's interest in him; historian David Levering Lewis writes, "Professor Locke had a weakness for his male students and for intelligent males in general."[35] Locke was also a part of Washington, D.C.'s literary and artistic communities. He participated in the famed Saturday Nighters salon in the home of the writer Georgia Douglas Johnson in the period before the start of the Harlem Renaissance.[36]

Just as there are places associated with African American intellectuals from the Harlem Renaissance, expanding historical research is also highlighting places associated with African American LGBTQ entertainers—where they lived and where they performed.

Blues/Jazz-Era African American LGBTQ Entertainment

The field of entertainment has long served as a safe haven for the LGBTQ community, including African Americans. From the rise of the bawdy blues performers to the proliferation of drag balls, to the emergence of jazz era entertainers hiding in plain sight, to the performances on the disco stage, to the house club, the African American LGBTQ community has made its presence in entertainment known. In many ways, ragtime/jazz artist Antonio "Tony" Jackson and blues artists Gladys Bentley and Gertrude "Ma" Rainey were pioneers in visibility and openness.

It was during the era of the Great Migration that Jackson moved from the Storyville community of New Orleans (the original home of jazz) to the Bronzeville community of Chicago.[37] According to the famed jazz musician Jelly Roll Morton, a contemporary of Jackson, Jackson made the move because he believed that both his music and his sexuality would be better appreciated in Chicago.[38] It was rumored that his 1916 song "Pretty Baby" originally referred to one of Jackson's male lovers.[39] Gladys Bentley also was known in Bronzeville for her tuxedo-clad performances and suggestive lyrics that alluded to bisexual tastes, but she really made her mark in Harlem.[40] Rainey, who maintained her base primarily in her hometown of Columbus, Georgia, hid in plain sight, using her lyrics to suggest certain truths.[41]

Rainey, like Jackson, performed as blues emerged at the turn of the twentieth century. Beginning her career in Columbus, and following her marriage to Will "Pa" Rainey, Ma Rainey toured with her husband's company, the Rabbit Foot Minstrels. She was one of the earliest blues artists to record her performances, earning her the title of "Mother of the Blues." On a trip to Chattanooga, Tennessee, Rainey discovered a young Bessie Smith, who later would become the "Empress of the Blues." Though it was research that revealed Rainey's bisexuality (and that of her protégé, Smith), her bisexuality was in her lyrics for anyone to hear. Rainey's song "Prove It on Me Blues" "speaks directly to the issue of lesbianism. In it, she admits to her preference for male attire and female companionship, yet she dares her audience to 'prove it' on her."[42] Rainey was able to be explicit on stage and on her records while maintaining her intimate relationships with women in private spaces. Rainey's successors, including Bessie Smith, Alberta Hunter (a student of Tony Jackson), Josephine Baker, and Ethel Waters followed her lead in their subsequent relationships with women, adopting heterosexual public personas [like Rainey], most favoring a "red hot mama" style. Bentley and comedienne Jackie "Moms" Mabley were notable exceptions who were much more open with their sexuality.[43]

That several of these female entertainers donned men's clothing during their performances was not surprising, considering that drag balls (and smaller performances with female/male impersonators) in the

African American community were quite popular in the first half of the twentieth century. Independent of the annual drag balls, "in cities with high black populations some nightclubs featured female impersonators. New York's 101 Ranch, Detroit's Uncle Tom's Cabin, and Chicago's Joe's Deluxe Club were among biggest."[44] Langston Hughes recalled his time attending the Hamilton Club Lodge Ball at the Rockland Palace with A'Lelia Walker: "It was fashionable for the intelligentsia and social leaders of both Harlem and the downtown area to occupy boxes at this ball and look down from above at the queerly assorted throng on the dancing floor, males in flowing gowns and feathered headdresses and females in tuxedos and box-back suits."[45] *Ebony* magazine published a report of a New York drag ball: "Harlem's annual drag ball at the Fun Makers Social Club was a hit in 1944. The men who don silks, satins and laces for the yearly masquerades are as style conscious as the women of a social club planning an annual charity affair or a society dowager selecting a debutante gown for her favorite daughter."[46] Back in the 1930s, years before *Jet* and *Ebony* magazines existed, Finnie's Club in Chicago hosted drag balls, eventually becoming so popular that they had to move them to the Pershing Hotel's Ballroom.[47] In the 1950s, *Ebony* did a feature on Harlem Renaissance–era drag king and lesbian, Gladys Bentley. By that time Bentley had moved to the West Coast, and had a fairly successful performance career in California;[48] she later demonized lesbianism in her retirement.[49] It is clear that the drag ball scene was all the rage in the early twentieth century. Unfortunately, very few drag ball sites from that dynamic era remain extant. One that does remain is New York City's Webster Hall, which hosted bohemian masquerade balls and drag balls in the 1910s and 1920s.[50]

The openness of the 1920s and 1930s eventually gave way to the struggles of the Great Depression, which certainly affected many African Americans. Though popular magazines like *Ebony* and *Jet* featured stories on LGBTQ events, the overarching scene was becoming more underground. By the time jazz composer and pianist Billy Strayhorn was hitting his creative stride with Edward "Duke" Ellington in the late 1930s and into the 1940s, the quiet acceptance of and tolerance toward the African American LGBTQ community was beginning to wane.

Strayhorn was one of the few openly gay jazz men, yet his sexuality seemed to not be much of an issue—perhaps because he allowed Ellington to be the public face of their many collaborative efforts. Strayhorn composed "Take the 'A' Train," one of the most recognized songs of Ellington's orchestra. He also composed "Something to Live For" and "Lush Life."[51] During this prolific period, Strayhorn was partnered with

Aaron Bridgers, another openly gay pianist and composer, and they lived together in the Hamilton Heights neighborhood of Manhattan from 1939 until Bridgers moved to France in 1948.[52]

As with other African American LGBTQ historic places from the Harlem Renaissance, many of the places associated with African American LGBTQ entertainers from the early decades of the twentieth century have been lost or have not been considered for historic designation. The Apollo Theater, listed on the NRHP, was an important performance venue for almost every African American LGBTQ entertainer throughout the twentieth century—an aspect of its history omitted from its nomination.[53] Important places that survive include the home of Billy Strayhorn and Aaron Bridgers, where Strayhorn composed some of his most recognized work, and the home of singer and actress Ethel Waters. Further research may provide information for places associated with Jackie "Moms" Mabley and Gladys Bentley (who moved to California in the 1930s), who were open lesbians in the 1920s and 1930s, or for places associated with more private African American LGBTQ entertainers, like Josephine Baker and Alberta Hunter.

Middle/Late Twentieth-Century African American LGBTQ Activism and Activists

Though there have been continual efforts to ensure full equality and freedom for African Americans since the nation's founding, the mid-twentieth century represented a high-water mark for organizational and activist success. This same time period also proved to be a watershed for the LGBTQ community.[54] Despite the fact that African American LGBTQ individuals played important roles in both movements, it was not until 2016 that places associated with them as African American and LGBTQ people were nationally recognized. An increasing scholarship is not only helping to identify and/or confirm African American LGBTQ participants, but also revealing associated historic places that can be considered for possible future historic designations. It is important to note that the nation's first LGBTQ civil rights organization, the Society for Human Rights founded by Henry Gerber in Chicago, had an African American president, John T. Graves. Beyond Graves's dealings with Gerber at the Henry Gerber House, there are no known extant places associated with Graves. Perhaps continued research on the Society for Human Rights and Gerber will reveal relevant places for this important figure in African American LGBTQ history.[55]

Pauli Murray, who was active in the civil rights movement, coined the term "Jane Crow" and noted that "Black women faced with these dual barriers, have often found that sex bias is more formidable than racial bias."[56] Gender nonconforming, Murray was open about her relationships with women, but she never identified as a lesbian. In her work, she offered critiques of both society and the civil rights movement for their discrimination based on gender. Murray went on to become one of the cofounders of the National Organization for Women. Her childhood home in Durham, North Carolina, was designated a NHL in January 2017.[57]

Bayard Rustin was a contemporary of Pauli Murray and, like her, was a member of the Fellowship of Reconciliation (FOR) and the Congress of Racial Equality (CORE). They both participated in efforts to test the 1946 Supreme Court ruling that deemed segregation in interstate bus travel unconstitutional (predating the Freedom Rides by almost twenty years). Bayard Rustin's New York City residence is the only National Register listing for an African American LGBTQ participant in the civil rights movement.[58] Rustin, an openly gay, yet discreet, man is perhaps best known as the principal organizer of the 1963 March on Washington for Jobs and Freedom. He was also the person who introduced nonviolence as a key principle for the Civil Rights Movement, helped to usher in direct action protest tactics, and restored the legitimacy of mass protesting.[59] Because of Rustin's sexuality, he was asked to step back from public work in the civil rights movement, and he was nearly erased from public memory. Fortunately, the LGBTQ community has helped to ensure that that erasure was not successful, and there has been a resurrection of Rustin's name as a significant civil rights and gay rights activist.[60]

Writers James Baldwin and Lorraine Hansberry used their pens and their voices to advance civil rights. Baldwin, who was openly gay, followed in Richard Bruce Nugent's footsteps when he wrote a gay protagonist into his novel, *Giovanni's Room* (1956). In 1957, Baldwin was given an opportunity to report about the South for the *Partisan Review*. It was through his reporting that he became a national voice of both the civil rights movement and the broader African American community. Hansberry, in her play *A Raisin in the Sun,* articulated the struggles of African American families striving for upward mobility. An activist from her time as a student at the University of Wisconsin, Hansberry continued that activism into the civil rights era. A 1963 meeting of Attorney General Robert Kennedy with civil rights activists, including Baldwin and Hansberry, held in the aftermath of brutal police attacks on peaceful demonstrators in Birmingham, Alabama, became contentious when Hansberry challenged Kennedy to use his authority (and that of President Kennedy) more forcefully to protect African American demonstrators—or risk those demonstrators resorting to violence in frustration. "This memorable moment of emotionality, radical refusal and principled resolve," writes historian Kevin Mumford, "ought to be seen as a signal beginning of modern black gay activism."[61]

Neither Baldwin nor Hansberry has National Register–listed or NHL-designated places associated with them, despite the survival of several locations. Two places survive in New York City associated with Baldwin: his apartment in Greenwich Village, where he wrote *Another Country*, and his home on the Upper West Side that he owned until his death in 1987, where he wrote *Tell Me How Long the Train's Been Gone*.[62] Hansberry spent her first years living in Chicago's South Side; in 1937, her parents purchased a home in an all-white neighborhood. They were sued for violating the restrictive covenant preventing African Americans from moving there. The case went to the United States Supreme Court (Hansberry v. Lee), which decided in favor of the Hansberry family.[63] However, it was in New York City's Greenwich Village that Hansberry wrote *A Raisin in the Sun*, and it is also where she lived as she more fully explored her interests in women.[64]

With its listing on the NRHP in 1999, the Stonewall Inn was the first explicitly LGBTQ historic site to gain historic designation specifically for its central place in American LGBTQ history.[65] The bar was a place where minorities could be patrons without encountering the levels of racism found at other gay bars. According to historian Martin Duberman, the Stonewall bouncer Ed Murphy reportedly "had a soft spot in general for Hispanics . . . and also for blacks; indeed, later gay bar owners who employed Murphy would worry that he would 'turn the club black' and—since racism has always been alive and well in the gay world—frighten off white clientele."[66] The Stonewall Inn was also a place where transgender and gender-nonconforming patrons felt safe to be themselves without judgment from those in the LGBTQ community who disapproved of their appearance. Kevin Mumford offered this assessment of Duberman's approach to the subject of the riots: "In Duberman's telling, the 1969 police raid of a gay bar signaled not only the usual violent repression, but also an emergent coalition of the respectable activist, the street drag queen, and the bar fly, alongside black and Hispanic gays."[67] Scholarship, as well as the personal recollections of Stonewall participants, such as the late Marsha P. Johnson and Miss Major, reveals that the first designated LGBTQ historic site is also an African American (and Hispanic) LGBTQ historic site.

The activism of writer and poet Audre Lorde straddled the era of the Stonewall Riots; she published her first work of poetry, *The First Cities,* in 1968. But it was in the post-Stonewall era and with the rise of the black power, women's, and gay liberation movements that Lorde gave voice to the intersections that defined the experiences and perspectives of African American lesbians. In her works—for example, *Zami: A New Spelling of My Name* (1982) and *Sister Outsider: Essays and Speeches* (1984)—Lorde offered searing critiques of these liberation movements from a black lesbian feminist perspective. Lorde also influenced the work of activist Barbara Smith, who cofounded the Combahee River Collective in 1974 (see below) and, in 1980 (at the suggestion of Lorde), Kitchen Table: Women of Color Press, the nation's first publishing company dedicated solely to works by women of color. Writer Joseph Beam, disillusioned not only with the racism of the broader LGBTQ movement, but also with the invisibility of African American gay male voices, "predicted that 'black gays are soon to follow the lead of black lesbians; our voices, from a whisper to a scream,' would soon be recorded, collected, and published."[68] It was Beam who took on that project (with mentoring from Barbara Smith), resulting in *In the Life: A Black Gay Anthology.* The publication was the first of its kind: all of the contributors were African American gay men writing about their experiences for an African American gay male audience.[69]

There are places associated with Lorde, Smith, and Beam that are extant. For example, the home Lorde shared with her partner, Dr. Frances Clayton, and where she wrote *Zami* and *Sister Outsider* is located on Staten Island, New York. There are several places in Boston and New York City associated with Smith (who among the three is the only one still living), which may be good candidates for NRHP or NHL nomination. Beam was based in Philadelphia, and his home in the Rittenhouse Square neighborhood, where he produced *In the Life,* remains extant. As with Rustin, Murray, Baldwin, and Hansberry, these African American LGBTQ activists and artists (and this is far from a complete list) have had national impacts on American and LGBTQ history.

Post-Stonewall and HIV/AIDS-Era African American LGBTQ Organizations

In the flurry of LGBTQ activism that arose after the Stonewall uprising, many members of the African American LGBTQ community found themselves, and issues important to them, excluded or not represented.

Finding racism in the existing LGBTQ organizations and homophobia in existing African American organizations, they organized among themselves.[70] Several of these organizations were the first of their kind in American history.[71]

The nation's oldest African American lesbian organization, the African Ancestral Lesbians United for Social Change (AALUSC) has a somewhat labyrinthine origin story. Having begun as the Black Lesbian Caucus of the Gay Activists Alliance (which itself formed from the splintering of the Gay Liberation Front), in 1974 the organization became the Salsa Soul Sisters, Third World Wimmin Incorporated Collective. In 1990, they changed their name to the AALUSC.[72] The year 1974 was also when the Combahee River Collective (CRC), another African American feminist lesbian organization, was established. They began as the Boston chapter of the National Black Feminist Organization with the express purpose of providing a space where African American feminist lesbians could be themselves wholly, without having to sublimate any aspect of their identities.[73] The members of the CRC "held seven retreats in the northeast between 1977 and 1980."[74] The *Combahee River Collective Statement,* written by members Barbara Smith, Demita Frazier, and Beverly Smith in 1977, came out of the first retreat. The statement highlights the importance of the intersecting identities of African American women (particularly around race and sexual orientation) in feminist organizing.[75] The subsequent retreats afforded the CRC opportunities to build upon principles established in its statement.

The nation's oldest national African American LGBTQ organization, the National Coalition of Black Lesbians and Gays, was founded as the National Coalition of Black Gays (NCBG) in Columbia, Maryland, in 1978 by bisexual activist ABilly S. Jones (now ABilly S. Jones-Hennin), Darlene Garner, and Delores Berry. The First National Conference of Third World Lesbians and Gays was organized by the NCBG at the former Harambee House Hotel at Howard University (now the Howard Center) the following year, with approximately 450 conference attendees, and in conjunction with the first National March on Washington for Lesbian and Gay Rights.[76] The NCBG also organized the 1986 National Conference on AIDS in the Black Community, the first national conference on HIV/AIDS focused specifically on the African American community.[77]

The National Conference of Third World Lesbians and Gays was a catalyst for the creation of the Lambda Student Alliance (LSA) at Howard University in 1979.[78] Interested students like Sidney Brinkley worked with faculty member James Tinney to establish the organization. In the January 1980 issue of *Blacklight,* the LSA's publication, Bill Stevens noted the challenges not only in publicizing the organization but also in gaining official recognition from the university. The organization initially advertised using posters under the (incorrect) assumption that African American LGBTQ students would recognize "Lambda" as being synonymous with gay. The uphill struggle for the LSA to gain university recognition was exacerbated by vocal opposition to the group, including the interruption of an LSA meeting by Muslim students.[79] In 1981, the LSA became the first LGBTQ student organization recognized by a historically black college or university. *Blacklight* was the nation's first African American LGBTQ publication.[80]

In 1986, as the HIV/AIDS crisis was raging, Rev. Charles Angel established Gay Men of African Descent (GMAD) to meet the holistic needs of African American gay, bisexual, and same-gender-loving men.[81] According to records in New York Public Library, "The organization represented the largest constituency of black gay men on the East Coast, and is the nation's largest and oldest black gay organization dedicated exclusively to the welfare of black gay men."[82] Though it wasn't created as an HIV/AIDS organization, it became one because of the need for an African American male-identified organization. Sadly, Rev. Angel himself succumbed to complications from HIV/AIDS in 1987.

This is far from an exhaustive listing of African American LGBTQ organizations, but the goal was to highlight those that may have national historic relevance. And with the emergence of the HIV/AIDS crisis, the LGBTQ community responded with the creation of organizations that had historic impacts in the various cities and states where they were established, like GMAD, and those organizations and their founding sites can be researched for NRHP and/or NHL designation.

Black Pride

Black Pride events have proliferated across the United States, providing African American LGBTQ communities the opportunity to celebrate both of their identities simultaneously. The first Black Pride event (though it was not called Black Pride at that time) was held Memorial Day weekend in 1975 at a bar called the Clubhouse in Washington, D.C.[83] The event was called the Children's Hour, which is a play on words: "Children" is often used in the African American LGBTQ community as a euphemism for themselves. The Children's Hour events were held annually at the Clubhouse from 1975 to 1990, when the venue closed its doors. Inspired by the Children's Hours, in 1991 Welmore Cook, Theodore Kirkland, and

Earnest Hopkins organized the first D.C. Black Pride event to use that name as an HIV/AIDS fundraiser.[84] It was held at Banneker Field, and served as the model for subsequent Black Pride events.[85] The locations of other cities' Black Pride events may also be considered significant. For example, Los Angeles held its first Black Pride event, called At the Beach, in 1988; New York City had its first Black Pride in 1997.[86]

African American LGBTQ Cruising / Sexual Engagement Sites

Clandestine liaisons, anonymous couplings, and sexual partner searches in public and/or partially private spaces have been central to the LGBTQ experience. Entertainment venues and bars—including the Stonewall Inn and Julius', both of which have been designated historic sites—have long been places where LGBTQ people have gathered and socialized.[87] In both cases, however, their historic designation rests primarily on the central role they played in the modern LGBTQ civil rights movement, not their roles as places of cruising or sexual engagement. Of course the possibility of cruising and sexual engagement drew patrons to these bars; however, could that aspect of an LGBTQ site's history contribute to its significance?[88]

There is precedence for places of sexual engagement being listed on the National Register. The Fort Laramie Three Mile Hog Ranch in Fort Laramie, Wyoming, served not only as a community center of sorts, providing patrons with access to alcohol and entertainment, but also as a bordello, a site of [hetero]sexual engagement.[89] The Fort Laramie Three Mile Hog Ranch "was one of the very few military bordellos left in the western United States at the time of its nomination to the National Register of Historic Places," in 1975.[90] The role of this place as one of sexual engagement was partially determinative in its designation. In 1973, Portland, Oregon's Hotel Alma building became home to the Club Baths bathhouse and a restaurant catering to a gay clientele; it continuously hosted gay bathhouses under several names until 2007, when the building was sold. While the Hotel Alma was listed on the NRHP with a period of significance of 1911, which is when it was built, the nomination does not shy away from the building's history as a gay bathhouse, and places it into the context of both LGBTQ life in Portland as well as the post-Stonewall era more broadly.[91]

One of the most significant African American LGBTQ historic sites related to cruising or sexual engagement is the Mount Morris Turkish Baths in Harlem.[92] The bathhouse was in operation from 1893 to 2003, and it was the only bathhouse in New York City that specifically catered to African American men (beginning in the 1930s). Primarily an African American LGBTQ space, it was also patronized to a much lesser extent by non-African American gay and bisexual men, and straight men of various races and ethnicities: According to owner (from the 1970s to 2003) Walter Fitzer, "Harlem royalty like Joe Louis and Sam Cooke used to sweat here years ago, and it [was] nothing to see French tourists, straight businessmen and Hasidic Jews perspiring in the steam room side by side."[93] Mount Morris Baths was one of the very few bathhouses across the country that was not closed down during the AIDS panic of the 1980s; instead of closing, Mount Morris provided public outreach and education about the disease. In 2003, organizations dedicated to HIV/AIDS education were conducting educational tours of the bathhouse.[94] The site currently is an apartment building with street-level retail space.

There are many other potentially significant sites of cruising and sexual engagement to the African American LGBTQ community. For example, in Washington, D.C., Meridian Hill Park, a National Historic Landmark, was an infamous site of cruising and sexual engagement prior to the park's restoration;[95] Marcus Garvey Park and the West Side Piers in New York City have storied places in the histories of African American same-gender-loving men.[96] The Wentworth, a bar located adjacent to the Apollo Theater, was in fact two bars: a straight bar in front, and then, behind it, with a separate side entrance, a Black lesbian bar.[97] It is likely that sites of cruising and sexual engagement related to African American same-gender-loving women, outside of lesbian bars, will be the private homes of African American women: Villa Lewaro, the New York estate of the Harlem Renaissance–era figure A'Lelia Walker, and the no longer extant Dark Tower home in Harlem are two examples.[98] Other examples could include the Georgia home of Ma Rainey, the Detroit home of LGBTQ activist Ruth Ellis, or the New York home of Ethel Waters.

Gail Dubrow wrote that "questions of morality . . . tend to come into play when the landmarks of GLBT history are proposed for designation, with queer folks claiming we need role models and homophobes arguing against the government legitimizing deviant lifestyles."[99] Therefore, it is understandable that the possibility of nominating African American LGBTQ historic sites related to cruising or sexual engagements may invite controversy. The impact of these places in creating community in the lives of the African American LGBTQ community members, however, cannot be underestimated. Both the Fort Laramie Three Mile Hog Ranch and the Hotel Alma are examples of places on the NRHP with explicit reference to their importance as places of cruising and sexual engagement; the inclusion of a similar African American LGBTQ site would not be breaking new designation ground.

Planning for Future African American LGBTQ Historic Places

With regard to the preservation of African American LGBTQ historic places, let the historic African American gay bar, Washington, D.C.'s Nob Hill, serve as a cautionary tale.[100] Nob Hill was the oldest gay bar in Washington, D.C., and one of the nation's oldest African American gay bars. Like so many other African American LGBTQ historic places, Nob Hill was part of the African American community of Columbia Heights. It opened in 1957. Significantly, it was an African American gay bar that was owned by gay African Americans until it closed in 2004 and passed out of African American gay ownership.[101] None of the other gay bars that catered to African Americans in D.C. was African American owned. When Nob Hill closed, the former middle-class African American neighborhood of the 1950s was known as an "up and coming" neighborhood for "urban pioneers" seeking to revitalize a Columbia Heights that went into decline following the assassination of Dr. Martin Luther King Jr. and the subsequent riots in 1968. The Wonderland Ballroom opened in the space a few months after Nob Hill's 2004 closing, and it is a vibrant community bar to this day. The new owners have been opposed to having the building nominated.

There are many African American LGBTQ historic persons and places that were not included in this chapter. This should not be taken as a judgment against the significance of any of those persons or places, but instead seen as a reflection of the limitations of space and current research. It is important that the African American LGBTQ community expand the discussion of historical legacies to include historic preservation. As noted throughout this study, historical research, scholarship, and local interest in African American LGBTQ historic places can be a boon for identifying individuals, organizations, and places that are historically important. But there should also be active consideration for what has happened in the more recent past, as well as what is happening currently in the African American LGBTQ community. For example, what is the status of the home of the late "Queen of Disco," Sylvester? What are the important addresses of Essex Hemphill, Marlon Riggs, and E. Lynn Harris, and have there been discussions around preparations for seeking historic designation for their homes? Who is prepared to ask Angela Davis or Alice Walker which places associated with them should be considered the most historically relevant to them? What are the historic preservation–related plans that will highlight the late Rep. Barbara Jordan's Houston-area home and her ties to the LGBTQ community in Texas? HIV/AIDS organizations like the Black AIDS Institute (Los Angeles) or Us Helping Us (Washington, D.C.) have been vital to the African American LGBTQ community, but what is being done to make sure that they will receive the historic recognition they deserve?[102] What will happen at the location of Jewel's Catch One nightclub (Los Angeles), now that it is closed?[103] These are just a handful of the questions that should be addressed when considering the historic preservation–based legacies of the African American LGBTQ historic places.

Conclusion

Throughout this chapter, I made it a point to highlight African American LGBTQ-related historic places that have been lost. So many of these historic places are located in African American neighborhoods across the country that are experiencing tremendous changes both physically and demographically, whether through revitalization (that does not explicitly acknowledge the African American LGBTQ historical relationship) or demolition; the historic places that remain are under direct threat. These include historic places from the Harlem Renaissance to the more recent past. With continued scholarship, there even may be opportunities to identify African American LGBTQ historic places preceding the twentieth century.[104] Though so many have already been lost, we have the opportunity to develop strategies to preserve African American LGBTQ historic places, including nominating them to the NRHP or for designation as NHLs. Though there are sure to be more places that will be lost, we have the chance now to help validate those places where members of the African American LGBTQ community could be themselves.

Mr. Jeffrey A. Harris is an independent historic preservation consultant and historian in Hampton, Virginia.

Notes

1. Montpelier, near Orange, Virginia, was added to the NRHP on 15 October 1966 and designated an NHL on 19 December 1960.

2. There are two historic districts in the Logan Circle neighborhood: the Logan Circle Historic District was added to the NRHP on June 30, 1972; the Fourteenth Street Historic District was added to the NRHP on November 9, 1994.
3. The Claude McKay Residence (Harlem YMCA) at 180 West 135th Street, New York City, New York, was listed on the NRHP and designated an NHL on 8 December 1976. The Pauli Murray Family Home at 906 Carroll Street, Durham, North Carolina, was designated a NHL on 11 January 2017. Villa Lewaro is located on North Broadway (US 9), Irvington, New York. It was added to the NRHP and designated an NHL on 11 May 1976.
4. The Apollo Theater is located at 253 West 125th Street, New York City, New York. It was added to the NRHP on 17 November 1983. The Langston Hughes House in Harlem, New York, was listed on the NRHP on 29 October 1982. The Dunbar Apartments in the Harlem neighborhood of New York City, New York, were listed on the NRHP on 29 March 1979. The Bayard Rustin Residence in the Chelsea neighborhood of New York City was added to the NRHP on 8 March 2016. The Ma Rainey House (now the Ma Rainey House and Blues Museum) is located at 805 Fifth Avenue, Columbus, Georgia; it was added to the NRHP on 18 November 1992. Azurest South, at 2900 Boisseau Street, Ettrick, Virginia, was added to the NRHP on 30 December 1993.
5. Azurest South now serves as the home of the Virginia State University Alumni Association.
6. "While the idea of privacy continues to be critical to protecting the right of queer folk to love whomever they choose, it is an increasingly problematic concept for public policy and practice, particularly when used as a rationale for the suppression of public discourse on controversial subjects." Gail Dubrow, "Deviant History, Defiant Heritage," The Friends of 1800 website, 2002, http://www.friendsof1800.org/VIEWPOINT/dubrow.html.
7. The White House, 1600 Pennsylvania Avenue NW, Washington, D.C., was designated an NHL on 19 December 1960. The United States Capitol building, Capitol Hill, Washington, D.C., was designated an NHL on 19 December 1960.
8. Charles I. Nero, "Why Are the Gay Ghettoes White?," in *Black Queer Studies: A Cultural Anthology,* ed. E. Patrick Johnson and Mae Henderson (Durham, NC: Duke University Press, 2005), 233.
9. Ibid., 234.
10. Alex W. Costley, "Editor's Note," in William G. Hawkeswood, *One of the Children: Black Gay Men in Harlem,* ed. Alex W. Costley (Berkeley: University of California Press, 1996), xii.
11. Timothy Stewart-Winter, *Queer Clout: Chicago and the Rise of Gay Politics* (Philadelphia: University of Pennsylvania Press, 2016), 19.
12. In his important work on the history of LGBTQ New York City, *The Gay Metropolis, 1940–1996,* Charles Kaiser stated the following regarding his focus:

"Some of the ordinary and extraordinary citizens who nurtured the spectacular growth of that larger metropolis are the main subjects of this book. While the women I have written about are among the most compelling characters in this saga, men gradually became my principal focus—because their story is also mine." See Charles Kaiser, *The Gay Metropolis, 1940–1996* (Boston: Houghton Mifflin, 1997), xii.

13. "As more researchers engage the queer turn, wholly new sexual landscapes promise to emerge, and yet one methodological flaw that limits both the older and recent scholarship has been inattention to questions of diversity and prejudice." Kevin J. Mumford, *Not Straight, Not White: Black Gay Men from the March on Washington to the AIDS Crisis* (Chapel Hill: University of North Carolina Press, 2016), 2.

14. Harlem was also something of a vice district, so there was a greater tolerance here by the city for what it considered salacious and licentious behavior. As historian George Chauncey noted, "The ascendency of Harlem's nightlife . . . also owed much to the willingness of city authorities to look the other way as the largely white-controlled 'vice industry' took shape in a poor black neighborhood." George Chauncey, *Gay New York: Gender, Urban Culture, and the Making of the Gay Male World, 1890–1940*, 3rd ed. (New York: Basic Books, 1994), 247.

15. Martin Duberman, *Stonewall* (New York: Penguin Group, 1994), 42.

16. According to Jack Dowling, who was interviewed by Charles Kaiser for *The Gay Metropolis, 1940–1996*, he and his friends used to patronize the Harlem club Lucky's. "It was a big bar where the waiters and waitresses would sing, and the patrons would sing, and people would come and listen to jazz. It was a straight bar, but there were a lot of gay people from downtown, and there were a lot of Black gay guys there." Kaiser, *The Gay Metropolis*, 122. Lucky's Rendezvous was located at 773 St. Nicholas Avenue and 148th Street, Harlem, New York City, New York. See Ulysses, "REMEMBER: Lucky's Rendezvous," *Harlem + Bespoke* (blog), 11 June 2012, http://harlembespoke.blogspot.com/2012/06/remember-luckys-rendezvous.html.

17. Chauncey, *Gay New York*, 253.

18. Shane Vogel, *The Scene of Harlem Cabaret: Race, Sexuality, Performance* (Chicago: University of Chicago Press, 2009), 4.

19. Hawkeswood, *One of the Children*, 154.

20. "A lesbian subculture seems to have developed earlier in Harlem than elsewhere, probably because blacks, knowing the pain of being treated as outsiders, had developed an attitude toward homosexuality relatively more tolerant than was characteristic of white heterosexual circles." Duberman, *Stonewall*, 42.

21. Historian David Levering Lewis and his works on the Harlem Renaissance and W. E. B. Du Bois have been particularly helpful in their detail.

22. Langston Hughes's residence on East 127th Street, New York City, New York, was listed on the NRHP on 29 October 1982. The Claude McKay Residence

(also known as the Harlem YMCA) is located at 180 West 135th Street, New York City, New York. It was listed on the NRHP and designated an NHL on 8 December 1976.

23. The Dunbar Apartments Complex is located along West 149th and West 150th Streets between Frederick Douglass and Adam Clayton Powell Jr. Boulevards, New York City, New York. It was added to the NRHP on 29 March 1979.

24. "This used to be the home and hangout of . . . so many of the literary luminaries of the Harlem Renaissance. Their former rooming house stood here until 2002, when New York City sold the peaked roofed brownstone, one of six in a matching row, to an investor in Rye, N.Y. The home came down, and a new one, no bigger, was built in its place, its most distinguishing feature being a driveway." Matt A. V. Chaban, "Much to Save in Harlem, but Historic Preservation Lags, a Critic Says," *New York Times,* 29 February 2016. The 267 House/Niggerati Manor (now demolished) was located at 267 West 136th Street, New York City, New York.

25. There was only one volume published, and there were only a few copies sold prior to a fire that destroyed the majority of the publication's copies. "'Fire!!' marked the first appearance in print of one of the most interesting minor characters of the Renaissance. Twenty-one year old Richard Bruce Nugent was a self-conscious decadent who had shortened his name to Richard Bruce to allay maternal embarrassment about his homosexuality." David Levering Lewis, *When Harlem Was in Vogue* (Australia: Penguin Books, 1997), 196.

26. David Lewis noted that it was Richard Bruce Nugent who suggested naming the salon after Cullen's poem "The Dark Tower." Ibid., 168–69. The Dark Tower (now demolished) was located at 108–110 West 136th Street, New York City, New York. This is now the location of the Countee Cullen Branch of the New York City Public Library.

27. David Levering Lewis, *W. E. B. Du Bois: The Fight for Equality and the American Century, 1919–1963* (New York: Henry Holt & Company, 2000), 224–25.

28. Villa Lewaro was added to the NRHP and designated an NHL on 11 May 1976.

29. The Rockland Palace (now demolished) was located at 280 West 155th Street, New York City, New York.

30. The Savoy Ballroom (now demolished) was located at 596 Lenox Avenue; Harry Hansberry's Clam House (now demolished) was located at 146 West 133rd Street, both in New York City, New York.

31. According to New York City's Landmarks Preservation Commission, as of February 2016, approximately 17 percent of properties in Harlem have protections through designations. That is in comparison with other Manhattan neighborhoods that have at least 60 percent of properties protected. Chaban, *Much to Save in Harlem.*

32. Carmen Mitchell, "Creations of Fantasies/Constructions of Identities: The Oppositional Lives of Gladys Bentley," in *The Greatest Taboo: Homosexuality in Black Communities,* ed. Delroy Constantine-Simms (Los Angeles: Alyson Books, 2001), 215.

33. Dr. Locke was chair of the philosophy department at Howard University. Locke Hall, 2441 Sixth Street NW, Washington, D.C., is named in his honor. Locke's home on R Street NW, Washington, D.C., is a contributing resource to the Fourteenth Street Historic District, added to the NRHP on 9 November 1994. When in New York City, Locke often stayed at the Hotel Olga, 42 West 120th Street.

34. Places associated with Langston Hughes include the Harlem YMCA (now the Claude McKay Residence), 180 West 135th Street, New York City, New York, added to the NRHP and designated an NHL on 8 December 1976; his residence on East 127th Street, New York City, New York, added to the NRHP on 29 October 1982; his residence on S Street NW, Washington, D.C., a contributing resource to the Dupont Circle Historic District, and added to the NRHP on 21 January 1978 (boundary increases 6 February 1985 and 10 June 2005); the 267 House on West 136th Street in New York City, New York, (now demolished) where he socialized with other members of the Harlem Renaissance; Rockland Palace (now demolished), 280 West 155th Street, New York City, New York, where he attended and wrote about the drag balls; and Yaddo in Saratoga Springs, New York, located within the Union Avenue Historic District (listed on the NRHP on 4 April 1978 and designated an NHL on 11 March 2013), where Hughes spent time as an artist in residence.

35. Lewis, *When Harlem Was in Vogue,* 87.

36. "In the living room of [Johnson's] S Street house . . . , a freewheeling jumble of the gifted, famous, and odd came together on Saturday nights. There were the poets Waring Cuney, Mae Miller, Sterling Brown, Angelina Grimke, and Albert Rose. There were the artists Richard Bruce Nugent and Mae Howard Jackson. Writers like Jean Toomer and Alice Dunbar-Nelson (former wife of Paul Laurence Dunbar), and philosopher-critic Locke came regularly to enjoy the train of famous and to-be-famous visitors." Ibid., 127. Johnson's home is located at 1461 S Street NW, Washington, D.C.

37. Jackson performed at the Beaux Arts Café on the second floor of the Pekin Theater (now demolished), 2700 South State Street, Chicago, Illinois. The Beaux Arts, which opened in 1911, was a "scandalous" venue where a racially diverse audience socialized and danced. See Kendall, "Bob Mott and the Pekin Theater," *The Chicago Crime Scenes Project* (blog), 17 January 2009, http://chicagocrimescenes.blogspot.com/2009/01/bob-mott-and-pekin-theater.html. In 2011, Jackson was inducted into Chicago's Gay and Lesbian Hall of Fame; see "Tony Jackson," Chicago LGBT Hall of Fame website, http://chicagolgbthalloffame.org/jackson-tony/.

38. Tristan Cabello, "Queer Bronzeville: African American LGBTs on Chicago's South Side, 1900–1985," *Windy City Times,* 29 February 2012, http://www

.windycitymediagroup.com/lgbt/Queer-Bronzeville-African-American-LGBTs-on-Chicagos-South-Side-1900-1985/36389.html.

39. David Ehrenstein, "Gay New Orleans 101," *Advocate*, 11 October 2005, 50.

40. Cabello, "Queer Bronzeville." Bentley performed at venues across the country, including Harry Hansberry's Clam House, 133rd Street, Harlem, New York City, New York; Rockland Palace (now demolished), 280 West 115th Street, New York City, New York; the Ubangi Club (now demolished), 131st Street at Seventh Avenue, New York City, New York; Joaquin's El Rancho, Vine Street, Los Angeles, California; and Mona's Club 440, 440 Broadway, San Francisco, California. Nan Alamilla Boyd, *Wide-Open Town: A History of Queer San Francisco to 1965* (Berkeley: University of California Press, 2003), 76.

41. Ma Rainey's home, now a museum honoring her legacy, is located at 805 Fifth Avenue, Columbus, Georgia.

42. Eric Garber, "A Spectacle in Color: The Lesbian and Gay Subculture of Jazz Age Harlem," American Studies at the University of Virginia website, http://xroads.virginia.edu/~ug97/blues/garber.html.

43. Ibid. Many of these performers, including Bessie Smith, "Moms" Mabley, and Ethel Waters, performed at the Apollo Theater, 253 West 125th Street, New York City, New York. The Apollo was added to the NRHP on 17 November 1983. Like Bentley, Mabley performed at the Ubangi Club (now demolished), 131st Street at Seventh Avenue, New York City, New York. In 1962, Mabley performed at Carnegie Hall, 881 Seventh Avenue, New York City, New York (added to the NRHP on 15 October 1966 and designated an NHL on 29 December 1962). Alberta Hunter got her big break performing at the Dreamland Café, 3518–3520 South State Street, Chicago, Illinois. In addition to the Apollo, Ethel Waters also performed at Edmond's Cellar, Fifth Avenue and 132nd Street, New York City, New York; she lived in the Crown Heights neighborhood of Brooklyn, New York. Both Josephine Baker and Ethel Waters performed at the Plantation Club, Broadway and 50th Streets, New York City, New York. See Aberjhani and Sandra L. West, *Encyclopedia of the Harlem Renaissance* (New York: Facts on File, 2003); Jonathan Gill, *Harlem: The Four Hundred Year History from Dutch Village to Capital of Black America* (New York: Grove Press, 2011).

44. Gregory Conerly, "Swishing and Swaggering: Homosexuality in Black Magazines during the 1950s," in *The Greatest Taboo*, ed. Delroy Constantine-Simms (Los Angeles: Allyson, 2000), 389. The 101 Ranch (now demolished) was located at 101 West 139th Street, New York City, New York; Joe's Deluxe Club (now demolished) was located at 6323 South Parkway, Chicago, Illinois.

45. Langston Hughes, *Autobiography: The Big Sea (The Collected Works of Langston Hughes)*, vol. 13, ed. Joseph McLaren (Columbia: University of Missouri Press, 2002), 208. Rockland Palace (now demolished) was located at 280 West 115th Street, New York City, New York.

46. Kaiser, *The Gay Metropolis,* 40–41. Gregory Conerly, in his essay "Swishing and Swaggering," focused his research on the mid-twentieth-century powerhouses of *Ebony* and *Jet* magazines. Generally, they focused their coverage on Halloween and Thanksgiving events that were held in Chicago and New York City.

47. Conerly, "Swishing and Swaggering," 387. The Pershing Hotel (now demolished) was located at 6400 Cottage Grove, Chicago, Illinois.

48. In San Francisco, where she played at the lesbian venue Mona's Club 440 during World War II, Bentley was "advertised as 'America's Sepia Piano Artist' and the 'Brown Bomber of Sophisticated Songs.'" Nan Alamilla Boyd, *Wide-Open Town,* 76. Mona's Club 440 was located at 440 Broadway, San Francisco, California.

49. "Bentley, at the time of the article written in 1952, was 'happily married and living a normal existence.' But, she claimed, 'I am still haunted by the sex underworld in which I once lived. I want to help others, who are trapped in its dark recesses by telling my story.'" Conerly, "Swishing and Swaggering," 391.

50. Webster Hall and Annex are located at 119–125 East 11th Street, New York City, New York.

51. Tom Vitale, "100 Years of Billy Strayhorn, Emotional Architect of Song," NPR, *Weekend Edition Sunday,* 29 November 2015, http://www.npr.org/2015/11/29/457598579/100-years-of-billy-strayhorn-emotional-architect-of-song.

52. Kevin Henriques, "Aaron Bridgers," *Guardian,* 21 December 2003. The home of Strayhorn and Bridgers was located within the Hamilton Heights Historic District, listed on the NRHP on 30 September 1983. Strayhorn's Childhood Home (now demolished) was at 7212 Tioga Street, Rear, Pittsburgh, Pennsylvania.

53. The Apollo Theater, 253 West 125th Street, New York City, New York, was added to the NRHP on 17 November 1983.

54. See Megan E. Springate, "LGBTQ Civil Rights in America," in *LGBTQ America: A Theme Study of Lesbian, Gay, Bisexual, Transgender, and Queer History* (Washington, DC: National Park Foundation and National Park Service, 2016), https://nps.gov/articles/lgbtqtheme-civilrights.htm.

55. The Henry Gerber House was designated an NHL on 21 July 2015. See Tammye Nash, "Henry Gerber: The Gay Rights Pioneer You Probably Never Heard Of," *Dallas Voice,* 17 February 2015, http://www.dallasvoice.com/henry-gerber-gay-rights-pioneer-heard-10190163.html.

56. Pauli Murray, "The Liberation of Black Women," in *Words of Fire: An Anthology of African-American Feminist Thought,* ed. Beverly Guy-Sheftall (New York: The New Press, 1995), 186–98.

57. The Pauli Murray Childhood Home is located at 906 Carroll Street, Durham, North Carolina. It was named a National Treasure by the National Trust for Historic Preservation in 2015, and is currently being developed as the Pauli Murray Center for History and Social Justice, with a planned opening to the

public in 2020. See National Trust for Historic Preservation, "National Treasures: Pauli Murray House," National Trust for Historic Preservation website, https://savingplaces.org/places/pauli-murray-house; Pauli Murray Project, "Pauli Murray Project," Duke Human Rights Center at the Franklin Humanities Institute website, http://paulimurrayproject.org/becoming-involved. The Pauli Murray Family Home was designated an NHL on 11 January 2017.

58. Bayard Rustin's residence in the Chelsea neighborhood of New York City, New York, was listed on the NRHP on 8 March 2016.

59. John D'Emilio, *Lost Prophet: The Life and Times of Bayard Rustin* (New York: The Free Press, 2003), 1.

60. See, for example, D'Emilio, *Lost Prophet*.

61. Mumford, *Not Straight, Not White*, 12–13.

62. Baldwin's residence on Horatio Street, Greenwich Village, New York City, New York, is within the Greenwich Village Historic District, listed on the NRHP on 19 June 1979. A plaque was unveiled at this location in 2015. The James Baldwin House is located on the Upper West Side, New York City, New York. Danielle Tcholakian, "James Baldwin Historic Plaque to Be Unveiled at 81 Horatio St.," *DNAinfo*, 6 October 2015, https://www.dnainfo.com/new-york/20151006/west-village/james-baldwin-historic-plaque-be-unveiled-at-81-horatio-st.

63. The Hansberry home on Chicago's South Side (now demolished) was at 5330 South Calumet Avenue, Chicago, Illinois. The home purchased by Lorraine's parents in 1937 was in Chicago's Woodlawn neighborhood. It has been designated a historic site at the local level. Alison Shay, "Remembering Hansberry v. Lee," *Publishing the Long Civil Rights Movement* (blog), 12 November 2012, https://lcrm.lib.unc.edu/blog/index.php/tag/hansberry-v-lee.

64. Her Greenwich Village residence was on Bleecker Street, New York City, New York. She also lived on Waverly Place, New York City. Though she did not live to see the Stonewall riots of 1969, Lorraine Hansberry's Bleecker Street home was less than two blocks away from the site. See New York City Landmarks Preservation Commission, *150 Years of LGBT History*, PowerPoint presentation, http://www.nyc.gov/html/lpc/downloads/pdf/LGBT-PRIDE_2014.pdf, 13.

65. Stonewall, at 51–53 Christopher Street, New York City, New York, was listed on the NRHP on 28 June 1999; designated an NHL on 16 February 2000; and declared the Stonewall National Monument on 24 June 2016.

66. Duberman, *Stonewall*, 183.

67. Mumford, *Not Straight, Not White*, 89.

68. Ibid., 140.

69. In this way, Joseph Beam's *In the Life: A Black Gay Anthology* (Boston: Alyson Books, 1986) is reminiscent of Wallace Thurman's *Fire!!*, which gave young Harlem Renaissance writers a place to produce art by and for themselves.

70. There were also concerns that existing LGBTQ organizations at that time simply weren't interested in working on "non-LGBTQ" issues that directly affected the African American LGBTQ community, like employment, police brutality, poverty, and health care.

71. Criteria considerations for both NRHP and NHL nominations exist that allow researchers to nominate places where the significant events took place less than fifty years prior. See Megan E. Springate and Caridad de la Vega, "Nominating LGBTQ Places to the National Register of Historic Places and as National Historic Landmarks: An Introduction," in *LGBTQ America: A Lesbian, Gay, Bisexual, Transgender, and Queer History* (Washington, DC: National Park Foundation and National Park Service, 2016), https://nps.gov/articles/lgbtqtheme-nominating.htm.

72. The Salsa Soul Sisters, Third World Wimmin Incorporated Collective included African American and Latina women. They met primarily at a private residence near Washington Square Park in Greenwich Village, New York City, New York. The AALUSC currently meets at the Lesbian, Gay, Bisexual & Transgender Community Center, 208 West Thirteenth Street, New York City, New York. Third World Gay Women, Inc., "Salsa Soul Sisters Pamphlet," *Greenwich Village History* website, http://gvh.aphdigital.org/items/show/1159.

73. In the mid-1970s, the Combahee River Collective met at the Women's Center, 595 Massachusetts Avenue, Cambridge, Massachusetts.

74. The retreats themselves took place "mostly in private homes," which is reflective of the overarching theme of this study, highlighting the spaces where members of the African American LGBTQ community could be themselves. Duchess Harris, "From the Kennedy Commission to the Combahee Collective: Black Feminist Organizing, 1960–1980," in *Sisters in the Struggle: African American Women in the Civil Rights-Black Power Movement*, ed. Bettye Collier-Thomas and V. P. Franklin (New York: New York University Press, 2001), 295.

75. See also Megan E. Springate, "A Note about Intersectionality, LGBTQ Communities, History, and Place" (this volume).

76. Robert Crisman, "History Made: First Lesbians/Gays of Color Conference," *Freedom Socialist Party* website, Winter 1979, https://socialism.com/fs-article/history-made-first-lesbiansgays-of-color-conference/. The Harambee House Hotel was located on the 2200 block of Georgia Avenue NW, Washington, D.C.

77. See "ABilly S. Jones-Hennin," Rainbow History Project Digital Collections website, https://rainbowhistory.omeka.net/exhibits/show/pioneers/2007aw ardees/jones-hennin. The National Conference on AIDS in the Black Community was held at the Washington Convention Center (now demolished), 909 H Street NW, Washington, D.C. Gil Gerald, "Speech to the Southern Christian Leadership Conference Women's Conference on AIDS," in *Speaking for Our Lives: Historic Speeches and Rhetoric for Gay and Lesbian Rights*

(1892–2000), ed. Robert B. Marks Ridinger (New York: Harrington Park Press, 2004), 515.

78. Howard University is located at 2400 Sixth Street NW, Washington, D.C.
79. Bill Stevens, "The Gay Movement Comes to Howard University," *Blacklight,* 2014, http://www.blacklightonline.com/howard.html.
80. Mumford, *Not Straight, Not White,* 157.
81. GMAD was located at 540 Atlantic Avenue, Brooklyn, New York. The term "same-gender-loving" includes those African American men who engage in same-sex sexual contact, but do not identify as gay or bisexual, particularly at sites of cruising/sexual engagement.
82. New York Public Library, "Gay Men of African Descent, Inc. records, 1986–1998" [Finding aid], New York Public Library, Schomburg Center for Research in Black Culture, http://archives.nypl.org/scm/21213.
83. The Clubhouse was located at 1296 Upshur Street NW, Washington, D.C. In 2016, the building was surveyed by the Historic American Buildings Survey. Amber Bailey, *Historic American Buildings Survey: 1296 Upshur St NW (The Clubhouse), HABS No. DC-884* (Washington, DC: Historic American Buildings Survey, 2016), https://www.nps.gov/places/upload/The-ClubHouse-1.pdf.
84. Frank Muzzy, *Gay and Lesbian Washington, D.C.,* Images of America Series (Charleston, SC: Arcadia Publishing, 2005), 51.
85. Banneker Field is part of the Banneker Recreation Center, 2500 Georgia Avenue NW, Washington, D.C. It was added to the NRHP on 28 April 1986.
86. Atlanta held its first Black Pride event in 1996. Les Fabian Brathwaite, "Black Pride Matters," *Advocate,* June/July 2016, 55.
87. Stonewall and Julius', both in New York City, are listed on the NRHP. See note 65 for Stonewall's address and listing dates. Julius', at 159 West 10th Street, New York City, New York, was listed on the NRHP on 21 April 2016.
88. For discussions of the importance of places associated with cruising and sexual engagement to LGBTQ history, see, for example, Christina B. Hanhardt, "Making Community: The Places and Spaces of LGBTQ Collective Identity Formation," in *Communities and Place: A Thematic Approach to the Histories of LGBTQ Communities in the United States,* ed. Katherine Crawford-Lackey and Megan E. Springate (New York: Berghahn Books, 2020); David K. Johnson, "LGBTQ Business and Commerce," in *LGBTQ America: A Theme Study of Lesbian, Gay, Bisexual, Transgender, and Queer History,* ed. Megan E. Springate (Washington, DC: National Park Foundation and National Park Service, 2016), https://nps.gov/articles/lgbtqtheme-business.htm; Tracy Baim, "Sex, Love, and Relationships," in Springate, *LGBTQ America;* and Jen Jack Gieseking, "The Geographies of LGBTQ Lives: In and Beyond Cities, Neighborhoods, and Bars," in Crawford-Lackey and Springate, *Community and Place.* See also Gail Dubrow, "Taking Action: An Overview of LGBTQ Preservation Initiatives," in *Preservation and Place: Historic Preservation by and of LGBTQ Communities in the United States,* ed. Kather-

ine Crawford-Lackey and Megan E. Springate (New York: Berghahn Books, 2019), for a discussion regarding pushback to having LGBTQ places added to the NRHP and designated as NHLs.

89. The Fort Laramie Three Mile Hog Ranch, located outside Fort Laramie, Wyoming, was added to the NRHP on 23 April 1975.

90. "National Register of Historic Places: Fort Laramie Three Mile Hog Ranch," Wyoming State Historic Preservation Office website, http://wyoshpo.state .wy.us/NationalRegister/Site.aspx?ID=179.

91. Hotel Alma (now the Crystal Hotel), 1201–1217 SW Stark Street, Portland, Oregon, was added to the NRHP on 9 September 2009. For more on the importance of periods of significance, see Springate and de la Vega, "Nominating LGBTQ Places."

92. Mount Morris Turkish Baths were located at 28 East 125th Street, New York City, New York.

93. Alan Feuer, "Mount Morris Journal; A Gay Bathhouse in Harlem? Hey, It's No Secret," *New York Times,* 19 January 2003.

94. With the arrival of HIV/AIDS, it is not a surprise that Mount Morris moved beyond its role as a site of cruising/sexual engagement, and became a site of education for men in the LGBTQ community. "Speakers from advocacy groups like the Gay Men's Health Crisis and the Minority Task Force on AIDS discuss topics of particular interests to gay men. There are lectures on being gay in high school and on gay men raising families." Ibid.

95. Anonymous, "The Secret Garden," *Washington City Paper,* 25 August 2000, http://www.washingtoncitypaper.com/news/article/13020626/the-se cret-garden. Meridian Hill Park (also known in the African American D.C. community as Malcolm X Park), 2400 Fifteenth Street NW, Washington, D.C., was added to the NRHP on 25 October 1974 and designated an NHL on 19 April 1994.

96. Marcus Garvey Park, formerly Mount Morris Park, 18 Mount Morris Park West, New York City, New York, is part of the Mount Morris Park Historic District, added to the NRHP on 6 February 1973, with a boundary increase 24 May 1996. The West Side Piers, individual piers, are located along the Hudson River, Greenwich Village, New York City, New York.

97. Duberman, *Stonewall,* 42.

98. Lesbian dancer Mabel Hampton recalled Walker's "funny parties," "the more intimate gatherings at The Dark Tower, [that] illustrate the extent to which the millionaires was willing to participate in Harlem's sexual bohemia." In Devon W. Carbado, Dwight A. McBride, and Donald Weise, eds., *Black Like Us: A Century of Lesbian, Gay, and Bisexual African American Fiction* (New York: Cleis Press, 2002), Section 1: "1900–1950: The Harlem Renaissance," 1–106.

99. Gail Dubrow, "Deviant History, Defiant Heritage." See also Gail Dubrow, "Invisibility and Representation: An Introduction to LGBTQ Historic Preservation" and "Taking Action: An Overview of LGBTQ Preservation and Initiatives," in Crawford-Lackey and Springate, *Preservation and Place.*

100. Nob Hill was located at 1101 Kenyon Street NW, Washington, D.C. Nob Hill was the subject of a short survey by the Historic American Buildings Survey; see Amber Bailey, *Historic American Buildings Survey: 1101 Kenyon St. NW (Nob Hill), HABS No. DC-882* (Washington, DC: Historic American Buildings Survey, 2016), https://www.nps.gov/places/upload/Nob-Hill-1.pdf.

101. Sean Bugg and Randy Shulman, "Closed for Business," *Metro Weekly*, 25 February 2004, 2016, http://www.metroweekly.com/2004/02/closed-for-business.

102. The Black AIDS Institute was founded in 1999 as the African American AIDS Policy Training Institute. It is currently located at 1833 West Eighth Street, Los Angeles, California. Us Helping Us was founded in 1985 by Rainey Cheeks with the support of African American gay and bisexual men to provide holistic support for those affected by HIV/AIDS. They met at the Clubhouse (1296 Upshur Street NW, Washington, D.C.) until it closed in 1990, when they began meeting in Rainey's D.C. apartment. Their first formal location was a rented house near the Washington Navy Yard in D.C.'s Southeast. Us Helping Us is currently located at 3636 Georgia Avenue NW, Washington, D.C. See "About Us," Black AIDS Institute website, https://www.blackaids.org/about-the-institute; "About Us," Us Helping Us, People Into Living, Inc. website, http://www.uhupil.org/#!about/cttm.

103. Jewel's Catch One, 4067 West Pico Boulevard, Los Angeles, California, was the nation's first black gay and lesbian disco, opened in 1972 by Jewel Thais-Williams. When the club closed in 2015 with Jewel's retirement, it was the last black-owned gay club in the city.

104. A great example of scholarship providing new information on nineteenth-century African American LGBTQ lives is Farah Jasmine Griffin, ed., *Beloved Sisters and Loving Friends: Letters from Rebecca Primus of Royal Oak, Maryland, and Addie Brown of Hartford, Connecticut* (New York: Knopf, 1999). Unfortunately, there are no known extant historic places associated with Primus or Brown.

Bibliography

Aberjhani, and Sandra L. West. *Encyclopedia of the Harlem Renaissance*. New York: Facts on File, 2003.

Anonymous. "The Secret Garden." *Washington City Paper*, 25 August 2000. http://www.washingtoncitypaper.com/news/article/13020626/the-secret-garden.

Bailey, Amber. *Historic American Buildings Survey: 1101 Kenyon St. NW (Nob Hill), HABS No. DC-882*. Washington, DC: Historic American Buildings Survey, 2016. https://www.nps.gov/places/upload/Nob-Hill-1.pdf.

———. *Historic American Buildings Survey: 1296 Upshur St NW (The Clubhouse), HABS No. DC-884*. Washington, DC: Historic American Buildings Survey, 2016. https://www.nps.gov/places/upload/The-ClubHouse-1.pdf.

Baim, Tracy. "Sex, Love, and Relationships." In *LGBTQ America: A Theme Study of Lesbian, Gay, Bisexual, Transgender, and Queer History,* edited by Megan E. Springate. Washington, DC: National Park Foundation and National Park Service, 2016. https://nps.gov/articles/lgbtqtheme-love.htm.

Beam, Joseph, ed. *In the Life: A Black Gay Anthology.* Boston: Alyson Books, 1986.

Black AIDS Institute. "About Us." https://www.blackaids.org/about-the-institute.

Boyd, Nan Alamilla. *Wide-Open Town: A History of Queer San Francisco to 1965.* Berkeley: University of California Press, 2003.

Brathwaite, Les Fabian. "Black Pride Matters." *Advocate,* June/July 2016.

Bugg, Sean, and Randy Shulman. "Closed for Business." *Metro Weekly,* 25 February 2004. http://www.metroweekly.com/2004/02/closed-for-business.

Cabello, Tristan. "Queer Bronzeville: African American LGBTs on Chicago's South Side, 1900–1985." *Windy City Times,* 29 February 2012. http://www.windy citymediagroup.com/lgbt/Queer-Bronzeville-African-American-LGBTs-on-Chicagos-South-Side-1900-1985/36389.html.

Carbado, Devon W., Dwight A. McBride, and Donald Weise, eds. *Black Like Us: A Century of Lesbian, Gay, and Bisexual African American Fiction.* New York: Cleis Press, 2002.

Chaban, Matt A. V. "Much to Save in Harlem, but Historic Preservation Lags, a Critic Says." *New York Times,* 29 February 2016.

Chauncey, George. *Gay New York: Gender, Urban Culture, and the Making of the Gay Male World, 1890–1940.* 3rd ed. New York: Basic Books, 1994.

Chicago LGBT Hall of Fame. "Tony Jackson." *Chicago LGBT Hall of Fame.* http:// chicagolgbthalloffame.org/jackson-tony/.

Crisman, Robert. "History Made: First Lesbians/Gays of Color Conference." Freedom Socialist Party website, Winter 1979. http://www.socialism.com/ drupal-6.8/articles/history-made-first-lesbians-gays-color-conference.

Conerly, Gregory. "Swishing and Swaggering: Homosexuality in Black Magazines during the 1950s." In *The Greatest Taboo: Homosexuality in Black Communities,* edited by Delroy Constantine-Simms, 384–95. Los Angeles: Allyson, 2000.

Costley, Alex W. "Editor's Note." In William G. Hawkeswood, *One of the Children: Black Gay Men in Harlem,* edited by Alex W. Costley (Berkeley: University of California Press, 1996).

D'Emilio, John. *Lost Prophet: The Life and Times of Bayard Rustin.* New York: The Free Press, 2003.

Duberman, Martin. *Stonewall.* New York: Penguin, 1994.

Dubrow, Gail. "Deviant History, Defiant Heritage." Friends of 1800 website, 2002. http://www.friendsof1800.org/VIEWPOINT/dubrow.html.

———. "Invisibility and Representation: An Introduction to LGBTQ Historic Preservation." In *Preservation and Place: Historic Preservation by and of LGBTQ Communities in the United States,* edited by Katherine Crawford-Lackey and Megan E. Springate. New York: Berghahn Books, 2019.

————. "Taking Action: An Overview of LGBTQ Preservation Initiatives." In *Preservation and Place: Historic Preservation by and of LGBTQ Communities in the United States*, edited by Katherine Crawford-Lackey and Megan E. Springate. New York: Berghahn Books, 2019.

Ehrenstein, David. "Gay New Orleans 101." *Advocate*, 11 October 2005.

Feuer, Alan. "Mount Morris Journal: A Gay Bathhouse in Harlem? Hey, It's No Secret." *New York Times*, 19 January 2003.

Garber, Eric. "A Spectacle in Color: The Lesbian and Gay Subculture of Jazz Age Harlem." American Studies at the University of Virginia, n.d. http://xroads .virginia.edu/~ug97/blues/garber.html.

Gerald, Gil. "Speech to the Southern Christian Leadership Conference Women's Conference on AIDS." In *Speaking for Our Lives: Historic Speeches and Rhetoric for Gay and Lesbian Rights (1892–2000)*, edited by Robert B. Marks Ridinger, 515–18. New York: Harrington Park Press, 2004.

Gieseking, Jen Jack. "The Geographies of LGBTQ Lives: In and Beyond Cities, Neighborhoods, and Bars." In *Communities and Place: A Thematic Approach to the Histories of LGBTQ Communities in the United States*, edited by Katherine Crawford-Lackey and Megan E. Springate. New York: Berghahn Books: 2020.

Gill, Jonathan. *Harlem: The Four Hundred Year History from Dutch Village to Capital of Black America*. New York: Grove Press, 2011.

Griffin, Farah Jasmine, ed. *Beloved Sisters and Loving Friends: Letters from Rebecca Primus of Royal Oak, Maryland, and Addie Brown of Hartford, Connecticut*. New York: Knopf, 1999.

Hanhardt, Christina B. "Making Community: The Places and Spaces of LGBTQ Collective Identity Formation." In *Community and Place: A Thematic Approach to the Histories of LGBTQ Communities in the United States*, edited by Katherine Crawford-Lackey and Megan E. Springate. New York: Berghahn Books, 2020.

Harris, Duchess. "From the Kennedy Commission to the Combahee Collective: Black Feminist Organizing, 1960–1980." In *Sisters in the Struggle: African American Women in the Civil Rights-Black Power Movement*, edited by Bettye Collier-Thomas and V. P. Franklin, 280–304. New York: New York University Press, 2001.

Hawkeswood, William G. *One of the Children: Black Gay Men in Harlem*, edited by Alex W. Costley. Berkeley: University of California Press, 1996.

Henriques, Kevin. "Aaron Bridgers." *Guardian*, 21 December 2003.

Hughes, Langston. *Autobiography: The Big Sea (The Collected Works of Langston Hughes)*. Vol. 13. Edited by Joseph McLaren. Columbia: University of Missouri Press, 2002.

Johnson, David K. "LGBTQ Business and Commerce." In *LGBTQ America: A Theme Study of Lesbian, Gay, Bisexual, Transgender, and Queer History*, edited by Megan E. Springate. Washington, DC: National Park Foundation and National Park Service, 2016. https://nps.gov/articles/lgbtqtheme-business.htm.

Kaiser, Charles. *The Gay Metropolis, 1940–1996*. Boston: Houghton Mifflin, 1997.

Kendall. "Bob Mott and the Pekin Theater." *The Chicago Crime Scenes Project,* 17 January 2009. http://chicagocrimescenes.blogspot.com/2009/01/bob-mott-and-pekin-theater.html.

Lewis, David Levering. *W. E. B. Du Bois: The Fight for Equality and the American Century, 1919–1963*. New York: Henry Holt & Company, 2000.

———. *When Harlem Was in Vogue*. Australia: Penguin, 1997.

Mitchell, Carmen. "Creations of Fantasies/Constructions of Identities: The Oppositional Lives of Gladys Bentley." In *The Greatest Taboo: Homosexuality in Black Communities,* edited by Delroy Constantine-Simms, 211–25. Los Angeles: Alyson Books, 2001.

Mumford, Kevin J. *Not Straight, Not White: Black Gay Men from the March on Washington to the AIDS Crisis*. Chapel Hill: University of North Carolina Press, 2016.

Murray, Pauli. "The Liberation of Black Women." In *Words of Fire: An Anthology of African-American Feminist Thought,* edited by Beverly Guy-Sheftall, 186–98. New York: The New Press, 1995.

Muzzy, Frank. *Gay and Lesbian Washington, D.C.* Images of America Series. Charleston, SC: Arcadia Publishing, 2005.

Nash, Tammye. "Henry Gerber: The Gay Rights Pioneer You Probably Never Heard Of." *Dallas Voice,* 17 February 2015. http://www.dallasvoice.com/henry-gerber-gay-rights-pioneer-heard-10190163.html.

National Trust for Historic Preservation. "National Treasures: Pauli Murray House." National Trust for Historic Preservation website. https://saving places.org/places/pauli-murray-house.

Nero, Charles I. "Why Are the Gay Ghettoes White?" In *Black Queer Studies: A Cultural Anthology,* edited by E. Patrick Johnson and Mae Henderson, 228–48. Durham, NC: Duke University Press, 2005.

New York City Landmarks Preservation Commission. *150 Years of LGBT History*. New York: New York City Landmarks Preservation Commission, 2014. http://www.nyc.gov/html/lpc/downloads/pdf/LGBT-PRIDE_2014.pdf.

New York Public Library. "Gay Men of African Descent, Inc. records, 1986–1998" [Finding aid]. New York Public Library, Schomburg Center for Research in Black Culture, http://archives.nypl.org/scm/21213.

Pauli Murray Project. "Pauli Murray Project." Duke Human Rights Center at the Franklin Humanities Institute. http://paulimurrayproject.org/becoming-involved.

Rainbow History Project. "ABilly S. Jones-Hennin." Rainbow History Project Digital Collections. https://rainbowhistory.omeka.net/exhibits/show/pioneers/2007awardees/jones-hennin.

Shay, Alison. "Remembering Hansberry v. Lee." *Publishing the Long Civil Rights Movement,* 12 November 2012. https://lcrm.lib.unc.edu/blog/index.php/tag/hansberry-v-lee.

Springate, Megan E. "LGBTQ Civil Rights in America." In *LGBTQ America: A Theme Study of Lesbian, Gay, Bisexual, Transgender, and Queer History*. Washington, DC: National Park Foundation and National Park Service, 2016. https://nps.gov/articles/lgbtqtheme-civilrights.htm.

——. "A Note About Intersectionality, LGBTQ Communities, History, and Place." In *Identities and Place: Changing Labels and Intersectional Communities of LGBTQ and Two-Spirit People in the United States*, edited by Katherine Crawford-Lackey and Megan E. Springate. New York: Berghahn Books, 2020.

Springate, Megan E., and Caridad de la Vega. "Nominating LGBTQ Places to the National Register of Historic Places and as National Historic Landmarks: An Introduction." In *LGBTQ America: A Lesbian, Gay, Bisexual, Transgender, and Queer History*. Washington, DC: National Park Foundation and National Park Service, 2016. https://nps.gov/articles/lgbtqtheme-nominating.htm.

Stevens, Bill. "The Gay Movement Comes to Howard University." *Blacklight*, 2014. http://www.blacklightonline.com/howard.html.

Stewart-Winter, Timothy. *Queer Clout: Chicago and the Rise of Gay Politics*. Philadelphia: University of Pennsylvania Press, 2016.

Tcholakian, Danielle. "James Baldwin Historic Plaque to Be Unveiled at 81 Horatio St." *DNAinfo*, 6 October 2015. https://www.dnainfo.com/new-york/20151006/west-village/james-baldwin-historic-plaque-be-unveiled-at-81-horatio-st.

Third World Gay Women, Inc. "Salsa Soul Sisters Pamphlet." Greenwich Village History website, n.d. http://gvh.aphdigital.org/items/show/1159.

Ulysses. "REMEMBER: Lucky's Rendezvous." *Harlem + Bespoke* (blog), 11 June 2012. http://harlembespoke.blogspot.com/2012/06/remember-luckys-rendezvous.html.

Us Helping Us, People Into Living. "About Us." http://www.uhupil.org/#!about/cttm.

Vitale, Tom. "100 Years of Billy Strayhorn, Emotional Architect of Song." NPR, *Weekend Edition Sunday*, 29 November 2015. http://www.npr.org/2015/11/29/457598579/100-years-of-billy-strayhorn-emotional-architect-of-song.

Vogel, Shane. *The Scene of Harlem Cabaret: Race, Sexuality, Performance*. Chicago: University of Chicago Press, 2009.

Activities

Katherine Crawford-Lackey

The following activities build on the content of previous chapters by examining the concept of "identity" and its implications in a historical and cultural context. These activities encourage readers to think critically about two-spirit, lesbian, gay, bisexual, transgender, and queer (LGBTQ) history and culture while exploring various aspects of their own identity. These education materials are intended for advanced college undergraduate and graduate students, and will prompt readers to delve deeper into the topic material by exploring different disciplines within the umbrella of public history. In addition to providing strategies for practically applying the knowledge included in the volume, these activities allow for self-reflection and provide opportunities to connect with others.

Defining Your Identity

Societal perceptions regarding categories of difference—race, class, gender, sexual orientation, ability, religion, etc.—are fluid and constantly changing with time. Methods for categorizing individuals have evolved, and, as a result, societal perceptions toward identity are different today than in the past.

Aspects of identity, including gender and sexual orientation, inform social interactions as well as the ability to partake in society—both professionally and personally.[1] Studying how an individual or group is treated by larger society based on these categories of difference allows scholars to study patterns of inequality in the historical record.

In the era of Jim Crow, for example, some towns and cities insisted on racial purity as a prerequisite for participation in white society. If an individual had African ancestry (even if they appeared Caucasian), they could be barred from white schools, jobs, and social gatherings.[2] Such practices forced people into categories by creating "standards" that enabled those in power.

Today, people are still placed in categories based on the color of their skin, their religious beliefs, and their access to wealth; however, individuals have more power to define their identities on their own terms.

Activity

What words would you use to describe yourself? How do they speak to who you are as a person? What do others think of you? Why?

Fill out the following chart to explore how your identity categories shape who you are and how this compares with others.

Identity Category:	How it impacts you:	How it impacts others you know:

Now that you have listed some aspects of your identity, consider how they influence your lived experiences.

- What are some of your identity categories? How do they impact your day-to-day experiences?

- Are your experiences similar to others who share those aspects of your identity? Why or why not?

- How has mainstream society responded to your identity categories historically? Has this changed today? Why or why not? Does this influenced the way you navigate the world? Why or why not?

- What can you learn about yourself by considering how your identity categories have changed over time?

Notes

1. For a more in-depth analysis on how intersectionality acts on individuals and communities, see Megan E. Springate, "A Note on Intersectionality" (this volume).
2. Daniel J. Sharfstein explores the complexities of identity formation in nineteenth- and early-twentieth-century America in his book *The Invisible Line: A Secret History of Race in America*. The author examines how three families attempted to negotiate their place within society because of (or in spite of) their racial identity. Daniel J. Sharfstein, *The Invisible Line: A Secret History of Race in America* (New York: Penguin Group, 2011).

Explore a Place

Our personal and cultural identities are influenced by place, meaning that we are shaped by the spaces of our past and present—our childhood home, a local restaurant, our place of worship, the workplace, and more. Part of our individuality is informed by the places where we live, and this context is essential for our own self-expression as well as for how we make connections with others on a local and national scale.[1]

Physical meeting locations afford opportunities to socialize, protest, mourn, and celebrate. More visible lesbian, gay, bisexual, transgender, and queer (LGBTQ) communities formed in the mid to late twentieth century due in part to the establishment of queer-tolerant public spaces, which facilitated the emergence of a collective identity.[2]

Queer meeting spaces were subsequently targeted by the police, and, as a result, these places became sites of resistance. One of the most notable is Stonewall Inn in Greenwich Village, New York City, where in 1969 a group of gay, lesbian, bisexual, and transgender individuals fought back against police brutality. Many historians consider the Stonewall Uprising the start of the modern gay rights movement. Stonewall continues to serve as a symbolic place for many LGBTQ communities, and, in 2016, President Barack Obama recognized its importance in the larger narrative of American history by designating it a National Monument.

In addition to serving as an invitation for socialization, resistance, and remembrance, place can also instill a sense of belonging. Urban historian Dolores Hayden argues that public spaces in particular have the potential to "nurture" a sense of citizenship.[3] Place is powerful because it serves as a tangible link between past, present, and future, allowing us to connect more deeply to a shared heritage that strengtheners the bonds of citizenship and civic duty.

Studying history based in place has the power to reach a more diverse audience by tapping into our emotional connections to space. The National Park Service (NPS) in particular uses this approach in its parks and programs.[4] NPS interpretation aims to discover the untold stories of historically significant places. A new interpretive resource created through a collaboration of National Park Service professionals, titled the "Discovery Journal," is one such tool for discovering the many stories of a place. Intended for preservationists, interpreters, educators, and historians both inside and outside the National Park Service, the journal inspires the creation of new interpretation that addresses the untold stories of a place in order to facilitate healing and change.

The heart of this process entails exploring a place from a new perspective. When we become familiar with a place, we often begin to make assumptions, and we forget to ask questions about other uses and meanings of the space.[5] The following diagram is intended to inspire new inquiry by encouraging you to think about your place and its connection to larger themes in American history.

Activity

Pick a place that has meaning to you and fill out the diagram.

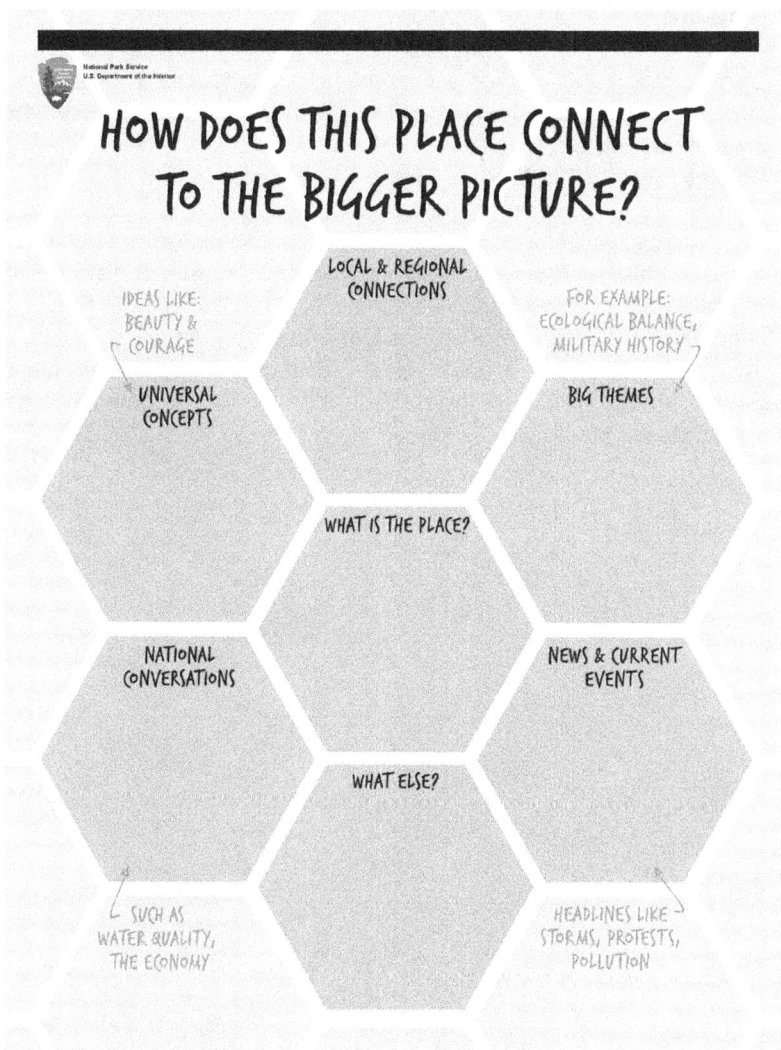

Figure A.1. "How does this place connect to the bigger picture?" National Park Service product. Diagram graphic designed by Mickey Shin. "Discovery Journal: Giving Voice to America's Places," National Park Service, n.d.

Notes

1. Kath Browne and Eduarda Ferreira, "Introduction to Lesbian Geographies," in *Lesbian Geographies: Gender, Place and Power*, ed. Kath Browne and Eduarda Ferreira (New York: Routledge, 2016). Kath Browne and Gavin Brown, "An Introduction to the Geographies of Sex and Sexualities," in *The Routledge Research Companion to Geographies of Sex and Sexuality* (New York: Routledge, 2016).

2. Gay, lesbian, bisexual, and transgender citizens would often frequent bars, taverns, and restaurants, and, while not necessarily welcome, gender and sexual minorities usually received service. Genny Beemyn, *A Queer Capital: A History of Gay Life in Washington D.C.* (New York: Routledge, 2015); John D'Emilio, *Sexual Politics, Sexual Communities: The Making of a Homosexual Minority in the United States, 1940–1970* (Chicago: The University of Chicago Press, 1983).

3. Dolores Hayden, *The Power of Place: Urban Landscapes as Public History* (Cambridge, MA: MIT Press, 1997), 9.

4. The Teaching with Historic Places program, for example, offers lesson plans based on historic properties listed on the National Register of Historic Places. https://www.nps.gov/subjects/teachingwithhistoricplaces/index.htm.

5. Katie Crawford-Lackey and Barbara Little, "Exploring American Places with the Discovery Journal: A Guide to Co-Creating Meaningful Interpretation," *George Wright Forum* 34, no.3 (2017), http://www.georgewright.org/343 crawford-lackey.pdf.

Essay Prompt: The Impact of the Legalization of Same-Sex Marriage

Queer people have long formed loving and meaningful romantic relationships. The emergence of a queer culture in the early to mid twentieth century led to greater social acceptance of same-sex couples in later decades. Despite the growing visibility of same-sex couples, the federal government did not legally recognize these unions.

The right to legally marry was an important demand of queer activism in the 1970s and 1980s. As a result of the Stonewall Uprising in Greenwich Village in New York City in 1969, lesbian, gay, bisexual, transfender, and queer (LGBTQ) Americans all over the country began demanding civil rights. As part of this movement, a number of queer people attempted to get married under state and federal law but were denied valid marriage licenses.[1]

Federally recognized marriages have important legal connotations. In the decades before the 2010s, queer people developed relationships without the support of the legal system. The lack of legal infrastructure often made life more difficult for those in same-sex partnerships in contrast to their heterosexual counterparts. There are countless examples of queer Americans unable to provide support for and make decisions on behalf of medically ill loved ones. The process of adopting children was also further complicated due to the lack of legislation recognizing queer unions.[2]

The fight for marriage equality eventually paid off in the twenty-first century after decades of protest. As a result of the Supreme Court cases *United States v. Windsor* (2013) and *Obergefell v. Hodges* (2015), same-sex marriage was legalized across the country.[3]

The debate concerning gay marriage caused many heterosexual and homosexual communities alike to question the definition and meaning of marriage. The legalization of same-sex marriage continues to raise questions about how this decision will impact queer society in the future.

Activity

Write an essay on the history of same-sex marriage in the United States and its implications on queer communities in the present. Use the following questions to prompt your inquiry.

- How have societal expectations regarding marriage changed over the past several decades?

- Does the prospect of marriage influence how we look for and select romantic partners? What does this subsequently mean for queer people?

- What does the legalization of same-sex marriage mean for same-sex couples specifically? How do these Supreme Court decisions have the power to change queer culture in America?

- Does the legalization of same-sex marriage imply that queer couples will face greater expectations to marry instead of forming life-long partnerships outside of the law?

Scholars, legal experts, and members of LGBTQ communities have yet to fully witness the effects of *United States v. Windsor* and *Obergefell v. Hodges*. The ability of people to marry partners of the same sex, while a step toward greater civil rights, also has the power to potentially alter queer culture in the decades to come.

Notes

1. Marc Stein, "Historical Landmarks and Landscapes of LGBTQ Law," in *Communities and Place: A Thematic Approach to the Histories of LGBTQ Communities in the United States*, edited by Katherine Crawford-Lackey and Megan E. Springate (New York: Berghahn Books, 2020).
2. Ibid.
3. "United States v. Windsor," SCOTUSblog, http://www.scotusblog.com/casefiles/cases/windsor-v-united-states-2/; "Obergefell v. Hodges," SCOTUSblog, http://www.scotusblog.com/casefiles/cases/obergefell-v-hodges.

Families of Choice

The concept of what defines a "family" has changed over time and differs based on cultural context. While some people have historically had the right to marry, many others have forged romantic relationships, raised children, adopted, and developed nonbiological familial bonds outside the legal institution of marriage. As queer Americans became more open in expressing same-sex love and desire in the second half of the twentieth century, the process of family-making shifted in American social life. Homosexual and bisexual men and women began to establish new relationships with same-sex partners after having children from previous marriages. In proceeding decades, queer couples also began to adopt children or choose artificial insemination. In many instances, the legal system did more to hinder than help lesbian, gay, bisexual, transgender, and queer (LGBTQ) Americans in creating families. Despite lack of legal support, queer people sought out ways to constitute their own families.[1]

Many Americans today create families of choice (also referred to as chosen families), this means they chose nonrelatives to treat as family. Families of choice are particularly important to those who identify as LGBTQ. Queer Americans are too often disowned by friends and family upon "coming out." The lack of acceptance often prompts LGBTQ individuals to develop close relations with people outside of their biological families.

In other cases, LGBTQ Americans do have the support of their biological family members; however, they build close relationships with others with similar experiences and interests.

Anyone, whether LGBTQ or heterosexual, can create a family of choice.[2]

Activity

Answer and discuss the following questions:

- How has your own understanding of the concept of "family" changed over your lifetime?

- Why is it important for there to be laws supporting lesbian, gay, bisexual, transgender, and (LGBTQ) Americans in constituting families of choice, such as through marriage, adoption, and artificial insemination?

- Why are chosen families important?

- Are there nonrelatives in your life that you consider family? Why are you close to these individuals?

- What are some of the benefits and challenges in constituting families of choice, both legally and socially?

Notes

1. Tracy Baim, "Sex, Love, and Relationships," in *LGBTQ America: A Theme Study of Lesbian, Gay, Bisexual, Transgender, and Queer History*, edited by Megan Springate (Washington, DC: National Park Foundation, 2016), 17–52.
2. For more information about families of choice and LGBTQ relationships, see Baim, "Sex, Love, and Relationships."

Exploring Intersectionality

Individual identities are shaped by factors such as gender, age, ethnicity, sexual orientation, religion, and ability. These categories of difference also inform social interactions as well as the ability to partake in society—both professionally and personally.

In her chapter on intersectionality, Megan E. Springate explains that categories of difference (race, gender, and sexual orientation) are interconnected. Identifying as a Black gay man, for example, entails a different experience than living as a white gay woman. These categories of difference are continually acting on each other to define an individual's identity.[1] Studying how an individual or group is treated by larger society based on these categories of difference allows scholars to study patterns of inequality in the historical record.

Activity: Part 1

Consider two or three categories of difference that apply to yourself.

How do they impact your daily experiences?

Categories of Difference	Impact on Lived Experience

Do you think one or more of these parts of your identify influence your life more than others? Why?

How do external factors, such as geographic location, change the meaning of parts of your identity?

Activity: Part 2

After identifying your categories of difference, write one or more of them down on individual scraps of paper. Ask your peers to do the same.

When finished, place all of your scraps of paper in a hat. Select several pieces of paper from the hat and read aloud.

Pretend these are all aspects of one individual's identity. Consider the benefits and challenges this individual may experience due to their categories of difference. What kinds of stereotypes may that person experience in twenty-first-century America? Why? What does this reveal about our culture?

Notes

1. For a more comprehensive analysis of intersectionality, see Megan Springate, "A Note About Intersectionality" (this volume).

Create a Toolkit: Talking about the "Tough Stuff" in History

Most Americans today recognize that the history of the country includes the stories of diverse individuals and communities. Acknowledging the nation's diversity is the first step to delving deeper into the root of our differences, which can be used to facilitate inequality. Individual identities, including gender, race, class, sexual orientation, religion, and ability, affect how people engage with society. These categories of difference also influence one's participation within cultural institutions, both personally and professionally.[1]

Racism, for example, became an inherent part of the system of slavery in the United States. Even after the passage of the Thirteenth Amendment abolishing slavery, racist attitudes shaped the freedoms of Black Americans politically, socially, and economically. Today, society continues to struggle with systemic and social forms of racial discrimination. Similarly, political and cultural institutions in America have also sought to regulate gender and sexual expression through legal means by instituting anti-sodomy laws.[2] Many lesbian, gay, bisexual, transgender, and queer (LGBTQ) Americans also continue to face homophobia, even after the passage of legislation protecting and expanding the rights and civil liberties of queer people.

While society has made progress in identifying and addressing inequality, many professionals and members of the public continue to grapple with how to talk about topics such as race, gender, sexual orientation, religion, ability, and much more.

Cultural institutions such as museums, libraries, and historic sites often act as places of healing where diverse groups can interact and express themselves in a supportive and welcoming environment.[3] These conversations should also be occurring in the home, at school, and in the workplace. In many cases, it is up to members of the public to address these topics within their social circles, among their colleagues, and with their families.

Providing a toolkit for engaging in difficult conversations—whether about race, class, sexual orientation—can help others take the initiative to discuss such topics with people they know and care about.

Activity

A toolkit is a guide to creating and implementing educational content about a topic. Using the information from the book, create a guide for how people can engage in conversations that facilitate healing and change instead of eliciting divisiveness and hostility.

Initiating a Dialogue: Steps and Suggestions

- Identify your audience: who is this toolkit for? The campus community? Local organizations—such as a public library? Or community social groups?

- Identify some challenges: what kinds of topics are people usually uncomfortable discussing? Why?

- Identify strategies to overcome discomfort: how can these topics be addressed in a way that promotes healing and change?

- Open lines of communication: remind everyone that this is a constructive conversation.

- Create safe spaces: establish a safe environment where people feel comfortable sharing their thoughts and feelings.

- Other things to consider:

  _____

  _____

  _____

  _____

  _____

Notes

1. Megan E. Springate, "A Note on Intersectionality" (this volume).
2. Dale Carpenter, *Flagrant Conduct: The Story of Lawrence v. Texas* (New York: W. W. Norton & Company, 2012).
3. Nina Simon, *The Participatory Museum* (Santa Cruz: Museum 2.0, 2010); Susan Ferentinos, "Interpreting LGBTQ Historic Sites," in *Preservation and Place: Historic Preservation by and of LGBTQ Communities in the United States,* edited by Katherine Crawford-Lackey and Megan E. Springate (New York: Berghahn Books, 2019); David W. Young, "Expanding Interpretation at Historic Sites," in *Interpreting African American History and Culture at Museums and Historic Sites,* edited by Max A. Van Balgooy (Lanham, MD: Rowman & Littlefield, 2015).

Essay Prompt: Transgender Identities

The formation of queer communities as a collective minority in the mid-twentieth century empowered sexually variant and gender-nonconforming Americans to become legitimate participants in civic life. By constituting communities, queer people were able to make demands for equal treatment under the law.[1] Lesbian, gay, bisexual, transgender, and queer (LGBTQ) Americans were also able build relationships with others with similar characteristics and goals, yet not all queer identities benefited equally from the legal victories of the last several decades.[2]

Today, society often refers to gender and sexual minorities using the collective "LGBTQ" label, yet there is no one single "LGBTQ" community as the term encompasses a diversity of identities and communities.[3] This term encourages camaraderie and collective action among similar stakeholders, yet it can also obscure the agency of distinct communities. For example, transgender Americans, particularly those of color, are more vulnerable to violence than other queer communities.[4]

Susan Stryker, scholar and author of "Transgender History in the U.S. and the Places that Matter," explains that gender-variant Americans actively participated in the modern gay rights movement in order to combat negative stereotypes. Much of the queer social activism of the mid to late twentieth century was accomplished by transgender men and women, including Sylvia Rivera and Marsha P. Johnson, who founded the Street Transvestite Action Revolutionaries (STAR) and STAR House.[5]

Activity

After reading this volume on queer identities, describe how lesbian, gay, bisexual, transgender, and queer Americans can collaborate across cultures and social groups to achieve greater civil liberties for all sexual and gender minorities.

What challenges do transgender Americans face that cisgender queer people do not?

How can cisgender lesbian, gay, bisexual, and queer people better advocate for the rights of transgender Americans? What actions can heterosexual communities take to better advocate for transgender Americans?

How has the visibility of transgender individuals in the media and in popular culture impacted societal perceptions?

Notes

1. John D'Emilio, *Sexual Politics, Sexual Communities: The Making of a Homosexual Minority in the United States, 1940-1970* (Chicago: University of Chicago Press, 1983); Marc Stein, "Historical Landmarks and Landscapes of LGBTQ Law," in *Communities and Place: A Thematic Approach to the Histories of LGBTQ Communities in the United States,* edited by Katherine Crawford-Lackey and Megan E. Springate (New York: Berghahn Books, 2020).
2. Current scholarship on LGBTQ communities often ignores the diversity of the queer experience. The three books included in this series attempt to address this and provide a broader understanding of those who are underrepresented in current scholarship.
3. In the last decade, scholars continue to reaffirm that the label "LGBTQ" refers to many different communities. Due to the complexity of queer identities, referring to one single community oversimplifies how categories of difference—such as race, gender, class, age, ability, religion, etc.—influence how queer communities are constituted. Megan E. Springate, "A Note on Intersectionality" (this volume); Susan Ferentinos, "Interpreting LGBTQ Historic Sites," *Preservation and Place: Historic Preservation by and of LGBTQ Communities in the United States,* edited by Katherine Crawford-Lackey and Megan E. Springate (New York: Berghahn Books, 2019).
4. Susan Stryker, *Transgender History* (Berkley: Seal Press, 2008), 142–43.
5. Susan Stryker, "Transgender History in the U.S. and the Places that Matter" (this volume).

Studying Identity through Objects

Archaeology is the study of past humans through the examination of material remains and built structures. Artifacts and other physical remnants, often referred to as material cultural, are "the tangible, preserved evidence of past human activities."[1] Physical traces—whether in the form of material objects, built structures, or altered landscapes—allow practitioners to study the culture, traditions, and even the behavior of past societies.

Archaeology is most effective when studying groups rather than the lives of individuals. As a result, practitioners are not necessarily looking for queer people and behavior in the archaeological record. Historical archaeologist Megan E. Springate explains that practitioners must not assume that past cultures were exclusively heterosexual or acknowledged only two genders.[2]

The type of objects an individual or culture values reveals information about the role of different genders, ethnicities, and classes within a society.[3] Professionals in the field are beginning to question if it is indeed possible to discern individual identities by examining what was left behind. Investigation at the household level is most effective, and, while archaeologists "cannot necessarily identify specific objects with specific people living in a household, it is possible to see changes both within and between households."[4]

Activity

What do your possessions reveal about you? Consider the following questions:

- What types of material culture can be found in your home?

- What impression might an outsider get when visiting your house? Why?

- How did you come into possession of these objects? Are these modern-day artifacts the result of personal purchases? Did you inherit any of these items?

As you consider your personal possessions and what they might reveal about you, complete the following steps with your peers:

Step 1: Bring in an object that represents an important aspect of your identity (gender, culture, religion, ethnic region, race, ability, etc.)

Step 2: Place all of the objects in the center of a circle. Take a few minutes to examine each one.

Step 3: Choose one item to investigate further and answer the following questions:

- What size is the object?

- Shape?

- What material is it made from?

- How might this object be used and for what purpose?

- Can you identify the object? How?

- Do you think archaeologists a hundred years from now would be able to identify the purpose of the object? Why or why not?

- What conclusions might future archaeologists make about your group based on the objects you shared? What do you want them to know about your object and your identity?

Notes

1. Douglas T. Price, *Principles of Archaeology* (Boston, McGraw-Hill, 2006), 101.
2. Megan E. Springate, "Beyond Identity: An LGBTQ Archaeological Context," in *Preservation and Place: Historic Preservation by and of LGBTQ Communities in the United States*, edited by Katherine Crawford-Lackey and Megan E. Springate (New York: Berghahn Books, 2019).
3. Ian Hodder, *Reading the Past: Current Approaches to the Interpretation of Archaeology* (Cambridge: Cambridge University Press, 1986).
4. Springate, "Beyond Identity."

Activities Bibliography

Baim, Tracy. "Sex, Love, and Relationships." In *LGBTQ America: A Theme Study of Lesbian, Gay, Bisexual, Transgender, and Queer History,* edited by Megan E. Springate. Washington, D.C.: National Park Foundation, 2016.

Beemyn, Genny. *A Queer Capital: A History of Gay Life in Washington, D.C.* New York: Routledge, 2015.

Browne, Kath, and Gavin Brown. "An Introduction to the Geographies of Sex and Sexualities." In *The Routledge Research Companion to Geographies of Sex and Sexuality,* edited by Gavin Brown and Kath Browne. New York: Routledge, 2016.

Carpenter, Dale. *Flagrant Conduct: The Story of Lawrence v. Texas.* New York: W. W. Norton & Company, 2012.

Crawford-Lackey, Katie, and Barbara Little. "Exploring American Places with the Discovery Journal: A Guide to Co-Creating Meaningful Interpretation." *George Wright Forum* 34, no. 3 (2017). http://www.georgewright.org/343 crawford-lackey.pdf.

D'Emilio, John. *Sexual Politics, Sexual Communities: The Making of a Homosexual Minority in the United States, 1940-1970.* Chicago: University of Chicago Press, 1983.

Ferentinos, Susan. "Interpreting LGBTQ Historic Sites." In *Preservation and Place: Historic Preservation by and of LGBTQ Communities in the United States,* edited by Katherine Crawford-Lackey and Megan E. Springate. New York: Berghahn Books, 2019.

Hayden, Dolores. *The Power of Place: Urban Landscapes as Public History.* Cambridge: MIT Press, 1997.

Hodder, Ian. *Reading the Past: Current Approaches to the Interpretation of Archaeology.* Cambridge: Cambridge University Press, 1986.

Price, Douglas T. *Principles of Archaeology.* Boston, McGraw-Hill, 2006.

Sharfstein, Daniel J. *The Invisible Line: A Secret History of Race in America.* New York: Penguin Group, 2011.

Simon, Nina. *The Participatory Museum.* Santa Cruz: Museum 2.0, 2010.

Springate, Megan E. "Beyond Identity: An LGBTQ Archeological Context." In *Preservation and Place: Historic Preservation by and of LGBTQ Communities in the United States,* edited by Katherine Crawford-Lackey and Megan E. Springate. New York: Berghahn Books, 2019.

———. "A Note About Intersectionality, LGBTQ Communities, History, and Place." In *Identities and Place: Changing Labels and Intersectional Communities of LGBTQ and Two-Spirit People in the United States,* edited by Katherine Crawford-Lackey and Megan E. Springate. New York: Berghahn Books, 2020.

Stein, Marc. "Historical Landmarks and Landscapes of LGBTQ Law." In *Communities and Place: A Thematic Approach to the Histories of LGBTQ Communities in the United States,* edited by Katherine Crawford-Lackey and Megan E. Springate. New York: Berghahn Books, 2020.

Stryker, Susan. *Transgender History.* Berkley: Seal Press, 2008.

———. "Transgender History in the U.S. and the Places That Matter." In *Identities and Place: Changing Labels and Intersectional Communities of LGBTQ and Two-Spirit People in the United States,* edited by Katherine Crawford-Lackey and Megan E. Springate. New York: Berghahn Books, 2020.

Young, David W. "Expanding Interpretation at Historic Sites." In *Interpreting African American History and Culture at Museums and Historic Sites,* edited by Max A. Van Balgooy. Lanham, MD: Rowman & Littlefield, 2015.

"United States v. Windsor," SCOTUSblog, http://www.scotusblog.com/case-files/cases/windsor- v-united- states-2/.

"Obergefell v. Hodges," SCOTUSblog, http://www.scotusblog.com/casefiles/cases/obergefell-v- hodges.

Index

www.ingramcontent.com/pod-product-compliance
Lightning Source LLC
Chambersburg PA
CBHW070612030426
42337CB00020B/3770